The Social Life of Pots

The Social Life of Pots

Glaze Wares and Cultural Dynamics in the Southwest, AD 1250–1680

edited by
Judith A. Habicht-Mauche, Suzanne L. Eckert,
and Deborah L. Huntley

The University of Arizona Press
Tucson

The University of Arizona Press
www.uapress.arizona.edu

We respectfully acknowledge the University of Arizona is on the land and territories of Indigenous peoples. Today, Arizona is home to twenty-two federally recognized tribes, with Tucson being home to the O'odham and the Yaqui. Committed to diversity and inclusion, the University strives to build sustainable relationships with sovereign Native Nations and Indigenous communities through education offerings, partnerships, and community service.

© 2006 by The Arizona Board of Regents
All rights reserved. Published 2006
First paperback edition 2024

ISBN-13: 978-0-8165-2457-0 (cloth)
ISBN-13: 978-0-8165-5355-6 (paper)
ISBN-13: 978-0-8165-5106-4 (ebook)

Cover images: top and middle of front cover, and back cover: Sityatki design style; bottom of front cover: Rio Grande Glaze A design style.

Publication of this book is made possible in part by the proceeds of a permanent endowment created with the assistance of a Challenge Grant from the National Endowment for the Humanities, a federal agency.

Library of Congress Cataloging-in-Publication Data
　The social life of pots : glaze wares and cultural dynamics in the Southwest, AD 1250–1680 / edited by Judith A. Habicht-Mauche, Suzanne L. Eckert, and Deborah L. Huntley.
　　p.cm.
　Includes bibliographical references and index.
　ISBN-13: 978-0-8165-2457-0 (hardcover : alk. paper)
　ISBN-10: 0-8165-2457-2 (hardcover : alk. paper)
　1. Pueblo pottery—Themes, motives. 2. Pueblo pottery—Antiquities. 3. Zuni pottery—Themes, motives. 4. Zuni pottery—Antiquities. 5. Pottery craft—Southwest, New. 6. Glazes—Southwest, New. 7. Glazing (Ceramics)—Southwest, New. 8. Southwest, New—Antiquities. I. Habicht-Mauche, Judith A., 1959– II. Eckert, Suzanne L., 1970– III. Huntley, Deborah L., 1969–
　E99.P9s66 2006
　666'.609790902—dc22
　2005037306

Printed in the United States of America
♾ This paper meets the requirements of ANSI/NISO Z39.48-1992 (Permanence of Paper).

To the memory of Anna O. Shepard,
within whose long shadow we all work.

Contents

Preface   ix

1 The Social History of Southwestern Glaze Wares
   Judith A. Habicht-Mauche   3

2 Glaze Ware Technology, the Social Lives of Pots, and
   Communities of Practice in the Late Prehistoric Southwest
   Miriam T. Stark   17

3 The Production and Distribution of Glaze-Painted Pottery in
   the Pueblo Southwest: A Synthesis   Suzanne L. Eckert   34

4 The Social Contexts of Glaze Paint Ceramic Production and
   Consumption in the Silver Creek Area   Thomas R. Fenn,
   Barbara J. Mills, and Maren Hopkins   60

5 Decorating Glaze-Painted Pottery in East-Central Arizona
   Scott Van Keuren   86

6 From Recipe to Identity: Exploring Zuni Glaze Ware
   Communities of Practice   Deborah L. Huntley   105

7 The Decline of Zuni Glaze Ware Production in the Tumultuous
   Fifteenth Century   Gregson Schachner   124

8 Glaze Wares and Regional Social Relationships on the
   Rio Alamosa   Toni S. Laumbach   142

9 Black-on-White to Glaze-on-Red: The Adoption of
   Glaze Technology in the Central Rio Grande Valley
   Suzanne L. Eckert   163

10 Inferring Social Interactions from Pottery Recipes: Rio Grande
   Glaze Paint Composition and Cultural Transmission
   Cynthia L. Herhahn   179

11 Lead, Paint, and Pots: Rio Grande Intercommunity
   Dynamics from a Glaze Ware Perspective   Kit Nelson and
   Judith A. Habicht-Mauche   197

12 Rio Grande Glaze Ware Technology and Production:
   Historic Expediency   Patricia Capone   216

13 Directionality and Exclusivity of Plains-Pueblo Exchange during
   the Protohistoric Period, AD 1450–1700   Kathryn Leonard   232

14 Rio Grande Glaze Paint Ware in Southwestern Archaeology
   Linda S. Cordell   253

Notes   273
Bibliography   277
Contributors   315
About the Editors   317
Index   319

Preface

Anna O. Shepard published her landmark monograph *Rio Grande Glaze Paint Ware: A Study Illustrating the Place of Ceramic Technological Analysis in Archaeological Research* (1942) more than sixty years ago, yet it stands as the most comprehensive treatment of southwestern glaze-painted pottery ever written. Over the last decade, this unique ceramic tradition has been the subject of renewed interest and attention by specialists in southwestern ceramics. This renaissance in southwestern glaze ware studies has been spurred, in part, by a broader revival of interest, after many decades of neglect, in the Late Precontact and Early Contact periods in the American Southwest. The late thirteenth through fifteenth centuries are now recognized as a time of unprecedented and dynamic social change in the region. Glaze-painted pottery has much to tell us about these changes, as a record of changing aesthetics, ideologies, and ritual practices and as a marker of technological practices and local knowledge that shifted as people moved through this dynamic social landscape. In addition, the increased availability of a new generation of instrumental techniques for the geochemical analysis and characterization of ceramic materials, including instrumental neutron activation analysis (INAA), electron microprobe, and inductively coupled plasma mass spectroscopy (ICP-MS), has added greatly to the tool kit of those studying southwestern ceramics. These techniques have begun to allow us to study technological practice at previously unimagined levels of detail and at multiple scales. Thus, the time seems more than ripe to reassess the state of southwestern glaze ware research and what it has contributed to our evolving understanding of the relationship between technological practice and social change in the late precontact to early contact Southwest.

In order to begin this conversation, the editors organized a symposium, entitled "The Social Life of Pots: Glaze Wares and Cultural Transformation in the Late Prehistoric Southwest" for the 2002 Meetings of the Society for American Archaeology, held in Denver, Colorado. At this symposium, fifteen scholars met to present their research on southwestern glaze-painted pottery. These researchers included a mix of graduate students, recent PhDs, and more experienced ceramic analysts, trained in a variety of analytical techniques and working on projects that spanned the entire temporal range and geographic breadth of late precontact to early contact glaze ware production in the Southwest. Linda Cordell and Miriam Stark provided important commentary on how our work fit into the broader history of southwestern archaeology and ceramic technology studies, respectively.

This half-day symposium generated a lively series of discussions and debates among the participants. After the meetings, papers were revised, circulated, and revised again. After two rounds of peer review and additional revisions, the current volume finally took shape and was accepted for publication by the University of Arizona Press. We would like to thank our four anonymous reviewers, whose extensive and detailed critical comments helped us to mold these somewhat eclectic symposium papers into a more focused and coherent volume, which we hope will make a significant and lasting contribution to both southwestern culture history and ceramic technology studies. Amanda (Amy) Scherer provided invaluable assistance in helping to proofread and format the manuscript for publication. Helen Cole of Graphic Services at UCSC redrafted a number of the figures for this volume. We are grateful for her artistic skill and professionalism, which greatly enhanced the overall look of our book. We also appreciate the thorough attention to detail provided by our copyeditor, John Mulvihill. A special thanks to Suzanne Eckert's husband, Keith Maggert, our "MacWizard" and all-around "knight in shining armor," who saved the day by helping us debug an earlier version of the manuscript that managed to get infected by a computer virus. And finally, many thanks to the editorial staff at the University of Arizona Press, and most especially

Allyson Carter and Chris Szuter, for their patience and support throughout this project.

Judith A. Habicht-Mauche
Suzanne L. Eckert
Deborah L. Huntley

The Social Life of Pots

1
The Social History of the Southwestern Glaze Wares

Judith A. Habicht-Mauche

The Late Precontact, or Pueblo IV, period (AD 1275–1400) in the American Southwest was marked by a series of demographic upheavals throughout the Pueblo world that resulted in the formation of a radically new social landscape. Massive migrations led to the displacement and reorganization of local communities and regional social networks as some areas, such as the Four Corners and Colorado Plateau, were completely depopulated, while others, such as the Zuni area and the Rio Grande Valley, received substantial influxes of new populations (see fig. 1.1). In many areas, people from diverse ethnic, linguistic, and cultural backgrounds were forced to come together to remake their social worlds from the shreds and tatters of existing cultural traditions. The proliferation and spread of new social and religious institutions and their associated rituals restructured the relationship between the individual, society, and the cosmos, leading to major transformations in notions of community, individual and corporate identity, and the nature of leadership and power in Pueblo society.

Associated with these social transformations we see dramatic changes in decorated ceramic traditions throughout the Southwest. These changes reflect a distinct break with the aesthetic and technological traditions of the past. Aesthetic changes include the introduction of new polychromatic color schemes, the use of new paints and painting techniques to add depth, texture, shading, and outline, changes in overall design struc-

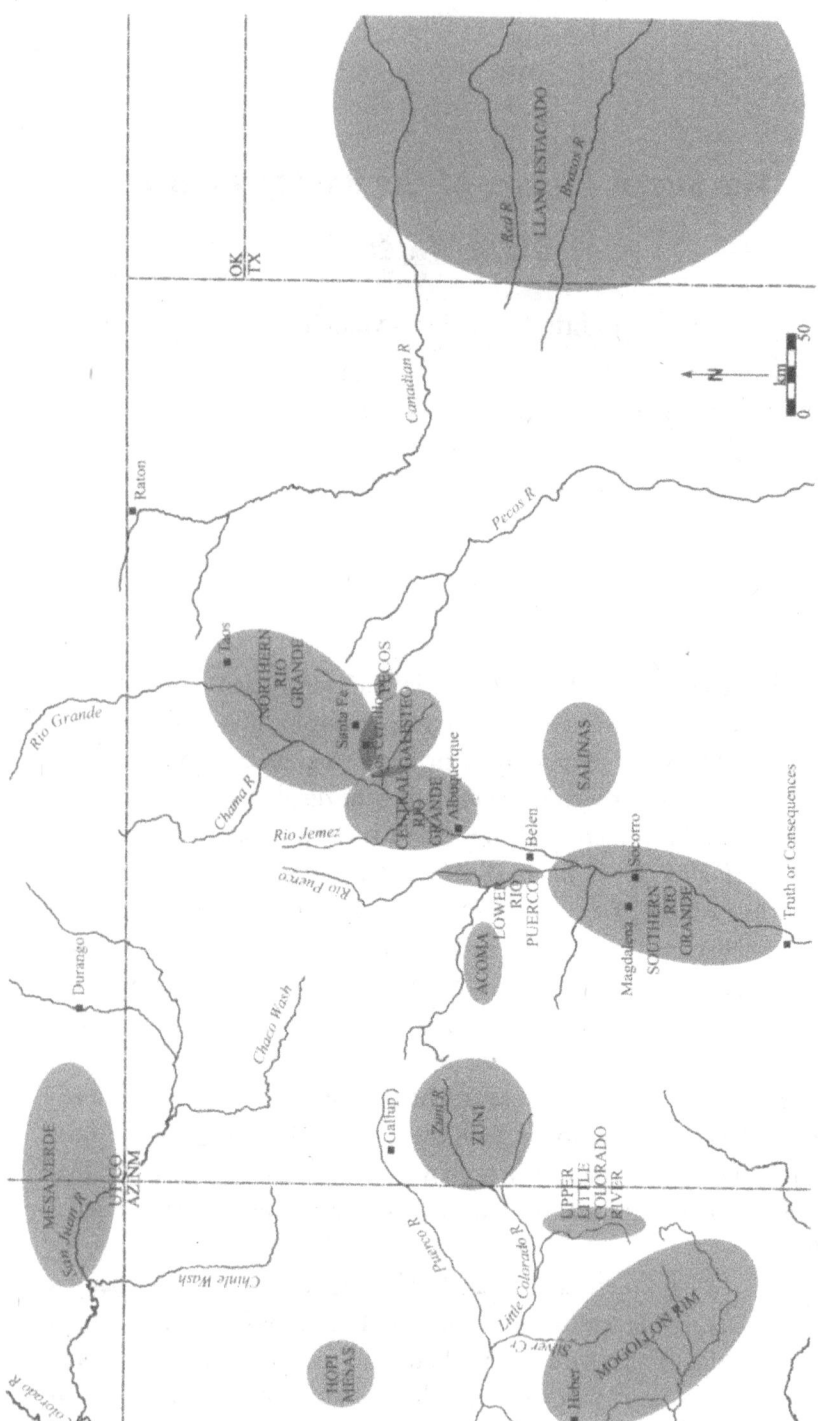

Fig. 1.1. Archaeological regions discussed in this volume.

ture and symmetry, and a greater emphasis on iconographic and representational imagery. From a technological perspective, some of these new decorated wares appear to be characterized by a greater efficiency and standardization of production, suggesting that they may represent the products of more specialized household and community-based industries (Motsinger 1992). They tended to be traded over longer distances and through broader regional and interregional networks of exchange than the earlier local black-on-white ceramic types (Habicht-Mauche 1993a). There is also increasing evidence that the context of use of these vessels may have extended beyond the domestic sphere and that they may have played important public roles in ritual displays and community feasts (Spielmann 1998).

Beginning in the late thirteenth century, first in east-central Arizona and then spreading eastward through the Zuni and Acoma regions to the central and southern Rio Grande, potters experimented with copper- and lead-based pigments that vitrified upon firing, forming a glossy glaze paint. Southwestern glaze-painted ceramics represent one of only a very few examples of glaze technology that developed indigenously in the Americas (see chap. 3). A glaze is a thin glassy substance that is melted and fused to the surface of a ceramic body (Rice 1987; Vandiver 1990). Ceramic glazes are commonly applied as a surface coating to decrease permeability and to enhance surface luster and texture. However, in the late precontact Southwest, glazes were applied as a paint to add texture and color to the vessel surface and as a bold outline to matte-painted and slipped designs.

Glazes are compositionally and technologically complex. The primary constituent of glazes is silica, which melts to form glass. Glazes also typically contain a variety of impurities, known as fluxes. Fluxes are essential to glaze production, because they lower the melting point of silica, allowing glass to form at relatively low temperatures. This is important because if a ceramic body is held at too high a temperature for too long it will begin to vitrify, causing the vessel to warp and melt. A common fluxing material is lead, which allows glazes to form at temperatures as low as 500–600° Celsius, well within the firing range of most nonindustrial potters. Lead is also popular because it produces a beautiful, clear, lustrous glaze. Oxides of metals, such as copper, iron, or manganese, are often added to glazes as colorants. However, these metal oxides also act as fluxes. In addition, most glazes contain some alumina, which controls the viscosity of the melted glass and prevents the glaze from becoming too runny. Because of the sophistication and uniqueness of this technological achievement, southwestern glaze wares have received considerable attention from archaeologists over the past three-quarters of a century (De Atley 1986; Hawley 1938; Kidder and Shepard 1936; Shepard 1942; Warren 1979). Much of this research has focused on resource acquisition and patterns of exchange of glaze ware vessels as traced through chemical and mineralogical characterization studies. However, despite the growing volume and sophistication of recent glaze ware analyses, less attention has been paid to synthesizing these studies within a broad social and historical framework. How did glaze ware production, distribution, and use articulate with transformations in social organization, notions of community, identity formation, regional alliance, and the spread of new ritual systems in the late precontact Southwest? What role did glaze ware pots play in Pueblo social life and in what contexts? How did these processes differ from one glaze-producing area to another and at different times? These are all questions that remain to be examined in detail.

This volume reflects an initial attempt to address some of these issues from a broad, pan-regional, and comparative perspective. The participants represent a diverse cross section of researchers working throughout the glaze-producing areas of the Southwest, including east-central Arizona, the Zuni region, the lower Rio Puerco of the East, and the central and southern Rio Grande Valley (figs. 1.1 and 1.2). The chapters cover the full historical range of glaze ware production from the late thirteenth century up through the Early Colonial period. The research reported on here utilizes a variety of analytical techniques, including typological and stylistic analyses, optical petrography, instrumental neutron activation analysis (INAA), electron microprobe analysis, and inductively coupled plasma mass spectroscopy (ICP-MS). Despite the diversity of approaches and perspectives, all the participants share a common objective to move beyond technical analysis and to begin to develop broader frameworks for examining the changing role of glaze-decorated ceramics in the social dynamics of the late precontact and early contact Southwest. In so doing, we also hope to make a contribution to theoretical studies of the creative interplay between material culture and processes of social formation and culture history.

Frameworks for Analysis

Arjun Appadurai (1986) has argued that specific objects or classes of things become charged with social potential as a result of their circulation within or among specific cultural and historical milieus. From this perspective, according to Appadurai, things, like persons, can be said to have "social lives." Such a view opens up a new way of thinking about the relationship between material culture and society.

As Dietler and Herbich (1998) have noted, archaeological approaches to the social significance of material culture have been mired in a false debate over whether things should be seen primarily as the passive reflection of cultural norms and social practices (e.g., Sackett 1990) or as more active "agents" in the dynamic construction of social relationships and cultural identities (e.g., Wiessner 1983; Wobst 1977). As they point out, such views "are not necessarily contradictory; they are merely partial." What is missing from these debates is an understanding of the reflexive, constitutive relationship between structure and agency (Sahlins 1981) and of the role of "practice," that is to say, human action in the material world, in mediating that relationship (Bourdieu 1977). As Appadurai (1986:5) puts it:

> Even if our own approach to things is conditioned necessarily by the view that things have no meanings apart from those that human transactions, attributions, and motivations endow them with, the anthropological problem is that this formal truth does not illuminate the concrete, historical circulation of things. For that we have to follow the things themselves, for their meanings are inscribed in their forms, their uses, their trajectories. It is only through the analysis of these trajectories that we can interpret the human transactions and calculations that enliven things. Thus, even though from a theoretical point of view human actors encode things with significance, from a methodological point of view it is the things-in-motion that illuminate their human and social context.

Things are made, exchanged, used, and discarded by people as part of material transactions and performances that make up the day-to-day, rough-and-tumble of human social life. The choices, strategies, and actions mobilized by people in the context of these material transactions and performances are largely conditioned by socially mediated views of

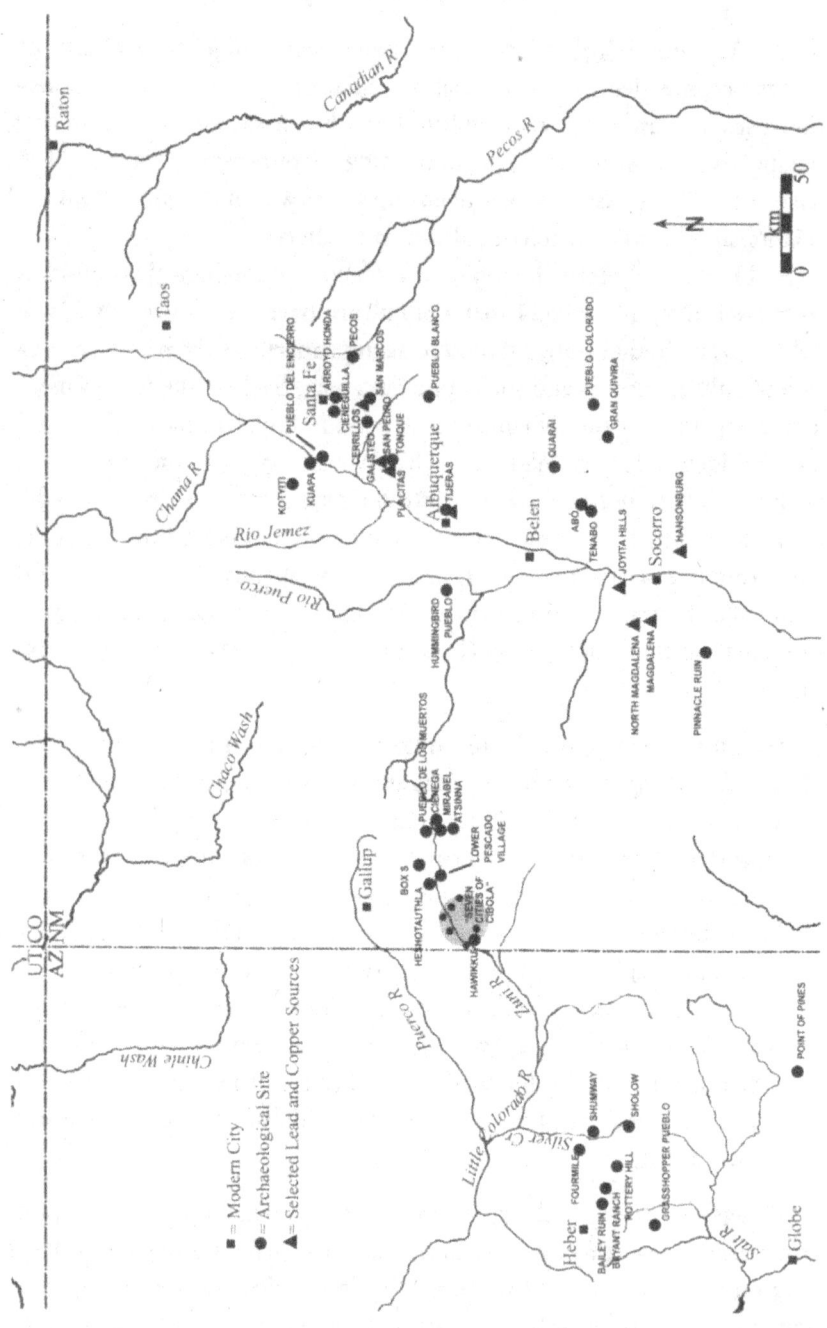

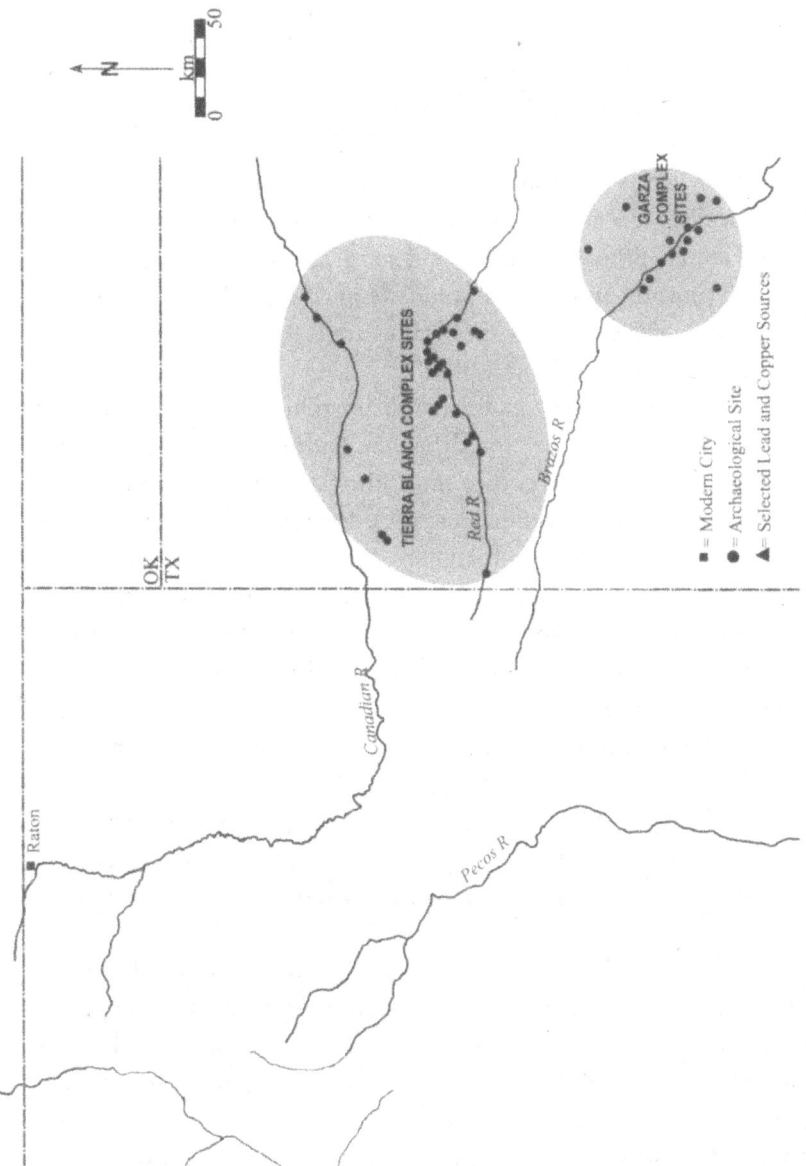

Fig. 1.2. Archaeological sites and ore sources discussed in this volume.

how the world works and how things should be done (Lemonnier 1986). But personal experience often fractures or disrupts our socially derived understandings of the world, opening a window of creative ambiguity, an opportunity for innovation and change, especially in response to contradiction, competition, and conflict. Thus, if we want to understand the role of material culture in this creative process of cultural formation and social transformation, we need to examine, in detail, the conditions and contexts in which specific objects or classes of objects are made and then circulate within and among different cultural and social arenas, both across space and through time. In Appadurai's words, we must trace these "things-in-motion" as they move through the various trajectories of human interaction that construct their "social lives."

Appadurai (1986:34) makes a further distinction between the cultural biography of things and their social history. Cultural biographies trace the flow of specific objects "as they move through different hands, contexts, and uses," creating a unique historical trajectory or life history for each individual object from production to discard. Such an approach incorporates, but moves beyond, the detailed reconstruction of production sequences or *chaîne opératoire* method currently favored by French archaeologists (see Stark, chap. 2, this vol.) by considering the entire use life of an object and its shifting social contexts and significances. Social histories, on the other hand, relate to whole classes or types of things as their technologies of manufacture, networks of exchange, contexts of use, and social meanings shift over broader domains of time and space. In order to fully examine the social dynamics of certain classes of things, such as glaze-painted pots, we must constantly toggle between these various scales and contexts of analysis.

The "social history" approach provides a potentially powerful framework for examining the relationship between glaze-painted pottery and the social dynamics of the late precontact and early contact Southwest. One of the advantages of this approach is that it forces us to look at material culture from an integrated and longitudinal perspective. We cannot divorce discussions of resource selection and production from those of distribution or from those of use, since each of these processes represents potential arenas of social action where cultural meanings may be inscribed and social relationships and identities may be negotiated. Thus, this approach dissolves the false distinction that is sometimes made between technological and economic approaches to the study of material culture, on the one hand, and social and symbolic (or "stylistic") approaches on the other.

The studies presented in this volume build on the work of earlier pioneers in the anthropology of technology and material culture, especially Heather Lechtman (Lechtman 1977; Lechtman and Steinberg 1979) and Pierre Lemonnier (1986). Lechtman argued that the choices and strategies mobilized by specific groups of artisans during the process of production constituted a culturally embedded set of techniques and practices, or a particular "technological style," that reflected deeply held symbolic and structural beliefs about how the world worked. Similarly, Lemonnier (1986:54) pointed out that technological systems were defined by a combination of materials, tools, actions, and knowledge, where such knowledge "is at the same time know-how, manual skills, procedures, but also . . . a set of cultural representations of 'reality.'" For both Lechtman and Lemonnier, cultural "meaning" is embodied, either consciously or unconsciously, in all aspects of technology, including those aspects, such as resource selection and processing, that are associated primarily with material function and performance. However, neither scholar has fully articulated how specific techniques or technological styles become embedded, or are subsequently reproduced, within particular communities of artisans or how or why they are shared, or not shared, among such communities.

In order to begin to address these questions, technology studies must attempt to examine not only how specific technologies are structured by, but also structure, their specific cultural and social milieus. We follow Stark (1998, chap. 2, this vol.) in defining technology as a series of culturally embedded techniques or practices. This view of "technology as practice" allows us to begin to integrate studies of technological style with the social history approach to the study of material culture by defining technology not only in terms of materials, methods, and know-how, but also as a site or arena of dynamic social action. It brings technology into the realm of what Bourdieu (1977) referred to as *habitus*, our internalized, embodied view of how the world works and how things should be done. Habitus is both constituted and manifest in daily practice. Thus, practice, including technological practice, creates a series of "strategic moments" (Lemonnier 1986:154) where habitus is continually either reproduced or transformed.

All of the chapters in this volume are engaged in interrogating this nexus between technological practice and social reproduction and transformation. Glaze-painted pottery was made in multiple regions throughout the northern and eastern Southwest during the Late Precontact and Early Contact periods by peoples with varying social histories and from diverse cultural origins. The production, distribution, and use of glaze ware vessels, however, linked these diverse peoples into multiple and intersecting "communities of practice" (Gosselain 1998; Stark 1999, chap. 2, this vol.) that at some times reinforced and at other times transcended local identities and social boundaries. The authors in this volume use a variety of analytical approaches to trace the circulation of ideas, techniques, raw materials, and finished vessels through networks of social interaction and shared cultural practice of varying context and scale. In turn, these authors explore how these networks functioned as arenas of social reproduction that transformed practices of community and identity formation during the Late Precontact and Early Contact periods.

The Social History of Southwestern Glaze Wares

Beginning in the latter half of the thirteenth century, potters in the upper Little Colorado area of Arizona began experimenting with the development of mineral-based pigments that vitrified upon firing to create a glossy, textured paint. As noted by Suzanne Eckert in chapter 3, earlier potters in the Four Corners area may have experimented with glaze paint technology, but these efforts were fairly short lived and extremely limited in their influence. In contrast, the reinvention of glaze paint technology at the end of the thirteenth century represented a radical technological and aesthetic innovation in southwestern pottery that spread widely and rapidly throughout much of the postmigration Pueblo Southwest (see chap. 3 for an overview of the various regional glaze ware series).

Both Colin Renfrew (1986) and Brian Hayden (1995) have argued persuasively that the impetus for many technological innovations may be as much social and political as economic or functional. In addition, Pamela Vandiver (1990) has noted that in most societies, "glazed ceramics were a prestige good—something that remained beyond the reach of common people because the necessary materials, know-how, and manufacturing skill were often difficult to acquire." Southwestern glaze wares are found widely scattered throughout the midden trash and room fill of late precontact villages. They were clearly used in a variety of domestic contexts to perform many mundane food preparation, service, and storage activities.

As a result, they do not appear to represent an "elite" or "prestige" technology in the traditional sense. Nevertheless, the complexity, and possibly restricted distribution, of the technological knowledge needed to produce glaze-painted pots may have been part of what determined their cultural and social value and what made them either desirable or appropriate for use in such socially charged public contexts as ritual and feasting.

For example, Thomas Fenn, Barbara Mills, and Maren Hopkins (chap. 4), present morphological data that indicate that glaze-painted vessels in the Silver Creek area were used in consumption events that, by the end of the thirteenth century, incorporated large numbers of people. They link these trends to the diversification of religious institutions and practices in the area and the construction of new social identities. Fenn and his colleagues argue that the maintenance of diverse glaze paint recipes in the Silver Creek area was a strategy for negotiating social distinctions and identities in the postmigration period. In contrast, Cynthia Herhahn (chap. 10) sees the increasing homogeneity of glaze formulas in the central and southern Rio Grande Valley as evidence for the cultural transmission of specialized knowledge within and among groups of potters. In turn, these patterns of cultural transmission are explored as clues to the nature and scale of social interaction in the late precontact Rio Grande. In a complementary study, Scott Van Keuren (chap. 5) uses design execution analysis to infer patterns of learning, social interaction, and style miscoding among producers of Fourmile-style pots along the Mogollon Rim. His results hint at changes in the organization of pottery manufacture in the area, possibly linked to the specialization of knowledge. All three studies suggest that under certain circumstances specialized technological knowledge can function as a socially valued commodity whose control or transmission acts to define social relationships and identities, both within and among communities of producers and consumers.

Many of the glaze-producing areas witnessed the arrival of large numbers of immigrants from depopulated regions of the Southwest during the thirteenth and fourteenth centuries. Absorbing and integrating these immigrant populations placed enormous strains on the social fabric of local indigenous groups. Several of the contributions to this volume address the problem of community formation and the construction of new group identities in the postmigration environment. Suzanne Eckert (chap. 9) examines the differential production and distribution of black-on-white versus glaze-painted ceramics at several villages in the lower Rio Puerco and central Rio Grande regions during the late thirteenth century. She explains this variation as the result of diverse strategies mobilized by members of these newly aggregated villages to define their own unique community identity at the same time that they negotiated their participation in various intervillage social networks.

Conversely, Gregson Schachner (chap. 7) examines evidence for a dramatic decline in the production of Zuni Glaze Ware during the fifteenth century. This decline coincides with significant population and settlement shifts within the region, including the founding of many of the historic Zuni towns, possibly triggered by a wave of new migrations into the area. Schachner argues that changes in the relative ratio of glaze-painted to matte-painted ceramics, and their related stylistic and technological traditions, reflect a reshuffling of pan-regional social ties and the emergence of a new, corporate "Zuni" identity.

Kit Nelson and Judith Habicht-Mauche (chap. 11) also address the theme of intercommunity interaction and regional integration in the central Rio Grande. Their results indicate that while finished glaze ware pots circulated through social networks that tended to reinforce emerging local identities, lead for glaze paint was acquired or exchanged over a much broader area that crosscut these apparent social boundaries. When examined from the perspective of each individual community, networks of exchange and social interaction in this region appear to be much more diverse and historically dynamic than suggested by previous research. Nelson and Habicht-Mauche argue that these results challenge existing models of regional integration and polity formation and suggest that most economic decisions and social strategies within and among central Rio Grande communities were being negotiated at the level of individual households or social segments in response to shifting local conditions.

In a similar vein, Deborah Huntley (chap. 6) uses the spatial and temporal distribution of glaze paint recipes to interpret the scale of social group membership and the strength of regional social integration in the Zuni region during the late thirteenth through fourteenth centuries. On the one hand, she argues that the development of lead-based glaze recipes "was a conscious technological choice that allowed potters more latitude in the production of distinctive and socially meaningful color combinations" that may have been related to local processes of identity formation within the Zuni region itself. On the other hand, Huntley's isotopic characterization and sourcing of the lead used in glaze paint production demonstrates that Zuni potters pursued long-distance resource-acquisition strategies that must have brought them into contact and possible competition with the rapidly expanding towns of the central and southern Rio Grande.

Both Toni Laumbach's and Kathryn Leonard's contributions (chaps. 8 and 13) examine the relationship between trade and intercommunity interaction on a larger, interregional scale. Laumbach's work at Pinnacle Ruin in the southern Rio Grande shows that while the masonry architecture and early carbon-painted ceramics from the site have been interpreted as evidence for an immigrant Mesa Verde community, the trade ware ceramics, including most of the imported glaze ware, from the site indicate strong and sustained social ties with the Western Pueblos. In contrast, connections with the central Rio Grande Pueblos appear to have been much more limited. Her work opens up some interesting questions about the relationship between local migration histories and the maintenance of long-distance interethnic and interregional interactions.

Kathryn Leonard's study uses the distribution of Rio Grande glaze-painted pottery on the southern High Plains to examine how exchange relationships were negotiated between Pueblo farmers and Plains bison hunters. She suggests that these relationships were characterized by strong alliances between specific Rio Grande communities and particular local bands or residence groups on the Plains that had deep historical roots. Leonard argues that these alliances were based on formal trade partnerships that were negotiated on a largely individual level between specific households and local residential groups.

The mode of production and scale of craft specialization that characterized glaze ware manufacture at different places and times is a subject of ongoing debate. Kit Nelson and Judith Habicht-Mauche's petrographic studies suggest that the intensity and scale of community specialization among Rio Grande Glaze Ware producers may have been exaggerated by earlier studies. Patricia Capone (chap. 12) also uses petrographic analysis to examine dynamic changes in expedient technology, scale and intensity of production, and the selection of raw materials among the late precontact Rio Grande glaze wares. She compares and contrasts these processes with those of the later Mission, Revolt, and Reconquest periods in order to examine the relationship between the organization of production and the historical and social dynamics in this region.

As this brief overview suggests, the research presented in this volume reflects diverse analytical approaches and methodological strategies for examining the role of glaze ware pottery in the social lives of the late precontact and early contact Pueblos. By tracing the circulation of specialized knowledge, raw materials, and the glaze-painted pots themselves, through interactive networks of varying sizes and scales, these researchers reveal how glaze ware production, distribution, and use articulated with a variety of dynamic historical and social processes, including migration, community formation, constructions of local and regional identity, intercommunity interaction and alliance, organization of production, and the proliferation of new religious systems and ritual practices. What is emerging from these studies is a diverse and complementary series of local "social histories" of the glaze wares that allow us to track both similarities and differences in how these articulations played out in different times, places, and contexts across the late precontact and early contact Southwest. Finally, by comparing and contrasting these diverse social histories, we hope to move toward a more synthetic understanding of the mutually constitutive relationships that linked material culture, technological practice, and the complex processes of social formation and culture change.

2

Glaze Ware Technology, the Social Lives of Pots, and Communities of Practice in the Late Prehistoric Southwest

Miriam T. Stark

In the last century, southwestern ceramics have been subjected to a staggering amount of research. Southwestern archaeologists have used ceramics to study social boundaries and organizational change, and have devoted extensive attention to understanding variability in stylistic decoration at the community and regional levels (e.g., Graves 1998; Hill 1970; Kintigh 1985b; Longacre 1970; S. Plog 1980). Articles in this volume concentrate on one ceramic technological tradition, glaze-decorated ceramics, which were manufactured and used across a broad swath of the northern Southwest after the mid-thirteenth century AD.

The protohistoric ceramic glaze ware tradition described in this volume is not the first appearance of this technology in the Puebloan Southwest or in the greater region (Eckert, chap. 3). Potters in the Four Corners region began using glaze paints on their white wares in the eighth and ninth centuries AD, and potters in western Mexico manufactured glaze wares by the tenth century AD. The salience of this protohistoric technology lies instead in its widespread adoption, its four-century-long tradition of manufacture, and its co-occurrence with macro-organizational shifts across the precontact North American Southwest.

This volume's chapters use glaze ware ceramics to examine two such changes: (1) the establishment and growth of large towns, particularly along the Rio Grande; and (2) a series of migrations both within the Western Pueblo region and between the Western Pueblos and communities within the Rio Grande region. That we see the introduction of a new ceramic technology, and specifically the appearance of glaze-paint-decorated pottery in this region by the late thirteenth century AD, compels researchers to investigate the link between technological and organizational change. This ceramic technological tradition was adopted within a generation in the upper Little Colorado, Zuni, and Acoma regions and spread to the central and southern Rio Grande within a few decades.

A primary goal of this volume is to develop broader frameworks for examining changing roles of ceramic technology during a period of organizational change in the late precontact Southwest. Archaeologists have used ceramics to track episodes of migration during this period into large aggregated settlements in many parts of the Puebloan Southwest (see Schachner, chap. 7, and Laumbach, chap. 8). These shifts correlate with the appearance of a new ceramic technology and specifically the use of copper- and lead-based paints that produce glaze decoration. The volume's contributors explore various articulations between technological and organizational shifts. Monitoring the "social lives of pots" involves considering social and ideological contexts of production, distribution, and consumption in a framework that transcends the confines of a normative "ceramic ecology" approach (following Arnold 1985). Authors in this volume use glaze ware ceramics as a proxy indicator for studying other processes, including the movement of peoples, interregional interaction, the formation of communities, and social and political reorganization.

My objective in this chapter is to contextualize studies of glaze wares into a broader anthropological framework, and to illustrate how studying glaze wares is relevant to areas beyond the precontact Southwest. Conceptual approaches from the anthropology of technology offer useful frameworks for contemplating the nature of glaze ware innovation and adoption, and ideas from practice theory offer alternative perspectives for analyzing examples of ceramic change and for conceptualizing social units that leave archaeological signatures. A new wave of ethnoarchaeological studies, done in concert with laboratory research, strengthens archaeological inferences about the contexts of technological change (see Stark 2003). The fact that recent ceramic ethnoarchaeological research has applied technological and practice frameworks provides intriguing directions for future research on glaze ware ceramics from the precontact Southwest.

Two goals structure this chapter. I first review conceptual frameworks from the anthropology of technology (Pfaffenberger 1992) and practice theory (Ortner 1984) to provide a framework for thinking about the patterning that the authors of this volume have so deftly identified. Second, I illustrate why these approaches enrich our understanding of social and political changes in the late precontact northern Southwest. My objective here is to encourage southwestern archaeologists to integrate an anthropology of technology framework with practice theory approaches to better understand processes of long-term change.

Anthropology of Technology, Practice Theory and Ceramic Studies

Archaeologists have begun to merge technologically informed conceptual frameworks of artifact variability (embodied in anthropology of technology approaches) within a broader theoretical framework called practice theory. Understanding this trend requires some background in two discrete intellectual traditions: technology studies and practice theory as archaeologists use it. Below I discuss the French techniques and culture school (with the *chaîne opératoire* concept), the concept of technological style, and practice theory.

Anthropology of Technology Framework

Increased attention to an "anthropology of technology" framework has emerged in the last decade (e.g., Dietler and Herbich 1998; Hegmon 1998; Lemonnier 1986, 1992; Loney 2000; Pfaffenberger 1992; Rice 1996a:186–87; Stark 1998:5–7). This approach has both an eclectic following and a varied intellectual history in both European and Anglo-American archaeology (Loney 2000; Schiffer et al. 2001). Much recent research, however, derives from a European scholarly tradition whose lineage originated in work by Marcel Mauss (Schlanger 1998), and which Andre Leroi-Gourhan operationalized using the chaîne opératoire concept (Audouze 2002:286–88; Pelegrin, Karlin, and Bodu 1989). More archaeologists working in Europe than in North America have adopted the chaîne opératoire as an analytical research methodology (Dobres 2000:167–70); it bears some resemblance to the behavioral chain or life-history approaches used in behavioral archaeology (e.g., Schiffer and Skibo 1997). While the ceramic ethnoarchaeological literature using this approach has burgeoned recently (Stark 2003:211–13), more archaeological applications have focused on lithics until recently (e.g., Knecht 1993; Pelegrin 1990; Sellet 1993). Their publication in French (rather than English) may also explain why such work remains poorly known among Americanist archaeologists.

At the same time the French developed their *techniques et culture* approach, some Americanist specialists have fused art, technology, and structuralist theory to examine the articulation between technological aspects of manufacture and symbolic systems (e.g., Hegmon 1998:266–68; Lechtman 1984; Lechtman and Steinberg 1979). Integral to this approach is the concept of technological style (following Lechtman 1977), which represents the aggregate of multiple choices during the manufacturing sequence and challenges the conventional style-function dichotomy that characterizes much Americanist research (see Stark 1998). Ethnoarchaeological studies indicate that technological styles are expressed through a wide variety of manufactured objects, including iron-smelting furnaces (Childs 1991; Childs and Killick 1993:330–33), social uses of space (Hitchcock and Bartram 1998), and earthenware ceramics (Hosler 1996; see also Stark 2003 for review). The use of technological approaches provides a methodology for studying technical choices in the archaeological record. By tracking differences and similarities in the production sequence across geographic regions, archaeologists can identify discrete technological traditions, technological innovations, and even some migration events in the archaeological record (Frankel 2000; Stark, Clark, and Elson 1995). A technological approach that combines practice theory with a chaîne opératoire framework, and that draws from comparative ethnoarchaeological studies, can help us understand the social contexts of glaze ware ceramic manufacture, circulation, and use in the precontact North American Southwest.

Practice Theory in Archaeology

Archaeologists' increased attention to practice theory is one significant outgrowth of the recent tumult in North American archaeology over critiques of processual archaeology. Practice theory, as archaeologists envision it (Dobres and Robb 2000:4–9; Dornan 2002; Roscoe 1993: 111–14), originated in ideas of Pierre Bourdieu (1977) and Anthony Giddens (1979) and were mainstreamed into anthropology by Sherry Ortner (1984). In this conception, practice theory focuses on the routinized activity of individuals as they undertake their daily activities: these practices are thus cultural constructions. Practice theory emphasizes individual action, rather than a society's institutions, as the driving force of behavior. This perspective views society as the aggregate of practices of its individuals and asserts that cultural and technological transformations unfold through practice (Dobres 2000:127).

While practice theory overlaps with agency theory (Dobres and Robb 2000), the two are not synonymous, since agency theory views people as mindful participants and practice theory does not focus as closely on individual intent as it does on outcomes. Yet individual action and choice matters in both frameworks, and practice consists of a series of choices that reflect what James Watson (1990:22) calls "cultural diacritics" (see also S. Jones 1997:87–92). These acts may be conscious, subconscious, or unconscious (e.g., Wobst 1999), but their implementation leaves material manifestations that reflect multiple levels of group identity.

Previous authors have summarized Pierre Bourdieu's work authoritatively (e.g., Calhoun, LiPuma, and Postone 1993; Harker, Wilkes, and Mahar 1990; Jenkins 1992; J. F. Lane 2000; van der Leeuw 1993:238–42), and readers are urged to consult these sources (see also Habicht-Mauche, chap. 1, this vol.). Bourdieu's practice theory was founded in ethnographic experience, and he focused on the constitution and reproduction of unequal power relations among people. His approach combined notions of structure and practice in the concept of *habitus*. Habitus describes the cultural embodiment of structures during socialization that reflect wider symbolic systems (Lemonnier 1993). Habitus is constituted and manifested in practice. Techniques used to manufacture goods like the ceramics discussed in this volume are often unconscious (Dietler and Herbich 1998:244–48). These techniques—motor habits, gestures, and behaviors—are social productions that are transmitted within and across generations. Ethnoarchaeologists and archaeologists can observe the practices that habitus produces. Increasing numbers of archaeologists, particularly those who study technology and culture, have adopted aspects of practice theory as a conceptual tool for studying the archaeological record (e.g., Dobres 2000; Dobres and Hoffman 1994; Dobres and Robb 2000).

There may be several explanations for the increase in archaeologists turning to practice theory. First, as a sort of middle-level theory (following Schiffer 1988), practice theory has the potential to transcend otherwise disparate theoretical programs (see also Dobres and Robb 2000:6–8). Archaeological applications of practice theory have thus far been dominated by postprocessual and postmodernist approaches and lumped under the "agency" rubric (Pauketat 2001a:79), but this approach is not restricted to such a narrow group of practitioners. Archaeologists with interests as divergent as meaning and evolutionary ecology are now concerned with aspects of social and cultural reproduction, individual action, and historical contingency. Their interest takes different forms and involves different analytical units, but practice theory and the closely related agency theory are beginning to penetrate the recesses of Anglo-American archaeology.

A second reason that archaeologists have recently embraced practice theory lies in the appeal of its conceptual framework, which is both familiar and accessible to Americanist archaeologists. Notions like habitus arguably have parallels deep in the culture historians' debate over typology. Most notably, Rouse's (1939) concept of mode, which emphasized techniques "analogous to habits" (1939:19), closely resembles the techniques that Lemonnier and his colleagues describe. Even some New Archaeology formulations of classification emphasized the importance of "measuring what people actually do, rather than what they think (the latter being difficult at best)" (Hill and Evans 1972:266). James Sackett's camp in the style debates of the 1980s and 1990s (Sackett 1977, 1982, 1985, 1986, 1990) emphasized "isochrestic variation," which bears some relationship to habitus. Finally, the use of practice theory enables us to conceptualize social boundaries as "something people do" (following Hegmon 1998:272) rather than simply as a set of cognized categories that many archaeologists believe is inaccessible in the ancient past.

A third reason why archaeologists like practice theory lies in its methodological approach, which lends itself to archaeological data. Practice theory stipulates that people reproduce their culture and social positions through daily practice, that daily practice is structured by basic organizational principles, and that daily practice is expressed through habitus. Daily practice leaves patterned traces in the archaeological record (Shennan 1993:55); the challenge lies in developing appropriate interpretations of material culture patterning. Examples from historical archaeology (e.g., L. Ferguson 1992; Lightfoot, Martinez, and Schiff 1998) and from ethnoarchaeological research (e.g., Dietler and Herbich 1998; Gosselain 1998, 1999, 2000; Hitchcock and Bartram 1998) provide controlled case studies that link particular social units to discrete material signatures and demonstrate the potential of a practice theory framework for archaeological research.

Some archaeologists using practice theory focus on learning frameworks (e.g., Crown 2001; Minar and Crown 2001) and blend earlier cognitive theory research by Jean Lave and Etienne Wenger (Lave and Wenger 1991; Wenger 1998) with practice theory (e.g., Sassaman and Rudolphi 2001:408). Others use practice theory to study historical process insofar as this reflects a process of tradition building, or cultural construction through practice (Pauketat 2001b:4). Finally, archaeologists have begun to use practice theory as a conceptual framework for studying social groups in the archaeological record: as "ethnic groups" (S. Jones 1997:87–92), "ethnic cores" (Emerson and McElrath 2001), or "communities of practice" (Lightfoot, Marinez, and Schiff 1998; Minar 2001).

The Anthropology of Southwestern Glaze Ware Technology

The southwestern glaze ware ceramic tradition has a long and hallowed history of research (chap. 3, this vol.) and is well suited for studying the social life of pots. Several chapters in this volume (e.g., Fenn, Mills, and Hopkins; Huntley; Nelson and Habicht-Mauche) summarize the development of glaze ware technologies in particular regions of the northern Southwest. Other chapters (e.g., Schachner, Capone) focus on contexts of technological change. Several other chapters (Fenn, Mills, and Hopkins; Herhahn; Laumbach; Van Keuren) examine the existence and movement of glaze ware manufacturing artisans and their communities. I first discuss the social lives of pots and then turn to ideas related to practice theory. The formation and maintenance of artisan communities, and their movement across space, provides a central theme for the volume's chapters.

The Social Lives of Pots

This volume's editors emphasize the social lives of pots, and it is this social lens through which contributors have been encouraged to view their data. As the dust now clears from the processual-postprocessual debates of the 1990s, most of us now agree that ceramics are not simply passive reflectors of style or even simply of ideological movements (see review in Rice 1996a, 1996b). Many among us still feel uncomfortable with the kinds of interpretive leaps that characterized symbolic-structural studies of ceramics in the 1980s (Stark 1993), precisely because of their nonempirical methodologies. Most ceramicists now agree, nonetheless, that potters do not make their goods in a cultural void, nor do consumers use pots in a social vacuum. We still face methodological challenges in studying these issues in an archaeological context.

The context-laden nature of ceramic technology is particularly evident in ethnographic settings; ceramic ethnoarchaeology provides guidance in constructing methodologies for studying archaeological ceramics. Ceramics, like other manufactured objects, reflect technical choices that leave material traces for archaeologists to study (Sillar 1997; Sillar and Tite 2000). Ethnoarchaeological research strategies enable archaeologists to observe potters making technical choices throughout the manufacturing process, from the processing of raw materials (e.g., Gosselain 1999; Livingstone Smith 2000) and particular shaping techniques (e.g., Mahias 1993; Pétrequin and Pétrequin 1999; Stark 1999; van der Leeuw 1993) to preferences in fuel for firing pottery (Sillar 2000). Some of these steps in the manufacturing process, such as shaping, are remarkably resistant to change, while others (such as stylistic decoration) vary. Subsequent laboratory testing permits the identification of material correlates of some of these technical choices in raw materials selection (Aronson, Skibo, and Stark 1994; Stark, Bishop, and Miksa 2000).

Several contributors to this volume focus on technological choices in the operational sequence that inform on the social lives of glaze ware pots. For example, Scott Van Keuren (chap. 5) focuses on brushstroke sequence to contemplate learning frameworks and emulation among potters who made White Mountain Red Ware. Deborah Huntley (chap. 6) argues that change to lead-based glazes was a conscious choice by fourteenth-century Zuni potters to produce meaningful color combinations. Looking somewhat later in time, Patricia Capone (chap. 12) tracks temporal changes in raw materials processing and shaping techniques in Salinas area ceramic technologies that reflect expediently produced and less standardized ceramics from the pre-Mission to Mission period.

That some of pottery's social life lies in the creation of social relationships is revealed through ceramic ethnoarchaeological research. For example, ceramic circulation forms certain types of communities that are predicated on potter-consumer relationships (e.g., Kramer and Douglas 1992; Longacre and Stark 1992). Moreover, the social relations of producer-consumer relationships may override geographic distance in determining the directionality of ceramic circulation and the shape of the distributional network. Few ceramic studies focus specifically on the relationship between producers and consumers, in part because such interactions are difficult to discern in regions where multiple communities are involved in ceramic production.

Three examples from this volume exemplify how pottery can create social relationships. First, Kathryn Leonard's study of fifteenth- to eighteenth-century Plains-Pueblo relations provides a fine case study (chap. 13). Limitations of the archaeological record, however, make it exceedingly difficult to know whether the Pueblo groups who formed trade partnerships with Plains groups manufactured their own pots, or whether they imported ceramics to use in exchange transactions. Second, compositional analyses of central Rio Grande ceramics (Nelson and Habicht-Mauche, chap. 11) demarcate different geographic clusters formed through the circulation of finished vessels and raw materials. Analysis of ceramic distributional data suggest that, during the Pueblo IV period, people were more likely to interact with others in their local settlement cluster than with populations beyond it (see also Creamer 2002:101–7). Finally, Schachner's chapter (chap. 7) suggests that the appearance of Matsaki Buff ceramics may have heralded the beginning of a newly formed and heterogeneous social unit that integrated long-term residents and relative newcomers into more unified Zuni communities.

Archaeological Units and Communities of Practice

In some respects, the chapters contribute more directly and substantively to archaeological understandings of communities of practice. Such communities are visible ethnographically as potter communities, in which artisans share a set of manufacturing techniques that are guided by local tradition and that reflect a shared habitus (e.g., Gosselain 1998; Stark 1999). Archaeological ceramicists who study communities of practice combine ideas of habitus and technological style to study stability in particular motor skills and identify bounded social units (e.g., Crown 2001; Minar 2001; Sassaman and Rudolphi 2001). With respect to glaze ware ceramics, Scott Van Keuren draws from the ceramic sociology tradition of the New Archaeology (following S. Plog 1983) to discuss shared learning and cognitive frameworks among potters who made White Mountain Red Ware vessels. Also in the Mogollon Rim region, Fenn and his colleagues explicitly link particular glaze paint compositions to localized technical traditions that they call "pottery production groups."

What, exactly, is the scale of a community of practice? It is becoming increasingly evident that we cannot directly move from this identification to certain types of social units like villages or communities, "cultures," or ethnic groups. These communities may not be isomorphic with villages, since artisans' technological traditions may appear in several settlements. Ceramic ethnoarchaeological research suggests that scalar variability exists in communities of practice (e.g., Gosselain 1998, 1999, 2000). Most communities of practice that have been documented ethnoarchaeologically are found at the local level (Graves 1994a,b; Stark 1999), and compositional studies suggest that these units leave tangible evidence (e.g., Arnold, Neff, and Bishop 1991; Arnold et al. 1999; Stark, Bishop, and Miksa 2000).

The fact that ethnographically documented communities of practice may not be isomorphic with villages or communities has archaeological implications for understanding southwestern glaze wares and their makers. Using archaeological research from elsewhere in the precontact North American Southwest (Elson, Stark, and Gregory 2000), we have offered the term *local system* as a more suitable alternative to village or community, since this term can encompass multiple residential clusters whose occupants share some practices (and presumably some social links) with others across the clusters. In the Tonto Basin (east-central Arizona), archaeological correlates for local systems include shared raw material sources for temper and perhaps even for clays (e.g., Miksa and Heidke 2001; Stark and Heidke 1998). Nelson and Habicht-Mauche (chap. 11, this vol.) use the term *local settlement cluster* to demarcate a similar social unit and source pottery to a particular district, a cluster of sites, or (in some cases) a specific manufacturing settlement.

Beyond the local system lie larger and meaningful social units that are not self-ascribed ethnic groups (contra Emerson and McElrath 2001; S. Jones 1997), since shared technological traditions, rather than language or other emblemic indicators of group affiliation, unite these producers into a social unit. The notion of the regional system, linked through kinship, alliances, and ideology, provides a more useful conceptual alternative to that of ethnic group (also see Neitzel 2000). Using an example from the Sepik Coast of New Guinea, Welsch and Terrell (1998) describe such a system as a social field or a "community of culture."

Archaeological research using a suite of compositional techniques provides a valuable approach for identifying regional systems in the northern Southwest. Broad-scale ethnoarchaeological research has identified macrogroups through systematic documentation of manufacturing techniques that crosscut communities and link them in a broader entity (e.g., Gosselain 1998, 2000). Work by Nelson and Habicht-Mauche provides a first step in this direction, as they identify geographic clusters in the

Rio Grande in which social links are established and reaffirmed through the circulation of raw materials and finished goods involved in ceramic production. And Leonard's analysis of Plains-Pueblo relationships also identifies larger social units than the local system, bound together by the circulation of ceramics (and likely other materials), and perhaps intergenerational in depth, between culturally discrete groups. Because ceramics constituted one small part of a much broader material culture inventory, it is imperative to cast a wider net that includes other material categories in such research.

The Timing and Nature of Change

Linda Cordell (chap. 14) reminds us that identifying the origins of southwestern glaze wares is interesting, but exploring processes behind their widespread adoption is of paramount importance. Research presented in this volume suggests, first, that potters adopted the glaze ware tradition within a single generation across most of what was to become the Western Pueblo region. Secondly, Eckert's synthesis (chap. 3) indicates that glaze ware technology peaked in popularity (where popularity is measured by the diversity of types produced at one point in time) between ca. AD 1424 and 1450. Within the next generation, this technological tradition waned in some areas (i.e., Little Colorado, Zuni, Acoma) and intensified in areas along the Rio Grande.

Chapters in this volume discuss the coevolution of glaze ware traditions among upper Little Colorado groups and the Zuni and Acoma potters' manufacture of Zuni Glaze Ware types indistinguishable from those made at Zuni, and sixteenth-century Zuni potters' emulation of Rio Grande Glaze Ware vessel forms. Understanding the "social lives" of these pots requires additional study of their changing social and political contexts, and of the development of intraregional and interregional relationships through time.

A technological approach provides an appropriate methodological framework for interpreting some aspects of innovation in southwestern glaze ware ceramics; it also offers a set of theoretical tools. Envisioning southwestern glaze wares as the outcome of discrete manufacturing steps (of a particular chaîne opératoire) provides a finer-grained perspective on technological innovation, persistence, and change over a four-hundred-year span. Along the Mogollon Rim, glaze ware technology was adopted relatively rapidly in the late thirteenth century (Fenn, Mills, and Hopkins, chap. 4); in the fifteenth-century Zuni region, the glaze ware tradition disappeared rather abruptly and was replaced by a buff ware tradition (Schachner, chap. 7). Potters adopted technological innovations associated with glaze ware manufacturing at different rates; in areas like Zuni, some potters may have decided not to adopt high-lead glaze recipes while neighboring artisans did (Huntley, chap. 6).

Studies in this volume also describe the nature of technological changes in glaze ware ceramics through time. Habicht-Mauche's introduction and Eckert's synthesis of glaze ware traditions suggest that Pueblo IV technological changes involved primarily decorative techniques (e.g., introduction of polychromatic color schemes, the use of new painting techniques, and changes in design structure/symmetry) and surface treatments (i.e., adoption of copper and lead-based pigments that formed glaze paints upon firing). Potters' experimentation with glaze paint recipes along the Mogollon Rim (Fenn, Mills, and Hopkins, chap. 4) required them to also modify their firing regimes. Potters made similar changes across the northern Southwest to accommodate their new glaze paint technology. Whereas previous generations of potters used a reducing (or neutral) firing atmosphere to manufacture their white ware ceramics, potters making glaze ware ceramics fired their vessels in an oxidizing atmosphere to produce yellow wares, red wares, and polychromes. These technological innovations required modifications to their firing technologies, the use of different fuels, and perhaps even the introduction of new firing features.

From an anthropology of technology framework, such changes involved both modifications to an extant ceramic manufacturing tradition and also technological transformations; the latter often reflects the influx of new producers. As such, our focus should be on factors that encouraged potters to modify their traditions as much as on documenting particular migration events. Several of this volume's chapters provide empirical evidence for the influx of immigrants into the region, from the thirteenth-century Mogollon Rim (Fenn, Mills, and Hopkins, chap. 4) to the fifteenth-century Zuni region (Schachner, chap. 7) and beyond to the Rio Grande Valley (Eckert, chap. 9). But, as Cynthia Herhahn (chap. 10) also points out, we cannot explain technological change simply or exclusively through processes of migration.

Contexts of Change

Another theme in the volume's chapters concerns the social contexts of technological change. Technological change does not simply correlate with, or serve as proxy indicator of, broader organizational changes. It instead operates at different rates, responds to multiple stimuli, and results from a complex mixture of internal and external pressures. Technological change is not ideologically determined, although we may detect relationships between certain types of change and the emergence of ideological movements. Instead, technological change reflects individual and aggregate decisions to innovate and adopt new strategies. Technological change thus represents a delicate interplay of agency and constraints; some aspects of technology are remarkably resistant to change (Aronson and Fournier 1993; Nicklin 1971; Stark 1991).

Documenting the nature of shifts through time is a necessary prerequisite for understanding the contexts of technological change. Extensive work across the northern Southwest, summarized ably by Suzanne Eckert (chap. 3), has helped bracket an approximate start date for the introduction of this new technological tradition. Research along the Mogollon Rim by Fenn, Mills, and Hopkins provides intriguing evidence of the inception of innovation, replete with compositional evidence for a trial-and-error period of experimentation. So, too, does Cynthia Herhahn's study of the earliest Rio Grande potters' efforts to use glaze paint recipes. Work by Mills (1995) and Schachner (chap. 7) illustrates the "life cycle" of the Zuni Glaze Ware technological tradition, which underwent significant technological shifts through time.

Some of the volume's chapters also identify shifts in glaze ware technology, including a shift from mineral to carbon to glaze paint during the twelfth through fourteenth centuries in the middle and northern Rio Grande region (Eckert, chap. 9), to a shift from relatively low-lead and high-copper to relatively high-lead and low-copper glaze paints in the fourteenth-century Zuni region (Huntley, chap. 6), and in the transition from more intensive to less intensive temper processing from the fifteenth to seventeenth century in the Salinas area (Capone, chap. 12). In the Rio Grande area, at least, potters pursued multiple strategies of production (possibly including household-based specialization) and engaged in trade throughout the region from the fourteenth to early sixteenth century AD.

The adoption of glaze ware technology across much of the northern precontact Southwest did not entirely overwhelm local ceramic technological practices. Fenn and his colleagues provide convincing evidence for the replacement of Cibola White Ware with red ware along the Mogollon Rim by ca. AD 1300. On the other hand, Suzanne Eckert's study suggests that white ware production continued in the thirteenth and fourteenth centuries at some communities in the central Rio Grande, while other settlements witnessed a replacement of white ware with glaze ware manufacture.

These sorts of empirical findings make valuable contributions, and help us consider whether, why, when, and which potters adopted new technological traditions (and abandoned old ones) at different rates. Questions remain concerning the origins of southwestern glaze wares and the differential adoption of this technology across the region. Why did potters during the Protohistoric period opt to modify certain production steps but not others? Perhaps some potters made deliberate choices to distinguish their wares from those of others in their regions (e.g., Huntley, chap. 6), while others made less conscious technological accommodations to changing raw material availability (for review, see also Hensler and Blinman 2002:377–79). To what extent did social and demographic factors (including immigration) stimulate this shift? Understanding these processes requires us to think about cultural transmission, or how information and techniques are transferred from one person to the next.

Cultural Transmission

The study of cultural transmission—and in this case, how technological knowledge passes from one artisan to another—is critical for understanding the development, spread, and disappearance of the glaze ware ceramic series. Herhahn's chapter views glaze ware as a technological style, and tracks its movement from west to east and then throughout the Rio Grande. Cultural transmission can take many forms, including vertical transmission through intergenerational learning frameworks (Van Keuren), horizontal transmission through emulation and exchange (Herhahn, Huntley), and through population movement (Schachner). Migrant potters' adoption of new technologies and their experimentation with unfamiliar raw materials across the late precontact Puebloan Southwest stimulated changes in local technological traditions (see also Schachner, chap. 7). The fact that migration and diffusion are complementary rather than contradictory processes is essential; Herhahn suggests that intergroup interaction might have occurred more frequently than physical migration in parts of the Rio Grande.

The Rio Grande, however, remains an ideal setting in the precontact North American Southwest for studying the movement of populations and migration-stimulated changes in local manufacturing traditions. Yet the response varied, and artisans adopted new technologies differentially: the influx of immigrants in the fourteenth-century Rio Grande led to some settlements adopting glaze wares, while other settlements remained committed to white ware manufacture (Eckert, chap. 9). Eckert also illustrates that some indigenous potters adopted the glaze ware technology from Western Pueblo potters (at least at Hummingbird Pueblo), and that potters sometimes used the same clays for local glaze ware and white ware production. Along the thirteenth-century Mogollon Rim (Fenn, Mills, and Hopkins, chap. 4) and in fifteenth-century Zuni (Schachner, chap. 7), the addition of nonlocal populations is clear from the archaeological record, which contains not only divergent burial traditions but discrete ceramic traditions that reflect distinctive technological styles. In each case, migration may have stimulated the emergence of new identities in the immediate postmigration period, the intensification and diversification of ritual life, and ultimately changes in the local ceramic technological tradition.

The Direction of Future Research

This volume's chapters contain a truly impressive amount of primary data using different analytical techniques. We now know more about southwestern glaze ware ceramic traditions than we do about any other ceramic technological tradition from precontact North America. Yet the contributors themselves suggest directions for future research; I leave substantive questions aside for regional specialists to consider.

On a methodological level, work remains to be done to integrate divergent data sources. Despite myriad compositional studies, more work is needed to merge technical and stylistic approaches into more holistic studies. Exploring communities of practice requires more integrated research that includes the entire range of steps in the operational sequence rather than focusing predominantly on decorative steps (Van Keuren, chap. 5). Stylistic and compositional studies must be combined to provide a proper baseline for studying the nature of change over the four-century period when southwestern glaze wares were manufactured.

Linda Cordell (chap. 14) bemoans the lack of theoretical guidance that a technology-and-agency approach provides, since it focuses primarily on issues surrounding ceramic production. Her point is well taken: we clearly need more theoretical work on ceramic distribution and consumption.

A growing corpus of ethnoarchaeological literature on ceramic distributional networks (for references, see Kramer 1985:82–83, Stark 2003:208–9) provides a starting point for understanding the range of factors that affect how ceramics circulate. So, too, does recent ceramic ethnoarchaeological research on ceramic use or consumption (see Stark 2003:209–13).

On a conceptual level, using a technological approach raises the bar for archaeological ceramicists, even in a region like the North American Southwest where the analytical caliber of such work is already outstanding. Concepts like technological style and habitus are useful to archaeologists, but require refinement and incorporation into a dynamic framework. Likewise, work to define, identify, and track communities of practice in the archaeological record has just begun. Bridging the source fields of these concepts and the archaeological correlates we study requires hard work by archaeologists. Southwestern archaeological ceramicists are well situated to undertake such work, particularly those working on glaze wares, as work in this volume illustrates.

On a theoretical level, archaeological ceramic studies can and should contribute to our understanding of the social life of things in general (following Appadurai 1986) and of pots in particular. Thus far, regrettably, the exchange has been largely unidirectional: archaeologists are generally consumers of external theory more than we are producers (Yoffee and Sherratt 1993). The bold questions of this volume's chapters concerning glaze paint ceramics in the Pueblo IV period test the limits of our conventional interpretive analysis. The precontact North American Southwest is deservedly famous for its archaeological research tradition, particularly in the realm of methodology. Southwestern archaeology contains some of the world's finest-grained chronologies, most precisely dated ceramics, and best-documented sites. This region is particularly well suited to pushing conceptual and theoretical boundaries.

In her chapter, Suzanne Eckert (chap. 3) calls for models that map complex relationships between material culture and social practices, models that archaeologists must build. Southwestern archaeologists working with glaze wares have an excellent opportunity to use fine-grained data sets to tack between the archaeological record and comparative ethnoarchaeological approaches. Doing so not only refines methodologies and encourages ethnoarchaeologists to undertake more relevant research; it contributes to our understanding of the social lives of pots across the precontact North American Southwest, and of the artisans who made them.

Acknowledgments

I would like to thank Judith Habicht-Mauche, Suzanne Eckert, and Deborah Huntley for inviting me to join their SAA session on glaze ware ceramics and to participate in this volume, and for their comments on my chapter. I am also grateful to James Bayman, Judith Habicht-Mauche, Suzanne Eckert, and Deborah Huntley for comments on an earlier draft of this chapter. I take full responsibility, however, for its final form.

3

The Production and Distribution of Glaze-Painted Pottery in the Pueblo Southwest

A Synthesis

Suzanne L. Eckert

> Archaeologists derive scant comfort from the fact
> that over and above the certainties of death and taxes,
> they are blessed with the additional constant of a
> seemingly limitless quantity of sherds to classify.
> —Prudence M. Rice (in D. H. Thomas 1999: 119)

Although a glaze-painted white ware was produced in the Four Corners region in the eighth and ninth centuries (Blinman and Wilson 1993; Shepard 1939; Wilson 1996), glaze-painted polychrome pottery was produced in west Mexico ca. AD 900 (Weigand 1975), and glaze-painted vessels were produced during the Medio period (AD 1150–1450) at Casas Grandes (Di Peso, Rinaldo, and Fenner 1974), none of these events approached the temporal and spatial scale of protohistoric glaze-painted pottery production. At its peak, glaze-painted pottery was made throughout much of the Pueblo Southwest; further, production lasted for approximately four hundred years. The introduction of glaze paint in some Pueblo areas was accompanied by changes in other material traits, suggesting that changes in pottery production were part of a suite of behaviors associated with specific social processes such as migration (E. K. Reed 1949:169–70; Shepard 1942:197–99; Warren 1976), expanding exchange networks (Habicht-Mauche 1995; Snow 1981), or the spread of new ritual systems (Crown 1994; Graves and Eckert 1998:279; Spielmann 1998). The goal in this chapter is to present a current understanding of the production and distribution of glaze-painted pottery throughout the Pueblo Southwest. Authors in the remainder of this volume address the broader issues of production, regional interaction, migration, and other social dynamics surrounding glaze-painted pottery.

Archaeologists working in the Southwest United States have not developed a single typology for glaze-painted pottery. Instead, two different *archaeological* traditions of decorated ceramic analysis exist, each focusing on different decorative and technological attributes. In general, archaeologists classifying glaze-painted vessels in the Western Pueblo region focus primarily on slip color, design layout, and design elements when recording ceramic types (Carlson 1970; Woodbury and Woodbury 1966). In the Rio Grande region, archaeologists focus more on rim form and temper type (Kidder and Shepard 1936; Mera 1935; Shepard 1942). In some areas, such as the Acoma area, a combination of these two traditions has been attempted (Seventh Southwestern Ceramic Seminar 1965). Further, *within* each of these overarching typological traditions, separate ceramic types and type variants have been identified. While these approaches to ceramic typology are useful for the regions in which they were developed, none are without problems. I do not presume to choose between these traditions, or solve the problems inherent to each. Rather, I present a brief summary of the five glaze ware series recognized by southwestern archaeologists (figs. 3.1 and 3.2), and provide references for more detailed descriptions of specific ceramic types. I focus on bowl forms, as they are the most common and temporally sensitive form in each series.

White Mountain Red Ware Series

Originally defined by Colton and Hargrave (1937) as the red-slipped pottery produced and distributed in east-central Arizona and west-central New Mexico, White Mountain Red Ware has been most thoroughly described by Carlson (1970). Glaze-painted pottery types in this series include late St. Johns Polychrome, Pinedale Black-on-red and Polychrome, Cedar Creek Polychrome, and Fourmile Polychrome (table 3.1). In general, St. Johns Polychrome bowls are red or orange slipped, with matte-painted designs in the Tularosa style (see fig. 3.3A) on the interior, and white-painted, broad-lined geometric designs on the exterior (Carlson 1970). Glaze- and subglaze-painted examples of St. Johns Polychrome,

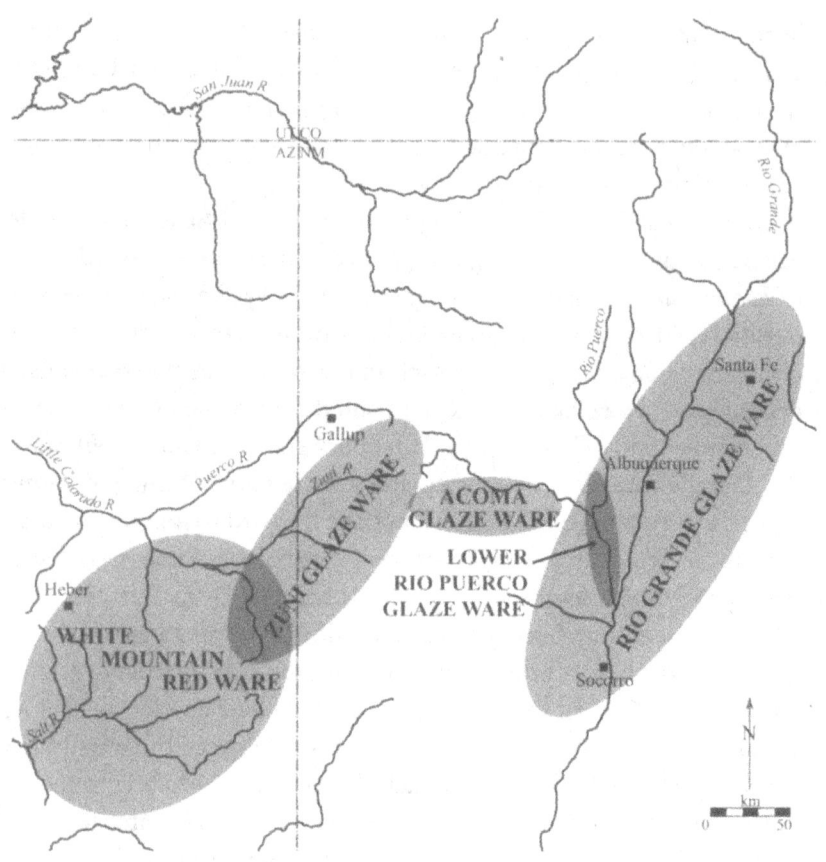

Fig. 3.1. Map of the Pueblo Southwest showing believed production areas of Pueblo Glaze Ware series.

assumed to postdate AD 1250, have been identified in the Zuni area (Kintigh 1985b; Huntley, chap. 6, this vol.). St. Johns Polychrome vessels with glaze and subglaze paint have been recovered from at least two sites with absolute dates, Atsinna and NA 11530. The earliest tree-ring date from Atsinna, located in the El Morro National Monument, is AD 1274rG (Robinson 1981); the latest tree-ring date at NA 11530, located on the modern-day Zuni Indian Reservation, is AD 1277 (Zier 1976). Although there is no direct association between these tree-ring samples and glaze-painted St. Johns Polychrome pottery within each site, the dating of these sites nevertheless suggests that the beginning of glaze paint production was at approximately AD 1275 (also see Fenn, Mills, and Hopkins, chap. 4,

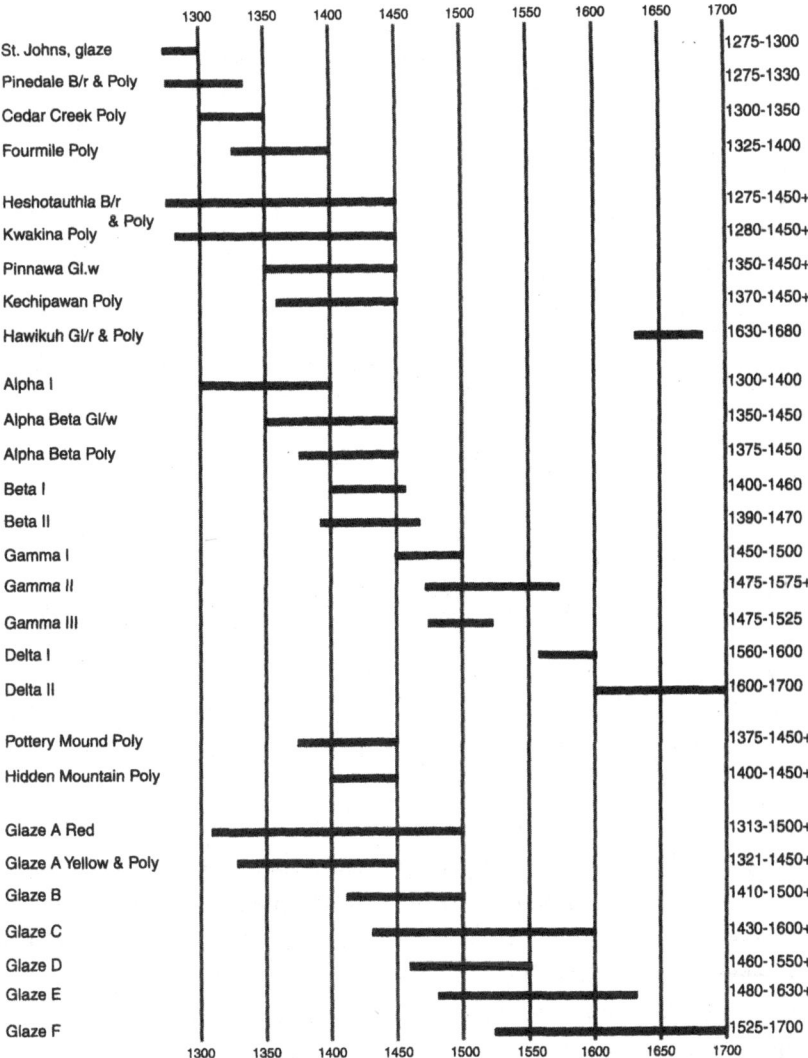

Fig. 3.2. Time line showing date ranges of major types in each glaze ware series.

this vol., where the authors argue that the glaze paint on pre-1275 Cibola White Ware types is not a "true" glaze compositionally, but rather an accidental product).

Pinedale Black-on-red and Polychrome bowls are red or orange slipped with glaze-painted designs in the Pinedale style (see fig. 3.3B) on the interior (Carlson 1970). White paint may be incorporated into the interior

Table 3.1

Summary of Glaze-Painted Pottery Types in the White Mountain Red Ware Series

Type	Date Range	Interior Decoration		Exterior Decoration	
late St. Johns Polychrome	1275–1300	slip:	red to orange	slip:	red to orange
		paint:	glaze	paint:	white
		design:	Tularosa style	design:	geometrics
Pinedale B/r and Polychrome	1275–1330	slip:	red to orange	slip:	red to orange
		paint:	glaze; may also have white	paint:	none, glaze, or glaze on white background
		design:	Pinedale style	design:	none or simple unit designs
Cedar Creek Polychrome	1300–1350	slip:	red	slip:	red
		paint:	glaze and white	paint:	glaze and white
		design:	Pinedale style	design:	banded
Fourmile Polychrome	1325–1400	slip:	red	slip:	red
		paint:	glaze and white	paint:	glaze and white
		design:	Fourmile style	design:	banded

design on Pinedale Polychrome. On the exterior, Pinedale Black-on-red may have no design or may have a simple glaze-painted unit design such as an X or a spiral. On Pinedale Polychrome, these unit designs are outlined in white paint. Although most frequently found in east-central Arizona along the Mogollon Rim, Pinedale types have been found as far north as the Homol'ovi area, as far south as Casas Grandes, and as far east as the Rio Puerco of the East. A cluster of tree-ring dates between AD 1270 and 1285 (Duff 2002; Mills et al. 1999) associated with Pinedale types places the beginning of production at this time. The latest associated tree-ring sample, dated to AD 1330, was recovered from Pinedale Pueblo (Haury and Hargrave 1931).

Cedar Creek Polychrome bowls are red slipped with glaze- and white-painted designs in the Pinedale style (see fig. 3.3B) on the interior (Carlson 1970). A continuous, banded design normally occurs around the exterior of bowls. This exterior design has glaze-painted elements as well as fine white lines. Cedar Creek Polychrome is most commonly found in

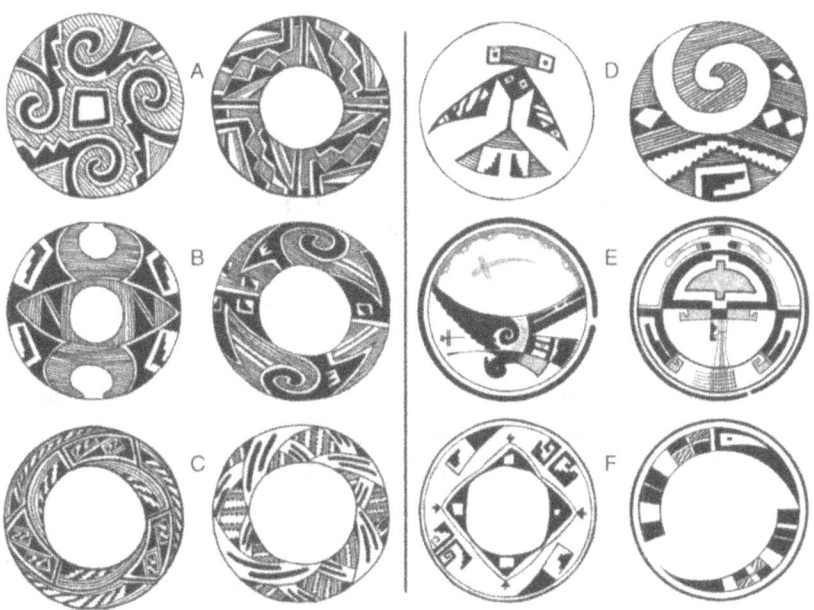

Fig. 3.3. Examples of various design styles common to protohistoric glaze-painted pottery in the Pueblo Southwest: (A) Tularosa, (B) Pinedale, (C) Heshotauthla, (D) Fourmile, (E) Sityatki, and (F) Rio Grande Glaze A (after Carlson 1970; Eckert 2003; and Woodbury 1966).

east-central Arizona along the Mogollon Rim. The relative frequency of Cedar Creek Polychrome compared to Pinedale Polychrome and Fourmile Polychrome in Mogollon Rim site assemblages, combined with tree-ring cross-dating (Carlson 1970:63), suggests that the type's period of production was AD 1300–1350.

Fourmile Polychrome bowls are red slipped with glaze- and white-painted designs in the Fourmile style (see fig. 3.3D) on the interior (Carlson 1970; Van Keuren, chap. 5, this vol.). Fourmile style is a departure from previous design styles on White Mountain Red Ware, as it is asymmetrical and often features zoomorphs and anthropomorphs (E. C. Adams 1991; Carlson 1970). Exterior designs are similar to Cedar Creek Polychrome, but may be more elaborate. The distribution of Fourmile Polychrome is concentrated in the area immediately above and below the Mogollon Rim but is common as far north as the Homol'ovi area (Carlson 1970:69). The earliest tree-ring date associated with Fourmile Polychrome is a cutting date of AD 1326 from Canyon Creek Ruin (Haury

1934). The type was produced until abandonment around AD 1390 in the Silver Creek area (Mills et al. 1999), and possibly in the upper Little Colorado area (Duff 2002). After AD 1400, in the Point of Pines area below the Mogollon Rim, Point of Pines Polychrome was produced. Production of this Fourmile Polychrome copy continued until approximately AD 1450 (Carlson 1970) and marks the end of the White Mountain Red Ware tradition.

Zuni Glaze Ware Series

Zuni Glaze Ware types were an outgrowth of St. Johns Black-on-red and Polychrome, and represent parallel decorative developments with glaze-painted types in the White Mountain Red Ware series. Different archaeologists have described various Zuni glaze-painted pottery types (Bushnell 1955; Bushnell and Digby 1955; Carlson 1970; Hodge 1924; Mera 1939); however, Reed (1955) and Woodbury and Woodbury (1966) are the most common references. Early glaze-painted types in the Zuni Glaze Ware series include Heshotauthla Black-on-red and Polychrome, Kwakina Polychrome, Pinnawa Glaze-on-white, and Kechipawan Polychrome (table 3.2). These types were produced and distributed from the upper Little Colorado River area in the west to the El Morro Valley in the east.

Heshotauthla Black-on-red and Polychrome bowls are bright red or orange slipped with glaze-painted designs in the Heshotauthla style (see fig. 3.3C) on the interior (Carlson 1970; Seventh Southwestern Ceramic Seminar 1965). Heshotauthla Polychrome has white-painted thin-lined geometric designs on the exterior. As Heshotauthla style is often confused with Pinedale style, a brief description seems warranted here. Heshotauthla style has designs normally laid out in a thin band, often divided into quarters, around a circular open base. Designs are normally geometrics, with more painted surface than unpainted (creating a "negative" effect), often incorporating solid fill, "eyes," lightning, and stepped motifs. Unlike in the Pinedale style (Carlson 1970; Crown 1994), hatched motifs are almost never present in the Heshotauthla style. The earliest tree-ring date for Heshotauthla Polychrome comes from Rattlesnake Point Pueblo, with a cutting date of AD 1272+rG (Duff 2002). Further, Heshotauthla Black-on-red and Polychrome share the same early dates as the glaze-painted St. Johns types described above: namely, AD 1274 (Robinson 1981) and AD 1277 (Zier 1976). Production of Heshotauthla types ended during

Table 3.2
Summary of Pottery Types in the Zuni Glaze Ware Series

Type	Date Range	Interior Decoration		Exterior Decoration	
Heshotauthla B/r and Polychrome	1275–1450+	slip:	red to orange	slip:	red to orange
		paint:	glaze	paint:	none or white, occasionally glaze
		design:	Heshotauthla style	design:	none or geometrics
Kwakina Polychrome	1280–1450+	slip:	white	slip:	red to orange
		paint:	glaze	paint:	none or white
		design:	varies; Pinedale, Tularosa, and Heshotauthla styles not uncommon	design:	none or geometrics
Pinnawa Gl/w	1350–1450+	slip:	white; may have red on center of bowl	slip:	white
		paint:	glaze	paint:	none or glaze
		design:	simple bands or Sityatki style	design:	none or unit designs
Kechipawan Polychrome	1370–1450+	slip:	white; may have red on center of bowl	slip:	white
		paint:	glaze with matte red used as filler	paint:	none or glaze and matte red
		design:	simple bands or Sityatki style	design:	none, unit designs, or simple bands
Hawikuh Gl/r and Polychrome	1630–80	slip:	dark red or white	slip:	dark red, white, or both
		paint:	none	paint:	glaze, sometimes with matte red
		design:	none	design:	banded

the mid-1400s (Kintigh 1985b; Woodbury and Woodbury 1966; Schachner, chap. 7, this vol.).

Kwakina Polychrome marks the introduction of white slips on glaze-painted pottery in the Western Pueblo region. Bowls of this type are white slipped on the interior and red or orange slipped on the exterior (Carlson 1970; Woodbury and Woodbury 1966). Glaze-painted designs on the interior may be in any number of styles (Carlson 1970), including Tularosa, Pinedale, or Heshotauthla (see fig. 3.3A,B,C). Exterior designs are white-painted, thin-lined geometrics nearly identical to exterior designs on Heshotauthla Polychrome. Kwakina Polychrome appears to have been produced starting at about the same time as, or only slightly after, the production of Heshotauthla Polychrome (Kintigh 1985b). Seriation of these two types is complicated by the fact that differences in relative frequencies of Kwakina Polychrome and Heshotauthla Polychrome at sites in the Zuni area may reflect group affiliation rather than a temporal trend (Huntley and Kintigh 2004; Huntley, chap. 6, this vol.). Kwakina Polychrome appears to have been produced until the mid-1400s (Kintigh 1985b; Woodbury and Woodbury 1966; Schachner, chap. 7, this vol.).

Pinnawa Glaze-on-white and Kechipawan Polychrome have similar decorative features. Both types are white slipped (although Woodbury and Woodbury [1966] report occasional Kechipawan Polychrome vessels with pale buff slips), with some late examples having a red slip on the center of bowl interiors. Early examples of both types (prior to approximately AD 1400) tend to have well-executed, glaze-painted designs with birds and geometric motifs prominent. Later examples of both types tend to have complex designs in the Sityatki style (see fig. 3.3E), or have a simple anthropomorph or zoomorph in the center of the bowl (Woodbury and Woodbury 1966). Stylized feathers and birds are common on both Pinnawa Glaze-on-white and Kechipawan Polychrome. The defining difference lies in the use of red paint as motif filler in Kechipawan Polychrome designs, while Pinnawa Glaze-on-white designs are only executed in glaze paint. Although production of Pinnawa Glaze-on-white may have begun a decade or so earlier than Kechipawan Polychrome (Kintigh 1985b), both types are believed to have been produced starting in the mid-1300s. Both are present at Rattlesnake Point Pueblo, where the latest tree-ring date is AD 1377 (Duff 2002). Production of these white-slipped types continued to the mid-1400s, when glaze-painted pottery ceased to be produced in the Zuni area for almost two hundred years (Kintigh 1985b; Schachner, chap. 7, this volume; Woodbury and Woodbury 1966).

Hawikuh Glaze-on-red and Polychrome (Mera 1939; Mills 2002a; Seventh Southwestern Ceramic Seminar 1965) are glaze-painted types that were produced in the Zuni area, but were neither temporally nor technologically continuous with earlier glaze-painted types (Schachner, chap. 7, this vol.). Instead, Hawikuh Glaze-on-red and Polychrome appear to have been the result of the *reintroduction* of glaze paint technology into the Zuni area from the Rio Grande region (Mills 1995, 2002a; Woodbury and Woodbury 1966). Designs include one or two bands on the exterior of bowls or jars, normally broken into panels. Stylized feathers are common motifs (Mera 1939). Hawikuh types began to be produced in the six historic Zuni villages after the construction of two Spanish missions in AD 1629, and ceased to be produced after the Pueblo Revolt of 1680. This marks the end of the glaze ware tradition in the Zuni region.

Acoma Glaze Ware Series

The Acoma Glaze Ware series has been only nominally discussed in print (Seventh Southwestern Ceramic Seminar 1965), but current understanding suggests that early types in the series share traits with the Zuni Glaze Ware series (Schachner, chap. 7, this vol.), while later types in the series share traits with the Rio Grande Glaze Ware series. Ceramic types in this series include Heshotauthla Black-on-red and Polychrome (Acoma variants), Alpha I, Alpha Beta Glaze-on-white and Polychrome, Beta I, Beta II, Gamma I types, Gamma II types, Gamma III, Delta I types, and Delta II types (table 3.3). Estimated date ranges for these types provided in figure 3.2 are based on seriation and ceramic cross-dating (Seventh Southwestern Ceramic Seminar 1965).

Heshotauthla Black-on-red and Polychrome (Acoma variant) bowls often have a deep red to maroon slip, with glaze-painted designs in the Heshotauthla style (see fig. 3.3C) on the interior. Although Heshotauthla Black-on-red is more common in the Acoma area than in the Zuni area, Heshotauthla Polychrome is not uncommon. This type has white-painted thin-lined geometric designs on the exterior, often with a single line of glaze paint near the rim. Alpha I (early Kwakina Polychrome, Acoma variant) bowls have a bright white slip on the interior and a deep red to maroon slip on the exterior. Exterior designs are normally absent; when present, they may be identical to Heshotauthla Polychrome (Acoma variant), or a simple glaze-painted X, or a pair of glaze-painted slashes. Both Alpha I and Acoma variants of Heshotauthla types have Rio Grande Glaze A rim forms (see fig. 3.4).

Alpha Beta Glaze-on-white (Pinnawa Glaze-on-white, Acoma variant) and Alpha Beta Polychrome (Kechipawan Polychrome, Acoma variant) are almost identical to their Zuni Glaze Ware series counterparts.

Table 3.3
Summary of Pottery Types in the Acoma Glaze Ware Series

Type	Date Range (Rim Form)	Interior Decoration		Exterior Decoration	
Heshotauthla B/r and Polychrome, Acoma variant	1275–1450+ (A rim)	slip: paint: design:	red to dark maroon glaze Heshotauthla style	slip: paint: design:	red to dark maroon none or white and glaze none, or geometrics in white with single glaze line, X's, or slashes
Alpha I	1300–1400 (A rim)	slip: paint: design:	bright white glaze varies: Pinedale, Tularosa, and Heshotauthla styles not uncommon	slip: paint: design:	red to dark maroon none, white, white and glaze, or glaze none, or geometrics in white with single glaze line, X's, or slashes
Alpha Beta Gl/w	1350–1450 (A rim)	slip: paint: design:	bright white glaze normally simple bands	slip: paint: design:	bright white none or glaze none or unit designs
Alpha Beta Polychrome	1375–1450 (A rim)	slip: paint: design:	bright white glaze with matte red used as filler normally simple bands	slip: paint: design:	bright white glaze with matte red used as filler normally simple bands
Beta I	1400–1460 (C rim)	slip: paint: design:	bright white with red round rim glaze varies, usually banded design	slip: paint: design:	red to dark maroon none or glaze none or simple unit design
Beta II	1390–1470 (beveled rim)	slip: paint: design:	red to dark maroon glaze varies, usually banded design	slip: paint: design:	bright white none or glaze none or simple unit design

Table 3.3

Continued

Type	Date Range (Rim Form)	Interior Decoration		Exterior Decoration	
Gamma I	1450–1500 (C rim)	slip:	dark red or bright white	slip:	dark red or bright white
		paint:	glaze, sometimes with matte red	paint:	uncertain
		design:	simple band	design:	uncertain
Gamma II	1475–1575+ (C rim)	slip:	dark red	slip:	dark red
		paint:	none	paint:	glaze, sometimes with white
		design:	none	design:	banded
Gamma III	1475–1525 (A rim)	slip:	dark red	slip:	dark red
		paint:	glaze	paint:	uncertain
		design:	uncertain	design:	uncertain
Delta I	1560–1600 (E and F rims)	slip:	dark red or bright white	slip:	dark red or bright white
		paint:	none	paint:	glaze
		design:	none	design:	banded
Delta II	1600–1700 (F rim)	slip:	dark red or bright white	slip:	dark red, bright white, or both
		paint:	none	paint:	glaze
		design:	none	design:	banded

Slips are always bright white on both types. Alpha Beta Polychrome bowls often have glaze-outlined designs filled with red paint on the exterior. Rim forms on these two types are normally the same as Rio Grande Glaze A, although later rim forms have been noted.

Beta I (Kwakina Polychrome, Acoma variant) is a "continuation of Alpha I" (Seventh Southwestern Ceramic Seminar 1965:7). The major difference between Alpha I and Beta I bowls is that, on the latter, the exterior red slip comes up over the rim into the bowl interior. The resulting effect is of a red band around the interior rim of the bowl. Further, Beta I never has thin white-lined geometrics on the exterior. Beta I rim forms are similar to Rio Grande Glaze C. Beta II (reverse Kwakina Poly-

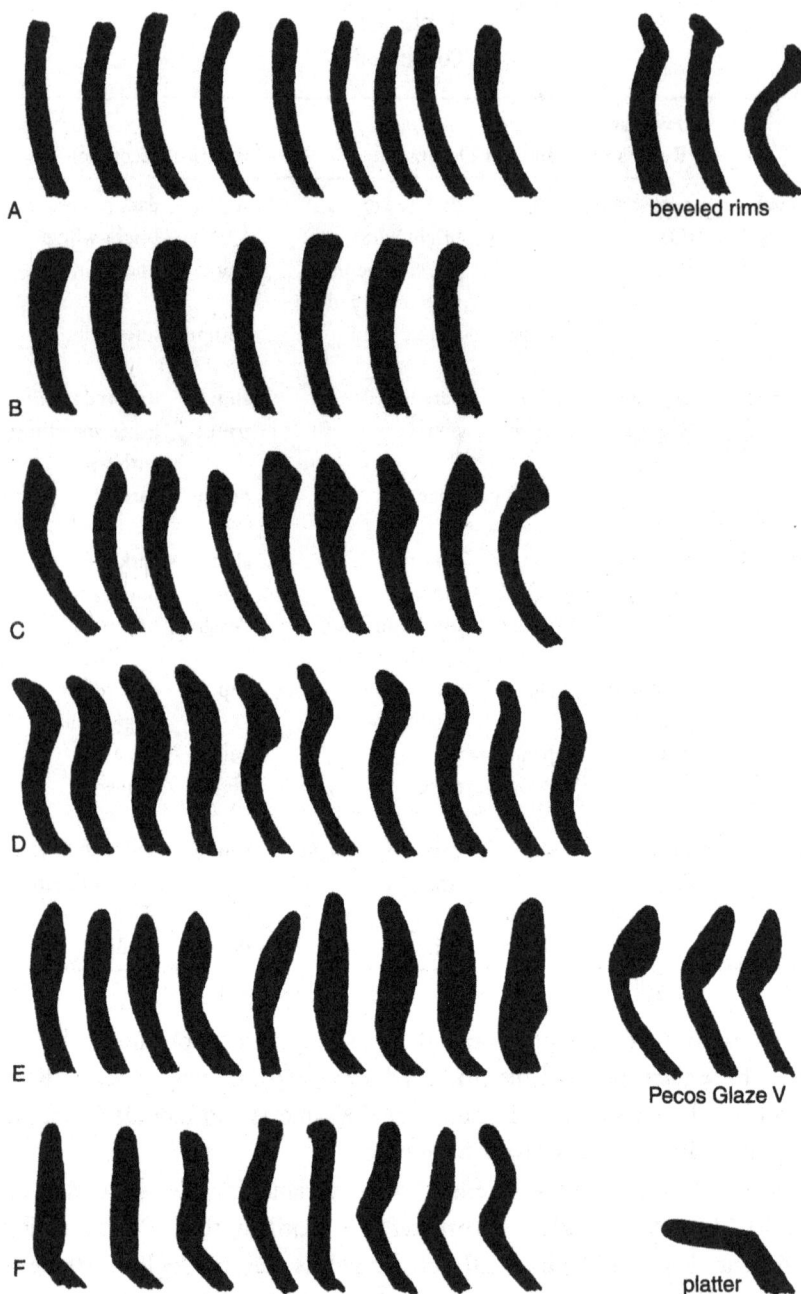

Fig. 3.4. Rio Grande Glaze Ware rim forms (after Eckert 2003).

chrome, Acoma variant) has a deep red slip on the interior of bowls and a white slip on the exterior. This slip color combination also occurs on pottery sherds recovered from the Middle Village excavations at Zuni Pueblo (Mills 2002b), as well as on pottery from the lower Rio Puerco of the East (described below). Originally described as unique (Seventh Southwestern Ceramic Seminar 1965), the rim form on Beta II is actually the same as the "beveled rim" on Rio Grande Glaze A (see fig. 3.4) (Eighth Southwestern Ceramic Seminar 1966). Glaze-painted designs occur on the interior of bowls and are similar to Beta I. The glaze paint on Beta II seems to mark a change in the composition of glaze paint in the Acoma area, as this and later glaze paints are more likely to erode when compared to earlier glaze-painted types (Seventh Southwestern Ceramic Seminar 1965).

Gamma I Black-on-red, Glaze-on-white, and Polychrome and Gamma II Glaze-on-red and Polychrome all have Rio Grande Glaze C rim forms and temporally overlap with this type (Snow 1989). Gamma I and II types are distinctive from Rio Grande types in that they do not have pastel-colored slips, but continue to have the dark red and bright white slips present on earlier glaze-painted types. Occasionally, some vessels have a light cream-colored slip. Gamma I types are believed to have been produced a decade or so earlier than Gamma II and seem to have had a more restricted temporal range of production (see fig. 3.2) (Seventh Southwestern Ceramic Seminar 1965). Gamma I and Gamma II types are distinctive in that the former have designs focused on bowl interiors, while the latter have designs focused on bowl exteriors. Not much is known about Gamma III Glaze-on-red other than it has a dark red slip and Rio Grande Glaze A rim forms (Seventh Southwestern Ceramic Seminar 1965). The production of Gamma III Glaze-on-red may be related to the apparently long period of production of Glaze A Red in the southern portion of the Rio Grande region (discussed below).

Very little description has been provided for the Delta types. Delta I types begin to "resemble glazes E and F from the Rio Grande," while Delta II types are "almost a duplicate of glaze F" (Seventh Southwestern Ceramic Seminar 1965:8). All Delta types have design predecessors in the earlier Acoma Glaze Ware types; however, the introduction of the "indented jar bottom" on Delta II-type jars may have been introduced from the Rio Grande area (Seventh Southwestern Ceramic Seminar 1965:8).

Table 3.4
Summary of Pottery Types in the Lower Rio Puerco
of the East Glaze Ware Series

Type	Date Range (Rim Form)	Interior Decoration		Exterior Decoration	
Pottery Mound Polychrome	1375–1450+ (A rim)	slip:	yellow buff	slip:	red
		paint:	glaze with matte red used as filler	paint:	none or glaze
		design:	Sityatki style	design:	none, X's or slashes
Hidden Mountain Polychrome	1400–1450+ (A and C rims)	slip:	red	slip:	bright white
		paint:	none	paint:	glaze on white
		design:	none	design:	banded around rim

Lower Rio Puerco of the East Glaze Ware Series

Although potters in the lower Rio Puerco of the East area produced glaze-painted pottery that shared traits with the pottery produced by their neighbors to the west and east, they also produced two types unique to the area: Pottery Mound Polychrome (Eckert 2003; Voll 1961) and Hidden Mountain Polychrome (table 3.4) (Eckert 2003). Pottery Mound Polychrome bowls are slipped yellow-buff on the interior and red on the exterior. Decoration is with both glaze and matte red paint, most often in the Sityatki design style (see fig. 3.3E) (Brody 1964; Colton 1955). Stylized birds and feathers are common motifs. Hidden Mountain Polychrome bowls have a dark red-slipped interior and bright white-slipped exterior. Although the slip-color combination is similar to that of Beta II from the Acoma glaze series, the focus of the design on Hidden Mountain Polychrome is on a band on the exterior of the vessel; the interior of bowls has either a very simple design or, more commonly, no design. Serpent, eye, and lightning motifs are common. Both types have Rio Grande Glaze A rim forms, including the beveled rim. Hidden Mountain Polychrome may also have Glaze C rim forms. Production of both types was restricted to the late fourteenth- and fifteenth-century village of Pottery Mound. Both types were exported to Hummingbird Pueblo, another village along the lower Rio Puerco of the East (Eckert 2003). Further, Pottery Mound Polychrome has been recovered from sites in the Rio Grande region (Hayes, Young, and Warren 1981).

The Pecos and Rio Grande Glaze Ware Series

The earliest seriation of glaze-painted pottery found in the Rio Grande region was by Nels C. Nelson (1914), who examined design elements and stratigraphic data to establish a chronology of three glaze-painted types at San Cristobal. Kidder (1917b) employed similar techniques to create an initial seriation of glaze-painted pottery types at Pecos Pueblo. Mera (1933) noted that application of these typologies was problematic when applied to the greater Rio Grande area and proposed the Rio Grande Glaze Ware series. This series, which was based primarily on bowl rim forms, consisted of six ceramic types, Glaze A–F (see fig. 3.4). Kidder and Shepard's subsequent work at Pecos Pueblo adopted this system of classification to establish the Pecos Glaze Ware series, which also consisted of six ceramic types, Glaze I–VI (Kidder and Shepard 1936). The Pecos and Rio Grande Glaze Ware series are, for the most part, considered equivalent; however, Mera's terminology has become the standard for Rio Grande archaeologists (table 3.5) (Eighth Southwestern Ceramic Seminar 1966). Within each rim form type, subtypes have been defined and named based on slip color, decoration, and temper. Bowl rim form, however, remains the primary classification system for glaze-painted pottery recovered in the Rio Grande area (Eighth Southwestern Ceramic Seminar 1966; Snow 1989; Warren and Snow 1976).

The Rio Grande Glaze Ware series is often divided into three temporal phases: early (A, B), intermediate (C, D), and late (E, F). These divisions are based on the observation that certain changes, other than rim form, occur over time (Eighth Southwestern Ceramic Seminar 1966). Both glaze paint composition (Herhahn, chap. 10, this vol.) and temper type (Shepard 1942) become more standardized. Color and texture of glaze paint also change, although it is important to note that later traits are simply added to the list of characteristics. In other words, earlier traits never completely drop out. Early glaze paint ranges in color from black to brownish black to greenish black, and occasionally bright green; intermediate glaze paint ranges from greenish brown to yellowish brown to brown to dark brown, to brownish black; and late glaze paint ranges from brown to brownish black to black, and occasionally apple green (Eighth Southwestern Ceramic Seminar 1966). The texture of the paint also changes: early glaze paint tends to be lustrous, may bead, and "holds to line of original application" (Eighth Southwestern Ceramic Semi-

Table 3.5
Summary of Pottery Types in the Pecos and Rio Grande Glaze Ware Series

Date Range	Interior Decoration		Exterior Decoration	
Glaze A Red types (Agua Fria Gl/r; Los Padillos Poly; Sanchez Gl/r)				
1313–1500+	slip:	red to orange	slip:	red to orange
	paint:	well-controlled, lustrous glaze ranging in color from black, brownish black, greenish black, to bright green	paint:	none, white, or glaze
	design:	Heshotauthla style or Rio Grande Glaze A style	design:	none, or geometrics in white, X's, or slashes
Glaze A Yellow types (Cienguilla Gl/y and Poly; Sanchez Gl/y and Sanchez Poly)				
1321–1450+	slip:	white to yellow	slip:	white to yellow
	paint:	well-controlled, lustrous glaze ranging in color from black, brownish black, greenish black, to bright green	paint:	none or glaze
	design:	Heshotauthla style or Rio Grande Glaze A style	design:	none, X's, or slashes
Glaze A Gl/poly types (San Clemente Poly)				
1321–1450+	slip:	white to yellow	slip:	red to orange
	paint:	well-controlled, lustrous glaze ranging in color from black, brownish black, greenish black, to bright green	paint:	none or glaze
	design:	Heshotauthla style or Rio Grande Glaze A style	design:	none, X's, or slashes
Glaze B types (Largo Gl/r, Gl/y, and Poly; Medio Poly)				
1410–1500+	slip:	red, white, or yellow	slip:	red, white, or yellow
	paint:	well-controlled, lustrous glaze ranging in color from black, brownish black, greenish black, to bright green	paint:	well-controlled, lustrous glaze ranging in color from black, brownish black, greenish black, to bright green
	design:	paneled band below rim	design:	X's or slashes

Table 3.5

Continued

Date Range	Interior Decoration		Exterior Decoration	

Glaze C types (Espinosa Gl/r and Poly; Kuaua Poly)

1410–1600+	slip:	soft red, fawn, tan, orangish, reddish, red brown	slip:	soft red, fawn, tan, orangish, reddish, red brown
	paint:	slightly runny, dull to lustrous glaze ranging in color from greenish brown, yellowish brown, brown, dark brown, to brownish black; matte red	paint:	slightly runny, dull to lustrous glaze ranging in color from greenish brown, yellowish brown, brown, dark brown, to brownish black; matte red
	design:	paneled band below rim, may have matte red line below rim	design:	matte red figures with glaze outline; may have rim ticking

Glaze D (San Lazaro Poly)

1460–1550+	slip:	soft red, fawn, tan, orangish, reddish, red brown	slip:	soft red, fawn, tan, orangish, reddish, red brown
	paint:	none or slightly runny, dull to lustrous glaze ranging in color from greenish brown, yellowish brown, brown, dark brown, to brownish black; matte red	paint:	slightly runny, dull to lustrous glaze ranging in color from greenish brown, yellowish brown, brown, dark brown, to brownish black; matte red
	design:	none or paneled band below rim, may have matte red line outlined in glaze below rim	design:	matte red figures with glaze outline; may have rim ticking

Glaze E types (Puaray Gl/r, Gl/y, and Poly; Trenaquel Poly; Escondido Poly; Tiguex Poly; Encierro Poly; Pecos Poly)

| 1480–1630+ | slip: | whitish, tannish, yellowish, reddish, fawn, thin fawn, tan | slip: | whitish, tannish, yellowish, reddish, fawn, thin fawn, tan |

Table 3.5

Continued

Date Range	Interior Decoration		Exterior Decoration	
	paint:	runny, semilustrous to lustrous glaze ranging in color from brownish, brownish black, to black, and occasionally apple green; matte red	paint:	runny, semilustrous to lustrous glaze ranging in color from brownish, brownish black, to black, and occasionally apple green; matte red
	design:	unpaneled band below rim, may have matte red line outlined in glaze below rim	design:	matte red figures with glaze outline

Glaze F types (Kotyiti Gl/r, Gl/y, and Poly; San Marcos Gl/r and Poly; Cicuye Gl/r and Poly; Yunque Gl/r; Polvadera Gl/r and Gl/y

1520–1700	slip:	whitish, tannish, yellowish, reddish, fawn, thin fawn, tan	slip:	whitish, tannish, yellowish, reddish, fawn, thin fawn, tan
	paint:	runny, semilustrous to lustrous glaze ranging in color from brownish, brownish black, to black, and occasionally apple green	paint:	runny, semilustrous to lustrous glaze ranging in color from brownish, brownish black, to black, and occasionally apple green
	design:	simple linear designs, often zigzags, below rim	design:	simple geometric designs in line around rim and pendant birds

nar 1966:I1); intermediate glaze paint is dull to lustrous and sometimes slightly runny; and late glaze paint is semilustrous to lustrous with a "tendency to run and destroy design" (Eighth Southwestern Ceramic Seminar 1966:IV2). Finally, slip colors change through time. Early glaze types have orange red, red, yellow, white, and yellowish white slip colors. Intermediate glaze types often have more muted shades described as soft red, fawn, tan, orangish, reddish, and red brown. Late glaze types continue to have muted shades, including whitish, tannish, yellowish, reddish, fawn, thin fawn, and tan (Eighth Southwestern Ceramic Seminar 1966).

Glaze A types (Los Padillas Polychrome; Agua Fria Glaze-on-red;

Cienguilla Glaze-on-yellow and Polychrome; San Clemente Polychrome; Sanchez Glaze-on-red, Glaze-on-yellow, and Polychrome) are divided into three broad categories based on slip color: Glaze A Red, Glaze A Yellow, and Glaze A Polychrome. Early examples of these types often have Heshotauthla-style designs painted on the interiors (see fig. 3.3C), while later examples have Rio Grande Glaze A style designs (see fig. 3.3F). Glaze A Red was produced throughout most of the Rio Grande area (Shepard 1942). The earliest absolute dates associated with Glaze A Red are a tree-ring date of AD 1287rB from Tijeras Pueblo (Cordell 1975:49) and a group of cutting dates from the same site that cluster around AD 1313 (Cordell 1975:27). Glaze A Yellow appears to have been produced primarily in the Galisteo Basin, while Glaze A Polychrome was produced primarily in the Albuquerque and Los Lunas areas (Eighth Southwestern Ceramic Seminar 1966; Shepard 1942). Production of Glaze A Yellow and Polychrome began slightly later than Glaze A Red (Eighth Southwestern Ceramic Seminar 1966; Shepard 1942). Arroyo Hondo has the earliest tree-ring date, AD 1321r, associated with Glaze A Yellow and Polychrome (Lang 1993). Glaze A Yellow does not appear at Las Madres until after AD 1370 (C. Schaafsma 1969), and no Glaze A Polychrome is reported from the site. Creamer and colleagues (2002) have pointed out that the appearance of Glaze A is associated with a range of tree-ring dates, including AD 1322 for LA 4 (Mera 1940), AD 1330 for Galisteo Pueblo (Mera 1940), and AD 1348 for both Pueblo Blanco (Creamer et al. 2002) and Pindi Pueblo (Stubbs and Stallings 1953). They use this range of dates to argue that glaze technology took several decades to spread across the central Rio Grande area and therefore any assessment of the earliest occurrence of glaze paint must take geographic location into account (Creamer et al. 2002).

Mera (1933) originally suggested that the production of Glaze A had a terminal date of AD 1450. However, more recent research has indicated that this terminal date is far too early for Glaze A Red in some areas (Hayes, Young, and Warren 1981; Marshall 1987; Shepard 1942; Snow 1986). Glaze A Red appears to have been produced in some villages south of Albuquerque up through the contact period. Thus, while the absence of later rim forms generally means that a site dates to the 1300s or 1400s, surface collections from sites in some areas may lack later forms and still date to the 1500s (Creamer et al. 2002).

Glaze B pottery (Largo Glaze-on-red, Glaze-on-yellow, and Polychrome; Medio Polychrome) was never a popular form, but light-slipped vessels appear to have been produced predominantly in the Galisteo Basin, while minor production of red-slipped vessels occurred throughout the Rio Grande area (Mera 1933; Shepard 1942; Snow 1997). Baldwin (1983) has argued that Glaze B is contemporaneous with the production of Glaze A, while Snow (1997) has noted that its production considerably overlaps with the production of Glaze C. Creamer and colleagues (2002) find evidence that Glaze B may have been produced in small quantities up to the contact period. A spread of archaeomagnetic samples from Nuestra Señora de Dolores Pueblo associated with Glaze B puts production at least between AD 1350 and 1440 (Marshall 1982). The relatively rare occurrence of this rim form, along with the current uncertainty for its production span, makes Glaze B a poor temporal marker.

Although Glaze C pottery (Espinosa Glaze-on-red and Polychrome; Kuaua Polychrome) occurs in greater frequencies than Glaze B pottery (Mera 1933; Snow 1997), the type is never a major component of any Rio Grande ceramic assemblage. A great deal of variation has been noted for the Glaze C rim form, which appears to have developed from variants in the Glaze A rim form. In the Estancia Basin, Baldwin (1983) and Snow (1997) agree that Glaze C may simply be a variant of Glaze A. It is with the production of Glaze C that changes in Rio Grande exchange networks begin to occur, with Tonque Pueblo (LA 240) and villages in the Galisteo Basin becoming dominant manufacturers of this type (Shepard 1942; Warren 1969, 1979). Identification of a Glaze C rim during a recent examination of the Arroyo Hondo ceramic assemblage by the author and Judith Habicht-Mauche associates the type with a tree-ring date of AD 1410. Radiocarbon samples taken from floor features containing Glaze C at LA 31746 provided dates of 1570 ± 60 and 1610 ± 60 (Marshall 1987), suggesting that the type was produced until the late 1500s, and possibly into the 1600s (Snow 1997). Creamer and colleagues' (2002) research supports this argument with a finding of a substantial frequency of Glaze C in contexts from San Marcos associated with noncutting tree-ring dates of AD 1613, 1615, 1625, and 1633. A 1600s terminal date for Glaze C is much later than many previous researchers have supposed.

Glaze D (San Lazaro Polychrome) was produced in the Galisteo Basin (Shepard 1942), at Tonque Pueblo (LA 240) (Warren 1969, 1979), Abó, and Picuris (Snow 1989). Temporally, Glaze D overlaps considerably with Glaze C (Shepard 1942). Glaze D was a common type found at

Aguages, where tree-ring dates put the major construction of the site between AD 1457 and 1462 (Snow 1997). Mera (1940) originally believed that Glaze D was not produced past AD 1515; however, Snow (1997) argues Glaze D lasted into at least the late 1500s, and may have lasted as late as the 1600s. Glaze D rims have been recovered from the floor assemblage of a kiva that was constructed between AD 1507 and 1520 at Pueblo del Encierro (Snow 1976), as well as from deposits with radiocarbon dates between AD 1570 and 1670 at Nuestra Señora de Dolores Pueblo (Marshall 1982). The popularity of Glaze C and D vessels in the northern and southern Rio Grande regions, as well as on the Southern Plains, has led Snow to argue that these vessels were made "principally for specialized purposes" (Snow 1997:353) and were acquired through exchange networks with Tonque Pueblo and villages in the Galisteo Basin. As such, the absence of Glaze C and D at a site may reflect the lack of participation in certain social networks rather than temporal trends (Baldwin 1983; Snow 1997).

Glaze E (Puaray Glaze-on-red, Glaze-on-yellow and Polychrome; Trenaquel Polychrome; Escondido Polychrome; Tiguex Polychrome; Encierro Polychrome; Pecos Polychrome) was primarily produced in the Galisteo Basin (Shepard 1942) and at Tonque Pueblo (Warren 1969, 1979, 1981); however, it was also produced at Pecos Pueblo, Zia, Cochiti, Picuris, and in the Albuquerque area (Shepard 1942; Snow 1997; Warren 1969, 1979, 1981). The earliest absolute dates associated with Glaze E come from kiva assemblages at Pueblo del Encierro (Snow 1976), which suggest the type was first produced between AD 1480 and 1500; the type was clearly well established by AD 1520 (Snow 1997). Terminal dates for Glaze E are not well documented. Glaze E made up a substantial portion of the ceramic assemblage from a Spanish colonial site constructed between AD 1629 and 1631 (Snow and Stoller 1987). At Pecos, Kidder and Shepard (1936) recognized an "early" Glaze V (imported Glaze E) and a "late" Glaze V (local Glaze E called Pecos Polychrome), both of which were produced into the 1600s.

Glaze F (Kotyiti Glaze-on-red, Glaze-on-yellow, and Polychrome; San Marcos Glaze-on-red and Polychrome; Cicuye Glaze-on-red and Polychrome; Yunque Glaze-on-red; Polvadera Glaze-on-red and Glaze-on-yellow) was produced in the Galisteo Basin, Estancia Basin, at Pecos Pueblo, and Zia, with lesser amounts being produced in the Jemez area (Shepard 1942; Snow 1982). Some recovered Glaze F vessels have European forms. The earliest absolute date for Glaze F comes from postoccupational fill at an Abó Pass site with an archaeomagnetic date of AD 1520 ± 50 years (Snow 1997). Baldwin (1983) argues that Glaze F was produced as early as AD 1550 in the Rio Abajo, while Snow (1997) argues that it was probably produced starting around AD 1575 at sites farther north. Glaze F was produced until AD 1700, as it is found on Refugee period sites (Capone, chap. 12, this vol.). However, the restructuring of society, land grants, and settlements characteristic of the post-Revolt era resulted in the disappearance of glaze-painted pottery production. This may have been owing, in part, to Spanish control of mineral sources necessary for the production of glaze paint (Shepard 1942). Whatever the reason(s), the knowledge necessary for glaze paint manufacture was "so completely lost that no tradition of the source of the material can be found among present-day Rio Grande Indians" (Shepard 1942:208).

Ceramic Horizons

The discussion thus far has focused on the series of glaze-painted pottery defined for various regions of the Pueblo Southwest. These series are important conceptual constructs because they provide a means of understanding chronological changes in specific study areas. However, series are not the only means by which to classify pottery; understanding broader decorative horizons provides a different perspective that may allow insights into social dynamics on a scale greater than one allowed by examination of regional series alone. A complete understanding of the distribution, chronology, and meaning of these horizons is beyond the scope of this chapter. However, I present here three general horizons, and examples of each, that may be of interest for future research. These three horizons are based on slip color, paint combination, and design style.

Slip Color Variations

Three slip-color variations flourished in the fourteenth-century Pueblo Southwest, including the use of red slip, light-colored slip (white or yellow), and "contrasting" (application of both light-colored and red) slips (Carlson 1970; Crown 1994; Shepard 1942; Snow 1982). All of these combinations have been found in most regions. However, the frequency of any particular slip combination in any particular area varies greatly. Contrasting slips are far more common in the western portion of the Zuni area than in the eastern portion (Huntley and Kintigh 2004), while red slips are far more common in the southern Rio Grande area than light-colored slips (Snow 1982). These slip-color horizons are not limited to glaze-painted pottery. For example, Snow (1982) noted that the application of yellow slips on glaze-painted pottery produced in the Galisteo Basin may have been associated with the production of contemporaneous yellow-slipped, matte-painted pottery types produced in the Hopi area.

Researchers currently have a limited understanding of the social meanings behind slip-color horizons. Carlson (1970) argued that the light-colored slips found on various fourteenth- and fifteenth-century ceramic types in the Western Pueblo region reflected influence from northern Mexico, and Snow (1982) implied that the yellow slip tradition from the Galisteo Basin was an outgrowth of this influence. More recent researchers (Blinman 1988; Crown 1994; Graves and Eckert 1998) have suggested that slip color may reflect certain social affiliations such as ethnic groups or religious sodalities.

Paint Combinations

A second group of decorative horizons that crosscut various glaze ware series is paint combination. Multiple paints can be applied to pottery in several ways. Although other combinations occur, the most common combinations on glaze-decorated pottery include the use of glaze paint on the interior of bowls with white paint on the exterior, glaze paint designs with white paint outlines, and glaze paint designs with red paint filler. The first combination is most common in the Western Pueblo region, occurring on types in both the White Mountain Red Ware and Zuni Glaze Ware series. However, Snow (1989) notes that this combination is also fairly common in the southern Rio Grande area and suggests that it reflects a social affinity between this area and the Western Pueblo region. Glaze paint designs with red paint filler occur in all but the White Mountain Red Ware series, and also occur on contemporaneous matte-painted wares in the Zuni and Hopi areas. The use of red paint filler varies, occurring on the interior of bowls on some ceramic types and on the exterior of bowls on other types. The meaning of these paint combination horizons has not been widely explored. In his study of "polychrome complexes" in the Southwest, Carlson (1982) suggests that the development of multiple paint combinations throughout the greater Southwest may have corresponded to the increasingly complex role of pottery in ceremonial usage.

Morgan (2002) has argued that the "glaze outlined figures" with red filler that occur on the exterior of Rio Grande Glaze Ware types may emphasize symbols relating to a pan-southwestern ideology. Further, the occurrence of these figures on the exterior of bowls may have been an attempt to use shared symbols that fostered regional identities.

Design Styles

Explicit definitions of design style are difficult to find in the archaeological literature, but on pre-Hispanic southwestern pottery the term generally refers to a combination of design layout, elements, and motifs recognized to be consistently applied over either space or time (E. C. Adams 1991; Carlson 1970; Crown 1994). Various design styles have been recognized on glaze-painted pottery (see fig. 3.3) that crosscut various types within and between the regional series described above. For example, the Sityatki design style (Brody 1964; Colton 1955), common to Hopi and Zuni matte-painted pottery types, has been recognized on Pottery Mound Polychrome (Eckert 2003; Voll 1961). Similarly, the Heshotauthla design style has been recognized on glaze-painted pottery produced in both the Western Pueblo and Rio Grande regions (Carlson 1970; Eckert 2003; Seventh Southwestern Ceramic Seminar 1965; Snow 1989; Warren 1980). Problems with the study of design style abound, including vague definitions for some design styles, the inconsistent use of style names across some study areas, and the lack of names for some recognized styles in other areas. Although the occurrence of a specific design style probably indicates some form of interaction between groups spanning the spatial and temporal range of the style, the nature of this interaction remains, for the most part, unclear.

One design style that has received a great deal of attention in the past decade has been the Pinedale style (see fig. 3.3B). Pinedale style occurs on various glaze-painted types in the White Mountain Red Ware series, Zuni Glaze Ware series, and Rio Grande Glaze Ware series. Further, the style occurs on Salado Polychromes and potentially some Rio Grande white wares. Both Adams (1991) and Crown (1994) have argued that the Pinedale design style is related to the spread of specific ideologies throughout portions of the Pueblo Southwest during the fourteenth century. As defined by Adams (1991), the Pinedale style is a decorative characteristic that was shared throughout the Southwest from the upper Little Colorado River valley to northern Mexico. He traces the transition of the Pinedale style into the Fourmile style in the Western Pueblo region. He argues that this transition marked a unique development of an asymmetrical design layout that corresponded with the development of the Katsina cult. Crown (1994) examines the Pinedale style as part of her study of the appearance, distribution, and eventual disappearance of Salado Polychromes during the 1300 and 1400s. She concludes that the Pinedale style displays a suite of icons associated with fertility and weather control and was probably associated with the spread of an ideology and ritual system that integrated disparate groups. Although both Adams's and Crown's studies are important contributions, they each focus on a fairly narrow data set. Understanding the appearance of the Pinedale style across the Pueblo Southwest requires further exploration of the style on a larger scale than either study provides.

Concluding Thoughts

I have provided a synthesis of temporal and geographic trends in Pueblo glaze ware traditions, outlined strengths and weaknesses in the absolute dates associated with glaze ware types, and indicated possible directions for future research that may be effective in improving our understanding of the distribution of various glaze ware characteristics. Although it is my hope that this chapter is a fair representation of our current knowledge, it is by no means meant to be a final discussion. Our understanding of the production and distribution of Pueblo glaze wares can be greatly refined through the collection and analysis of further data.

Acknowledgments

This chapter would have been impossible without input from many colleagues. I would especially like to thank Gregson Schachner and Judith Habicht-Mauche for various long discussions concerning several aspects of this chapter. I am also indebted to Linda Cordell, Andrew Duff, Deborah Huntley, Keith Kintigh, Barbara Mills, David Snow, and two anonymous reviewers. However, any and all mistakes are completely my own.

4

The Social Contexts of Glaze Paint Ceramic Production and Consumption in the Silver Creek Area

Thomas R. Fenn, Barbara J. Mills, and Maren Hopkins

Glaze-painted ceramics were produced and used in the Silver Creek drainage of east-central Arizona during the thirteenth and fourteenth centuries. The Mogollon Rim region (see fig. 1.1) has some of the earliest glaze-painted pottery in the Southwest, other than the short-lived Pueblo I use of glaze paints in the Four Corners area (Shepard 1939; Wilson 1996; Eckert, chap. 3, this vol.). The production of glaze paints in the Mogollon Rim region, especially the Silver Creek drainage, inspired a west-to-east adoption of the technology in the late thirteenth and early fourteenth centuries (Habicht-Mauche et al. 2000:709; Shepard 1956/1980). This chapter addresses the timing, composition, distribution, and morphology of glaze-painted ceramics to better understand the social contexts in which these wares were produced and used in this important area.

Several questions guided our analyses: When was glaze paint introduced? What is the composition of glaze paints in the Mogollon Rim area? Are there differences through time, across wares, and within sites in glaze paint recipes? How can these intrasite differences in glaze paint recipes be used to understand the learning and transmission of technological knowledge? And finally, what are the connections between glaze paint production and broader regional processes that are so important for the period, including migration, aggregation, and ritual reorganization. We consider the above questions within a theoretical framework that acknowledges the importance of understanding technology in its social context, or what some refer to as the social construction of technology (Hosler 1986, 1994; Pfaffenberger 1992; White 1970). It is clear that the social contexts of production, distribution, and consumption are integral to understanding variation in ceramic technology: who made the vessels and why some technological choices were made over others, how the objects moved from locations of production to consumption, and how they were used and in what social contexts.

Like Miriam Stark (chap. 2, this vol.), we view the literature on practice theory as strongly conducive to understanding how technological variation is transmitted and expressed (see also Dietler and Herbich 1998; Hegmon 1998). We also agree with Stark and Scott Van Keueren (chap. 5, this vol.) that the choices that are made in the production of ceramics are bounded by a number of factors, but that these factors are often spatially and socially clustered by what Jean Lave and Etienne Wenger (1991) call "communities of practice." These communities are framed by apprenticeship relationships between potters who learn within communities of craftspeople (Crown 2001; Wallaert-Pêtre 2001).

Communities of practice may be much smaller than residential communities, and in fact, the diversity and number of learning or potting communities may tell us a great deal about some of the key features of craft production. For example, distinctive recipes made at the same time may indicate that boundaries between potting groups were impermeable—either intentionally through social distance or perhaps because potters were spatially removed from each other. Alternatively, recipes that are similar to each other may indicate permeable social boundaries in which information about how to make pots a specific way and/or the materials used in each recipe were shared. As our analyses demonstrate, these communities of practice operated at social scales smaller than the village, and the scale and number of them at different sites are important indicators of the presence of different potting communities.

Lastly, we cannot underscore enough how important it is to acknowledge the influence of social contexts of consumption, as Appadurai's (1986) original "social lives of things" implied. Although pots do not have true social lives, the anthropology of consumption is as important for understanding technological variation as is the anthropology of production. Lave and Wenger (1991:100–105) write about the "transparency and sequestration" that is involved between the production of artifacts and their contexts of use. By transparency, they refer to how a single learning process involves not just how to make an artifact, but also how to use it and what the significance of that use is within the society. Sequestration, on the other hand, refers to a disconnect between knowledge acquisition related to production and knowledge related to the use of an object. At the end of this chapter we contextualize the changes that occurred in the Silver Creek area to understand the intersections of glaze paint production and consumption.

Although we are not able to reconstruct whether individual producers acquired knowledge of production at the same time as knowledge of the significance of pottery vessels, we can begin to understand the connections between social contexts of use and the potential importance of those events to the producers. We specifically address this issue by comparing how glaze-painted ceramics co-occur with the presence of large aggregated pueblos and other archaeologically documented indicators of suprahousehold consumption, especially those that have been suggested as hallmarks of feasting (Crown and Wills 2004). These include large serving vessels, the consumption of large game, and cooking features located in public areas such as plazas.

The Archaeological Setting

The ceramics that we discuss come from three sites excavated by the Silver Creek Archaeological Research Project (SCARP) in the Mogollon Rim region of east-central Arizona: Pottery Hill, Bryant Ranch Pueblo, and Bailey Ruin (see fig. 1.2). These three sites are roughly sequential in time, beginning with Pottery Hill at ca. AD 1200–1275 and ending with Bailey Ruin, dating to ca. AD 1275–1325. Temporally and spatially between Pottery Hill and Bailey Ruin is Bryant Ranch Pueblo. This site was originally dated to ca. AD 1250–1300, based on ceramic cross-dating. However, tree-ring dates place the construction of the kiva in the early 1280s, and we now date the site to ca. AD 1260–85. We also compare our compositional data from two of the three sites to microprobe results published by De Atley (1986) from the large site of Fourmile Ruin, which dates to ca. AD 1300–1400.

The above sequence of sites corresponds to the period in which migration, aggregation, and ritual diversification in architecture occurred in the Mogollon Rim area. Our sequence of sites captures the changes in settlement scale that are the hallmark of the Pueblo III to Pueblo IV transition, beginning with Pottery Hill at fifty rooms and ending with Fourmile Pueblo at five hundred rooms (Mills 1998).

The Bryant Ranch site is particularly instructive because it is relatively small, was occupied for a short duration, and falls at a critical period in the occupational history of the Mogollon Rim area. Its small size goes against the aggregation trend of the late 1200s. The site has only six rooms, of which four were excavated by SCARP. We think only three rooms were used at any one time. The three rooms on top of the hill are probably earlier than those on the bottom, judging by the lack of floor assemblages and the presence of stone-robbed walls. The three rooms at the base of the hill include two domestic rooms and one subterranean kiva.

Because the Bryant Ranch site is "out of phase" in terms of its size, it provides an excellent test of whether changes that we observe are independent of aggregation. The Bryant Ranch site also is important because it has perforated plates, one of the calling cards of migration from northeast Arizona, a small square kiva with an eastern bench, and extensive exterior cooking facilities. The low room-to-kiva ratio and the large number and size of exterior cooking features suggest that ritual, including suprahousehold feasting, was an important part of the activities conducted at this site. The Bryant Ranch Site is also significant because it was occupied when glaze paints were first incorporated into Silver Creek assemblages.

The Timing of Glaze Paint Introduction

Glaze paints were applied to vessels of two wares in the Silver Creek area: Cibola White Ware and White Mountain Red Ware. Both of these wares are predominantly sherd tempered and decorated with mineral paints with different recipes (Triadan 1997; Zedeño 1994). Previous analyses of the glaze paints on small samples of sherds from the Silver Creek area have been conducted, indicating that lead, copper, manganese, and silica were used in varying amounts (Carlson 1970; De Atley 1986; Haury and Hargrave 1931:34, 65; Hawley and Hawley 1938; Shepard 1942:220–21). One of our goals is to better understand when glaze paint recipes were incorporated into the technological repertoires of Mogollon Rim region potters and how they changed through time.

Only the latest types of Cibola White Ware and White Mountain Red Ware are generally acknowledged as being painted with glaze paints, which we define as the addition of fluxes such as lead or copper along with silica to form a glass. These types include Pinedale Black-on-white, Pinedale Black-on-red, Pinedale Polychrome, Cedar Creek Polychrome, and Fourmile Polychrome. Hays-Gilpin and van Hartesveldt (1998:98) refer to Pinedale Black-on-white as decorated in a matte glaze. Carlson (1970) also refers to some of the glaze pigments on White Mountain Red Ware types as matte glazes. We have observed that sherds of White Mountain Red Ware, especially Pinedale Polychrome, do show the characteristic crystalline growth and dull surface finish that characterizes true matte glazes. This effect is achieved by slowing down the cooling rate and by the addition of alumina, producing higher oxygen-silicon ratios (Kingery 1960:345).

Glazelike paints or "subglaze paints" are described for some vessels of earlier types of both Cibola White Ware and White Mountain Red Ware, such as Snowflake Black-on-white, Tularosa Black-on-white, and St. Johns Polychrome. The term "subglaze" paint is used to refer to glossy-looking paints that do not appear fully vitrified. Haury (1985:78) even describes the presence of a glazelike paint on a type from the Forestdale Valley painted in Red Mesa style that dates to the ninth century.

Shepard (1956/1980:47) observed that the earlier glossy pigments on Cibola White Ware are probably the result of the use of iron-manganese ores that contained enough lead to produce a glass. She thought that the glaze effect was an unintentional by-product of the use of these ores. We agree that the apparent glaze was the by-product of the choice of ores. The analyses that we present below, however, record lead in only trace amounts in the Pinedale Black-on-white (Cibola White Ware) paints at Bryant Ranch Pueblo. These paints have been called "subglazes" or "glazelike," but the glaze effect appears to have been the result of minute quantities of other elements that act as fluxes. In our samples, these subglazes are not from lead, as Shepard suggested, but from iron and/or manganese.

Although ceramic types with glaze paint are well dated by association with over one thousand tree-ring dates from the Mogollon Rim area (Mills and Herr 1999; table 4.1), since types are not necessarily coeval with the practice of glaze painting, the actual transition to glaze paints cannot be dated solely by the use of ceramic cross dates. Thus, we first conducted an analysis that visually identified the presence of glaze paints on sherds from Pottery Hill, Bryant Ranch, and Bailey Ruin ($n = 1,326$; fig. 4.1). In this case, "glaze" was defined as paint with apparent vitrification. Based

Table 4.1
Date Ranges of Production of Glaze-Painted Ceramic Types in the Mogollon Rim Region Based on Cross-Dating with Tree-Ring Dates

Ware	Type	Estimated Date Range of Production
Cibola White Ware	Pinedale Black-on-white	1270–1320
White Mountain Red Ware	Pinedale Black-on-red	1280–1330
	Pinedale Polychrome	1290–1330
	Cedar Creek Polychrome	1300–1350
	Fourmile Polychrome	1330–1390

on visual identification, the biggest jump in what *appears* to be the use of glaze paints occurs between the Bryant Ranch and Bailey Ruin assemblages, suggesting that the transition to glaze painting took place in the latter portion of the thirteenth century.

As our analyses demonstrate, however, the Cibola White Ware in our sample from Bryant Ranch Pueblo does not include enough low-temperature metal-bearing mineral fluxes to call them true glaze paints—despite the fact that these sherds visually look like they have glaze paints. Instead, intentionally added low-temperature metal-bearing mineral fluxes appear first on Pinedale Black-on-red and Pinedale Polychrome, both of which are White Mountain Red Ware types. White Mountain Red Ware is rare at any site in the Silver Creek area prior to the late 1200s, which contrasts with sites elsewhere in the upper Little Colorado (ULC) drainage, where the earlier type of St. Johns Polychrome is relatively common. Our previous research has concluded from this that Pinedale Black-on-red and Polychrome were the first White Mountain Red Ware types actually produced in the Silver Creek area (Mills et al. 1999). The production of Pinedale Black-on-red and Polychrome in the Mogollon Rim area marks the diversification of White Mountain Red Ware into a White Mountain series and a Zuni series (Carlson 1970; Eckert, chap. 3, this vol.). For the Silver Creek area, it marks not only the production of a new ware, but also the first intentional use of lead or other low-temperature metal-bearing mineral fluxes to produce glaze paint.

The Bryant Ranch assemblage represents the first site in our series of sites in which Pinedale Black-on-red and Polychrome appear in more than

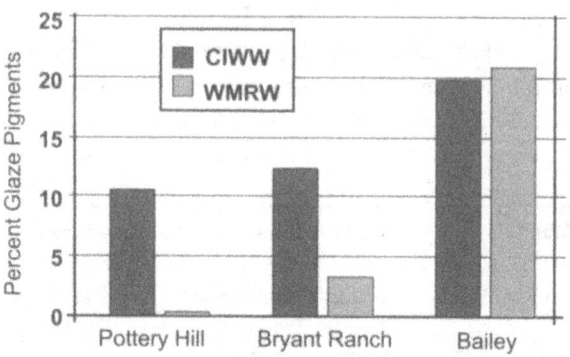

Fig. 4.1. Percentage of glaze pigments on Cibola White Ware (CIWW) and White Mountain Red Ware (WMRW) by site, based on visual identifications.

trace quantities. Based on tree-ring dates from the kiva at Bryant Ranch and similar associations and tree-ring dates from Chodistaas Pueblo in the Grasshopper region, we place this transition at ca. AD 1275–85. We now turn to the data on chemical composition to better understand intra- and intersite variation in glaze paint recipes and communities of practice.

Compositional Analyses and Interaction

Methodology

Sampling methods for the compositional analysis were designed to address two main research objectives. The first was to sample the same ceramic ware(s) from multiple-floor or near-floor contexts to understand intrasite variation in glaze paint recipes, while the second was to sample ceramic ware(s) from different sites to examine intersite patterns of variability. The primary ware sampled in this analysis was White Mountain Red Ware (WMRW), although another smaller set of samples was derived from Cibola White Ware (CIWW). We analyzed specimens from the two SCARP-excavated sites of Bryant Ranch and Bailey Ruin, but were also able to include results from a prior analysis conducted by Suzanne De Atley (1986) on samples from Fourmile Ruin.

Electron probe microanalysis (EPMA) of the SCARP samples was conducted on a Cameca SX electron probe in the Department of Planetary Sciences, University of Arizona. A 15 kV accelerating voltage and 20 nA sample current were utilized for most elements, though a 25 kV accelerating voltage and 30 nA sample current were used for lead analysis to maximize counting. The main sampling strategy consisted of analyzing multiple spots (eight to twelve was the ideal number when possible) on each sherd. This strategy was utilized to minimize anomalous values resulting from heterogeneity within the glaze paint of each sherd. Spot size of the electron beam was set at 10 μ (microns) to minimize contamination potential from the adjacent slip and paste. These multiple spot samples provide data on the potential range of glaze paint compositional variability within a single sherd. Averaging the results of the multiple spot samples for each sherd provides a more representative glaze paint composition for that sherd.

Chemical elements sought during all glaze paint compositional analyses were copper, lead, iron, manganese, silicon, aluminum, calcium, potassium, and magnesium, while sodium, sulfur, and titanium were also sought on some of the analyses. Computer software attached to the electron microprobe stoichiometrically balanced the chemical element data, and weight percentages are presented as oxides. Basic statistical analysis was conducted on raw oxide weight percentage data, while multivariate statistical analysis was conducted with transformed oxide weight percentage data. Data transformation consisted of standardizing the oxide weight percentages against silicon dioxide (SiO_2), as this compound was the most abundant in the glaze paints. It should be noted, however, that the relatively small sample size from each site (n_{Total} = 56: Bryant Ranch n = 18, Bailey Ruin n = 20, Fourmile Ruin n = 18) dictates that the multivariate statistical results be examined and interpreted with caution. Summary tables of the chemical analysis results, basic statistical results on WMRW weight percentages, and variance percentages for the principal component analysis are presented in tables 4.2 through 4.4.

Results and Interpretation

For the sake of discussion in this chapter, "pottery production group" will be defined as an individual or small group of individuals, probably with kinship ties, who share a common production technology, including a common general composition of the glaze paints employed. This may also be seen as equivalent to what Stark (chap. 2, this vol.) refers to as "potting communities." Multivariate statistical analyses of both published and new chemical composition data for paints from White Mountain Red

Table 4.2a

Electron Probe Chemical Composition Analysis Results for Cibola White Ware (CIWW) Glaze Paint Specimens from Bryant Ranch Pueblo and Bailey Ruin*

Room No.	Sample ID	SiO$_2$	MgO	Al$_2$O$_3$	K$_2$O	CaO	FeO	MnO	CuO	PbO	Total
2	0351b	47.825	1.068	17.391	2.258	1.880	21.888	0.547	0.018	0.026	94.063
	0453a	48.834	0.796	22.589	2.399	0.748	19.612	0.148	0.030	0.022	98.445
	0453b	53.856	0.654	26.833	3.128	1.239	3.986	0.084	0.052	0.014	91.129
	0453c	46.899	0.643	19.857	2.184	0.851	27.267	0.036	0.027	0.036	99.055
	0479a	35.541	0.606	13.910	2.287	0.761	39.573	0.299	0.028	0.014	93.859
	0479b	34.777	0.927	14.375	6.716	0.851	39.144	0.525	0.059	0.007	99.049
3	0422	64.488	0.372	17.815	2.340	0.895	6.044	0.074	0.016	0.016	93.347
	0451c	48.242	1.692	15.466	3.160	2.779	23.663	0.220	0.024	0.015	96.589
	0457a	35.307	1.300	11.466	1.707	0.780	41.117	0.327	0.026	0.034	98.782
	0457b	47.438	1.046	17.852	1.925	1.113	28.942	0.552	0.021	0.029	99.903
	1051	58.207	0.418	18.467	1.720	1.383	4.138	0.045	0.017	0.012	86.135
	1065b	16.232	0.998	7.110	0.196	0.226	72.279	0.435	0.098	0.017	98.249
	1071	34.908	0.609	9.977	1.826	0.658	39.983	0.625	0.395	0.016	90.123
4	0496	21.674	0.904	8.291	0.423	0.488	62.266	0.653	0.026	0.034	95.282
	1048	36.423	0.591	17.800	2.151	0.501	34.873	0.382	0.029	0.029	94.841
	1086a	68.738	0.254	13.385	2.625	1.741	3.284	0.072	0.010	0.034	90.894
	1086b	61.265	0.341	19.932	4.015	3.391	4.138	0.089	0.013	0.060	94.453
	1101	45.348	1.682	15.044	3.131	8.868	17.979	0.144	0.015	0.021	94.287
	1108	26.637	1.090	9.817	0.567	0.254	51.485	0.601	0.016	0.034	91.192
	1110b	30.872	1.015	9.710	1.760	0.830	44.728	0.260	0.021	0.033	89.899
	1116	49.468	0.542	16.257	3.964	5.690	6.535	0.103	0.036	0.025	89.185
	1137b	57.580	0.251	18.361	5.592	4.738	8.396	0.158	0.030	0.015	96.473

*Oxide weight percentages generated and stoichiometrically balanced by electron probe analysis software.

Table 4.2b
Electron Probe Chemical Composition Analysis Results for White Mountain Red Ware (WMRW) Glaze Paint Specimens from Bryant Ranch Pueblo*

Type Code	Room No.	Sample ID	SiO_2	MgO	Al_2O_3	K_2O	CaO	FeO	MnO	CuO	PbO	Total
PBR	2	0351a	39.435	0.999	10.492	1.861	1.559	4.887	0.093	31.532	3.900	95.743
	3	0420	28.294	0.803	6.906	1.212	0.964	2.927	0.081	36.015	9.216	87.127
	3	0451a	39.760	0.834	11.735	1.564	2.148	4.594	0.020	28.438	4.639	94.943
	3	0451b	29.674	0.638	7.480	1.927	0.956	5.614	0.169	41.041	6.948	95.180
	2	0452a	47.885	0.745	12.899	2.211	2.795	2.874	0.038	15.836	3.242	89.952
	2	0452b	41.603	0.903	13.303	2.142	1.814	7.018	0.142	15.665	7.093	90.795
	3	1029a	26.877	0.677	5.803	1.109	0.777	1.776	0.064	48.062	4.820	90.749
	3	1029b	39.899	1.010	10.111	1.760	1.284	3.115	0.105	29.116	4.060	91.444
	3	1029c	31.140	0.608	9.441	1.513	1.022	1.715	0.054	41.195	2.730	90.069
	3	1029d	24.180	0.741	7.564	1.259	0.809	7.316	0.131	38.936	7.984	89.414
PP	4	1137a	34.424	0.487	10.234	1.465	1.940	9.227	0.066	30.041	6.841	95.541
SJP	3	1065a	40.548	1.274	14.487	4.436	1.441	2.320	0.756	22.892	0.044	89.292
	4	1104	50.273	0.588	12.241	3.488	1.470	2.203	12.330	5.570	3.812	93.253
	4	1109	45.239	0.863	16.786	2.911	1.158	11.154	3.559	7.634	1.572	91.866
	4	1110a	49.012	1.062	19.317	3.689	0.591	5.119	0.032	6.037	0.016	86.732
SJP-PP	4	1001a	36.767	0.679	11.982	2.481	1.000	2.916	11.795	22.223	0.059	90.683
	3	1029e	42.206	0.519	12.463	1.995	1.057	33.951	0.428	0.032	0.018	93.875
SLP	4	1001b	38.084	0.988	17.995	2.392	1.038	4.242	11.853	17.948	0.030	96.130

*Oxide weight percentages generated and stoichiometrically balanced by electron probe analysis software.
**See table 4.3 for explanations of type code abbreviations.

Table 4.2c

Electron Probe Chemical Composition Analysis Results for White Mountain Red Ware (WMRW) Glaze Paint Specimens from Bailey Ruin*

Type Code	Room No.	Sample ID	SiO_2	MgO	Al_2O_3	K_2O	CaO	FeO	MnO	CuO	PbO	Total
PBR	1	2045–PBR	37.873	0.790	17.821	3.218	0.567	19.400	0.050	8.576	3.596	92.535
	2	3047–PBR1	40.254	0.823	12.062	2.130	0.787	4.665	0.083	25.329	9.054	95.181
	2	3047–PBR2	25.188	0.430	6.420	0.529	0.998	1.795	0.032	15.946	36.433	87.757
	4	3157–PBR	25.484	0.441	8.223	2.008	0.544	1.334	0.043	39.965	16.193	94.223
	4	3163–PBR	36.198	0.756	11.138	2.437	1.275	2.406	0.043	23.425	17.784	95.445
	5	3216–PBR1	36.991	0.548	12.181	1.883	0.548	4.207	0.228	38.307	4.295	99.189
	5	3216–PBR2	39.131	1.163	18.451	3.279	1.192	5.887	6.871	5.435	0.094	94.768
PP	1	1087–PP	29.293	0.576	10.309	1.686	1.079	2.555	0.025	2.835	44.824	94.152
	1	1091–PP	40.677	2.403	13.114	2.973	1.886	3.900	0.038	14.149	12.150	91.289
	1	1096–PP	46.858	0.925	12.831	2.898	2.016	2.946	0.024	11.973	15.120	96.587
	1	2045–PP	34.379	0.560	12.527	1.441	0.859	3.662	0.029	22.792	16.116	92.358
	2	3033–PP	40.797	0.887	20.775	4.347	0.432	14.291	0.023	7.770	0.584	90.609
	2	3047–PP	41.852	0.757	15.154	2.527	1.682	1.641	3.136	29.021	0.508	96.280
	4	3145–PP	33.335	0.807	11.918	1.094	1.598	1.438	1.867	35.516	4.321	91.895
	4	3163–PP	22.400	0.503	8.621	1.747	1.913	27.955	0.035	29.401	1.679	95.110
	5	3196–PP	32.763	0.663	19.025	2.213	1.776	7.544	1.367	30.948	2.483	99.421
	5	3216–PP	35.343	0.851	17.151	2.945	2.520	20.421	0.168	2.968	0.034	89.686
PP/PBR	2	3075–PP/PBR	40.951	0.604	14.652	3.206	0.860	4.352	0.020	23.533	5.001	93.170
	4	3118–PP/PBR	34.878	1.069	13.525	1.897	1.266	4.113	1.483	25.000	12.059	95.827
	5	3142–PP/PBR	56.388	1.802	22.373	3.116	0.770	7.059	0.700	1.224	0.027	94.632

*Oxide weight percentages generated and stoichiometrically balanced by electron probe analysis software.
**See table 4.3 for explanations of type code abbreviations.

Table 4.3
Basic Statistics for the Main Metallic Oxides for
Cibola White Ware (CIWW) and White Mountain Red Ware (WMRW)
Glaze Paint Chemical Composition Analysis Data

Site (No. of Specimens), Ceramic Ware, and Type(s)	Oxide	Mean[a]	Standard Deviation (1s)[a]	Min.[a]	Max.[a]	Range[a]
Bryant Ranch Ruin (n = 22)	CuO	0.05	0.08	0.01	0.39	0.38
Cibola White Ware	PbO	0.02	0.01	0.01	0.06	0.05
	FeO	27.33	20.07	3.28	72.28	69.00
	MnO	0.29	0.21	0.04	0.65	0.62
Bryant Ranch Ruin (n = 7), Early[b] WMRW	CuO	11.76	9.10	0.03	22.89	22.86
Springerville-like Polychrome (SLP)	PbO	0.79	1.45	0.02	3.81	3.80
St. Johns Polychrome (SJP)	FeO	8.84	11.49	2.20	33.95	31.75
St. Johns/Pinedale Polychrome (SJP/PP)	MnO	5.82	5.89	0.03	12.33	12.30
Bryant Ranch Ruin (n = 11), Late[b] WMRW	CuO	32.35	10.20	15.66	48.06	32.40
Pinedale Polychrome (PP)	PbO	5.59	2.12	2.73	9.22	6.49
Pinedale Black-on-Red (PBR)	FeO	4.64	2.45	1.72	9.23	7.51
	MnO	0.09	0.05	0.02	0.17	0.15
Bailey Ruin (n = 20)	CuO	19.71	12.34	1.22	39.97	38.74
Pinedale Polychrome	PbO	10.12	12.17	0.03	44.82	44.80
Pinedale Black-on-Red	FeO	7.08	7.44	1.33	27.96	26.62
Undifferentiated PP/PBR	MnO	0.81	1.65	0.02	6.87	6.85
Fourmile Ruin (n = 18)[c]	CuO	11.14	8.82	0.25	34.39	34.14
Four Mile Polychrome (FMP)	PbO	4.66	5.90	0.11	17.25	17.14
	FeO	6.30	2.04	2.77	10.52	7.75
	MnO	1.85	4.03	0.10	16.65	16.55

[a] Based on stoichiometrically balanced oxide weight percentages.
[b] "Early" and "late" as used here refer only to the Bryant Ranch Ruin. As discussed in the main body of the paper, the "early" WMRW types are all probably imported, while the Late represent types that may have been made at the site or at least within the Silver Creek Drainage.
[c] Calculated from data published in De Atley 1986.

Ware (WMRW) and Cibola White Ware (CIWW) sherds indicate that different chemical "recipes" can be identified within and between these wares at the intrasite level and temporally within wares at the intersite scale.

On the intrasite scale, for example, paint compositions from Bryant Ranch vary between ceramic wares *and* between archaeological contexts.

Table 4.4a
Total Variance Percentage Explained and Component Matrix for the Principal Component Analysis (PCA) Results Plotted in Figures 4.2 and 4.3

	Total Variance Explained		
Component	Initial Eigenvalues Total	Percent of Variance	Cumulative Percent
1	2.485	31.063	31.063
2	1.788	22.347	53.410
3	1.145	14.312	67.722
4	1.035	12.940	80.662
5	.778	9.724	90.386
6	.480	5.995	96.381
7	.179	2.242	98.623
8	.110	1.377	100.000

Component Matrix*

Oxide	Component 1	2	3	4
PbO	-.820	.418	.052	.151
CuO	-.816	.382	.189	.247
Al_2O_3	.744	-.047	.170	.199
FeO	.667	.653	-.118	.048
MgO	.317	.766	-.158	.470
MnO	.092	-.171	.737	.399
CaO	-.190	-.306	-.703	.394
K_2O	.056	-.572	-.042	.612

*Only components with an eigenvalue greater than one were extracted.

This is well illustrated when the chemical compositional data are compared using principal components analysis (see fig. 4.2). Clear groups occur within the bivariate plot of components 1 and 2 for both White Mountain Red Ware paints and Cibola White Ware paints. These clusters have strong correspondence with both the ceramic wares and the archaeological contexts. The earlier White Mountain Red Ware types form a group discrete from two other groups formed by the later White Mountain Red Ware types. The Cibola White Ware specimens also plot away from the later White Mountain Red Ware types.

Table 4.4b
Total Variance Percentage Explained and Component Matrix for the Principal Component Analysis (PCA) Results Plotted in Figure 4.5

	Total Variance Explained		
Component	Initial Eigenvalues Total	Percent of Variance	Cumulative Percent
1	3.028	37.851	37.851
2	1.777	22.217	60.068
3	1.056	13.200	73.268
4	.784	9.805	83.073
5	.600	7.501	90.574
6	.367	4.583	95.156
7	.202	2.524	97.681
8	.186	2.319	100.000

Component Matrix*			
	Component		
Oxide	1	2	3
PbO	.864	.177	.122
CuO	.771	.463	.080
Al_2O_3	-.729	.269	.145
K_2O	-.657	.482	.031
MnO	-.642	.116	-.345
MgO	.245	.864	.212
FeO	-.058	-.594	.742
CaO	.498	-.339	-.546

*Only components with an eigenvalue greater than one were extracted.

When the archaeological contexts of these paints are compared, the patterns are equally revealing (see fig. 4.3). The earlier White Mountain Red Ware types originate mainly from Room 4, with two specimens from Room 3 (the kiva). One of the two later White Mountain Red Ware groups was recovered only from Room 3, while the second group consists of mainly Room 2 and Room 3 specimens. The Cibola White Ware specimens also form clusters that correspond to their archaeological contexts. For example, relatively discrete groups are formed for Room 2 and for Room 3, and two groups are formed from Room 4. Thus, it is clear that at

Table 4.4c

Total Variance Percentage Explained and Component Matrix for the Principal Component Analysis (PCA) Results Plotted in Figure 4.8

Total Variance Explained

Component	Initial Eigenvalues Total	Percent of Variance	Cumulative Percent
1	2.065	25.816	25.816
2	1.374	17.174	42.990
3	1.122	14.029	57.018
4	.981	12.261	69.280
5	.844	10.555	79.834
6	.676	8.455	88.290
7	.523	6.543	94.833
8	.413	5.167t	100.000

Component Matrix*

Oxide	Component 1	2	3
Al_2O_3	.791	-.002	.164
K_2O	.760	.361	-.124
PbO	-.577	.202	.008
MgO	.129	.710	-.384
CuO	-.434	.577	-.040
MnO	.338	-.484	-.475
CaO	-.149	-.141	.606
FeO	.433	.335	.581

*Only components with an eigenvalue greater than one were extracted.

the intrasite scale, even with this small sample of analyses, variability can be recognized both within and between ceramic wares as well as between archaeological contexts.

The separation of the Cibola White Ware and White Mountain Red Ware specimens appears to be based on paint recipes that are at least partially based on solutions for different firing regimes. A White Mountain Red Ware pot is red after firing; this is achieved by intentionally slipping the exterior of the vessel with an iron-rich slip, probably containing limonite, which fires red in an oxidizing atmosphere. However, Cibola White Ware vessels achieve their white color as the result of being

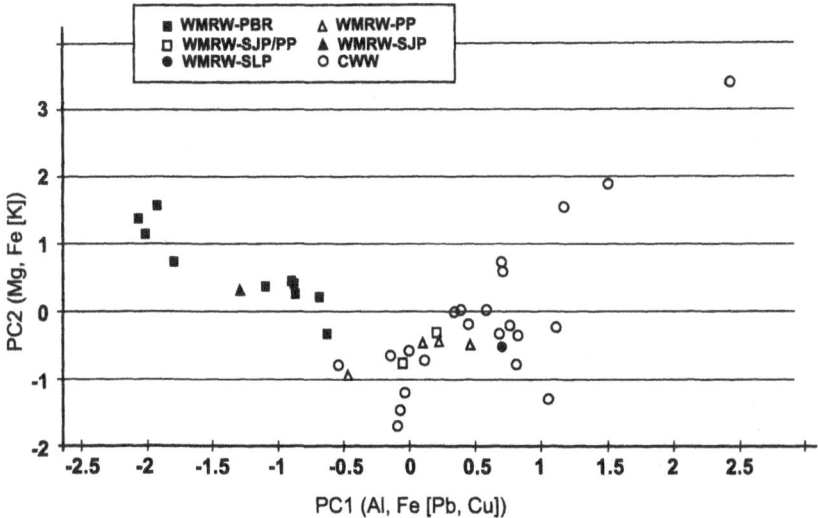

Fig. 4.2. Bivariate plot of glaze paint Principal Components 1 and 2 for White Mountain Red Ware (by type) and Cibola White Ware from Bryant Ranch Pueblo.

fired in a neutral to reducing atmosphere. Likewise, the composition and firing atmosphere also affect the color and final appearance of the glaze paints.

As a result, a White Mountain Red Ware pot, fired in an oxidizing environment, needed to have a paint composition that would remain black, the desired color, in those conditions. If the glaze paints were iron-rich they would fire red like the limonite-based slip on the White Mountain Red Ware vessels. This has been corroborated by refiring experiments on Cibola White Ware sherds (Daniela Triadan 2002, personal communication). However, when common copper minerals, such as malachite and azurite, are oxidized at temperatures below their melting points, they convert primarily to tenorite, a black copper oxide mineral, and, thus would have been suitable for making black paints on the White Mountain Red Ware vessels. Alternatively, Cibola White Ware pots are fired in a neutral to reducing atmosphere, and iron, which turns black to gray in an oxygen-poor environment, would have been perfectly adequate as the black colorant in the paints. Some of these oxides are black in their native state and would stay so in neutral or reducing atmospheres. The copper and iron would have served not only as colorants but as fluxes along with the lead, sodium, and potassium in the paint recipes.

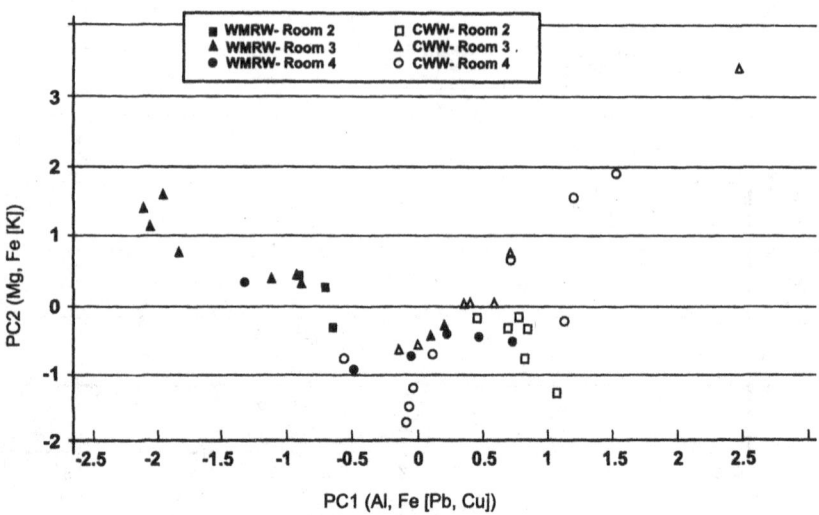

Fig. 4.3. Bivariate plot of glaze paint Principal Components 1 and 2 by room for White Mountain Red Ware and Cibola White Ware from Bryant Ranch Pueblo.

The technological correspondence between iron in Cibola White Ware paints and lead and copper in White Mountain Red Ware glaze paints also is well illustrated in a bivariate plot of the copper versus lead oxide weight percentages in glaze sherds from Bryant Ranch (see fig. 4.4). The Cibola White Ware sherds, which have virtually no lead or copper in their paints but high amounts of iron, plot in the lower left corner, indicating only trace levels, while the White Mountain Red Ware sherds, which contain relatively high concentrations of copper and lead in their paints, plot in the upper right corner. A few of the earlier White Mountain Red Ware sherds have significantly lower levels of copper and lead in their paints, including one as low as the Cibola White Ware sherds.

When the Cibola White Ware pottery is removed from the Bryant Ranch data set and the principal component analysis recalculated (see fig. 4.5), the principal components form two discrete clusters of points that are primarily divided based on the relative proportions of copper and lead to iron and manganese. The group on the left side of the figure is unique within the Bryant Ranch sample, as it consists of all early White Mountain Red Ware polychromes. It contains a Springerville-like polychrome, four St. Johns Polychrome specimens, and two specimens of a

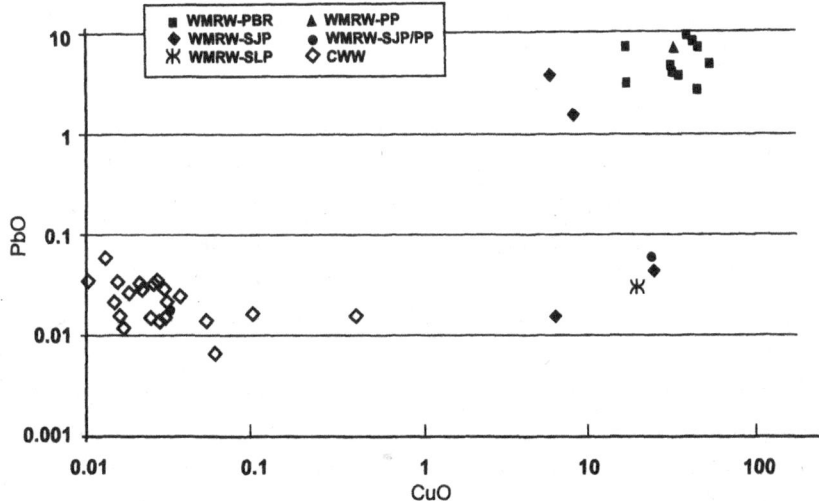

Fig. 4.4. Bivariate plot of copper vs. lead (stoichiometrically balanced) for both White Mountain Red Ware and Cibola White Ware glaze paints from Bryant Ranch.

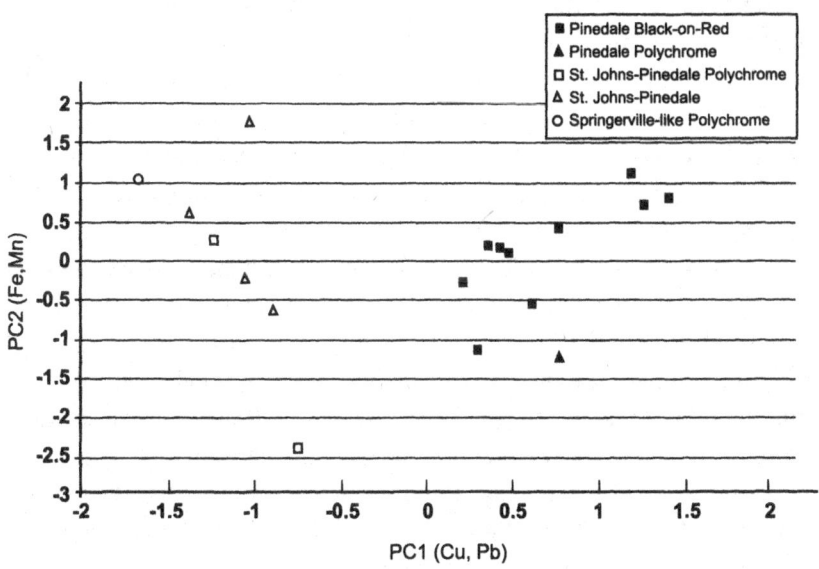

Fig. 4.5. Bivariate plot by ceramic type of two principal components for White Mountain Red Ware from Bryant Ranch (standardized vs. SiO_2).

transitional type with characteristics common to both St. Johns and Pinedale polychromes. The group on the right side of the figure consists of later White Mountain Red Ware types: Pinedale Black-on-red specimens and the one definite Pinedale Polychrome sherd. Thus, these two temporally distinct ceramic types, the St. Johns/Springerville-like polychromes and the Pinedale-style sherds, clearly utilized different recipes for their paints. These differences are based on the intentional addition of low-temperature metal-bearing mineral fluxes and indicate that the transition to a true glaze paint recipe took place during the occupation of Bryant Ranch Pueblo.

We can examine variability in glaze paint recipes through time and space in the Silver Creek area by comparing the Bryant Ranch data set with data from two other sites, Bailey Ruin and Fourmile Ruin. As noted earlier, Bailey Ruin temporally overlaps with the end of Bryant Ranch Pueblo and continues for a few generations, while Fourmile Ruin temporally overlaps with the end of Bailey Ruin and continues for several generations after that. Thus, by comparing White Mountain Red Ware from these three sites, we can examine the changes in glaze paint recipes through time from three different pueblos within the Silver Creek area that span a maximum of about 140 years of occupation.

Multivariate statistical comparisons of the glaze paint compositions of White Mountain Red Ware sherds from these three sites suggest that temporally significant trends may be identified (see fig. 4.6). In figure 4.6, first note that the zero-zero point on the axes is in the center of the graph. The earliest White Mountain Red Ware types in the data set, the St. Johns and Springerville-like polychromes, still maintain a correspondence to each other (positive principal component 1 [PC1], negative PC2; mainly the lower right quadrant of fig. 4.6). Likewise, the Pinedale-style sherds from Bryant Ranch also maintain a relatively good correspondence to each other (negative PC1, positive PC2; mainly the upper left quadrant of fig. 4.6). When considering the Bailey Ruin sherds, which consist only of Pinedale Black-on-red and Polychrome, we can see that they share a correspondence with the Pinedale-style sherds from Bryant Ranch but also extend into the positive half of principal component 1 (PC1). Finally, the latest White Mountain Red Ware type from Fourmile Ruin is confined primarily to the negative half of principal component 2 (PC2).

We interpret these clusters and distributions within figure 4.6 as further evidence for the transition to intentionally added low-temperature

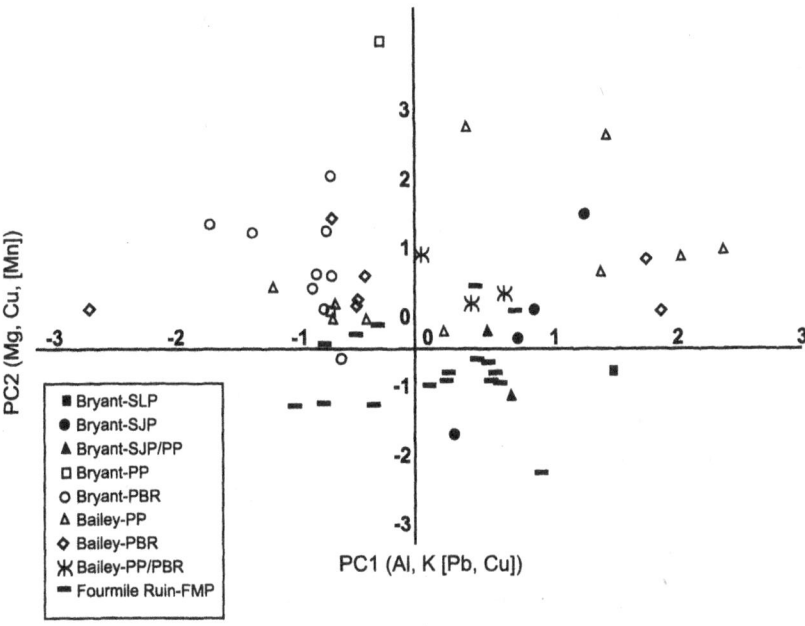

Fig. 4.6. Bivariate plot by ceramic type of first two principal components for White Mountain Red Ware from Bryant Ranch Pueblo, Bailey Ruin, and Fourmile Ruin.

metal-bearing mineral fluxes to paint recipes during the Bryant Ranch occupation. The Pinedale-style sherds from Bryant Ranch show a dramatic increase in the amount of copper and lead with a corresponding decrease in iron and manganese, represented here by the upper left quadrant of figure 4.6. The Pinedale-style sherds from Bailey Ruin also contain significant lead and copper, but not as much copper and more lead than at Bryant Ranch. This is represented by the Bailey specimens, which plot almost exclusively in the positive half of PC2. And finally, in the later Fourmile Ruin specimens the copper levels continue to drop, as do the lead levels, while manganese increases, resulting in the specimens plotting exclusively in the negative half of PC2. The increase in manganese within the latest White Mountain Red Ware types is particularly interesting. Manganese is another element that forms black minerals in its native state, and its color is preserved when oxidized. This again shows the range of materials available to the ancient potters and the level of technological knowledge employed by the potters in the Silver Creek area.

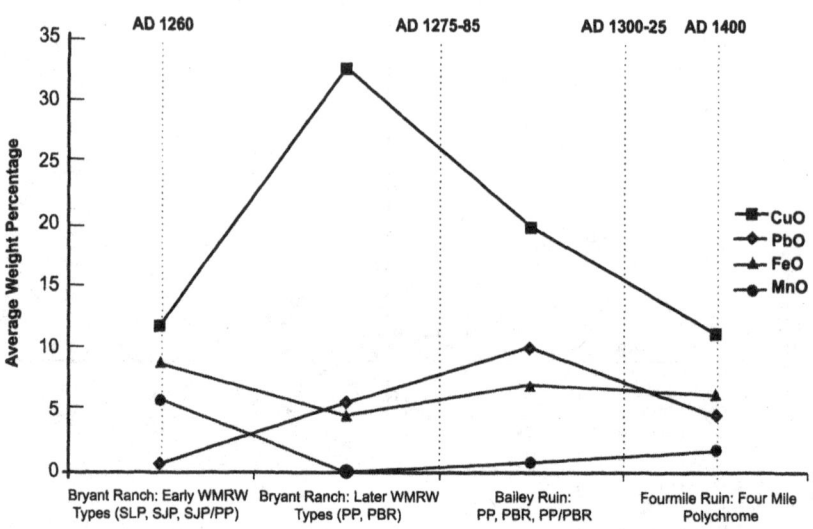

Fig. 4.7. Temporal variation in the average oxide weight percentage of the four main metallic colorants/fluxes in the White Mountain Red Ware specimens from three sites in the Silver Creek drainage. The x axis lists the sites and WMRW types within Bryant Ranch in chronological order. (Note: temporal spans are not to scale, and dates are approximate.)

A simplification of the key information from this analysis is presented in figure 4.7. Again, the trend is that the early White Mountain Red Ware types at Bryant Ranch contain, in decreasing order of oxide weight percentage, copper, iron, manganese, and lead. The later WMRW types at Bryant Ranch exhibit a dramatic increase in copper (from 11.76 percent to 32.35 percent) and lead (from 0.79 percent to 5.59 percent), with a decrease both in iron and manganese. Within the Bailey Ruin sample, the lead content has almost doubled (to 10.12 percent), while the copper content has decreased (to 19.71 percent) and iron and manganese have both increased slightly. Finally, at Fourmile Ruin, both the lead and copper contents decrease (to 4.66 percent and 11.14 percent, respectively), while the manganese content doubles and the iron content decreases slightly. The parallel behavior of the average weight percentages for both the iron and manganese oxides through time suggests that these colorants/fluxes were contained within the same mineral pigment samples. This is supported by the fact that manganese oxide is a very common impurity in limonite (Dana 1932:505–6), at times as high as 5 percent manganese (Hurlbut and

Klein 1977:287), as well as in hematite (Hurlbut and Klein 1977:269). Additionally, manganese ore deposits often have limonite and hematite caps. Thus, the likelihood of these elements paralleling each other in relative proportions in mineral pigment specimens is very good. Finally, a manganese ore deposit is located approximately twenty-five miles west of Bailey Ruin and Bryant Ranch, while a second iron and manganese ore deposit is located just south of the Mogollon Rim approximately twenty-one miles southwest of Bailey Ruin and Bryant Ranch (Keith et al. 1983:16, 30, map).

The compositional data presented here illustrate not only the level of technological knowledge held by the pottery producers, but also suggest that a series of trial-and-error experiments must have preceded this knowledge as part of a technological learning process to discover the appropriate mineral paint recipes for the appropriate firing regimes. If the goal was a red pot fired in an oxidizing atmosphere, then iron-oxide paints were not the best solution. Moreover, the visual performance characteristics (Schiffer and Skibo 1997) of a glaze on a red slip are significantly different from those of a black organic or mineral paint.

These data also indicate that there are discrete glaze paint recipes being used by contemporaneous pottery-producing groups, or "potting communities," and that the main pigment constituents in these recipes changed through time. The compositional data support that the transition to glaze paints occurred on White Mountain Red Ware during the occupation of Bryant Ranch Pueblo, or ca. AD 1260–85. Even within this small site, there were two different glaze paint recipes being used, which may indicate the presence of two different learning frameworks—one for white ware and another for red ware.

Although sample sizes are small, later sites show that there may also have been a diversity of recipes related to different potting communities within each settlement. At Bailey Ruin, for example, the sample of twenty sherds comes from four different rooms and two different ceramic types. Not unexpectedly, there are no clusters that correspond with the two different White Mountain Red Ware types of Pinedale Black-on-red and Pinedale Polychrome. Several recipes apparently were used in the production of the black glaze paint on bichromes as well as on polychromes, a few of which were the same for both wares.

When glaze recipes are looked at in terms of rooms of recovery at Bailey, there are some hints at clusters. A majority of the Room 4 sherds fall into the northwest quadrant of the graph, while the majority of the Room 5 sherds are in the northeast quadrant. These differences are along the PCI axis, summarizing relative differences in aluminum, potassium, lead, and copper in the glazes from these two contexts. Again, sample sizes are too small to definitely identify, but the distribution of samples by room is less random than is the distribution by type, suggesting that spatial differences are present.

The Social Contexts of Consumption

Now we address our final question: What were the social contexts in which glaze ware vessels were used? To look at the social contexts of consumption, we focus on the differences in vessel form and the relationship of those changes to patterns of aggregation, faunal consumption, and ritual features. We focus on the case of Bryant Ranch Pueblo, where the transition to intentionally produced glaze paints first appears, followed by Bailey Ruin, where glaze paint ceramics reached widespread use.

Based on our sequence of sites, it is clear that Cibola White Ware bowls, whether glazed or not, are replaced by red ware bowls, whether glazed or not. This is shown in figure 4.8, which charts the proportions of the four most common decorated wares in the bowl assemblages of our three sequent sites: Pottery Hill, Bryant Ranch, and Bailey Ruin. By about 1300, when Bailey was occupied, White Mountain Red Ware bowls replaced Cibola White Ware bowls. Roosevelt Red Ware, a nonglazed painted ware, still dominated the decorated bowl assemblages of the late thirteenth century, but decreased slightly during the occupation of Bailey Ruin as the proportion of White Mountain Red Ware increased.

When we compare bowl sizes of these different wares, the average bowl size of White Mountain Red Ware is always larger (see fig. 4.9), followed by Roosevelt Red Ware and the earlier Showlow (Puerco Valley) Red Ware. Cibola White Ware bowls are always the smallest size class. We interpret these differences between wares as evidence for differences in the social contexts of consumption. Differences in bowl sizes have been related to variation in household size and feasting in other areas of the Southwest (Mills 1999; Potter 2000; Spielmann 1998). These studies have also suggested that changes in feasting are correlated with aggregation.

An important result of the bowl size analyses from our sequence of sites, however, is that the largest average bowl sizes are not at the most aggregated site, Bailey Ruin, but at Bryant Ranch Pueblo. In addition, the

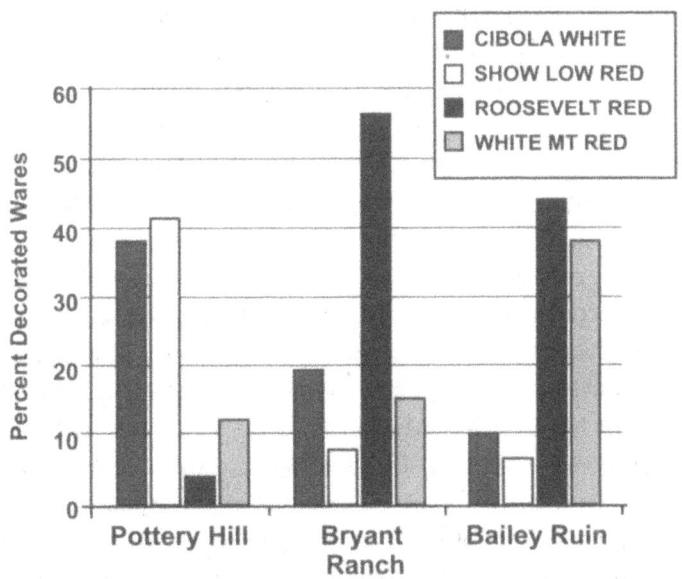

Fig. 4.8. Percentages of decorated wares in the Pottery Hill, Bryant Ranch, and Bailey Ruin bowl assemblages.

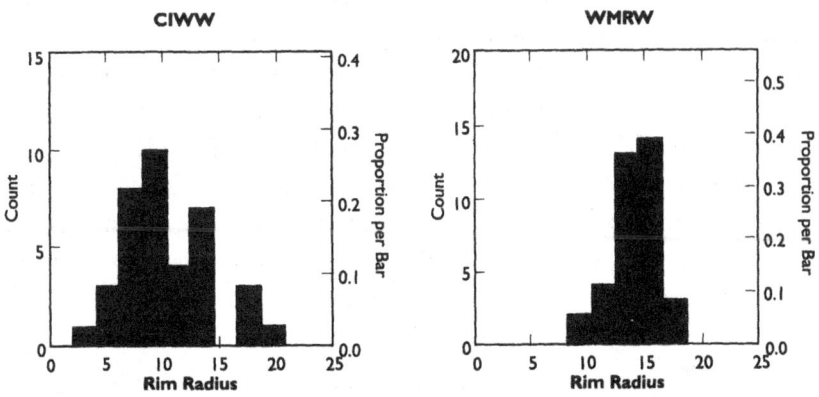

Fig. 4.9. Histograms of Cibola White Ware and White Mountain Red Ware bowl rim radii at Bryant Ranch.

separation of Cibola White Ware and White Mountain Red Ware bowl sizes is most evident at the latter site, suggesting that each ware was used in different social contexts. Ritual feasting at Bryant Ranch is supported by the faunal analysis conducted by Rebecca Dean (2001), comparing Pottery Hill, Bryant Ranch, and Bailey Ruin assemblages. She shows that consumption of large animals was highest at Bryant Ranch Pueblo. The concentration of large extramural cooking features provides further evidence for communal feasting at Bryant Ranch. Suprahousehold feasting was also widely practiced at Bailey Ruin, where large quantities of deer bone were recovered. The enclosed plaza and a plaza roasting feature at this site are additional evidence of public consumption events.

Cumulatively, the faunal data, ceramic bowl sizes, and the concentration of large roasting features show that suprahousehold feasting was an important activity at Bryant Ranch Pueblo. In this case, aggregation alone does not appear to explain changes in the incidence of feasting, the use of larger bowl sizes, or the adoption of glaze paint technology. Although Bryant Ranch Pueblo has evidence of extensive suprahousehold feasting with its high concentration of large roasting features in the plaza, the site is small and was briefly occupied. Instead of aggregation being the independent variable (cf. Potter 2000), we suggest that migration, the emergence of new identities in the immediate postmigration period, and the intensification and diversification in ritual sodalities were the most important factors in the changes to larger red ware bowls and the practice of suprahousehold feasting.

Like potters in the Zuni area, Silver Creek area potters began to use glaze paints on their vessels in the last quarter of the thirteenth century (see Huntley, chap. 6, this vol.), but on vessels with distinctive layouts and decorative styles. This parallel use of glazes, both similar yet different from the Zuni area, was likely an intentional difference that marked regional social distinctions during the dynamic late thirteenth century. These differences continued throughout the fourteenth century, culminating with the production of Fourmile Polychrome (see Van Keuren, chap. 5, this vol.).

Conclusion

We conclude that although glazelike paints may have had precedence on Cibola White Ware vessels in the Mogollon Rim region in the mid-1200s, this was an unintentional result of incidental fluxing at high firing temperatures of some iron and manganese mineral colorants. By AD 1275–85, however, low-temperature metal-bearing mineral fluxes were intentionally added to the paint recipe and applied to White Mountain Red Ware vessels in the Mogollon Rim region that were distinct from other White Mountain Red Ware glaze-painted ceramics found in the Zuni area.

In the Silver Creek area, this first use of glaze paints corresponds to a period of ritual intensification, as evidenced by changes in vessel size, the use of communal cooking features, and the consumption of large game at both small and large sites. Glaze-paints were used on the largest vessels in these assemblages and only on White Mountain Red Ware. Ritual intensification was not necessarily a product of aggregation, but was part of the process of reorganization associated with migration into the area. Briefly occupied sites like Bryant Ranch Pueblo, which are atypical of the period, allow us to track these changes more closely. This site allows us to look at the intentional use of glaze paints on vessels whose "social lives" extended beyond everyday domestic contexts to use in special occasions marked by feasting.

Our case study illustrates how important it is to look at technological changes in their social contexts. The diversity of wares, design layouts, and paint recipes so evident during this period suggests that ceramics were used in different social contexts and marked regional and local social distinctions. But, we would not know about the more specific contexts in which these vessels were used without looking more broadly at differences in the faunal, architectural, and feature data.

Finally, our analyses underscore that compositional analyses are highly suited to looking at potting groups or communities of practice. It is clear that these communities operate at the intra- as well as intersite level. Some of the glaze recipes are quite distinctive owing to transmission of knowledge about ore and other material sources, about how to mix glaze paints, and perhaps even owing to exchange of the ores themselves. These factors must be disentangled to better understand the social networks of transmission. For example, do the ore sources for the higher lead content glazes found on later White Mountain Red Ware types and Fourmile Polychrome derive from the Cerrillos and Magdalena sources, as has been suggested for the Zuni area glaze-painted ceramics (see Huntley, chap. 6, this vol.), or are they local? Each scenario has different implications for understanding more completely the social contexts of production and how production and consumption might intersect.

5
Decorating Glaze-Painted Pottery in East-Central Arizona

Scott Van Keuren

In her seminal essay introducing the concept of technological style, Lechtman (1977:14) reminds us that "culturally accepted rules of performance are embodied in the events that lead to the production of an artifact." For her, technological know-how is embedded within other realms of social knowledge relating to belief systems, social or political relationships, and cultural identity (Lechtman 1977:13–15). Recent essays expand her original ideas (e.g., Dietler and Herbich 1998; Dobres 2000), but Lechtman's early statement is useful as a starting point for thinking about the dynamic between technology and decorative style in painted ceramics. The application of decoration should not be viewed as a subroutine in a larger chain of artifact production, nor should we treat decorative knowledge as completely divorced from technological know-how in considering the manufacture of painted ceramics. The social rules that guide the manufacture of pots are complexly situated in cultural experience, historical circumstances, and worldview. In a real sense, decoration and technological styles are rooted in overlapping modes of social practice (Hegmon 1998). In this chapter, I examine these relationships as they relate to early glaze-painted pottery production and, specifically, how the structure of painted decoration complexly embodies group membership, identity, and social boundaries.

In the Western Pueblo region, the technological and decorative features of glaze-painted pottery echo a new social environment of production, one in which potters enjoyed new opportunities to exchange knowledge, observed each other crafting, and experimented with new manufacturing techniques and decorative layouts. These new ceramic traditions were inextricably linked to broader transitions in the Pueblo world (Crown 1996, 1998), and glaze-painted ceramics are important to studying broad patterns of community reorganization during this period. Most authors in this volume discuss glaze-painted ceramics in terms of provenance, paint recipes, or other technological issues. I deviate slightly and examine instead the decorative structure and layout of early glaze-painted ceramics in east-central Arizona (see fig. 1.1). I focus on Fourmile-style White Mountain Red Ware, a widely circulated pottery type in the region that is cited by archaeologists as a marker of new ritual belief systems in the early fourteenth century (e.g., E. C. Adams 1991).

This area underwent important cultural changes at the end of the thirteenth century when groups from within and outside the region resettled at a handful of large aggregated pueblos. This "postmigration" setting set the stage for changes in pottery traditions, which culminated with the appearance of the new iconographic (Fourmile) style on glaze-painted pottery by the 1320s (see fig. 5.1).[1] Here I discuss how these pots were painted, rather than what the painted images symbolize, and what these patterns say about the exchange of crafting-knowledge within early Pueblo IV potter networks. In contrast to the expansiveness of Pinedale style and other earlier ceramic styles (see Crown 1994), the new decorative layouts were not as consistently executed or rendered by potters in the region. The decorative variability of these glaze ware assemblages thus suggests that crafting-knowledge *within* pottery-producing communities was not as freely shared.

I examine these changes in glaze-painted pottery production by treating ancient Pueblo communities not strictly as historical entities associated with specific villages, clustered settlements, or even political alliances, but rather as intersecting modes of social practice. Using a term discussed by Etienne Wenger (1998), I view the social boundaries within these Pueblo landscapes in terms of *communities of practice* rather than of place. This analytical perspective not only yields a more dynamic understanding of the context in which iconographic glaze-painted ceramics were produced, but also demonstrates how the methodological gap between studies of technological and decorative style can be bridged in archaeological interpretation.

Fig. 5.1. Pinedale Polychrome (top), Fourmile Polychrome (middle), and Grasshopper Polychrome bowls (bottom).

The Setting of Ceramic Change

The abandonment of portions of the Four Corners region by the late 1200s began a period of important changes in ceramic production and use in surrounding areas of the Ancestral Pueblo world. Villages along the Mogollon Rim in east-central Arizona were shaped both by local population movement and immigration of groups from surrounding areas. By the first decade of the fourteenth century, these Pueblo peoples were living at a handful of large villages, including Fourmile Ruin, Showlow Ruin, Grasshopper Pueblo, and Point of Pines Pueblo. Most were large plaza-oriented settlements occupied by groups from diverse historical backgrounds (Haury 1958; Mills 1998; Reid 1998). The "co-residence" of these groups set the stage for the innovation and fusion of ceramic traditions (Crown 1996; Zedeño 1995), and this ceramic record, in turn, offers important evidence of broader patterns of community reorganization. How we define a Pueblo community in east-central Arizona is still open to debate.

Networks of ceramic circulation in east-central Arizona indicate that fourteenth-century villages along the eastern Mogollon Rim participated in a socioeconomic interaction sphere that is distinguishable from surrounding areas (Carlson 1982; Duff 2000). Pueblo communities in other parts of the Pueblo IV Southwest are characterized by the clustering of settlements. These clusters were likely based on common historical ties to landscapes, shared resource use areas, the movement of marriage partners or relocation of relatives, and channels of economic exchange (Duff 2000; Upham, Crown, and Plog 1994). Unfortunately, such entities are difficult to recognize in the study area discussed here, owing in part to the complex histories of individual villages. My colleagues and I refer to an emergent Silver Creek cluster that encompasses the socioeconomic relationships among the villages that produced White Mountain Red Ware (Kaldahl, Van Keuren, and Mills 2004). This loosely defined cluster was apparently separate from settlement clusters south of the Mogollon Rim.

Although our interpretation of this landscape may approximate that of the groups who occupied this area during the fourteenth century (i.e., the cluster as a multivillage community), I am certain that Pueblo groups also drew important distinctions in the social boundaries between closely residing groups. For instance, Fourmile Ruin, Grasshopper Pueblo, and other large settlements were likely occupied by diverse ethnic groups

(Ezzo, Johnson, and Price 1997; Haury 1958; Reid 1998). It is possible, then, that the "co-residence" of local and migrant households led to new social boundaries *within* individual settlements. These boundaries are occasionally made obvious in the archaeological record by way of extraordinary events in the past (e.g., the abrupt exodus of the Ancestral Pueblo enclave at Point of Pines Pueblo). Typically, however, these internal settlement boundaries at Pueblo IV sites are much less obvious.

Pottery works well as a proxy of socioeconomic interaction at regional scales, but how do we identify a cultural landscape that is defined by emergent social boundaries at smaller scales? This question must be answered before we fully understand why glaze-painted ceramics first appear and what their production implies about the organization of the Pueblo world. I argue that we must first understand the processes by which potters learn and express crafting-knowledge.

In this chapter, I discuss the appearance of Fourmile-style ceramics produced and circulated among fourteenth-century villages in east-central Arizona. The style emerged from the earlier, omnipresent Pinedale style that spread throughout the upland Southwest by 1300 but first appeared in the Mogollon Rim area slightly earlier. Both styles are among the first attempts by potters in east-central Arizona to produce glaze-painted pottery. Nearly all Pinedale- or Fourmile-style whole vessels surveyed in an earlier dissertation project (Van Keuren 2001) evidence a partial or full glazing of black mineral paints. In addition to experimenting with glaze paint technologies (see Fenn, Mills, and Hopkins, chap. 4, this vol.), White Mountain Red Ware potters also introduced new decorative layouts and symbolic images to their bowls. The new type, Fourmile Polychrome, quickly became one of the central red ware bowls in household assemblages throughout the area. Recent provenance studies place the production locality of this late type in the Silver Creek drainage (Mills et al. 1999; Triadan, Mills, and Duff 2002). Although further provenance work is needed in the region, particularly to discern mid- to late-fourteenth-century ceramic production and distribution, Fourmile Polychrome was likely produced at one or more of the latest villages in the Silver Creek area.

Unlike its ceramic precursors, Fourmile Polychrome was also widely copied in the Grasshopper region and other areas south of the Mogollon Rim (Triadan 1997; Wendorf 1950). This is an important event: the transition to Fourmile-style pots marks the first wide-scale copying of

Colorado Plateau glaze-painted ceramics in the Mogollon Rim area. As I discuss later in this chapter, these Fourmile "hybrids" often fail to replicate both the decorative and technological style of classic Fourmile Polychrome. Many do not achieve the glaze-, or subglaze-, painted appearance of classic White Mountain Red Ware, nor do they accurately imitate the iconographic imagery of Fourmile Polychrome bowl interiors. The transition to glaze-painted, iconographic pottery in east-central Arizona thus hints at the application of increasingly specialized knowledge.

In the next section, I present a model drawn from practice theory that articulates the connection between learning, activity, and social identity (Bleed 2001; Dietler and Herbich 1994; Lave and Wenger 1996; Sinclair 2000; van der Leeuw 1993). I then use the model to examine organizational changes in glaze-painted ceramic production in the Mogollon Rim area, and specifically, to identify style barriers that may have impeded the sharing and exchange of crafting-knowledge. These barriers are the key to modeling past communities of practice in east-central Arizona and surrounding regions of the Pueblo world.

Pottery Styles and Communities of Practice

Human communities are defined by fluid criteria: economic ties, familial contacts and ancestry, oral traditions, political affiliation, and spatial proximity, among others (Arensberg 1961; Murdock 1949). These historical qualities are typically inaccessible in the archaeological record of the Pueblo Southwest, and as I noted earlier, we rely on the spatial proximity of settlements to infer the composition of ancient communities (Kolb and Snead 1997). My task here is not to critique the utility of these approaches, but rather to examine community boundaries as they are expressed at smaller scales of interaction (e.g., within large aggregated settlements). I address the issue of community reorganization using an alternative perspective, one that examines how crafting-knowledge is learned and expressed among households at newly formed, ethnically diverse Pueblo IV settlements. This bottom-up analysis uses prehistoric whole vessels as objects for inferring social practice and how individuals think and act within their social worlds (see Hinde 1976).

Wenger (1998) and others (Chaiklin and Lave 1996; Minar and Crown 2001) use the phrase "community of practice" to conceptualize the relationship between social practice, learning, identity, and production activities. For Wenger (1998:5–6), communities are as much passive entities defined by historical criteria as they are active and changing collectives defined by the distribution of knowledge and participation in activities. Communities of practice designate a group, or groups of individuals, who are literally defined by a "sustained pursuit of a shared enterprise" (Wenger 1998:45). Understanding and knowing what is to be expressed through action is "inherent in the growth and transformation of identities" (Lave and Wenger 1991:122). In such a model, doing is a reflection of knowing and knowing is shaped by the social and spatial distance of interaction, the structure of learning events, and the identity and experience of the persons involved. Such models of social practice deal with complex, overlapping dimensions of thought and action, but I cite this approach with the specific intent of understanding how crafts reflect past learning frameworks and information exchange and, by extension, group affiliation or identity. In Wenger's (1998:4–5) model, she notes the importance of learning as participation in cultural worlds. In this sense, learning is predicated on many things, including idiosyncratic factors, physical aptitude, an individual's ethnic or cultural affiliation, and ability to communicate.

Returning to the Ancestral Pueblo world, a community of practice rather than of place model offers a platform for examining the active processes that shape crafting economies. I am particularly interested in interaction at scales that shape the co-residence of groups with diverse historical backgrounds, where the ability or inability to share crafting-knowledge was dependent on the fluidity of social boundaries, group membership, and the proximity of learning exchanges. Lave (1996:16) calls attention to "failed learning," or instances when one or more dimensions of social practice are incompletely emulated. Regardless of how they shape the production of objects or other actions, these processes are key to revealing the margins of communities of practice. This type of practice-based analysis delineates the fluid identities of smaller-scale groups, as reflected through learning and craft production.

As with many archaeological objects, painted ceramics carry inherent messages about social identity and experience that are not intended by their producers (Dietler and Herbich 1994; Hegmon 1998; Hegmon, Nelson, and Ennes 2000; Herbich 1987). It is at this discrete analytical level that prehistoric communities of practice are recognized. In the Southwest, potters learned by watching other potters, following verbal or nonverbal instruction and emulating the finished work of other potters

(Hagstrum 1995). The informality of these activities produced diverse results, reflective of both idiosyncrasies of individual potters and access to widely shared bodies of crafting-knowledge. The challenge in style research is to access levels of variability that best approximate the original learning process, apart from purely "individual styles" or, at the other end of the spectrum, cross-cultural parallels in style behavior. The sequence in which paint is applied to the vessel surface is one clue to the structure of these learning frameworks.

It is useful to think of pottery decoration in a larger sense as graphic behavior. Graphic representation proceeds in several cyclical stages: the perception of images, the operation of learning and memory, the expression of cognitive templates in painting and other motor actions, and the modification of these cognitive frameworks through feedback and error correction. Schemata are encoded in the learning process and determine the course of action during subsequent graphic behavior. Schemata are "generalized plan[s] for a class of movements" (J. A. Adams 1976:101) and form the cognitive foundation of perception, memory, and recall (Crozier and Chapman 1984; Summers 1989). Much of the graphic behavior that is guided by these schemata takes place at cognitive levels that are not explicitly altered during the execution of motor actions. In fact, the processes of perception, referencing and memorization, and expression and feedback that define the sequence of graphic behavior are largely "unavailable to consciousness" (Pratt 1985:52). The artisan may intentionally modify decoration at any stage of the painting process, but the underlying sequencing of graphic behavior is consistent. If the transmission of information is incomplete, individuals will modify and even miscode schemata according to their own internal modes of graphic behavior, ultimately structuring decoration differently. In the case of painted pottery, these cognitive processes guide (or even misguide) the hand during the application of paint.

The decorative process is not structured by the mixing and matching of traditional design elements, but rather by the application, directionality, and overall composition of individual painting gestures. Potters may think and converse about design elements, aesthetic presentation, color, symbolism, and techniques, but they rarely discuss the precise sequences of paint application (Friedrich 1970). These sequences are not random but are instead shaped by the original learning context(s), much like the sequence of written script that is encoded at a young age and resistant to change thereafter (Eden 1961). The basal unit of ceramic decoration is the brushstroke. Brushstroke sequences reveal the order of paint application, the organization of framing lines, and the spatial patterning of the decorative field, all of which collectively define the decorative event. If one is dealing with a whole vessel, the entire brushstroke sequence is a momentary expression of learned behavior by an individual potter.

The analytical basis for this approach is outlined elsewhere (Van Keuren 1999), but it is important to note here that the initial stages of vessel decoration are key to the analysis of painting sequences. There is a strong cross-cultural tendency among potters to start the painting process by delineating decorative space with framing lines or framing forms that are subsequently filled (Arnold 1970; Guthe 1925; Hardin 1983; Roe 1980). Much of the decoration applied after the painting surface is framed, including filler elements and motifs, is less consistently rendered. What is most relevant from an analytical standpoint, however, is the sequence in which the first set of (framing) brushstrokes is applied.

Although some of the variability in brushstroke sequences is associated with cross-cultural tendencies in graphic behavior (Washburn 1983), at least part of it encodes culture-specific or historical patterns of learning and information exchange. In the Southwest, the decoration of ceramics was influenced chiefly by the context of learning and the social experience of the artisan (Crown 1999). By definition, potters belonging to a community of practice share similar cognitive strategies for crafting pots. However, a potter copying a pot with little or no prior experience with the decoration may create a visual duplicate with similar design elements or motifs, but the underlying execution sequence of the copied pots will not be duplicated. In the latter instance, potters draw on improvised schemata to emulate decorative schemes, and this new structure imposed during the copying process may even alter the semantic content of the original design. These are instances of failed learning (see Lave and Wenger 1991), caused by what Margaret Hardin (1984:592–96) calls communication differentials, stylistic screens, and other "style barriers." These barriers influence how a variety of knowledge is translated, expressed, or even presented after the craft is produced. Artisans can (and do) misunderstand and misconstrue the underlying symbolic foundation of technological and decorative knowledge. These actions do not simply result in poor copying or mistaken expression, but in a real sense are misconstructions of others' cultural worlds. These processes can be inferred by studying microscale variation.

The Specialization of Glaze Ware Styles in East-Central Arizona

Recent provenance research in east-central Arizona reveals a high degree of spatial variability in fourteenth-century polychrome assemblages. Zedeño (1994) and Triadan (1997) demonstrate that southern Colorado Plateau ceramic technologies were copied south of the Mogollon Rim beginning in the late thirteenth century. The shift in production by the 1330s is unprecedented. For instance, the Grasshopper Pueblo decorated assemblage is dominated by black-on-white and polychrome pottery brought from the southern edge of the Colorado Plateau, but it is not until Fourmile Polychrome appears that a local, nonglaze-painted White Mountain Red Ware "hybrid" appears at this village. This new dimension of glaze ware imitation indicates a shift in the social environment of production and specifically in the structure of learning and information exchange among potters (Van Keuren 2000).

Painting Fourmile Style

In an earlier study, I showed that the execution of Pinedale style was fairly standardized. Potters who produced Cibola White Ware and perhaps Roosevelt Red Ware did so with a regular formula for applying decoration, signaled by the consistent sequencing of framing line execution, brushstrokes that are used to lay out the vessel decoration prior to the addition of solid or hachure filling (Van Keuren 1999). A more recent structural analysis of painted designs on Pinedale-style White Mountain Red Ware corroborates the earlier study (Van Keuren 2001). Figure 5.2 illustrates the basic decorative sequence displayed as stages of paint application (indicated by numbered arrows) on two Pinedale Polychrome bowls. Following the addition of the red slip, thin black framing brushstrokes were used to delineate the quartered layouts; additional design forms were then outlined in subsequent steps prior to the application of solid and hachure filler. The entire layout is framed first in a specific order, and the basic sequence is pervasive in Pinedale-style pottery throughout the Mogollon Rim area. These brushstroke recipes, along with the cognitive frameworks they are based on, were likely derived in part from the painting sequences of earlier Tularosa- and Kayenta-style pottery. These historical contingencies should be further explored, but it is clear that Pinedale-style pottery was produced in a fluid learning environment and possibly tied to a widespread belief system (Crown 1994).

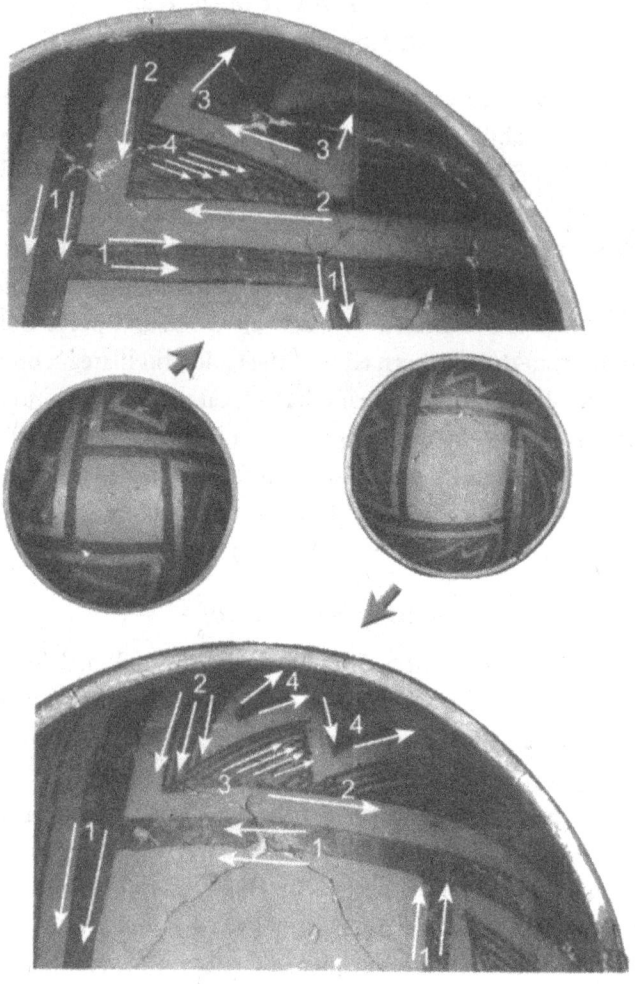

Fig. 5.2. Execution sequence of black brushstrokes on Pinedale-style bowl interiors.

The appearance of Fourmile Polychrome in the 1320s marks a change in the organization of interior bowl decoration. Bowl interiors still exhibit some underlying consistency in the application of brushstrokes in spite of the diverse subject matter conveyed by this new style. Most noteworthy, however, is the consistency with which bowl exterior panels are painted: no two Fourmile Polychrome bowls display the exact same decorative scheme, but the underlying brushstroke pattern is fairly regularized. Figure 5.3 shows the execution of an exterior panel. Potters began these vessels with long white horizontal framing lines to define the banded design field; next, brushstrokes were added to delineate individual panels, followed by the application of additional white lines or elements and two bands of black paint as filler. The banded design begins directly at or slightly below the rim. There are two important dimensions of brushstroke variability: panel to panel consistencies within the same vessel and similarities between vessels. Both patterns suggest that Fourmile Polychrome potters were painting with a standard mental template. These potters were innovators, utilizing different motifs, design elements, spatial organizations, and, perhaps most important, elaborate representational images on bowl interiors. However, the order of brushstrokes reveals a fundamental consistency in the painting sequence. I suggest that these sequences speak to a single or set of closely related learning pools among Fourmile Polychrome potters in the Silver Creek drainage. Future provenance studies may someday pinpoint these learning pools to specific villages or perhaps even potter workshops within villages, but current thinking does not place Fourmile Polychrome production at a single settlement in the Silver Creek drainage (Triadan, Mills, and Duff 2002). By way of their craft, however, I argue that these potters were tied to a single and distinct community of practice, possibly encompassing two or more villages.

Fourmile Polychrome hybrids appear in the Grasshopper and Q-Ranch areas, at Point of Pines Pueblo to the southeast and even within the Silver Creek drainage above the Mogollon Rim by the mid-1300s (Triadan 1997; Wendorf 1950; Whittlesey 1974). Although the potters who produced these hybrid vessels probably had regular social contact with White Mountain Red Ware producers, perhaps living alongside these potters at some villages (e.g., Fourmile Ruin), their efforts at copying Fourmile Polychrome were largely improvised. This is evident both in the structure of interior bowl decoration and the execution of line work on the exterior surface. Grasshopper Polychrome is the best known of these copies, owing in part to the extensive work at Grasshopper Pueblo (Reid and Whittlesey 1999) and Triadan's (1997) expansive provenance study of red ware vessels in the region. Grasshopper potters were clearly emulating Fourmile Polychrome bowls, drawing on crafting-knowledge they acquired through social ties to Pueblo villages to the north. There is also convincing evidence of ethnic co-residence between Mogollon Rim groups and Colorado Plateau peoples at Grasshopper Pueblo (Ezzo, Johnson, and Price 1997; Reid 1998; Riggs 2002). Nonetheless, local potters painted Fourmile-style

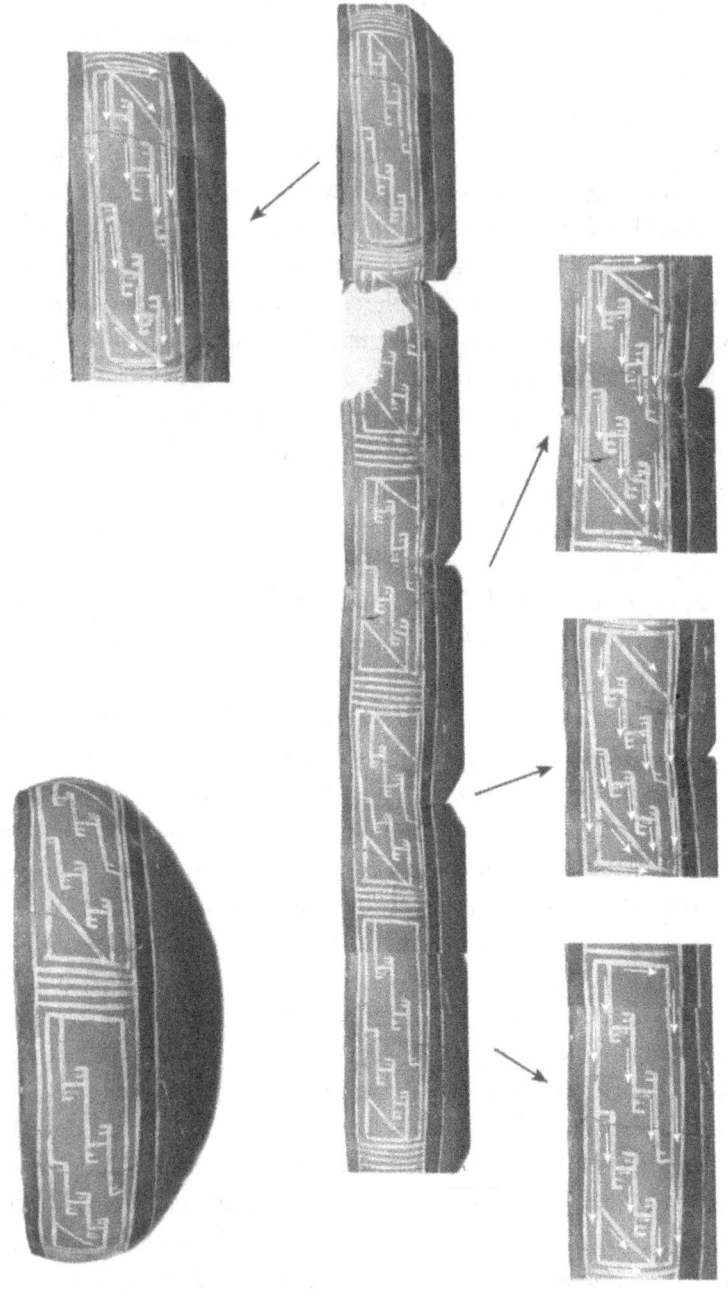

Fig. 5.3. Framing line execution, Fourmile Polychrome.

decoration differently than White Mountain Red Ware potters. Figure 5.4 illustrates these structural inconsistencies: the banded design drops below the rim; the overall execution of white and black paint is nonsequential (Fourmile Polychrome potters always framed the entire design field with white brushstrokes prior to later additions). The directionality and sequence of white brushstrokes are inconsistent from panel to panel, a key difference from Fourmile Polychrome. The essential banded exterior is recreated here, but with ad-lib brushstroke sequences. These copies are not decorative mistakes, but rather visual misconceptions of Colorado Plateau-produced Fourmile-style vessels.

The significance of these design errors or instances of "failed learning" to the prehistoric audience is impossible to know. Some may have offended the aesthetic sensibility of White Mountain Red Ware potters; others were deeply embedded decorative patterns that went unnoticed. They do, however, show that the sharing of crafting-knowledge among early Pueblo IV potters in the Mogollon Rim area was less fluid than with the earlier Pinedale style. These instances of copying were not restricted to Grasshopper Pueblo and other sites outside the production zone of White Mountain Red Ware. Fourmile-style hybrids are present in the large red ware whole-vessel assemblage recovered during the early excavation of Fourmile Ruin (Fewkes 1904). Many of these exhibit the same basic pattern of style miscoding seen in Grasshopper Polychrome. Some households at Fourmile Ruin, possibly the largest White Mountain Red Ware-producing village, produced Fourmile-style copies with authentic exterior banded design fields and interiors that resemble the Pinedale-derived Jeddito style recently discussed by Lyons (2003). Although preliminary paste and temper observations imply local production of these Fourmile Ruin hybrids, more work is needed to establish their provenance. Finally, it is important to note that nearly all Fourmile-style copies show improvisation of technological qualities. Grasshopper Polychrome bowls were often painted with organic-based paints (or a blend of organic- and mineral-based paints) and subjected to less stringent firing regimes (Triadan 1997). Very few of the painted designs on these local pots exhibit glazing.

Glaze Ware Communities of Practice

Why did potters throughout east-central Arizona begin copying glaze-painted wares in the fourteenth century? Practically speaking, shifting demographics and exchange networks made Fourmile Polychrome harder

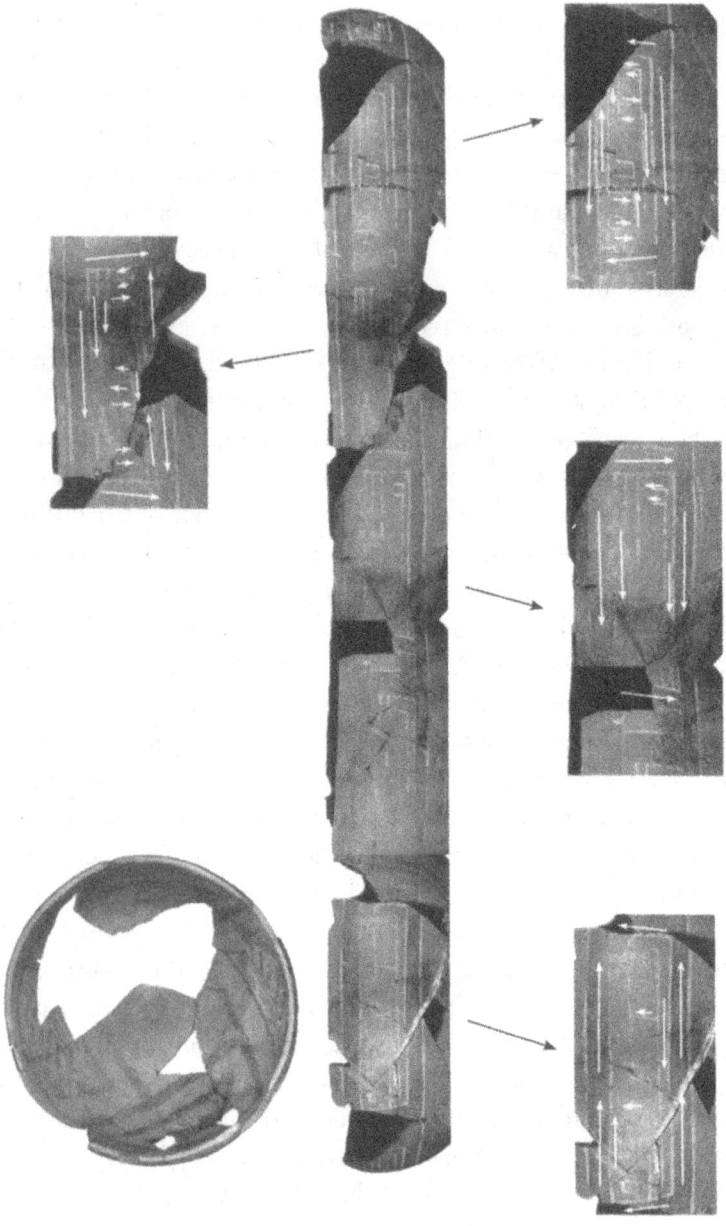

to come by, as indicated by the paucity of Fourmile Polychrome on late-abandoned household floors at Grasshopper Pueblo (Triadan 1997). Smaller numbers of vessels circulated from the Silver Creek villages to surrounding areas as White Mountain Red Ware potters relocated to fewer villages by the early to mid-1300s. But why were these hybrids painted with ad hoc brushstroke sequences? The emulation of glaze-painted pottery in east-central Arizona hints at a key shift in the sharing of both technological and decorative knowledge among potter groups.

Fourmile Polychrome bowls present complex imagery, analogous to the esoteric subject matter of kiva murals and other decorated media (E. C. Adams 1994; Hays 1989). These images must have embodied ritual knowledge that was complexly rooted within the broader cultural identity of Fourmile Polychrome potters. I have suggested elsewhere that some images may have evoked the allegories of specific clans or similar social groups (Van Keuren 2000). The potters who copied Fourmile Polychrome, on the other hand, were working with an unfamiliar visual lexicon. The end products are bowls that closely mimic the banded exteriors of Fourmile Polychrome, but replace interior images with geometric patterning that recalls the earlier Pinedale style. If, as Lave and Wenger (1991:52–54) suggest, the process of learning creates new social identities, then potters experimenting with glaze ware technology and style were emulating more than just the material culture of the Fourmile community of practice. Reproducing highly decorated polychrome bowls and perhaps also participating in the activities in which these vessels were displayed and utilized (e.g., communal feasts) may have resituated the social identity of these potters. As with any emulative behavior, however, making is not always "knowing" (Lave and Wenger 1991:123). Those potters who copied Fourmile Polychrome did so using variable raw materials and manufacturing techniques and fusions of Fourmile- and Pinedale-style decorative elements. The most relevant pattern noted here, and discussed in length elsewhere (Van Keuren 2001), is the improvised application of framing lines and other steps in early stages of paint application.

It is erroneous to think of White Mountain Red Ware copies from the Grasshopper region and other areas as inferior, since they were probably viewed as functional equivalents of Fourmile Polychrome bowls. They do, however, exhibit fundamental differences in application of paint that I attribute to the miscoding and misunderstanding of crafting-knowledge. Whatever the precise style barriers at work here, they did not restrict the copying of Fourmile-style bowls per se, but did influence the exchange of knowledge beyond the Fourmile Polychrome community of practice. Furthermore, we cannot separate the semantics of decoration from design execution or structure: "failures to learn" will pervade all dimensions of decorative behavior. Most Fourmile copies substitute geometric Pinedale-style layouts in place of iconographic imagery despite a literal imitation of the Fourmile Polychrome exteriors (see fig. 5.4). In the case of Fourmile-style copies, the central symbolic act was one in which one group emulated the cultural or ritual currency of another. In other words, Fourmile-style copiers were drawing on the symbolic resources of an "other," and this degree of miscoding, as I discuss at length elsewhere (Van Keuren 2000, 2001), seems to contradict the conventional wisdom about the role of unifying cults in the post-Pinedale-style Southwest.

With the community of practice model in mind, we can begin to identify style barriers that shape past learning processes and especially "failures to learn" and "failures to participate" (Wenger 1998:4–5). I apply a community of practice model because it emphasizes the individual as unit of study (Dobres 1999), can be operationalized using discrete and replicable analytical techniques, and extends the traditional scope of ceramic style research. As applied in this chapter, the framework not only helps reconstruct the environment of glaze-painted pottery production in east-central Arizona but also reshapes our understanding of broader ceramic changes in the Western Pueblo region. I suggest that the appearance of the final glaze ware type produced in the Mogollon Rim area marks a threshold in the sharing and expression of technological and decorative knowledge. Fourmile Polychrome pots appear to have been produced by a distinct community of practice, skilled in the use of specific glaze paint recipes (De Atley 1986) and the presentation of esoteric imagery (E. C. Adams 1991). These high-fired pots not only made reference to a broad ritual belief system, as Adams (1991) argues, but also signaled a shift to the specialized production of iconographic-style glaze-painted bowls within this limited geographic area. Those who copied this type in the Grasshopper region and elsewhere were working outside or on the periphery of this community of practice. That local potters at these villages copied Fourmile-style designs with hypothetical painting schemes hints at new access rules that limited the distribution of crafting-knowledge and perhaps even ideological concepts by the mid-1300s. This interpretation does not contest the integrative function of regional belief systems (expressed through regional pottery styles), but does call attention to the possible disintegrative processes that shaped fourteenth-century communities (Kaldahl, Van Keuren, and Mills 2004; Plog and Solometo 1997).

Conclusion

The changes in the environment of ceramic production that I discuss in this chapter took place at a time when ongoing migration and abandonment reshuffled the spatial organization of Pueblo peoples in the Silver Creek drainage and greater Mogollon Rim area. An initial aggregation of large villages was followed by a reconsolidation in the 1320s, leaving at least one major village abandoned (Bailey Ruin). The fusion of ceramic traditions that resulted in the Pinedale style that appears at the close of the thirteenth century was short lived. Within two decades some potter groups produced iconographic Fourmile Polychrome, while others emulated this type with improvised stylistic and technological strategies. Other wares once painted with Pinedale-style decoration take divergent pathways, moving away from the decorative content of glaze-painted pottery (e.g., late Salado Polychromes). It is no coincidence that potters failed to emulate both the technological and decorative aspects of early glaze-painted pots. I see this diversification of pottery traditions in east-central Arizona as reflecting broader organizational changes, tied to the increasing specialization of craft production, the exclusivity of ideological networks, and factionalism within large settlements. The latter process may have played a role in the abandonment of the region by Pueblo groups at the close of the fourteenth century (Kaldahl, Van Keuren, and Mills 2004). Ultimately, the ceramic style data discussed here are but one small part of an emerging picture of Pueblo community organization during this period, and these preliminary interpretations need to be evaluated with further work in the Mogollon Rim area.

In closing, it is helpful to address the overlaps between decorative and technological knowledge used to make glaze ware pottery. Pfaffenberger (1988:241) points out that "any technology is a set of social behaviors and a system of meanings." These sets of behaviors and systems of meanings are not divorced from the actual production of decoration (see Hegmon 1998; Schiffer and Skibo 1987, 1997; Zedeño 2002). The brushstroke method discussed in this chapter is one of many crossover techniques for characterizing the technological and decorative styles of glaze-painted ceramics.

At this analytical level, both technological *and* decorative gestures encode an artisan's learning history, familiarity with a subject matter, access to raw materials (including knowledge), and, most important, their exposure to and re-expression of new or unfamiliar cultural worlds. In the case of Fourmile-style pottery, I suggest that the cognitive processes that guide the application of brushstrokes (and other microscale manufacturing steps) are tied to the depiction of iconographic imagery and other instances of "active" stylistic expression. In closing, painted ceramics are central to our understanding of regional identities and community boundaries in the Pueblo Southwest, but traditional methods of ceramic analysis often fail to reveal the smaller-scale margins of social groups within large aggregated villages. One strategy for understanding early glaze-painted pottery production is to better integrate our analyses of technological and stylistic variability through careful attention to both process and practice (Bleed 2001; Sellet 1993; essays in Stark 1998).

6

From Recipe to Identity

Exploring Zuni Glaze Ware
Communities of Practice

Deborah L. Huntley

Across the northern Southwest, the Pueblo IV period (ca. AD 1275–1400) was a time of new social developments, as regional changes in settlement patterns resulted in the renegotiation of social boundaries, the redefinition of social identities, and the reestablishment of social connections at multiple scales. Archaeological studies of ceramic technological systems provide one means of elucidating these social connections.

In this chapter I explore the development of glaze paint recipes in the Zuni region of west-central New Mexico. During the Pueblo IV period, local potters developed lead-based glaze recipes that represent a departure from earlier copper-rich glazes used in the Zuni region and elsewhere in the Pueblo Southwest. I propose that this recipe shift was the result of conscious technical choices that allowed potters more latitude in the production of distinctive glaze ware vessels with socially meaningful color combinations. Zuni region potters appear to have used ores from multiple distant sources, although they initially focused intensively on the Cerrillos Hills deposits near Santa Fe. The diversity of ore resources used by Zuni region potters apparently increased through time, suggesting possible changes in the scale and direction of interregional social connections during the fourteenth century. At the same time that ore resource diversity increased, however, glaze paint recipes became more homogeneous overall, suggesting that Zuni region potters shared technical information widely and participated in extensive and overlapping communities of practice.

Regional Context

The Zuni region (see fig. 1.1), part of the larger Cibola cultural province of Arizona and New Mexico, includes some 4,500 km^2 of the Zuni River drainage, all of the present-day Zuni Reservation, the El Morro Valley to the east of the reservation, and Jaralosa Draw to the south of the reservation (Duff 2000; Kintigh 1996). The onset of glaze ware production in the Zuni region generally coincides with the development of a distinctive architectural pattern: the nucleated pueblo. Nucleated pueblos are the hallmark of the Pueblo IV period not only in the Zuni region, but in much of the northern Southwest as well. Beginning around AD 1250, at least twenty-eight large, nucleated pueblo villages were constructed and eventually abandoned in the Zuni region (Duff 2000; Kintigh 1985b, 1996; LeBlanc 2001; Watson, LeBlanc, and Redman 1980). A typical nucleated pueblo consisted of a single block of contiguous rooms (around 200 to 1,200 total) surrounding a central plaza (Kintigh 1985b; Spier 1917). Most nucleated pueblos clearly were planned and appear to have been built over a relatively short period of time, often with later additions (Anyon 1987; Duff 2000; Kintigh 1985b; Watson, LeBlanc, and Redman 1980).

Keith Kintigh and I (Huntley and Kintigh 2004) have shown that during the Early Pueblo IV period (AD 1275–1325), some nucleated pueblos in the Zuni region were clustered on the landscape, while others were relatively isolated. Clustering became more distinct during the Late Pueblo IV period (AD 1325–1375), with at least three identifiable subregional clusters: one in the El Morro Valley, one in the Pescado Basin area, and one to the south along Jaralosa Draw. We argue that temporal shifts in the spatial clustering of settlements within the Zuni region, as well as differences in the distribution of glaze-decorated ceramic types, suggest that social boundaries and interactions were regularly defined on a much smaller scale than that of the region (Huntley and Kintigh 2004). As discussed in this chapter, analysis of Zuni Glaze Ware paint compositions highlights the existence of multiple spheres of social interaction.

Zuni Glaze Ware

The two Zuni Glaze Ware types included in the present study, Heshotauthla Polychrome and Kwakina Polychrome, were made between AD 1275 and 1400 and are most commonly bowl forms (Carlson 1970; Woodbury and Woodbury 1966; see Eckert, chap. 3, this vol.). Both types developed from St. Johns Polychrome (Carlson 1970; Seventh Southwestern Ceramic Seminar 1965; see Eckert, chap. 3, this vol.), which was common in the Zuni region between AD 1200 and 1300. Potters began experimenting with glaze paints in the mid-1200s, and St. Johns Polychrome vessels exhibit a wide range of paint textures, ranging from matte mineral paints to well-vitrified glazes. As discussed by Habicht-Mauche (chap. 1, this vol.), the use of glaze paint by Pueblo potters represents a major technological innovation in that, given the relatively low firing temperatures obtainable in open-pit firings, glazes can be made only by using certain combinations of ingredients.

Zuni Glaze Ware is one example of a distinctive style of polychrome pottery that was made across the northern Southwest beginning around AD 1275 (Carlson 1970; Shepard 1942; see Eckert, chap. 3, this vol.). This new style included bowls with white-slipped interiors and red-slipped exteriors, many of which were decorated with glaze paint. Kwakina Polychrome and matte-painted Pinto Polychrome (in the Salado tradition) appear to be the earliest examples of the polychrome color scheme (Crown 1994:17–18; Kintigh 1985b:15). According to Crown (1994) this particular use of slip-color combinations was associated with the adoption of what she concludes was a southwestern regional cult. Since most of the polychrome vessels that she examined exhibited use wear, she argues that they were used in domestic contexts.

Glaze-decorated red ware bowls with both bichrome and polychrome color schemes were also made in the Rio Grande Valley during the Pueblo IV period. Here glaze ware bowls are proposed to have played an important role in the development of new ritual activities, such as communal feasts (Graves and Spielmann 2000; Spielmann 1998). To support this argument, Spielmann (1998) cites several examples of the ritual use of glaze ware bowls, including representations in prehistoric kiva murals (Hibben 1975; Smith 1952) and historic Isleta Pueblo paintings (Goldfrank 1970) and association with artifacts and ecofacts related to ritual food preparation and consumption, such as nonsubsistence fauna, at Quarai Pueblo in the Salinas district. Although Upham (1982) has argued that late prehistoric Western Pueblo decorated vessels were "elite" wares made by craft specialists, the fact that they are universally found in association with domestic refuse at excavated Pueblo IV sites throughout the Zuni region suggests that they were commonly used in everyday domestic contexts. Thus there is evidence that glaze-decorated bowls were used both for serving food within individual households and for certain community-wide integrative ritual activities.

The Development of Zuni Region Glaze Recipes

Glaze paint compositions are the result of the interplay of a number of factors, including the availability of raw materials and the conscious and unconscious manipulation of those materials. In creating glazes, potters must make a series of technical choices that result in chemically and visually distinctive products. For example, a potter who decides to use a lead flux must then also choose where to get the lead ore, its parent form (e.g., galena or another mineral, such as cerrusite), how much of the flux to use, and whether or not to mix it with other materials, such as an organic binder, a slip clay, or other mineral colorants. The outcome of these various technical choices is a particular glaze paint alternative that can be considered a recipe.

Distinctive glaze paint recipes might also be considered a form of technological style, a concept first employed by Heather Lechtman (1977), if they convey socially meaningful information. I use Rice's (1987:201) modified definition of technological style as a combination of experience and custom resulting in a body of information and practice governing the manufacture of material culture, which leads to a characteristic product with a unique range of properties. I argue that the socially meaningful information conveyed by glaze paint recipes pertains to learning frameworks that relate to the construction of group identity and social boundaries (Lemonnier 1992, 1993). In other words, meaningful, nonarbitrary technical choices are made in the context of learning frameworks, or communities of practice, in which potters participate. I define a community of practice as a social group within which a particular technique is learned and perpetuated through interaction among group members (Lave and Wenger 1991:50; Minar 2001; Sassaman and Rudolphi 2001; Stark 1999, chap. 2, this vol.; Wenger 1998). Importantly, communities of practice are complicated in that they may incorporate various overlapping group affiliations structured by spatial proximity (e.g., household or village membership) or along lines of kinship and/or ethnicity. The community of practice concept is especially useful for understanding glaze paint recipes since glaze paint manufacture is something that presumably must be learned firsthand (or at least via word of mouth) rather than through imitation of a finished product (Herhahn 1995; see also Herhahn, chap. 10, this vol.). In the following sections I use compositional analysis of glaze paints and isotopic sourcing of lead ores to identify glaze paint technological styles and explore the scale(s) of fourteenth-century Zuni Glaze Ware communities of practice.

Glaze Paint Compositions

I used an electron microprobe to determine the chemical compositions of glaze paints on over three hundred Zuni Glaze Ware and St. Johns Polychrome sherds from seven different Zuni region nucleated pueblos (see fig. 1.2). The microprobe utilizes a focused electron beam to determine the concentrations of elements, measured as relative percentages by weight of oxides, present within a given polished thick section sample. Reed (1993) provides a review of the technique. For the present analysis, taking five individual readings at different points on each sample averages out potential heterogeneities inherent in each glaze. The individual point values are then normalized to 100 percent, and an average percentage by weight for every oxide is calculated for each glaze sample. A complete discussion of sampling and analysis methods is presented in Huntley (2004).

The microprobe analysis reveals differences in the relative amounts of lead and copper present in Zuni region glazes. Paints on St. Johns Polychrome, the earliest type examined in this study, tend to have little or no lead and higher amounts of copper compared to paints on Kwakina Polychrome and Heshotauthla Polychrome. The average lead composition of the seventy sampled St. Johns Polychrome glaze paints is approximately 7 percent by weight, and half of those samples contain less than 1 percent lead by weight (see Huntley 2004:table 7.2). Copper ranges from less than 1 percent to 47 percent by weight in St. Johns Polychrome, with a mean of approximately 18 percent. This can be contrasted with a mean of around 28 percent by weight for lead and around 12 percent by weight for copper in Heshotauthla and Kwakina Polychrome. There also appears to be some variability within and among types in terms of minor glaze constituents, such as iron and manganese, as well as elements that may have been introduced in small quantities through their association with lead or copper ores (e.g., zinc and titanium).

The trend toward increasing lead and decreasing copper appears to have been a gradual development characterized by experimentation with lead-based glaze recipes at the late end of the White Mountain Red Ware sequence and the early end of the Zuni Glaze Ware sequence. The contexts from which sherds used in this study were selected can be classified as relatively early or late within the Pueblo IV period.[1] Figure 6.1 shows box-and-whisker plots of lead and copper percentages by weight for each type from early and late Pueblo IV contexts. Note that the box-and-whisker plots present median values rather than means and also highlight the presence of a few outliers for each pottery type. As these plots indicate, within earlier archaeological contexts from Zuni region sites, all three types— St. Johns, Heshotauthla, and Kwakina Polychrome—have lower median values for lead than do all three types from later contexts. The fact that St. Johns Polychrome glaze compositions overlap substantially with early Heshotauthla and Kwakina Polychrome glaze compositions indicates that this basic change in recipe represents a local developmental trajectory of White Mountain Red Ware in the Zuni region.

I performed a k-means nonhierarchical cluster analysis (Kintigh 2002) in order to identify groups of glaze samples with similar compositions. The analysis incorporated all samples independent of type or time period to create compositional groups. K-means analysis was performed using molecular proportions for each oxide, which are calculated by dividing an oxide's weight percentage by its molecular weight. The molecular proportion therefore represents the proportion of molecules for each oxide present in the mixture and ensures that heavy elements, such as lead, do not have disproportionate influence on statistical analyses. The cluster analysis was performed using standardized z-scores of the molecular proportion data.

In this analysis, a three-cluster solution exhibits the most pronounced difference from randomly generated data and confirms the major distinction between high- and low-lead paints. It also identifies a third, smaller compositional group characterized by high levels of manganese.[2] While other cluster solutions result in further partitioning of the two large compositional groups, these solutions largely highlight differences in minor elements, such as magnesium, titanium, and zinc, that are highly variable and may be present in glazes as impurities associated with other minerals. I choose to focus on the three-cluster solution because I believe that it distinguishes groups that are the result of intentional glaze preparation strategies used by Zuni region potters.

There are a number of significant differences between compositional groups, the most important of which are probably lead, copper, man-

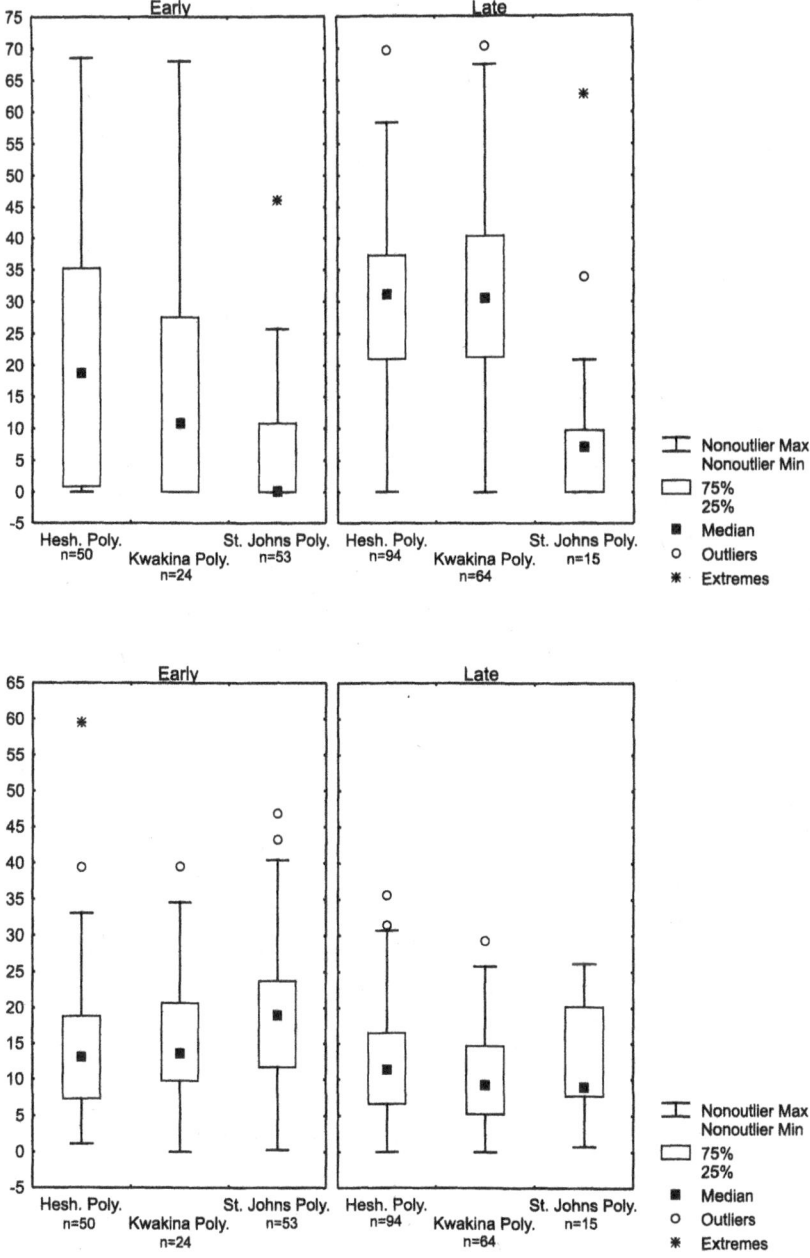

Fig. 6.1. Lead oxide weight percentages (top) and copper oxide weight percentages (bottom) by type for early and late contexts.

ganese, silica, and alumina concentrations.[3] A total of 60 percent of all sampled Heshotauthla Polychrome glazes and 61 percent of Kwakina Polychrome glazes are classified in Group 1. Only 11 percent of St. Johns Polychrome glazes are classified in this group. Group 3, the low lead group, contains 84 percent of all St. Johns Polychrome glazes and 33 percent and 34 percent, respectively, of Heshotauthla and Kwakina Polychrome glazes. Group 2 appears to be a somewhat lower-lead/higher-manganese version of Group 1 and contains relatively low frequencies of all three types, with Heshotauthla Polychrome glazes most common.

The relatively high copper and lower lead content of Group 3 glazes, which are predominantly on St. Johns Polychrome bowls, typically results in a paint that is dark brown or black in color. St. Johns glazes also tend to have more silica and alumina than Heshotauthla or Kwakina glazes, which may explain why many of the St. Johns glazes are not very glassy and may best be considered subglazes. Moreover, both Heshotauthla and Kwakina Polychrome from late contexts are less variable than are both types from earlier contexts, a trend that St. Johns Polychrome glazes do not share (see Huntley 2004:table 7.3). St. Johns glazes are consistently more heterogeneous (and lower) in lead compositions than Kwakina and Heshotauthla Polychrome.

Increased compositional homogeneity in Kwakina and Heshotauthla Polychrome glazes might be explained by increased standardization in glaze recipes through time, owing either to a reduction in the number of glaze producers or to a general consensus among Zuni region potters about the appropriate way to make a glaze. A more consistent glaze recipe, particularly if coupled with consistent ore sources and improved processing techniques, would have allowed potters to reliably achieve certain glaze qualities, such as glassiness and color brightness. Relatively high lead and silica compositions in many Heshotauthla and Kwakina glazes not only cause them to be more vitreous, but also promote more variety and brilliance in glaze color since these materials are essentially clear. Underlying slip color also has an effect on observed color. For example, green glazes on white-slipped Kwakina Polychrome appear brighter than they would on a red-slipped St. Johns or Heshotauthla Polychrome.

Intraregional Variability in Glaze Technological Styles

A closer look at intraregional patterning in glaze compositions reveals that while the basic glaze recipe seems to have changed over the course of the

Pueblo IV period at all of the sampled pueblos within the Zuni region, there may be some subtle differences among sites. I was able to identify probable production sources for a total of 118 sherds using instrumental neutron activation analysis (INAA) of sherd pastes. INAA data were obtained at the University of Missouri Research Reactor (MURR), and the results of the analysis are presented in Huntley (2004). The reader is referred to Duff (2002), Glascock (1992), Neff and Glowacki (2002), and Neff (2002) for detailed discussions of MURR sample preparation, instrumentation, and statistical procedures. For present purposes I assume that glaze paints found on sherds recovered from a particular pueblo were locally made. I also assume that batches, or prepared mixtures, of glaze paints were not traded independently of ceramic vessels, as has been suggested by Habicht-Mauche and colleagues (2000; see also Nelson and Habicht-Mauche, chap. 11, this volume, for a discussion of possible lead ore circulation mechanisms).

Low-lead paints (Group 3) are generally more common overall than high-lead paints (Group 1) on vessels recovered from early contexts (see Huntley 2004:table 7.8). However, in early contexts, high-lead glazes are common on vessels made from clays available in the Pescado Basin (where Heshotauthla Pueblo is located) but entirely absent on vessels most likely made in the El Morro Valley (Fisher's Exact $P = 0.06$).[4] In later contexts, high-lead paints are on average about twice as common on vessels produced in the Pescado Basin as on vessels attributed to the El Morro Valley or Jaralosa Draw in the southwestern portion of the Zuni region (Fisher's Exact $P = 0.05$). Thus, I argue that while there apparently was a strong temporal component to the use of lead- versus copper-based glaze recipes within the Zuni region as a whole, potters from pueblos in different parts of the region appear to have adopted the high-lead recipe at different rates. Indeed, some groups of potters may not have adopted it at all.

Ore Sources for Zuni Region Glaze Paints

The change in basic glaze recipe from low lead and high copper to high lead and low copper appears to coincide with changes in patterns of raw material utilization. In particular, there appears to have been diversification through time in the lead and copper ore sources used to make Zuni glazes.

I identified the geographic locations of copper and lead ores used to make glaze paints using inductively coupled plasma mass spectroscopy

(ICP-MS). The application of this technique to the analysis of glazes is based on the principle that lead ores from different geological sources—and copper ores associated with them—can be distinguished by their stable lead isotope "fingerprints." Judith Habicht-Mauche and others (Habicht-Mauche et al. 2000, 2002; Huntley et al. in press) have successfully used this technique to source lead ores and lead-based glazes from the Rio Grande Valley. I followed the methodology outlined by Habicht-Mauche and colleagues (2000; see also Huntley 2004).[5]

Lead and copper ores occur in association in a number of formations throughout New Mexico and Arizona. The Cerrillos source is one of the best-known lead and copper ore sources and was extensively utilized by Rio Grande potters (Habicht-Mauche et al. 2000). Other ore sources are located along the Rio Grande rift—several of these are shown in figure 1.2 along with the Cerrillos source. As the map indicates, probable lead ore sources used by Zuni region potters range from approximately 175 km to nearly 300 km distant. Copper ores were reportedly available locally in the Zuni Mountains (Ferguson and Hart 1985:49) and in parts of south-central Arizona (USGS 1969). There are no currently known lead ore sources in the Zuni region, however, and no lead ore samples from this area could be located in the geological and archaeological collections that I surveyed.

Lead isotope data are conventionally plotted in two-dimensional space using various combinations of stacked plots of pairs of ratios (e.g., ^{206}Pb/^{204}Pb and ^{207}Pb/^{204}Pb vs. ^{208}Pb/^{204}Pb). This provides a means of visually identifying ore source separation and correspondence between glazes and ore sources. Figure 6.2 shows isotopic ratios for lead ores from different mining districts. These data include ore isotope ratios reported by Habicht-Mauche and Ginn (2004), Habicht-Mauche and colleagues (2000, 2002), Huntley (2004), and Huntley and colleagues (in press). As the figure indicates, ore sources represented by multiple samples tend to plot as elongated, flattened ellipses with characteristic slopes. In the lower plot, for example, Cerrillos North and South samples are represented by the group of solid and open circles on the lower left. These samples show a distinct linear trend from lower left to upper right. Placitas district samples (represented by open squares) plot to the right of the Cerrillos ores but show a similar linear trend. Ores from central (Tijeras) and southern sources (Joyita Hills, Magdalena, North Magdalena, and Hansonburg) plot along a flatter, left-to-right trending line (note that the

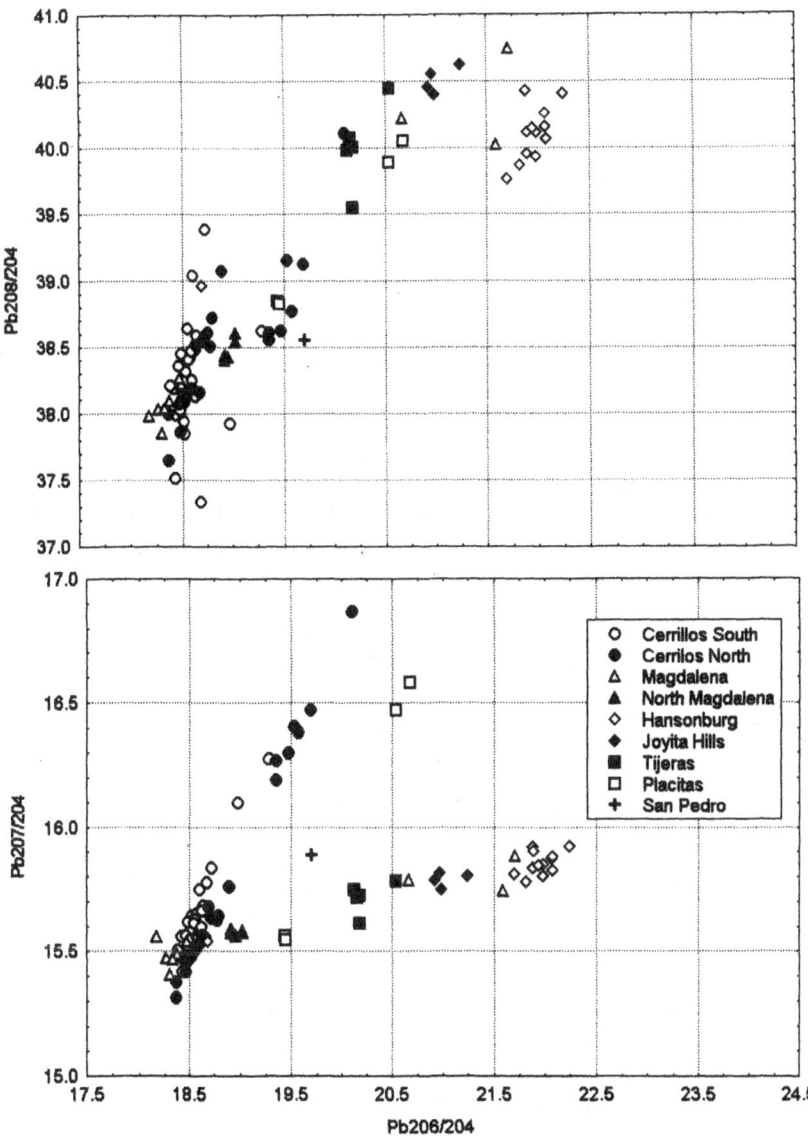

Fig. 6.2. Plot of ore lead isotope ratios by mining district (^{207}Pb/^{204}Pb over ^{206}Pb/^{204}Pb and ^{208}Pb/^{204}Pb over ^{206}Pb/^{204}Pb).

smaller groups of Tijeras, Joyita Hills, and North Magdalena ores cluster fairly tightly).

The Socorro area samples are somewhat problematic, since several samples from the Juanita, Kelly, and Mistletoe mines in the Magdalena district and one sample of unknown provenience from the Hansonburg district partially overlap the group of Cerrillos ores in the lower left corner of the plot. This overlap is not surprising given that the Cerrillos and Magdalena ore deposits are similar in geologic age and depositional context (Virgil Leuth, personal communication). Thus, since some of the southern ore samples overlap with some of the Cerrillos ore samples, I assign glaze paint samples to ore source groups with caution.

Figure 6.3 plots lead isotope ratios for Heshotauthla Polychrome, Kwakina Polychrome, and St. Johns Polychrome. In this figure, the lower plot also includes ellipses showing the spatial distribution of Cerrillos and southern (Joyita Hills, Magdalena, North Magdalena, and Hansonburg) ore samples from figure 6.2. The upper plot shows an enlarged view of the area covered by the rectangle in the lower plot and includes regression lines[6] for Cerrillos and southern ore source groups. Most of the St. Johns glazes (twenty-seven of thirty-five samples) show the same general linear trend as the Cerrillos ore source group. Of the eight St. Johns Polychrome sherds that clearly fall within the area of the southern ore source group, five are from late contexts, four have unusual interior and/or exterior design motifs, and three may actually be classified as late St. Johns transitioning to Heshotauthla Polychrome. Glazes on Heshotauthla Polychrome and Kwakina Polychrome more frequently plot in the ellipse defined by the southern ore sources.

There are several reasons why caution must be applied when assigning glaze paints to ore sources. First, as discussed above, some of the southern ore samples appear to overlap with the Cerrillos ore samples. Additionally, I cannot rule out the possibility that some of the glazes I analyzed were made using other ore sources that have not been sampled. It is also likely that potters regularly mixed materials from multiple ore sources to make glaze paints. This seems particularly likely given that the ore sources known to have been available to Zuni region potters were very far away. Whether potters visited ore sources themselves or acquired ores via trade with groups living near ore sources, materials from various sources were probably stockpiled and used as needed. Habicht-Mauche and colleagues (2000) argue that such stockpiling and mixing behavior explains

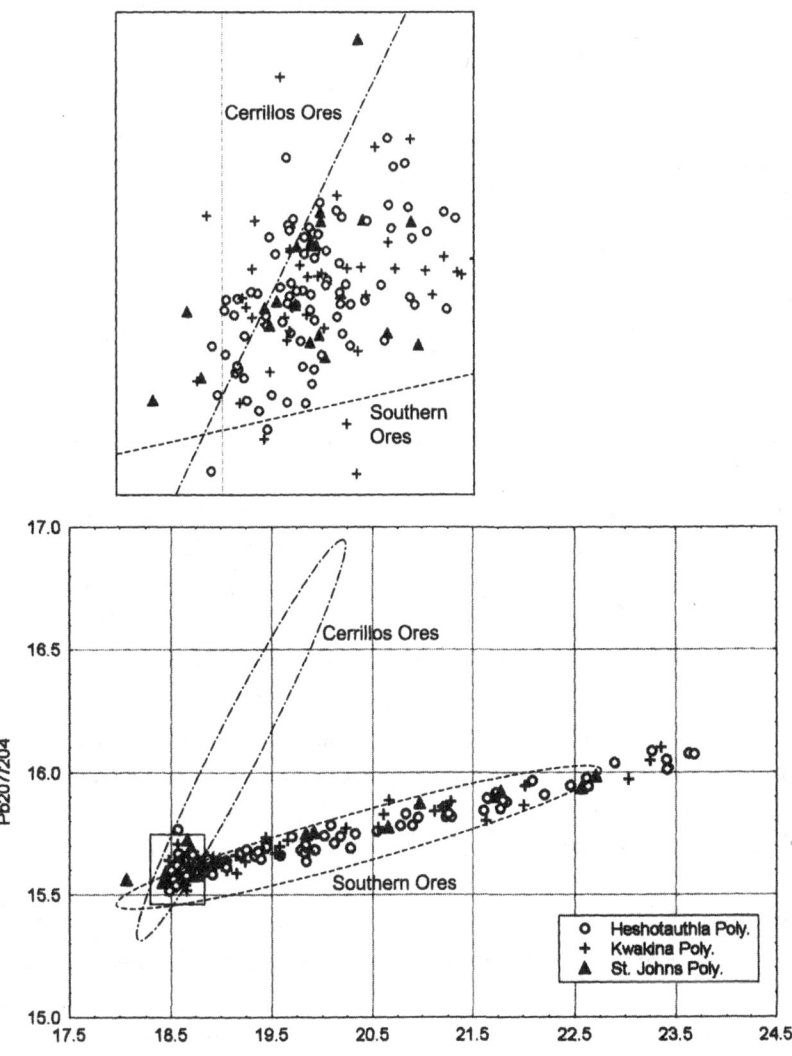

Fig. 6.3. Plot of lead isotope ratios (^{207}Pb/^{204}Pb over ^{206}Pb/^{204}Pb and ^{208}Pb/^{204}Pb over ^{206}Pb/^{204}Pb) for Heshotauthla, Kwakina, and St. Johns Polychrome. Top plot is area denoted by rectangle in bottom plot.

Table 6.1
Ceramic Type Frequencies by Ore Source Group (All Sites Combined)

Ceramic Type	Ore Source Group (Counts)				
	Cerrillos	Hansonburg	Magdalena	Indet.	Total
St. Johns Polychrome	15	2	12	6	35
Heshotauthla Polychrome	37	3	69	30	139
Kwakina Polychrome	18	2	32	23	75
Total	70	7	113	59	249

some of the isotopic variability seen in glaze paints from Galisteo Basin pueblos.

Bearing in mind these caveats, table 6.1 presents probable ore source classifications for glaze paint samples based on visual examination of multiple bivariate plots of isotope ratios. A slightly higher proportion of St. Johns Polychrome glazes are attributed to the Cerrillos ore source (fifteen of thirty-five samples) than to other sources. While the Cerrillos source continues to be quite commonly used for Kwakina Polychrome and Heshotauthla Polychrome glazes, potters appear to have more commonly used ores from southern sources for these types. As noted by Laumbach (chap. 8, this vol.) Zuni Glaze Ware sherds (or local copies thereof) are found on Magdalena area sites, providing additional evidence of contact between these two regions. Glazes attributed to ores from the Hansonburg mining district are much less common among all three types. Fifty-nine glaze samples (six St. Johns Polychrome, thirty Heshotauthla Polychrome, and twenty-three Kwakina Polychrome) could not be classified into a single source group. Most of these samples may be attributed to either the Cerrillos or Magdalena ore source. A few plot near the Tijeras or Placitas ore samples for one or more pairs of isotope ratios, but also fall close to the regression line for the southern ore source group.

On the whole, isotope sourcing of glaze paints indicates that Zuni region potters used a variety of distant ore deposits—particularly for lead, which may not have been locally available. A large number of glaze paints used to decorate St. Johns Polychrome and early Heshotauthla and Kwakina Polychrome vessels appear to have been made using ores from the Cerrillos Hills mines near Santa Fe, although some early glazes were made with ores from the Socorro area. It is perhaps not very surprising that

Table 6.2
Distribution of Ore Sources among Glaze Paint Compositional Groups

	Glaze Comp. Group (Column Percentages)			
Ore Source	1 (high Pb) $n = 141$	2 (high Mn) $n = 16$	3 (low Pb) $n = 81$	Total $n = 238$
Cerrillos	24.1	31.3	33.3	27.7
Hansonburg	2.8	—	3.7	2.9
Magdalena	48.2	43.8	42.0	45.8
Indeterminate	24.8	25.0	21.0	23.5
Total	100	100	100	100

Pueblo IV Zuni region potters utilized the Cerrillos source since Zunis reportedly obtained copper and turquoise from Cerrillos in historic times (Ferguson and Hart 1985:49). What is somewhat surprising is that the isotope data suggest regular, sustained contact between the Western and Eastern Pueblo regions by the mid-1200s, especially since other lines of evidence indicate that the Zuni region was relatively isolated throughout the Pueblo IV period. Later Zuni region glaze paints are commonly made using ores from southern sources, suggesting an overall expansion of social networks, and perhaps increased emphasis on social networks focused on the Socorro area, during the early to mid-1300s. By this time San Marcos in the Galisteo Basin, which is located near the Cerrillos ore source, became a major producer of Rio Grande Glaze Ware (Shepard 1942). If Galisteo Basin pueblos exercised control over the Cerrillos lead source, Zuni region potters may have found these ores more difficult to obtain and consequently utilized alternative sources more frequently (Nelson and Habicht-Mauche, chap. 11, this vol.).

Comparison of glaze paint compositions with probable ore sources indicates that high-lead and low-lead paints are not strongly patterned by ore source. Of the 313 samples for which glaze chemical compositions were determined, 238 also have lead isotope data. The distribution of ore sources among glaze paint compositional Groups 1, 2, and 3 is very similar (table 6.2). Nearly half (48.2 percent) of all glazes in Group 1 (high lead) are attributed to Magdalena ores and approximately 24 percent were likely made from Cerrillos ores; 2.8 percent are from Hansonburg ores and 24.8 percent are of indeterminate ore source. The proportions of Cerrillos ores are somewhat higher and the percentages of Magdalena ores somewhat lower in Groups 2 (high manganese) and 3 (low lead/high copper). Fisher's Exact test shows that equal or greater differences between observed and expected cell frequencies have a nearly 20 percent probability of occurring if the variables are independent ($P = 0.18$). Thus while it appears that high-manganese and high-copper paints were made less frequently using ores from Magdalena and other southern sources, I cannot say with certainty that this pattern is statistically significant. Differences in glaze paint compositions, then, cannot be attributed exclusively to the chemical properties of different ore sources. Rather, glaze compositions appear to be the result of technical choices made during glaze manufacture.

Summary and Interpretations

Few anthropologists would doubt that material culture plays an active role in the creation and maintenance of social identities. Most scholars agree that identity is a relatively fluid property and that individuals and groups consciously construct and maintain multiple social identities at different scales (e.g., Barth 1969; Dobres and Hoffman 1994; Hitchcock and Bartram 1998; Moerman 1965). Often at issue is whether or not social identities and group boundaries are typically visible to archaeologists, and, if so, what those identities and boundaries actual signify (e.g., see the chapters in Stark, ed., 1998, particularly Hegmon 1998; Stark 1998). The data presented in this chapter and others in this volume illustrate that we are beginning to disentangle the complicated networks of interaction and social identity within which glaze ware vessels circulated. For example, examining multiple lines of evidence allows us to document Pueblo IV Zuni region potters' technical choices and speculate as to how these choices may inform on social interaction and identity at the interregional, regional, and intraregional levels.

Despite apparent long-distance circulation of lead ores and the widespread adoption of a glaze paint tradition throughout much of the northern Southwest, data presented in this chapter and elsewhere in this volume (e.g., chap. 4 and chap. 10) point to the development of distinctive regional trends that may reflect larger ethnic or other social boundaries. Zuni glazes, particularly on Heshotauthla and Kwakina Polychrome vessels, typically have much higher lead and lower copper and iron than glazes on polychrome ceramics from the White Mountains (De Atley 1986:306;

Fenn, Mills, and Hopkins, chap. 4, this vol.; Hawley 1938; Shepard 1942), and lower lead and higher copper than Rio Grande Glaze Ware (Herhahn, chap. 10, this vol.; Herhahn and Huntley 1996; Huntley and Herhahn 1996; Shepard 1942).[7] Zuni Glaze Ware types also appear to be unique in overall design style and, compared to early Rio Grande Glaze Ware, in the wide range of colors—black, browns, brilliant greens, reds, yellows, and purples—that potters were able to produce.

The glaze paint compositional data indicate that there was a region-wide shift through time in the basic glaze recipe used to decorate Zuni Glaze Ware vessels. Potters initially made glazes with variable lead and copper compositions, but by the late Pueblo IV period typically chose to make glazes that were high in lead and low in copper. Lead- and copper-based recipes represent alternatives or variations in technological style that would produce broadly similar but not completely equivalent products. Glazes on Kwakina and Heshotauthla Polychrome also became less compositionally variable through time, suggesting standardization in processing techniques, firing, or reduction in the number of potters.

I argue that a broadly shared and relatively rapidly adopted glaze recipe reflects a shared conception about the "correct" way to make a glaze paint that may be tied to the proposed ritual functions of glaze ware vessels (see also Huntley 2004). This shared conception could only have been brought about by regular communication among potters. Although Zuni glazes are probably not so complex as to require formal instruction in glaze preparation, some degree of face-to-face communication would have been necessary in order to reproduce the basic recipe and proper firing conditions required to create a vitreous paint. Assuming that women were the primary producers of glaze-decorated pottery, much of this interaction was likely among groups of women. Thus, fourteenth-century Zuni potters must have maintained social ties with female kin living in other pueblos, and potting communities of practice may have regularly included a number of related women, including the wives and daughters of male relatives, from multiple pueblos.

Within the Zuni region there are also some minor intraregional differences in the distributions of high-lead and high-copper paints, suggesting that potters from pueblos in the Pescado Basin may have adopted the high-lead glaze recipe earlier and more fully than did potters in the El Morro Valley or the Jaralosa Draw area. Based on this pattern, I propose that within an overall regional pattern of shared glaze recipes there are indications of intraregional differences that may reflect more restricted spheres of interaction and identity. These spheres may have been influenced largely by spatial proximity, that is, by residence in a particular village or clustered group of villages.

In conclusion, I propose that the convergence of a high-lead glaze recipe with a wider range of colors and a major change in design style in Zuni Glaze Ware, particularly polychrome/bichrome-slipped Kwakina Polychrome, is socially significant on many levels. On one level, Zuni Glaze Ware is one particular manifestation of a larger stylistic and technological phenomenon possibly linked to pan-southwestern changes in social and religious organization. While participating in this large-scale development, Zuni region potters nevertheless developed their own unique glaze recipe that may have been an intentional expression of shared cultural identity. Thus, while the basic knowledge necessary to make glaze paints was something shared by a network of potters spread out across much of the Pueblo world, I argue that Zuni region potters made an attempt to distinguish their wares from those made in other regions. At the same time, ore resource utilization suggests even wider social ties that transcended regional boundaries and traditionally defined culture areas. I argue that Zuni region potters' communities of practice were largely defined by residence in a particular nucleated pueblo or cluster of pueblos, but must have periodically extended well beyond these geographic boundaries.

Acknowledgments

Analyzed sherds come from the following collections: the Heshotauthla Archaeological Research Project (directed by Keith Kintigh), the Cibola Archaeological Research Project (directed by Patty Jo Watson, Charles Redman, and Steven LeBlanc), and Lower Pescado Village (directed by Nan Rothschild and Susan Dublin). Funding for electron microprobe and ICP-MS analyses was provided by the National Science Foundation (grant number BCS-0003191) and the Wenner-Gren Foundation for Anthropological Research (Grant Number 6659). A. Russell Flegal, Rob Franks, Judith Habicht-Mauche, Mara Ranville, Dan Sampson, and Bruce Tanner provided valuable technical support for these analyses, which were conducted on equipment available in the Earth and Marine Sciences facilities at the University of California, Santa Cruz. Ryan Dean, Elizabeth Kerin, and Sarah Ginn performed the sample digestions for the lead isotope analysis. Lead ore samples were kindly provided by Homer Milford (formally of the Mining and Minerals Division of the New Mexico Department of Energy, Minerals, and Natural Resources, Santa Fe), Virginia McLemore and Robert Weber of the New Mexico Bureau of Geology and Mineral Resources, Socorro, and David Hill of Archaeological Research and Technology, Inc., Austin. Special thanks goes to Homer Milford and Robert Weber for answering my geology questions. Suzanne Eckert, Judith Habicht-Mauche, Keith Kintigh, and several anonymous reviewers provided helpful comments on earlier drafts of this chapter.

7

The Decline of Zuni Glaze Ware Production in the Tumultuous Fifteenth Century

Gregson Schachner

Archaeologists working in the Zuni region of the American Southwest have long noted the dramatic break in ceramic technology that coincided with the founding of the protohistoric Zuni towns, the famed "Seven Cities of Cibola," during the late fourteenth and early fifteenth centuries AD (Kintigh 1985b; Kroeber 1916; Reed 1955; Spier 1917) (see fig. 7.1). Potters residing in the Zuni area were among the first to utilize glaze paints in the Southwest, but in the AD 1400s, after a long period of technological development, glaze ware production declined precipitously and in all likelihood ceased. Glaze-painted white and red wares were rapidly replaced by matte-painted buff ware with new technological and stylistic conventions. This pattern is quite different from that of other glaze ware-producing areas of the Southwest, where glaze paints continued to be applied until the Pueblo Revolt in 1680 (see chap. 3).

In this chapter, I explore the demise of Zuni Glaze Ware production and its relationship to the historical processes and events that shaped Zuni society during the founding of the protohistoric towns. The first section introduces a framework for relating changes in material culture to the social transformations that often occur during migration and resettlement. Next, I reconsider the dating of the decline in glaze ware production at Zuni, which is necessary in order to place this shift in historical context. In the remainder of the chapter, I argue that the demise of glaze ware production at Zuni was linked to the development of new concepts of shared iden-

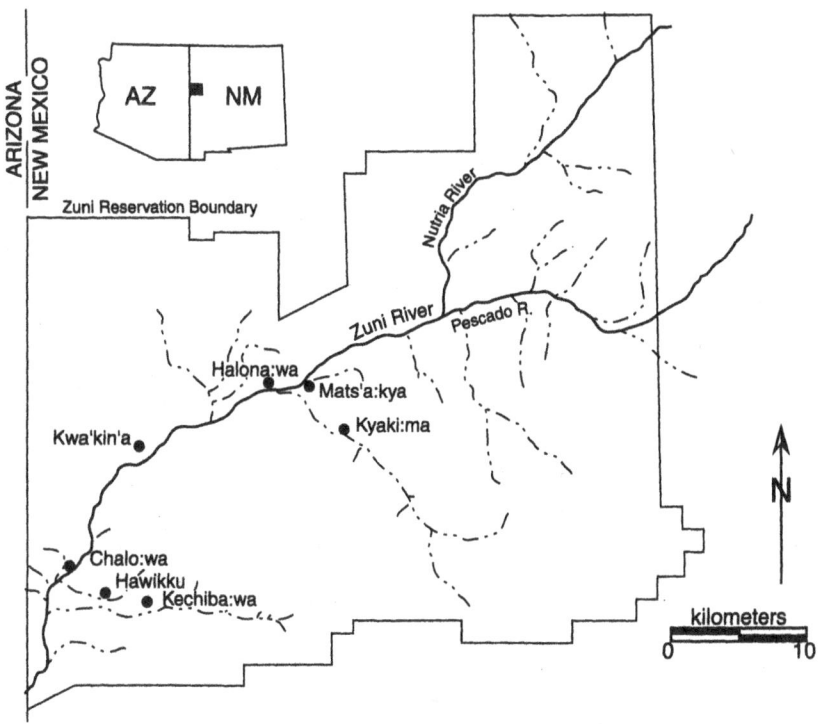

Fig. 7.1. Protohistoric Zuni Villages.

tity following the incorporation of migrant groups and significant shifts in Zuni settlement and society during the fifteenth century.

Linkages between Material Culture, Social Change, and Migration

Understanding how changes in material culture are linked to social transformations has long been one of the primary goals of archaeological research. In recent years our conception of processes of material culture change has been enhanced by ethnoarchaeological and archaeological studies of technological systems, styles, and choices (Childs 1991; Lechtman 1977; Lemonnier 1986, 1992; Stark 1998, 1999, chap. 2, this vol.). Empirical studies have provided a clearer view of the processes that lead to change, the pace at which it happens, and the material signatures that result from shifts in technological systems (Hardin and Mills 2000; Kalentzidou 2000; Stark 1999; Stark and Longacre 1993). For the most part these studies have shown "that technological styles are more resistant to change than are decorative aspects of material culture" (Stark 1999:29, citing Gosselain 1992:582–83; Rice 1984:252; Wiessner 1985). Changes in technological styles have been linked to both conscious decisions and external causes. Proposed causal mechanisms include shifts in subsistence practices, population size and structure, networks of interaction, the movement of potters between communities, colonization, and changing demand (Stark 1999:29–30). Documenting changes in technological choices represents a primary, although minimal, step toward explaining material culture shifts. These shifts must then be placed in social and historical context in order to delineate the processes of change and articulation of productive and social systems (Kalentzidou 2000:166–67). In this chapter, I examine a well-documented, relatively clear-cut case of technological change (from glaze- to matte-painted ceramics) in light of our growing understanding of changes in Pueblo IV Ancestral Puebloan society.

For good reason, the study of migration and its effects on society has recently proliferated within Southwest archaeology. This movement has been an intriguing product of our growing knowledge of the archaeological record, critical reengagement with anthropological (Clark 2001; Duff 1998) and archaeological models of migration (Cordell 1995; Reid 1998), and renewed appreciation of oral tradition and the centrality of migration in Native American identity and history (Bernardini 2002; Dongoske et al. 1997; Kuwanwisiwma 2002; Lyons 2003; Naranjo 1995). Recent studies of migration have attempted to address how migration, and mobility in general, often lead to and generate social change. In particular, these studies have focused on why new communities either formed by, or that incorporate, migrant groups are often the locus of significant shifts in settlement structure, identity, and ritual practice (E. C. Adams 2002; Cordell 1995; Lyons 2003; M. C. Nelson 2000; see Pauketat 2003 for a recent non-Southwest example). Large-scale population movements, such as those that occurred in the Southwest in the late fourteenth and early fifteenth centuries, fragmented existing social networks and groups, creating conditions ripe for the onset of social change as new social ties, communities, and identities were created by diverse social groups with varying traditions and goals (sensu M. C. Nelson 2000; Pauketat 2003).

Of particular interest to this study is the extensive documentation of shifts in ceramic technological choices and systems associated with the incorporation of migrant groups (Hegmon, Nelson, and Ruth 1998; Stark, Clark, and Elson 1995; Zedeño 1994; see Kalentzidou 2000 for a non-Southwest example). Migrant potters introduced new techniques, pursued novel uses of local materials, and provided a new pool of knowledge that often resulted in innovation in both local and migrant technological systems. However, as I will argue below, in the Zuni case, changes in pottery production were not simply technological shifts but closely linked to the renegotiation and creation of social identity during resettlement.

Migration and its effects must be included in discussions of the foundation of the historic Zuni villages and the creation of modern Zuni identity (Cushing 1896; Ferguson and Hart 1985; Kintigh 2000; Schachner 2001; Smith, Woodbury, and Woodbury 1966). Migration and the gathering of diverse groups are key aspects of Zuni oral traditions concerning the establishment of the historic Zuni villages and modern pueblo (Dongoske et al. 1997; Ferguson and Hart 1985). Frank Cushing was convinced that his studies of Zuni oral tradition attested to the composite character of historic Zuni society, which he felt comprised two peoples, one indigenous to the area and another more recently arrived from the southwest (Cushing 1896). Cushing dedicated most of his archaeological fieldwork at Zuni and in the Phoenix Basin to the exploration of this question. In the following sections I explore the archaeological evidence for the decline of Zuni Glaze Ware production and its relationship to migration and accompanying settlement shifts in the fifteenth century AD.

The Demise of Zuni Glaze Ware Production in the Fifteenth Century

Glaze paints began to be applied to Zuni area ceramics in the mid-1200s, with Zuni Glaze Ware comprising almost the entirety of Zuni decorated assemblages for the next two hundred years.[1] Zuni area potters first applied glaze paints to St. Johns Black-on-red and Polychrome types. Many pots from the late thirteenth century exhibit characteristics of both St. Johns types and one of the earliest Zuni Glaze Ware types, Heshotauthla Polychrome. Most archaeologists have seen these transitional examples as indicative of the roots of Zuni Glaze Ware in earlier White Mountain Red Ware traditions (Carlson 1970; Reed 1955; Seventh Southwestern Ceramic Seminar 1965; Woodbury and Woodbury 1966). All Zuni Glaze

Ware types exhibit combinations of glaze paint and red or white clay slips (frequently found on the same vessel), with all-over white slips coming to dominate glaze ware assemblages by the mid-1300s (see chap. 3).[2] In terms of decorative style, Zuni Glaze Ware shares some elements of Pinedale and Fourmile styles (Carlson 1970; Crown 1994), but also possesses an economy of design structure and motifs reminiscent of Rio Grande Glaze Ware (Carlson 1970; Woodbury and Woodbury 1966).

Prior to AD 1400, Zuni Glaze Ware production occurred over a much larger area than its name implies. Except for some overlap along the upper Little Colorado River, production areas of White Mountain Red Ware and Zuni Glaze Ware were distinct after AD 1300. Compositional studies conducted by Duff (2002) have demonstrated that all Zuni Glaze Ware types were produced in both the upper Little Colorado and Zuni regions. An often forgotten aspect of Zuni Glaze Ware is its relationship to ceramics produced at the same time in the Acoma area (Dittert 1959, 1998; Seventh Southwestern Ceramic Seminar 1965). Acoma potters produced analogues of Zuni Glaze Ware types that are frequently difficult to visually distinguish from those produced elsewhere. One could make the argument that Acoma types should be included in the Zuni Glaze Ware series, resulting in a production area spanning the Acoma, Zuni, and upper Little Colorado regions. However, this production distribution changed over time, covering the whole area from 1300 to 1400, becoming restricted to Zuni and Acoma after 1400, and continuing only at Acoma through the sixteenth century. Acoma potters did not participate in the switch to buff ware and continued to make glaze-painted pottery until the Pueblo Revolt.

Ceramic production in the fifteenth-century Zuni villages shifted radically, with a long tradition of glaze ware production being supplanted by the manufacture of matte-painted buff ware. At this time potters began making Matsaki Buff Ware, a buff-colored pottery decorated with brown, red, and white matte paints that is often considered a copy of Sikyatki-style Jeddito Yellow Ware (E. C. Adams 1991; Kintigh 1985b; Mills 1995; Reed 1955; Smith, Woodbury, and Woodbury 1966). Although the production of glaze and buff wares overlapped for a short period during the 1400s, stratigraphic evidence from Hawikku and Halona:wa (modern Zuni Pueblo) suggests the shift in dominance was rather abrupt, with Matsaki representing a small portion of the decorated assemblage before eclipsing glaze ware sometime in the fifteenth century (Mills 2002b; Smith, Woodbury, and Woodbury 1966). Matsaki Buff Ware comprised virtually all of the Zuni potters' decorated repertoire until the founding of missions in the area in 1629.

The best evidence for the shift from assemblages dominated by Zuni Glaze Ware to those dominated by Matsaki Buff Ware derives from the 1917 to 1923 excavations at Hawikku (Hodge 1937; Smith, Woodbury, and Woodbury 1966) and a recent Zuni Cultural Resource Enterprise project conducted as part of the reconstruction of portions of Zuni Middle Village (Mills 2002b). Hodge's crew excavated a trench 75 feet long, 11 feet wide, and 15 feet deep in one-foot levels in the plaza at Hawikku (Smith, Woodbury, and Woodbury 1966). Although the data from this trench are difficult to interpret owing to the mixing of deposits over the length of the trench, the use of arbitrary levels, and uncertainty about Hodge's typological categories (Kintigh 1985b:61–62), it still provides the longest unbroken stratigraphic sequence of ceramic material from the Zuni area. The Hawikku data are much more interpretable when viewed in concert with those from the recent Middle Village Project at Zuni Pueblo. Over nine thousand sherds from seven levels (other levels remain to be analyzed, including the two deepest) of a test trench to sterile soil near a plaza at Zuni Middle Village provide detailed evidence of ceramic change from at least the late fourteenth century to the mid-1500s (Mills 2002b:table 4).

Figure 7.2 shows Ford diagrams of the decorated assemblages from both the Hawikku and Zuni Middle Village trenches. Assuming different villages had access to similar ceramic types, a visual comparison of the proportions of decorated ceramics indicates that the Middle Village sequence is roughly contemporary to the lower levels at Hawikku, probably levels 9 or 10 through 14. The relative lack of Hawikuh Polychrome in the Zuni Middle Village assemblage indicates that deposition of this unit predates AD 1630 by an undetermined duration (see below).[3] The lowest levels from Zuni Middle Village may in fact predate those at Hawikku, although only a portion of Hodge's trench reached sterile soil (Smith, Woodbury, and Woodbury 1966:143). In the Zuni Middle Village trench, glaze ware dominates the assemblage in levels 6 through 10, but then decreases dramatically. Above level 6 Matsaki Buff Ware comprises the majority of the Middle Village decorated assemblage and glaze types steadily decline. Bearing in mind the significant possibility of mixing in the Hawikku trench deposits, primarily owing to the extremely large size of the trench itself, the Hawikku data illustrate a re-

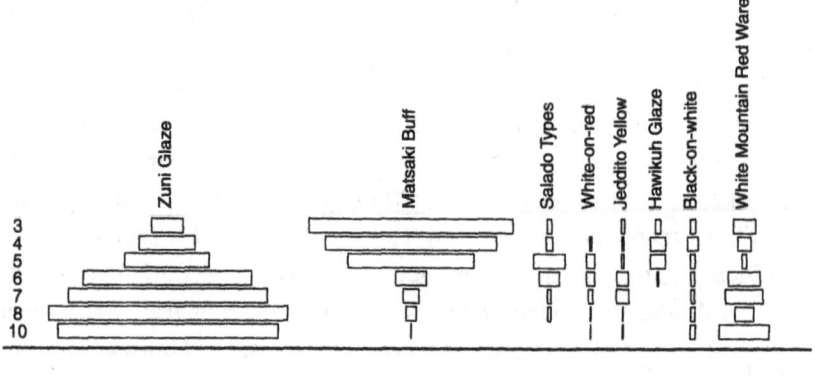

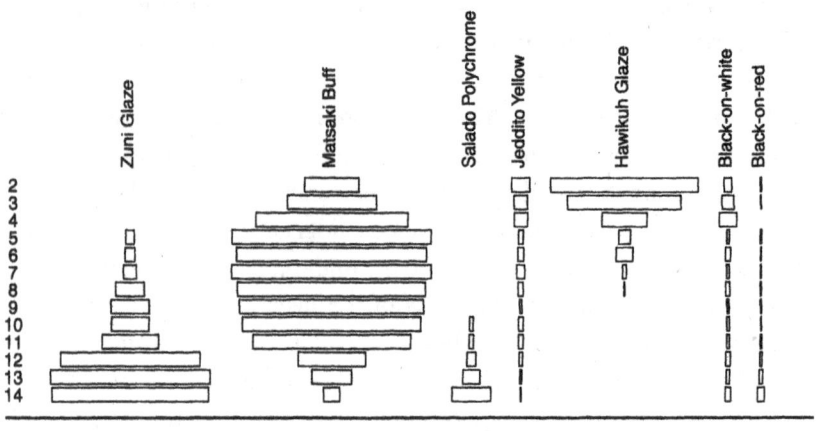

Fig. 7.2. Ford diagrams for Zuni Middle Village and Hawikku (data from Mills 2002b and Smith, Woodbury, and Woodbury 1966:170, respectively).

markably similar trajectory of change. In this case, the switch from glaze ware to buff ware occurs between levels 12 and 11. Thus we consistently have notably "quick" changes from glaze-ware-dominated to buff-ware-dominated decorated assemblages at both Zuni Middle Village and Hawikku.

At both Zuni Middle Village and Hawikku, Zuni Glaze Ware sherds continued to be deposited as trash after the transition to Matsaki-dominated assemblages. Zuni Glaze Ware proportions decrease significantly at each site, and in upper levels were either absent (Hawikku levels 2–4) or found in such low quantities that mixing of deposits seems a likely explanation for their presence (Hawikku levels 5–7, possibly Middle Village level 3). Thus at this time we cannot be sure that Zuni Glaze Ware production ceased entirely with the expansion of buff ware production, but it is quite clear that it had at least significantly decreased to the point of being a minor portion of Zuni potters' repertoire. Negligible, continued deposition would be expected as vessels in active use and those that were kept as heirlooms wore out and were deposited as trash. Additionally, some glaze ware vessels may have been obtained from Acoma.

The correlation of these changes with calendrical dates is somewhat difficult, but a few lines of evidence suggest the glaze ware to buff ware switch occurred during the mid-AD 1400s. Previous attempts at delineating chronological phases during the period from AD 1400 to 1630 at Zuni have been hampered by the lack of systematic, excavated ceramic collections from sites of interest (Kintigh 1985b; Mills 2002b). This interval was the longest undifferentiated period in Kintigh's (1985b:18–19) ceramic chronology for the Zuni area, marked largely by the presence of Matsaki Buff Ware and black ware, the plain utility ware that replaces gray corrugated ceramics after AD 1400. The new data from the Zuni Middle Village excavations provide an excellent opportunity to revisit the chronology of this period.

Barbara Mills's (2002b) thorough examination of chronological evidence from the Middle Village trench estimates that the deposits represent the period from approximately AD 1375 to 1550. The lowest analyzed level correlates well with Kintigh's (1985b:18) Complex G from AD 1375 to 1400, and thus provides a relatively solid beginning date. Significantly, this period is thought to predate the beginning of Matsaki Buff Ware production and the appearance of Salado Polychrome and Jeddito Yellow Ware at Zuni area sites (Kintigh 1985b:18–19; Mills 2002b).

Although the earliest levels from Zuni Middle Village appear to be solidly dated based on typological assessments, estimating chronological changes within the later, undifferentiated AD 1400–1630 period requires us to turn to other lines of evidence, primarily changes in vessel shape. Archaeologists working in the Zuni area have long noted that marked changes occur in vessel form during the production span of Matsaki Buff Ware between AD 1400 and 1680 (Reed 1955; Smith, Woodbury, and Woodbury 1966). Erik Reed (1955:187–88) proposed that later forms of

Matsaki were distinctive enough to warrant a separate type name, Concepción Polychrome. However, subsequent researchers found the delineation of these changes difficult owing to a lack of well-provenienced stratigraphic collections (Mills 1995, 2002b; Seventh Southwestern Ceramic Seminar 1965; Woodbury and Woodbury 1966). Working with both whole vessels and sherd collections, Barbara Mills has recently been able to document that Matsaki bowls and jars changed from hemispherical to shouldered forms over time (Mills 1995, 2002b; see Mills 1995, fig. 8.2, for depictions). The shouldered Matsaki vessels are reminiscent of relatively well dated, late Rio Grande Glaze Ware forms that postdate AD 1500 (Mills 2002b; Reed 1955) and, thus, provide a means of temporally subdividing the AD 1400–1630 period. Mills's (2002b) analysis of the Middle Village ceramics was among the first to systematically record rim form in a large stratigraphic collection and demonstrates the utility of the approach (see Mills 1995 for an application using whole vessels). Rim form was recorded for sherds from four levels in the Middle Village trench (3, 6, 7, and 8). All shouldered Matsaki jar rims were found in level 3 ($n = 10$), while 20 of 22 shouldered bowl rims also were recovered from level 3. Hemispherical rim forms were found in all levels. Thus, only the uppermost level appears to securely postdate AD 1500, although the persistence of hemispherical rims indicates it may not be much later than this date. Thus changes in vessel form, coupled with typological assessments, provide a means of bracketing the span of occupation represented by the Zuni Middle Village trench at approximately AD 1375–1550.

Correlating individual levels with calendrical dates is a bit more difficult; however, various lines of evidence suggest reasonable estimates. Mills (2002b:table 4) used changes in type frequencies (including utility wares not discussed here) in concert with shifts in Matsaki vessel shapes to estimate that levels 6 through 8 date to approximately AD 1400–1450, levels 4 and 5 to 1450–1500, and level 3 to AD 1500–1550. Although it is likely that these dates will be refined with further analysis of the Middle Village collections, they do provide a more secure framework for beginning to discuss the tempo of ceramic change during the glaze ware to buff ware transition at Zuni. Using these preliminary dates as a guide, the switch from glaze- to buff-dominated assemblages at Zuni Middle Village (between levels 5 and 6) can be estimated to have occurred sometime around AD 1450. The switch at Hawikku is likely to have occurred during the same interval judging from similarities in typological proportions at the two villages. Lower levels of deposition of glaze ware occurred in subsequent levels, suggesting production may have continued at an extremely small scale during the transition. By the 1500s, however, production of Zuni Glaze Ware most likely had ceased, as it was deposited in significantly diminished quantities in levels that appear to date to this period. Thus although much work remains to be done in order to securely date the transition from glaze ware to buff ware production at Zuni area villages, current, reasonable estimates place the change sometime during the mid-fifteenth century AD.

The production of Matsaki Buff Ware marks a major technological break in the Zuni area ceramic sequence (Mills 1995, 2003; Woodbury and Woodbury 1966). Although a few transitional vessels have been identified, such as examples that include glaze paints on buff slips, these are quite rare and most likely early in the Matsaki production span (Woodbury and Woodbury 1966:324, 330). The production of Matsaki Buff Ware required changes in slip color, paint color and type, and eventually significant changes in vessel form. Additionally, the selection of appropriate clays shifted when buff ware began to be produced. Mills's (1995:220–21) compositional analyses of protohistoric, post-AD 1400 Zuni ceramics demonstrate that Zuni Glaze Ware vessels were produced from a restricted suite of clays, possibly even a single source.[4] These clays may have been selected for their physical properties, especially the ability to withstand relatively high firing temperatures (Mills 1995:221). Matsaki Buff Ware, on the other hand, was produced using diverse clays of variable quality (Mills 1995:213–14). The diversity of clay sources used to produce Matsaki Buff Ware is reflected in the finished products, which exhibit a wide range of color, hardness, and crackling (Woodbury and Woodbury 1966:325–31). Although it is likely that the differences in glaze ware and buff ware ceramic technology may in part be a product of greater specialization of Zuni Glaze Ware production, possibly including the geographic localization of production (Mills 1995:214), the movement of new potters into the region with quite different learning networks and ceramic manufacturing techniques may have helped spur on experimentation with, and the eventual adoption of, a different technological regimen in the Zuni area (Hegmon, Nelson, and Ruth 1998; Kalentzidou 2000; Stark 1999; Stark, Clark, and Elson 1995). However, changes in ceramic production were not simply technological shifts, they were part of larger transformations in Zuni society that accompanied the formation of the protohistoric towns in the AD 1400s.

Correlating the Zuni Glaze Ware Decline with Migration and Its Aftereffects

Identifying migration events through archaeological evidence, particularly when those events may be implicated in radical changes in material culture that mask their occurrence and effects, is fraught with difficulties (Cordell 1995). We must turn to multiple lines of evidence, which in the Zuni case include shifts in settlement location, burial practices, and ceramic assemblages (other than the glaze-buff transition itself). The temporal coincidence of these processes provides some indication of the dramatic changes in Zuni society of which the glaze ware to buff ware transition was a part.

One of the most intriguing aspects of the shift to buff ware production is its correlation with the appearance of new ceramic types at Zuni. Researchers often comment on the limited number of ceramic types found in pre-1400 Zuni region assemblages compared to surrounding areas (Duff 2002; Kintigh 1985b, 2000; Mills in press). Trade wares are exceedingly rare, and decorated assemblages are usually dominated by two to three types that are often variations of a single stylistic and technological mode, differentiated from one another largely by slip color; Tularosa Black-on-white and St. Johns Polychrome during the AD 1200s are the best examples. In the 1400s, however, a relative explosion of ceramic diversity appeared in the Zuni area. Technological and decorative styles previously unknown to the region suddenly emerged alongside the Zuni Glaze Ware sequence. These include Salado Polychromes and various red wares such as smudged and white-on-red vessels (Kintigh 2000; Smith, Woodbury, and Woodbury 1966). These pottery types, with antecedents in central Arizona and the Mogollon Rim area, were present in the assemblages of the Zuni protohistoric villages during the transition from Zuni Glaze Ware to Matsaki Buff Ware in the 1400s, but appear to have gone out of use at about the time Matsaki came to dominate the assemblages (Woodbury and Woodbury 1966:315).

The Middle Village data provide an excellent example of this phenomenon, with Salado Polychromes and various white-on-red types spiking in proportion just prior to, and during, the switch to buff-ware-dominated assemblages (see fig. 7.2). Jeddito Yellow Ware also began to appear and then became slightly more common just before the switch. Mills (2002b, 2003) proposes a model by which both Salado Polychromes and Jeddito Yellow Ware began filtering into the Zuni area through exchange in the early fifteenth century, but suggests that the proliferation of both wares may be linked to migrants entering the area by the mid-1400s. Although the sample of vessels from Zuni sites is small ($n = 12$), recent compositional analyses by Duff (2002:155–56) indicate that some Salado Polychrome ceramics were likely manufactured in the western portions of the Zuni region during this interval, while others may have been produced in the upper Little Colorado River valley, a probable source area for migrants to Zuni. Many researchers have seen the appearance of nonlocal ceramics, particularly Salado Polychromes, as indicative of migration of populations from the Mogollon Rim and perhaps areas to the south to the Zuni region in the fifteenth century (Kintigh 2000; Mills in press; Reed 1955; Schachner 2001; Smith, Woodbury, and Woodbury 1966). At Acoma, where the buff ware shifts never occurred, Salado Polychromes never appeared (Dittert 1998:86).

Two other changes in the Zuni region archaeological record also coincide with the demise of Zuni Glaze Ware production and the increase in ceramic diversity in the 1400s. First, the appearance of a significant number of cremation burials at the protohistoric villages of Hawikku and Kechiba:wa has often been cited as evidence for migration from central and possibly southern Arizona (Kintigh 2000; Mills in press; Reed 1955; Rinaldo 1964; Schachner 2001; Smith, Woodbury, and Woodbury 1966). Cremations make up almost one-third of the over 1,200 burials excavated at these two villages (Kintigh 2000). In most cases at Hawikku, cremations were found in distinct cemeteries, or in groupings within cemeteries (Smith, Woodbury, and Woodbury 1966:187, fig. 37), which some have interpreted as the result of social distinctions between groups that followed different burial customs (Howell and Kintigh 1996; Kintigh 2000). Cushing's excavations of over 190 burials from Halona:wa South and Heshotauthla, two villages occupied immediately prior to the historic villages, failed to reveal a single cremation (Kintigh, personal communication 2001, based on Cushing's field notes), indicating the practice most likely did not predate AD 1400 in the Zuni area. The practice of killing vessels also appears to have become more common at Zuni with the founding of the historic villages. The Woodburys' analysis of the Hawikku and Kechiba:wa burial vessels recorded 117 killed vessels, 86 of which were Matsaki Buff Ware (Woodbury and Woodbury 1966:329). These vessels were usually associated with cremations.

The burial practices followed in the Zuni region during the AD 1400–1630 period were quite different from those in surrounding areas. Cremations have not been recorded in the archaeological record of Acoma (Dittert 1998:86). A few cremations have been found at various Pueblo IV sites outside of the Hohokam and Salado areas, such as Pottery Mound along the lower Rio Puerco of the East (Cordell 2002). However, the only burial population comparable to that of Hawikku and Kechiba:wa is that of Gran Quivira in the Salinas district east of the Rio Grande. Cremations were found there in a similar proportion to the Zuni villages (about 30 percent) (Hayes, Young, and Warren 1981:169–76). Hayes, Young, and Warren (1981:174) suggest that cremation of the dead did not occur at Gran Quivira until approximately AD 1550, long after the appearance of the practice in Zuni. Interestingly, the best archaeological analogue for protohistoric Zuni mortuary practices is from the Point of Pines area below the Mogollon Rim in Arizona. Residents of large pueblos in that region, some of which may have been occupied as late as AD 1450, practiced both cremation and inhumation. Burial populations from the area have ratios of inhumations to cremations (approximately 2:1) and vessel killing practices (Robinson and Sprague 1965) similar to those documented by excavations at Hawikku and Kechiba:wa.

The second major change that presages the demise of Zuni Glaze Ware and that I suggest is evidence for a major population shift at Zuni is the "settlement gap" at approximately AD 1400. Originally identified by Keith Kintigh (1985b:110–12) in his reconstruction of Pueblo IV Zuni settlement history (also see Spier 1917:303), this gap is marked in terms of ceramics by the shift from assemblages dominated by glaze ware to those with a majority of buff ware. Throughout most of the fourteenth century, most Zuni area populations were residing in a band of villages that runs east from Halona:wa (modern Zuni Pueblo) up into the El Morro Valley (see fig. 7.3a). In the late fourteenth and early fifteenth century all but one of these villages was abandoned and the focus of population in the Zuni region shifted west to an area between the modern Arizona–New Mexico border and a kilometer or two east of Halona:wa (see fig. 7.3b). This latter cluster includes all of the Zuni villages occupied when Coronado arrived in 1540. Interestingly the village that seems the best candidate to span this gap is Halona:wa, which except for a brief period after the Pueblo Revolt (Ferguson 2002) exhibits evidence of continuous settlement beginning at least in the late fourteenth century and continuing up to the present day (Kintigh 1985b; Mills 2002b).

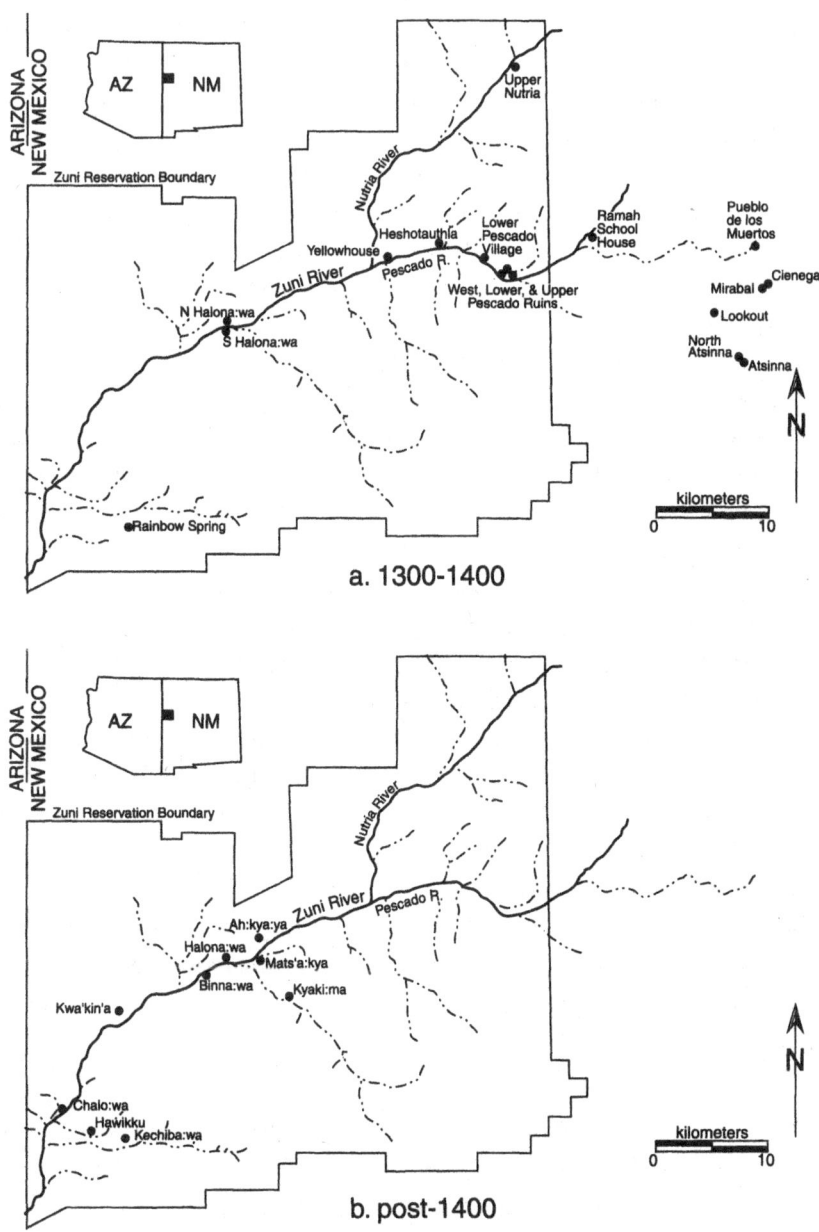

Fig. 7.3. Zuni-area villages from 1300 to 1540 (adapted from Kintigh 1985b: fig. 4.1).

Estimates of the total number of occupied pueblo rooms in the Zuni region during this period suggest that the shift in settlement location may have coincided with a noticeable decline in room counts (Kintigh 1985b:85–86; Spier 1917). Some researchers have associated the decline with a period of emigration from the Zuni area, possibly to the Rio Grande (Reed 1949, 1955). In 1985, Kintigh (1985b:110–12) suggested five possible scenarios to account for the shift in settlement and changes in room counts. These include abandonment of the region by its pre-1400 occupants and replacement by a new cultural group; the inability to identify significant pre-1400 components at large, protohistoric sites; massive pan-regional reorganization involving migration to and from multiple areas including Zuni; failure of Kintigh's seriation techniques; or a shift to settlement forms invisible in the archaeological record. Since the publication of Kintigh's study, numerous authors have documented the massive changes that occurred in regional settlement systems throughout the Southwest during the 1300s and 1400s and have taken particular note of the significant effects of large-scale migrations and local reorganization (E. C. Adams 1991, 2002; Bernardini 2002; Cordell 1995; Crown 1994; Dean, Doell, and Orcutt 1994; Duff 2002; Fish et al. 1994; LeBlanc 1999; Lyons 2003; Mills 1998; Nelson and Schachner 2002; Reid and Whittlesey 1999; papers in Spielmann, ed., 1998; Wilcox and Haas 1994). These studies have led recent research within the Zuni region to take a renewed interest in the effects of migration and reorganization within an area long thought to have been socially and economically isolated from other areas of the Southwest (e.g., Duff 2002; Mills in press; Kintigh 2000). Migration and reorganization (Kintigh's third scenario) is now the most likely candidate for explaining the apparent gap in Kintigh's original data (Duff 2002; Kintigh 2000; Mills in press; Schachner 2001).

Uniting the Evidence: The Glaze Ware to Buff Ware Transition and the Reorganization of Zuni Identity in the Tumultuous Fifteenth Century

By synthesizing the historical context of the shift from Zuni Glaze Ware production to that of Matsaki Buff Ware, we are able to begin to think about some of the social processes that may have led to significant technological change. During an approximately fifty-year period in the early to mid-1400s, residents of the Zuni area (who surely numbered in the thousands) participated in a dramatic shift in settlement location to the western portions of the region, which may have been accompanied by increased reliance on irrigation agriculture (Kintigh 1985b); significant changes in material culture, including the adoption of new ceramic technologies (matte-painted buff ware); and the expansion of exchange ties with surrounding regions, the departure of some migrant groups for areas to the east or to the Hopi Mesas, and the incorporation of migrant groups from diverse areas with different burial and, likely, social and ritual practices. In light of the significant changes that were occurring, fifteenth-century Zuni residents would have been starting anew, reconstituting villages and the sociopolitical organizations that structure social life. This process of resettlement would have been a prime opportunity for the initiation of key changes in social life (Pauketat 2003), which would have been apparent in a variety of forms, including shifts in technological style.

One of the most common assumptions about the adoption of Matsaki Buff Ware technology by Zuni potters is that it derived from the emulation of Sikyatki-style Jeddito Yellow Ware ceramics (E. C. Adams 1991:43; Reed 1955:187; Woodbury and Woodbury 1966:329). Mills (2003) notes that although Jeddito Yellow Ware production began on the Hopi Mesas at approximately AD 1325, Sikyatki style did not appear until the late 1300s at the earliest, at about the same time Matsaki Buff Ware was first produced. She suggests that instead of seeing "one [Sikyatki-style Jeddito Yellow Ware] inspiring the other [Matsaki Buff Ware], it seems more likely that the style itself is related to close interaction and shared ideology" brought about through migrations between the Hopi and Zuni areas and the shared experiences of migrants when they resided together along the upper Little Colorado and Mogollon Rim (Mills in press). Matsaki Buff Ware marks the first ceramic type at Zuni to include significant numbers of katsina figures and motifs that were relatively common on pottery in adjacent regions to the west and south during the AD 1300s (Mills in press). Following Duff (2002), I would suggest that the demise of communities in central Arizona in the fourteenth century led to the breakup of many local kin and social groups with ties to both the Zuni and Hopi areas. The incorporation of these migrants at Hopi and Zuni may have provided a new opportunity for the development of social ties between the areas and the creation of some semblance of shared history. How long these ties persisted and what form they took are questions for another time, best answered in consultation with the Hopi and Zuni people.

Barbara Mills (2003) has pointed out that one of the most important aspects of the shift away from glaze ware production was that Matsaki Buff Ware represented a dramatic break with the past technological styles of all groups, regardless of whether they were long-term residents or newly arrived migrants. She also noted the parallels between this significant, and likely conscious, shift and the rejection of glaze ware technology that may have become associated with the world under Spanish rule at Zuni and elsewhere following the Pueblo Revolt in 1680 (Mills 2002a, 2003). I would suggest that the widespread, rapid adoption of Matsaki Buff Ware by residents of the newly founded villages may have served to mark the emergence of a new, shared identity reflective of the integration of diverse groups. Older styles were left behind, and a new, shared means of producing and decorating pottery helped mark a growing, shared identity and tradition in the Zuni region.

Kintigh (2000) has interpreted variability in mortuary treatment and ceramic assemblages among protohistoric Zuni villages as indicative of the maintenance of social distinctions between migrant and resident groups. The preservation of these differences in ceramic assemblages was short lived however, with Matsaki Buff Ware completely replacing both Zuni Glaze Ware and types with southern antecedents by the late fifteenth century. Distinctions may have been maintained by other means, such as burial practices and through social groupings such as clans and ritual sodalities, but at least in terms of ceramics, a new common conception of appropriate technology and design was emerging. Thus, although we see a shift toward shared aspects of identity on one level, distinctions were likely maintained on others, much the same as in historic and modern Puebloan communities (Eggan 1950; Kroeber 1917; Ortiz 1969; Titiev 1944; Whiteley 1988).

In the fifteenth century, with the shift to buff ware production, residents of the Zuni area were forming a new "community of practice" (Stark, chap. 2, this vol.) encompassed by the protohistoric Zuni villages and incorporating both migrants and longtime residents. Communities were both rebuilt and created anew. These processes likely encouraged and solidified the formation of a new, shared Zuni identity and social organization. The demise of Zuni Glaze Ware production and resulting shift to buff ware technology is perhaps best seen as another aspect of the processes of community building and identity formation that were occurring in the Zuni area in the fifteenth century. Simultaneously, this shift marks the adoption of new technological and decorative styles, the former of which were novel for all groups involved, while the latter are indicative of shared experiences throughout the Western Pueblo world (Mills in press). The demise of Zuni Glaze Ware is largely inexplicable without placing it in context, linking pots to social life and the practices, events, resources, and traditions that were implicated in the formation of the fifteenth-century Zuni villages.

Acknowledgments

Barbara Mills deserves commendation for her valuable insights and for providing access to key data and papers during the course of this research. I would also like to thank Keith Kintigh, Andrew Duff, Michelle Hegmon, and the editors, discussants, and reviewers for their guidance and commentary.

8
Glaze Wares and Regional Social Relationships on the Rio Alamosa

Toni S. Laumbach

For years, the west-central New Mexico pueblo at Gallina Springs (LA 1178) has been a center of intrigue and controversy. The dominant pottery types of this D-shaped masonry site are a McElmo/Mesa Verde–like carbon paint ware and a variety of western glaze paint wares. These data have been interpreted as the result of a migrant population from the Mesa Verde culture area (Davis n.d., 1964; Ellis 1974). Therein lies the controversy. Research in the late 1970s concluded that the newly named "Magdalena" white ware was a "combination of traditions" and "represents a local ceramic tradition developed over some length of time" (Knight 1981:2; Tainter n.d.). By 1990, this interpretation had changed and the carbon paint pottery was attributed to Mesa Verde immigrants with reference to Laguna migration legends (Ellis 1974; Gomolak and Knight 1990:8–24). Sixty miles farther south, Pinnacle Ruin, with its compound masonry, carbon-painted pottery, and early glaze ware, overlooks the Rio Alamosa from a defensible vantage. Here too, the presence of an immigrant population from the Mesa Verde culture area is postulated (Lekson et al. 2002). Data from Pinnacle Ruin and nearby sites are evaluated against both the immigrant and nonimmigrant paradigms and provide researchers with new perspectives from which to view the early development and spread of the glaze paint tradition.

The Rio Alamosa is located in southwestern Socorro County, New Mexico, on the nebulous borderland between the Mogollon and northern Pueblo ceramic traditions. The ceramic sequence on the Cañada Alamosa includes northern and southern ceramic types from AD 700 through AD 1400. Site LA 2292, from here on referred to as Pinnacle Ruin (see fig. 1.2), has yielded the latest assemblage of this long sequence.

The Rio Alamosa, funneled between the northern projection of the Black Range on the west and the San Mateo Range on the east, becomes a perennial stream just below the 2,000-gallon-per-minute warm water spring known as Ojo Caliente. Immediately entering a deep canyon, known locally as the Cañada Alamosa, the stream dissipates sixteen miles later near the community of Monticello. Three miles downstream from the Ojo Caliente, the Rio Alamosa makes a hairpin bend around the high, rhyolitic outcrop on which Pinnacle Ruin was built. The location appears to be defensive. In places, definable walls of stone masonry are visible; other walls can only be guessed at beneath the undulating terraces of collapsed architecture. Several large depressions suggest the presence of subterranean rooms or plazas.

Recorded first by W. B. Morrow in 1940 and again by Lekson in 1991 (Laumbach 1992), Pinnacle Ruin was not formally tested until 1999 when four test pits were placed on a mound near a looted room (Laumbach 2000). More extensive excavations in 2000 and 2001 indicated that Pinnacle Ruin contains exceptional stratigraphic integrity, with superimposed floors and a stratified midden (Laumbach 2001; Nepstad-Thornberry and Lekson 2001). The ceramic assemblage is a mix of northern San Juan-style carbon-painted ware, Western and Rio Grande glaze wares, and utility and painted wares associated with the El Paso Phase of the Jornada Mogollon. The dominance (over 50 percent) of the northern San Juan-style carbon paint ware in combination with the compound masonry walls constructed of shaped elements and the stratified midden have led Lekson (2001a) to postulate that Pinnacle Ruin was home to a community of immigrants from the Mesa Verde culture area.

The larger research effort by the Cañada Alamosa Project has made available both survey and excavated data from nearby sites. Pertinent to this discussion are data from the nearby Victorio site, a 447-room multicomponent pueblo with a large thirteenth-century Tularosa Phase component (Laumbach and Wakeman 1999). Limited excavations have allowed a comparison of the ceramic assemblages from the Pinnacle and Victorio sites (Laumbach 2000).

The Pinnacle Ruin ceramic assemblage, like that of Gallinas Springs, reflects a population on the fringes of the glaze paint world making the transition from traditional black-on-white ceramics to the western glaze ware tradition. As such, it provides new perspectives on the dynamics of pueblo population and culture during the late thirteenth and early fourteenth centuries.

Excavated Features at Pinnacle Ruin

Feature 1 is located on an artificially leveled terrace on the slope of the Pinnacle outcrop. Exploration revealed well-defined strata filled with cultural trash, animal bones, and burned vegetable material. Corncobs from near the bottom of Feature 1 produced a radiocarbon date of 880 ± 100 BP that calibrated to a two-sigma span of AD 980–1290 (Beta 149237). This date and its clear association with the carbon paint wares indicate that the midden began to form prior to AD 1290.

Feature 2 is in a roomblock on the southeastern crest of the site (Laumbach and Wakeman 2001). Corncobs from the floor provide a radiocarbon date of 630 ± 40 BP that calibrates to a two-sigma span of AD 1290–1410 (Beta 149238). The associated ceramics include carbon paint ware and White Mountain Red Ware.

Feature 3, located on the flat top of Pinnacle Ruin, yielded a stratigraphic sequence of White Mountain Red Ware with carbon-painted Magdalena Black-on-white associated with superimposed floors. Corn cupules found on the upper floor produced a conventional radiocarbon date of 740 BP that calibrates to a two-sigma span of AD 1225–1300 (Beta 180685).

The Ceramic Types of Pinnacle Ruin

Thirty-three ceramic types were identified in the assemblage (tables 8.1–8.4).

Northern Pueblo Carbon Paint Ware

Magdalena Black-on-white (ca. AD 1200–1350) composes over 50 percent of the painted-ware assemblage. Like McElmo/Mesa Verde Black-on-white, Magdalena Black-on-white is characterized by a creamy white to gray white slip that frequently appears crackled, an organic pigment, and polishing over both slip and pigment. Stylistically, the Magdalena Black-

Table 8.1
LA 2292, Feature 1, Unit A, Ceramic Types and Number of Sherds by Level

Ceramic Type	Level 2	3	4	5	6	7	Total
Agua Fria Glaze-on-red	3						3
Chupadero Black-on-white	2		2				4
Heshotauthla Glaze Polychrome	2		2	1			5
Lincoln Black-on-red	2						2
Magdalena Black-on-white	45	16	14	7			82
Playas Red	11	18		6	2		37
Playas Red, cord marked		1					1
Playas Red, punctate variety	1						1
Reserve Black-on-white	5						5
Reserve Indented Corrugated	60	32	27	16	9		144
Reserve Plain	3		1				4
Reserve Plain Corrugated	12	1	7	1		1	22
Salado Red	2						2
Salt Smudged	3						3
Seco Corrugated	13	9	3	3		1	29
St. Johns Black-on-red					1		1
Three Rivers Red-on-terracotta		1					1
Too small to identify	21						21
Tularosa Black-on-white				1			1
Undif black-on-red				1			1
Undif brown smudged	99		25	22	3		149
Undif brownware	104	34	15	12	3		168
Undif corrugated	46		5	7			58
Undif El Paso	10	1	8	1			20
Undif El Paso Polychrome	7	1					8
Undif fillet rim	8		3	4			15
Undif red-slipped ware	1						1
Undif white ware	1						1
White Mountain Red Ware	2						2
Total	463	114	110	84	18	2	791

on-white from Pinnacle Ruin looks like McElmo Black-on-white or Santa Fe Black-on-white (ca. AD 1175–1425) from the central and northern Rio Grande.

Although not yet named, Magdalena Black-on-white was first recognized as a type with similarities to carbon paint ware of the "Mesa Verde

Table 8.2
LA 2292, Feature 1, Unit B, Ceramic Types and Number of Sherds by Level

Ceramic Type	1	2	3	4	5	6	7	8	9	Total
Agua Fria Glaze-on-red		1								1
Chupadero Black-on-white		1	1		1					3
Early El Paso Polychrome		1								1
Heshotauthla Glaze Polychrome		1		2						3
Kwakina Glaze Polychrome		1								1
Magdalena Black-on-white	2	27	23	7	15	3	1	3	1	82
Playas Red	3	7	13	1		3				27
Playas Red, incised variety			3		1	2	1			7
Playas Red, punctate variety						2	1			3
Reserve Indented Corrugated	49	1	28	7	73	25	8	5	1	197
Reserve Plain						2				2
Reserve Plain Corrugated	4				7	11	3	1		26
Reserve/Tularosa Corrugated series				14					2	16
Salado Red	2					1				3
Salt Smudged		2		1						3
Seco Corrugated	30		1	6	15	5			1	58
St. Johns Polychrome						1				1
Tularosa Patterned Corrugated					2					2
Undif black-on-red			1							1
Undif brown smudged	17	43	21	11	23	7	1	10	4	137
Undif brown ware	25	57	25	10	16	11	2	3		149
Undif corrugated	34	6	7	8	1	5		2	1	64
Undif El Paso			2	6	11		1		3	23
Undif El Paso Polychrome		4	1		4	4	1	2		16
Undif fillet rim	2				3	3	1			9
Undif red-slipped ware				1						1
Undif white ware	1	4	1							6
White Mountain Red Ware		1								1
Total	169	157	127	74	172	85	20	26	13	843

Tradition" by Emma Lou Davis (n.d., 1964) from samples she examined at Gallinas Springs Pueblo in the Gallinas Mountains, located about sixty miles north of Pinnacle Ruin. It was Davis who first suggested a similarity with Mesa Verde types and the possibility of "immigrants" from the Four Corners region settling at Gallinas Springs. Later, Warren (1974) described this carbon paint pottery as "southern" McElmo. Gomo-

Table 8.3
LA 2292, Feature 2, Ceramic Types and Number of Sherds by Level

Ceramic Type	1	2	3	4	5	6	7	6 lower half	Surface	Total
Agua Fria Glaze-on-red		2		5	2				5	14
Chupadero Black-on-white	1	1								2
Early El Paso Polychrome									2	2
El Paso Polychrome					1					1
Gila Polychrome									4	4
Heshotauthla Glaze Polychrome	1		1							2
Magdalena Black-on-white	6	4	6	9	3	4			2	34
Pinedale Black-on-red						1				1
Pinedale Polychrome			1	1			1		1	4
Playas Red	2	3	1		2		1		5	14
Playas Red, incised variety			1							1
Playas Red, punctate variety						7	5	1	1	14
Ramos Polychrome									1	1
Reserve Indented Corrugated	3		1	8	27	17	15	7	19	97
Reserve Plain	2	1	1		2					6
Reserve Plain Corrugated	2	1		1	1	1	1	1		8
Reserve/Tularosa Corrugated series				14						14
Salado Red					1	1				2
Seco Corrugated	9	17	4	14	11	3		2	20	80
St. Johns Black-on-red			1				3			4
St. Johns Polychrome	1						2			3
Tularosa Patterned Corrugated	1									1
Undif black-on-red									1	1
Undif brown effigy					3					3
Undif brown smudged	23	10	27	13	16	19	4		14	126
Undif brown ware	19	10		5	16	6	10	4	12	82
Undif corrugated	1	1	1	3	2	5		1		14
Undif El Paso			4			2		1	4	11
Undif El Paso Polychrome	3		1	1	3		2		1	11
Undif fillet rim	1	1			1	1			1	5
Undif red-slipped ware		1	7	2					3	13
Undif white ware	1									1
White Mountain Red Ware	1					1				2
Total	77	52	57	62	103	70	44	17	96	578

Table 8.4
LA 2292, Feature 3, Ceramic Types and Number of Sherds by Level

Ceramic Type	1	2	3	4	5	6	Total
Agua Fria Glaze-on-Red	4						4
El Paso Polychrome, early			2				2
Heshotauthla Black-on-red	2	4					6
Magdalena Black-on-white	4		7	1	1		13
Mimbres Classic Black-on-white (Type III)		1					1
Pinedale Polychrome	1						1
Playas Red			5	1			6
Playas Red, punctate variety			2				2
Puerco Black-on-red	1						1
Reserve Black-on-white	1						1
Reserve Indented Corrugated	10	11	18	6	1	1	47
Reserve Plain			2				2
Reserve Plain Corrugated	4	1		1		1	7
Seco Corrugated	8	11	1				20
Socorro Black-on-white				1			1
St. Johns Black-on-red				17		1	18
St. Johns Polychrome				48	1		49
Tularosa Patterned Corrugated		1		1			2
Undif corrugated	17	7	9	1			34
Undif El Paso				4			4
Undif El Paso Polychrome			10	3			13
Undif fillet rim	1	3					4
Undif plain	34	31	35	9	5	3	117
Undif plain with smudged interior	23						23
Undif red-slipped ware	7			2	1	2	12
White Mountain Red Ware	2			4	4	1	11
Wingate Polychrome				1			1
Total	119	70	95	96	13	9	402

lak and Knight formally described Magdalena Black-on-white. Knight's (1981:2; Tainter n.d.) initial interpretation of Magdalena Black-on-white was that it represents "a local tradition developed over some length of time." Later, Gomolak and Knight (1990:8–24) changed that interpretation, attributing the ceramic type to "proto-Laguna" and post-Mesa Verde immigrants, referencing Laguna migration legends documented by Ellis (1974).

Carbon-painted white ware is a phenomenon of the thirteenth century in north-central New Mexico. McElmo Black-on-white and Mesa Verde Black-on-white are produced in the Four Corners region. Stylistically similar, carbon-painted Santa Fe Black-on-white and Galisteo Black-on-white are found in the upper central Rio Grande and Galisteo Basin (Habicht-Mauche 1993a; Honea 1968). In the Rio Abajo (Marshall and Walt 1984) and on the Chupadero Mesa, Elmendorf Black-on-white is decidedly dissimilar in style from the northern carbon-painted wares. In this distribution, Pinnacle Ruin is situated on the far southwestern fringe of the carbon paint world and, other than Gallinas Springs, is distant from those areas where Mesa Verde-tradition ceramics were commonly distributed. Magdalena Black-on-white is clearly an anomaly in the otherwise mineral paint ceramic assemblage that characterizes the Cañada Alamosa sequence.

Glaze Wares

The glaze ware assemblage includes three groups, two of which are related. The related groups are the White Mountain Red Ware sequence (Carlson 1970) and the early Zuni Glaze Ware types (Woodbury and Woodbury 1966). The third group, numerically smallest, is made up of early Rio Grande Glaze Ware.

White Mountain Red Ware. Glazed red ware and the antecedent types from the White Mountain Red Ware tradition dominate the red ware assemblage. Post-AD 1200 White Mountain Red Ware (Carlson 1970) includes St. Johns Black-on-red and St. Johns Polychrome (AD 1175–1300), Pinedale Black-on-red and Pinedale Polychrome (AD 1275–1325), and Heshotauthla Glaze Polychrome (AD 1275–1325).

Early Zuni Glaze Wares. Kwakina Polychrome and Pinnawa Glaze-on-white are typically associated with the Zuni and Acoma areas (Dittert 1959; Woodbury and Woodbury 1966). Temporal range for Kwakina Polychrome is ca. AD 1275/1300 to 1375 and perhaps into the early 1400s. Dates for Pinnawa range from ca. AD 1325 to 1400 or later.

Early Rio Grande Glaze Wares. Two early Rio Grande glaze types, Agua Fria Glaze-on-red and San Clemente Glaze Polychrome, occur in small numbers. Agua Fria was made in the Albuquerque area and farther south in the Rio Abajo (Shepherd 1942). Like Agua Fria Glaze-on-red, San Clemente Glaze Polychrome was also made in the central Rio Grande region. Eckert (chap. 3, this vol.) provides an excellent discussion of glaze ware production and the dynamics of its exchange.

El Paso Polychrome

El Paso Polychrome is associated with the Jornada Mogollon culture area in south-central New Mexico. El Paso Polychrome is temporally distinguished by early and late jar rim styles. Whalen (1978:58–70) dates the early rim style, an expanded rim, to AD 1200–1300. The late rim style has an everted rim and dates to AD 1300–1400. Both early and late rim styles of El Paso Polychrome are present at Pinnacle Ruin.

The Corrugated Wares

Reserve Indented Corrugated (Rinaldo and Bluhm 1956), a brown ware, is the dominant corrugated utility ware. Reserve Indented Corrugated is associated with the Tularosa Phase (ca. AD 1175–1325).

Next in number is Seco Corrugated. The regional origin and cultural affiliation of Seco Corrugated is problematic. Originally described by Wilson and Warren (1973), the type is common on the large, fourteenth-century adobe pueblos of south-central and southwestern New Mexico. Usually found in association with the late variety of El Paso Polychrome, this type is often described as smudged obliterated or obliterated corrugated (Browning et al. 1992; Lekson and Rorex 1987:17; Nelson and Hegmon 1993:88).

Seco Corrugated is similar to obliterated corrugated types found on Salado sites in the Mimbres and Gila drainages (Nelson and LeBlanc 1986). There are also similarities with obliterated corrugated wares from the northern Rio Grande. Perhaps significantly, the northern Rio Grande obliterated corrugated wares are associated with Santa Fe Black-on-white (Honea 1968:126; Sudar-Murphy and Laumbach 1977:23). Santa Fe Black-on-white, like Magdalena Black-on-white, bears a marked resemblance to Mesa Verde pottery styles and has been interpreted as indicative of immigration from the Mesa Verde culture area (Cordell 1997:198, 405; Mera 1935:12; Wendorf and Reed 1955:131–73); however, Habicht-Mauche (1993a:89) maintains that "Santa Fe Black-on-white represents a uniquely local ceramic development."

Based on ceramic cross-dating, Seco Corrugated is a fourteenth-century type. Associated with Reserve Indented Corrugated in the stratigraphic record at Pinnacle Ruin, its debut was not much earlier than AD 1300, coinciding with the postulated arrival of the immigrant population.

Ceramic Types Found in Minor Quantities

Ceramics associated with the eleventh and twelfth centuries are found in small quantities. Early White Mountain Red Ware, Mimbres Classic Black-on-white, Socorro Black-on-white, and Reserve Black-on-white may be intrusive into the Pinnacle Ruin assemblage from nearby sites or simply reflect the earliest Pueblo period use of the site.

The thirteenth and fourteenth centuries are represented by a number of types from neighboring regions to the south and east. Potential sources of these sherds are the Rio Grande pueblos south of Socorro, New Mexico, and the adobe pueblos of the El Paso/Black Mountain Phase found immediately to the south and east.

Like Rio Grande Glaze Ware, limited quantities of carbon-painted Elmendorf Black-on-white suggest some contact with Rio Grande populations. Contact with the Rio Grande seems to have occurred on the cusp of the thirteenth and fourteenth centuries if Marshall and Walt's (1984:95) distinction between the early Elmendorf Phase (AD 950–1100) and the late Elmendorf Phase (AD 1100–1300) is correct. The post-1300 Ancestral Piro Phase on the Rio Grande begins with the emergence of the glaze ware ceramic industry. After a period of transition that may have lasted into the fourteenth century, Elmendorf Black-on-white is displaced by Rio Grande gray ware and the Rio Grande Glaze Ware tradition (Marshall and Walt 1984:138). Other types associated with this transitional period include Heshotauthla and Kwakina polychromes, both of which are represented in the Pinnacle Ruin assemblage.

Mineral-painted Chupadero Black-on-white, found in very limited quantities, is a widely traded type whose likely sources are the Salinas area and points eastward.

Four ceramic types reflect contact to the south and west. Ramos Polychrome and Playas Red represent northern Chihuahua and the Casas Grandes culture area. Fourteenth-century Salado painted ware, Gila Polychrome and Maverick Mountain Polychrome, also occur. Gila Polychrome, common in the Gila and Mimbres drainages (Nelson and LeBlanc 1986), was widely traded to the east into El Paso Phase villages (Carmichael 1986:67–72; Human Systems Research 1974:362–64; Lehmer 1948; Lekson and Rorex 1987:17–26; Whalen 1978:44). A sherd of Maverick Mountain Polychrome, collected by Morrow in 1940, was observed in the Laboratory of Anthropology collections from Pinnacle Ruin. Not commonly found in southwestern New Mexico, this type is associated with fourteenth-century Salado villages of southeastern Arizona. Lindsay (1987:192) has suggested that Maverick Mountain Polychrome is "stylistically analogous to types in the Kayenta area" of northeastern Arizona and that its presence in southern Arizona is owing to a migration of Kayenta Anasazi into southeastern Arizona. The fourteenth-century pueblos of the El Paso/Black Mountain Phase found along the Rio Grande and its Black Range tributaries are likely sources for all of these wares (Laumbach and Kirkpatrick 1983; Lekson 1989; M. C. Nelson and Hegmon 1993).

The Chronological Context for Pinnacle Ruin

Ceramic Assemblage

Magdalena Black-on-white is consistently found in the pre-AD 1300 context of the lower levels of Feature 1 and Feature 3 (Lekson 2001b). In that context, Magdalena Black-on-white is associated with Reserve Indented Corrugated and small numbers of Tularosa Black-on-white and St. Johns Polychrome. The fourteenth-century wares are significantly absent. Upper levels of Feature 1 have Magdalena Black-on-white and Seco Corrugated, Rio Grande Glaze Ware, White Mountain Red Ware, and early Zuni Glaze Ware.

Magdalena Black-on-white and Reserve Indented Corrugated are found throughout all levels of Feature 2 along with Seco Corrugated, Agua Fria Glaze-on-red, Gila Polychrome, Playas Red, Pinedale Polychrome, and Heshotauthla Polychrome. Corresponding to the ceramic assemblage from the upper levels of Feature 1, the Feature 2 ceramics are in a single dated context (AD 1290–1410). A few sherds of Tularosa Black-on-white and St. Johns Polychrome were found in Feature 2.

Although Magdalena Black-on-white does occur throughout Feature 3, middle and late White Mountain Red Ware dominate the assemblage. Stratigraphically, fill and floors separate the middle and late White Mountain Red Ware. The middle White Mountain Red Ware, St. Johns Polychrome and late St. Johns Polychrome, distinguished by the distinctive Pinedale style that lacks curvilinear elements, are found in association with Magdalena Black-on-white on the floors and the fill immediately above the floors. Corn found on the upper floor dates to AD 1225–1300 at two sigmas. Found in the trash in the upper fill of this feature are the latest of the White Mountain Red Ware found at Pinnacle Ruin, including Pinedale Polychrome and Heshotauthla Glaze Polychrome. Associated with these later types are sherds of Heshotauthla Black-on-red and Agua Fria Glaze-on-red.

Implications of Regional Associations

The Pinnacle Ruin ceramic assemblage indicates that the community had connections with four areas: the Cibola culture area to the west, the Gallina Springs Pueblo to the north, the central Rio Grande area to the east, and the southern Rio Grande and its Black Range tributaries to the south. To accurately evaluate the nature of those connections, we must first know if the thirteenth- and fourteenth-century inhabitants of Pinnacle Ruin were immigrants from the north as suggested by Lekson (2001a) or a local population with roots in the Cañada Alamosa. If the Pinnacle population stemmed from the Tularosa Phase component at the nearby Victorio site, then based on its precedent material culture, its connections would be to the west with the majority of the Tularosa Phase sites. However, the dominance of McElmo-style Magdalena Black-on-white in the Pinnacle Ruin assemblage, the compound masonry walls constructed of shaped elements, the well-developed midden, and the defensive location of the site are strong indications that populations from the Mesa Verde culture area were integral to the occupation of Pinnacle Ruin.

The concept of migrant communities from the Mesa Verde cultural area has suffered from a lack of evidence on the northern Rio Grande where much of the Mesa Verde population is assumed to have settled. Habicht-Mauche (1993a:87), in her report on the ceramics from Arroyo Hondo, states that "not a single site has ever been identified in the northern Rio Grande that contains an assemblage of features or artifacts that can be interpreted as evidence of a wholly immigrant community." Nevertheless, current data from Pinnacle Ruin suggest that migrants from the Mesa Verde culture area may have occupied all or part of this pueblo (Lekson 2001a).

When Did They Arrive?

If one accepts the data suggesting an immigrant population at Pinnacle, then the question becomes, "when did they arrive?" Regardless of the timing of their arrival, it seems logical that their primary outside connection would have been to the Gallinas Springs community located sixty miles to the north. If the immigrants arrived while the Victorio site was still occupied, then interaction with the Victorio site population would have encouraged development of secondary connections with the widespread and relatively numerous Tularosa Phase sites found to the west. Conversely, if the immigrants arrived to find an abandoned valley, then the system of Tularosa Phase pueblos would have been absent and contact would have been necessarily limited to those few aggregated villages that remained. These would have been limited to a few El Paso/Black Mountain phase sites in the Black Range drainages to the south (thirty miles), the late Elmendorf/Ancestral Piro sites on the central Rio Grande south of Socorro (fifty miles), and the Gallinas Springs Pueblo (presumably the "mother ship") located some sixty miles to the north. To the west and northwest, the nearest known sites of this period are eighty miles distant as the crow flies.

Assuming that at least some of the Pinnacle Ruin inhabitants were immigrants, what does their ceramic assemblage tell us about when they arrived? The dominant painted ware from the thirteenth- and early-fourteenth-century contexts is Magdalena Black-on-white. The design style of carbon-painted Magdalena Black-on-white at Pinnacle Ruin is primarily that of the temporally earlier McElmo Black-on-white and not that of Mesa Verde Black-on-white. McElmo Black-on-white began to be made around AD 1100, while Mesa Verde Black-on-white began one hundred years later. Production of McElmo Black-on-white continued well into the late thirteenth century, albeit in diminishing quantities (Breternitz, Rohn, and Morris 1974: 41–43). To date, the majority of the Magdalena Black-on-white at Pinnacle Ruin is in the McElmo style, although a few sherds have stylistic elements of Mesa Verde Black-on-white. Similarly, only a few of the Magdalena Black-on-white sherds from the Gallinas Springs ceramic assemblage are in the Mesa Verde style (Knight 1981:15).

Based on the stratigraphic position of the McElmo-style Magdalena Black-on-white and the associated radiocarbon dates, the data are ambiguous and allow for two possibilities. One scenario has the immigrants from the Mesa Verde culture area arriving in the early thirteenth century and becoming isolated, thereby missing the transition from a McElmo design style to a Mesa Verde design style (Laumbach and Laumbach 2001).

This scenario is supported by a model proposed by Duff and Wilshusen (2000), which contends that the departure from the Mesa Verde culture area began early in the 1200s. Tree-ring-based climatological evidence for harsh winters during the early thirteenth century has led some researchers to suggest that abandonment of the area began early in the 1200s (T. L. Jones et al. 1999; K. L. Peterson 1988; Salzer 2000). A second scenario sees the Mesa Verde community arriving late in the thirteenth century as refugees of the Great Drought or perhaps as a splinter colony from the larger Gallinas Springs colony. Each of these scenarios would have presented the immigrants with a different distribution of neighboring pueblos.

One factor affecting interpretation of pueblo relationships is that current dating of many unexcavated or partially excavated sites is based on very limited data. Thus contemporaneity between sites is rarely demonstrable. This data set is no exception.

The Contact Implications of an Early-Thirteenth-Century Arrival

An immigrant arrival in the early 1200s would have found the Victorio site and neighboring Tularosa Phase pueblos occupied. However, ceramic data suggesting contact between the two sites is currently limited. At Pinnacle Ruin, only a few sherds of Tularosa Black-on-white are found in association with the earliest levels containing Magdalena Black-on-white. The most common ceramic links between Pinnacle Ruin and the Victorio site are Reserve Indented Corrugated, St. Johns Polychrome, and a few sherds of early style El Paso Polychrome. If the two sites were contemporary, then there was little exchange during those early years. However, this cannot be used as an effective argument against an early arrival, since immigrant communities are often unwelcome and at a distinct disadvantage in terms of access to optimal agricultural land, often occupying defensive locations like the Pinnacle (Clark 2001:90–92). Migrant communities often become insular and maintain their old traditions (Kloberdanz 1975: 210–11) until that time when local relationships allow exchange and enculturation.

Interaction between the Pinnacle Ruin community and local Tularosa Phase populations is suggested by the continued use of Reserve Indented Corrugated after AD 1300. A perhaps analogous situation is found at the

Point of Pines in eastern Arizona where Haury (1958) and later Lindsay (1987) define the characteristics of an immigrant group from the Kayenta area of northern Arizona. At Point of Pines the immigrants are clearly using local utility wares while producing their traditional decorated wares with local resources (Haury 1958:416–17; Lindsay 1987:194).

St. Johns Polychrome is found on both the Victorio and Pinnacle Ruin sites, but the later White Mountain Red Ware types are found only on Pinnacle Ruin. Whether or not the presence of St. Johns Polychrome and Reserve Indented Corrugated at Pinnacle Ruin is indicative of contact with local populations is not clear at this time.

Contact Implications of a Late-Thirteenth-Century Arrival

Given a late-thirteenth-century arrival with the Victorio site already abandoned, the nearest Pueblo neighbors are at some distance, as there are no other occupied sites in the Rio Alamosa at this time. Nepstad-Thornberry (2001) notes that the macrobotanical remains from the Pinnacle Ruin midden indicate widespread use of all available plant communities, suggesting that there was little competition for resource areas. The faunal data lend support to this scenario. Large game is rare in the limited Victorio site assemblage but plentiful in the Pinnacle Ruin deposits (Cain 2002).

Connection to the North: Gallinas Springs Pueblo

Although Pinnacle Ruin is a much smaller pueblo, its ceramic assemblage leaves little doubt that it is related to Gallinas Springs Pueblo. Comparing the Gallinas Springs ceramics at the Laboratory of Anthropology (Santa Fe, New Mexico) with those from Pinnacle Ruin reveals a marked similarity between the assemblages. Specifically, the Magdalena Black-on-white from both collections has a "McElmo design style." Corrugated wares in both collections include Seco and Reserve Indented Corrugated. St. Johns Polychrome, Pinedale Black-on-red, and Heshotauthla Polychrome are present in both assemblages, although the Gallinas Springs St. Johns Polychrome, Pinedale Polychrome, and Heshotauthla Glaze Polychrome have been redefined as Magdalena Black-on-red and Magdalena Polychrome (Gomolak and Knight 1990:8:18–25). If the immigrants at Pinnacle Ruin were late arrivals from Gallinas Springs, they would have already begun to use St. Johns Polychrome and Reserve Indented Corrugated.

Connections to the West: The Cibola Area

Connections to the west appear to be strong both before and after the arrival of the immigrants, as evidenced by the high numbers of White Mountain Red Ware in both the Victorio and Pinnacle assemblages and the occurrence of Pinedale Polychrome and early Zuni Glaze Ware at Pinnacle Ruin. It seems logical that relationships between the immigrants and the local Tularosa Phase population during the thirteenth century would have meant developing relationships with the Tularosa Phase sister communities to the west. However, relationships with the west during the early fourteenth century could have developed independently, perhaps through the northern connection with the Gallinas Springs Pueblo. Alternatively, if Pinnacle Ruin was not an immigrant pueblo but was instead populated by the local antecedent Tularosa Phase population, then a strong relationship to the west would not be surprising.

Interpreting relationships of the Pinnacle Ruin community with communities to the west may be enhanced by examination of glaze paints and sources of raw materials used in making glaze paints. Recent preliminary studies (Huntley, chap. 6, this vol.) of thirteenth- and fourteenth-century pottery from the Zuni region have focused on compositional analysis of glaze paints and isotopic sourcing of glaze paint resources. Huntley (this vol.) reports that lead and associated copper ores from different geological resources can be distinguished. Lead ores from the Cerrillos Hills, situated in the central Rio Grande region, were identified as a significant source for Zuni potters making glaze paint wares. However, Huntley's data further suggest that for later glaze ware types, such as Heshotauthla Glaze Polychrome and Kwakina Polychrome, the glaze paint composition corresponds more frequently to ores recovered from the Magdalena and Hansonburg areas of south-central New Mexico. Huntley's research suggests the possibility of local production for Pinnacle Ruin glaze wares, particularly the later St. Johns, Heshotauthla, and Kwakina polychromes. If these late Zuni types were not produced at Pinnacle Ruin, then it is likely they were made at Gallinas Springs Pueblo.

Contact with the South-Central Rio Grande

Based on the occasional occurrence of Elmendorf Black-on-white, Chupadero Black-on-white, Agua Fria Glaze-on-red, and San Clemente Glaze Polychrome, it would appear that the Pinnacle Ruin community had a much more limited relationship with Rio Grande populations near Socorro and Albuquerque than it enjoyed with the Western Pueblos.

Connection with the Northern Fringe of the Casas Grandes World

The social connection to the southern adobe pueblos (in the Rio Grande and associated Black Range drainages) is interesting in that while those pueblos are geographically the closest, the small numbers of El Paso, Gila, and Ramos polychromes appear to reflect limited interaction. Interestingly, both the early (thirteenth century) and late (fourteenth century) jar rims of the El Paso Polychrome are in evidence.

Although Seco Corrugated is ubiquitous in El Paso/Black Mountain Phase sites to the south and east, its origins are unknown and problematic. Nevertheless, its presence at Pinnacle Ruin suggests some link to those southern sites.

Discussion

The Pinnacle Ruin ceramic assemblage seems most closely related to the pueblos found to the north and west. Whether this was owing to antecedent relationships that began during the Tularosa Phase occupation of the Cañada Alamosa or was born of the relationship between Pinnacle Ruin and Gallinas Springs Pueblo depends both on the validity of the immigrant hypothesis and, if valid, the arrival date and number of the migrants. What is significant is that the western relationship remained strongest even though the central Rio Grande, southern Rio Grande, and Black Range pueblos were geographically close. Thus the cultural identity of the Pinnacle Ruin population appears closely linked to that of the Western Pueblos. Further, it suggests that the recognition of significant cultural, political, and perhaps linguistic differences prevented closer relationships with neighbors to the east and south. This negative relationship seems to have been strongest with those adobe pueblos that ceramically and architecturally represent the northern edges of the Casas Grandes world (Hegmon et al. 1999:150–52).

The current data from Pinnacle Ruin present three possible interpretations. The first interpretation is that Pinnacle Ruin is not an immigrant pueblo. Instead, it represents an in situ development of the Tularosa Phase population wherein the locals became aware of socially related ceramic and architectural changes to the north and simply accepted the new horizon, integrating the new styles into their existing traditions (Tainter n.d.). The second interpretation also sees Pinnacle Ruin as a local development but one that has accepted a small number of immigrants, creating a site unit intrusion observable in the archaeological record. The intrusive group may have provided the catalyst for adaptation of the incipient glaze paint tradition because of social ties with western pueblos that had also accepted immigrant groups (see Schachner, chap. 7, this vol.). The third interpretation is that Pinnacle Ruin is, indeed, a community of migrants that either arrived early enough in the thirteenth century to have Tularosa Phase neighbors or who arrived late in the thirteenth century to find a deserted valley.

If the first scenario is correct and Pinnacle Ruin was constructed by the descendants of the Tularosa Phase occupation, the population appears to have been much reduced in size given the number of sizable Tularosa Phase communities in the area (Laumbach 1992; Laumbach and Kirkpatrick 1983). In addition, something must have forced them from the broad terraces to a defensive position on a rocky precipice. Adaptation of the glaze paint tradition would have been a natural evolution from the long-lived use of White Mountain Red Ware. However, there is no ready explanation for the adoption of an already dying carbon paint tradition.

The second scenario involving the addition of small immigrant family groups to a descendant Tularosa Phase pueblo population fits the northern San Juan population change model proposed by Duff and Wilshusen (2000) wherein small family groups began leaving the Four Corners early in the thirteenth century and joined populations with whom they were familiar. Because they were small family groups with existing social ties, these immigrants are virtually invisible on the northern Rio Grande where the primary evidence for migration is a dramatic increase in population. Habicht-Mauche (1993a:89) states the case: "None of these traits [primarily Mesa Verde-inspired architecture and ceramics] co-occur in a context that can clearly be identified as a site unit intrusion." The data from Pinnacle Ruin appear to stand in marked contrast to that from the northern Rio Grande. Perhaps the similarities between Santa Fe Black-on-white and McElmo Black-on-white made the merging more seamless in the northern Rio Grande, whereas on the Cañada Alamosa the addition of carbon-painted ceramics and compound masonry walls stands out against a background of mineral-painted red and white wares in a Tularosa design style and irregular cobble/clast wall construction. Low frequencies of Tularosa Black-on-white from Pinnacle Ruin suggest that the immigrant group joined the locals as they were abandoning production of Tularosa Black-on-white in favor of the later White Mountain Red Ware.

The third scenario sees Pinnacle Ruin representing an immigrant community that arrived either in the early thirteenth century to find a large community of Tularosa Phase neighbors or, alternatively, arrived late in the century, after the abandonment of the Victorio site. The first alternative, the early arrival, suggests a parallel situation to that described by Haury (1958) and Lindsay (1987) at Point of Pines. In the Point of Pines scenario, immigrants were welcomed and utilized local utility wares while maintaining their own decorated ceramic traditions and architectural styles. Haury (1958) suggested that this relationship ended badly with an intentional conflagration and subsequent defensive efforts by the locals. Conversely, Lindsay implies that the fire was likely accidental and that the immigrants again reoccupied the pueblo, only to move on after a short period, leaving the indigenous population and their ceramic tradition to continue in place (Lindsay 1987:195).

There are significant differences between the two situations. While the Pinnacle Ruin scenario might have been similar to that at Point of Pines in terms of the immigrants using local utility ceramics while maintaining the use of carbon paint wares, it seems clear that White Mountain Red Ware types were already a significant aspect of both the local and the immigrant assemblages. The proxemics also appear to have been different. At Pinnacle Ruin, the immigrants were isolated on what Lekson refers to as a "nasty knob," not welcomed into the structure of the nearby large pueblos or free to build on one of the broad, level, and available terraces. Given the number of Tularosa Phase villages, if anyone moved on, it was the indigenous population, not the immigrants. Even after the Tularosa Phase villages were abandoned, the immigrants stayed on their "knob" in what seems to be a defensive position.

The early-thirteenth-century alternative suggests that the immigrants and the indigenous population may have gone through a separate but similar transition from their respective thirteenth-century ceramic traditions of black-on-white decorated pottery to a near complete adoption of the White Mountain Red Ware tradition (and thus into the western glaze wares) during the early fourteenth century. The stratigraphy at Pinnacle Ruin indicates that the makers of Tularosa Black-on-white may have undergone that transition slightly earlier than the immigrants, perhaps because it was part of their own trajectory of material culture. Magdalena Black-on-white, even in its by then archaic McElmo style, continues into the upper levels, where it is associated with the later White Mountain Red Ware, notably Pinedale Polychrome and Heshotauthla Polychrome, neither of which have been found in clear temporal association with Tularosa Black-on-white in the Cañada Alamosa. One implication is that the immigrants maintained their own cultural identity well into the fourteenth century and did not join the indigenous population in their abandonment of the area. If that was the case, then the nearest pueblo neighbors were miles away until the construction of two, possibly descendant, glaze-tradition-period pueblos near the Ojo Caliente (Laumbach 1992:70).

Current data strongly support the late-thirteenth-century arrival of an immigrant group to a deserted valley. No carbon paint pottery has been found on the Victorio site. Plant remains from the Pinnacle midden indicate that there was little competition for wild plant resources or wild game. It is probable that Pinnacle Ruin was ancestral to two other pueblos located three miles upstream near the Ojo Caliente. These late sites may not have been abandoned until the fifteenth century, as indicated in surface collections that include later glaze wares than those found on Pinnacle Ruin. Neither site has been professionally excavated.

Thus, it seems that both the immigrants and the indigenous Tularosa Phase populations on the Rio Alamosa may have taken separate paths in following the ceramic lead of the Western Pueblo world. Whether or not that was the case, the makers of both the Tularosa and Magdalena ceramic traditions ultimately shared a common relationship manifested by the production of glaze paint ceramics. Following Schachner (chap. 7, this vol.), this common relationship may well have been owing to a realignment of social organization resulting from the influx of population into the Western Pueblo world during the thirteenth century.

Chronological control is critical in order to confidently evaluate these scenarios. Pinnacle Ruin and its associated sites provide us with an ideal field laboratory to assess models for recognizing immigrants in the archaeological record and for understanding the development and spread of the glaze paint tradition.

Acknowledgments

Several people helped to bring this chapter to fruition. Dr. Dennis and Trudy O'Toole and the Cañada Alamosa Institute provided the opportunity to do research in one of the most fascinating areas of New Mexico. Dr. Linda Cordell and Dr. Stephen Lekson provided stimulating suggestions and editorial comment. Karl W. Laumbach, director of the Cañada Alamosa Project, provided guidance and disciplined attention to the data.

9

Black-on-White to Glaze-on-Red

The Adoption of Glaze Technology in the
Central Rio Grande Valley

Suzanne L. Eckert

During the fourteenth century, the establishment and growth of large towns in the central Rio Grande region (including the lower Rio Puerco and Rio Grande Valleys from the Rio Chiquito in the north to the confluence of the Rio Puerco and Rio Grande in the south) resulted in a new social landscape that required navigation by various Pueblo groups (Eckert and Cordell 200). This demographic re-formation provided new arenas in which transformations in group identity, social organization, and ritual systems could be negotiated. During this period, new regional traditions evident in decorated ceramic style, ceramic technology, and architectural designs developed. However, the social processes that produced these new traditions in the central Rio Grande region remain a matter of debate.

The early Pueblo IV period (AD 1275–1400) in the central Rio Grande region is generally defined by the appearance of red-slipped, glaze-painted pottery apparently made in imitation of Western Pueblo Glaze Ware. Early glaze paint manufacture occurred along the central and lower Rio Grande from Cochiti south to Socorro (Eckert, chap. 3, this vol.; Snow 1982). This new ceramic tradition has been associated with immigration of Western Pueblo groups into the area (Reed 1949:169–70; Shepard 1942:197–99; Warren 1976), the spread of ideology and its associated rituals (Crown 1994:108; Graves and Eckert 1998:279; Spielmann 1998), and/or transformations in exchange networks (Habicht-Mauche 1995; Herhahn, chap. 10, this vol.; Snow 1981).

This chapter briefly explores the adoption of glaze-painted pottery at four fourteenth-century Rio Grande sites (see figs. 1.1 and 1.2) by examining various decorative and technological ceramic attributes. To explore which of the above social processes were related to the adoption of glaze technology, I examine how quickly glaze-painted pottery was adopted at each site, the production source for glaze-painted pottery, and changes in design style and iconography. I find that glaze ware production and distribution among these four villages varied greatly, and cannot be explained by a single social process.

Previous Explanations for the Adoption of Glaze Technology

In the central Rio Grande region, the shift from carbon-painted, white-slipped pottery to glaze-painted, red-slipped pottery was a dramatic transition for potters in terms of both production technology and decoration. Decoratively, the contrast between slip colors is probably the most visually striking difference. However, in many cases, the transition from white- to red-slipped pottery was also accompanied by a change in design layout and motifs (Graves and Eckert 1998). Technically, the switch from carbon-rich paints to paints composed of lead- and copper-bearing minerals is most notable. However, a switch from reducing atmosphere to oxidizing atmosphere when firing pottery was also required. In some areas, the shift in paint composition is also associated with a shift in temper choice (Warren 1976). These decorative and technical shifts required conscious choices on the part of Rio Grande potters.

The conscious adoption of glaze technology in the Rio Grande Valley has most commonly been explained through immigration from the Western Pueblo region (Reed 1949:169–70; Shepard 1942:197–99; Warren 1976), as a response to ritual developments sweeping over much of the Pueblo Southwest during the 1300s (Graves and Eckert 1998; Spielmann 1998), or as transformation in exchange networks (Habicht-Mauche 1995; Herhahn, chap. 10, this vol.; Snow 1981). Because glaze recipes and an oxidizing firing atmosphere must be learned either through trial and error or from another potter, the rapid appearance of glaze technology throughout much of the Rio Grande region as an apparently fully developed technique led early researchers to hypothesize the presence of Western Pueblo immigrants (Shepard 1942). More recent research has shown that glaze technology is not as difficult to learn as originally supposed (Herhahn 1995), and that massive immigration need not be used to explain its rapid spread throughout the Rio Grande region (Herhahn, chap. 10, this vol.).

Early glaze-painted vessels in the central Rio Grande region display iconic representations and distinctive slip-color combinations associated with the development and spread of a new ritual system in the early 1300s throughout much of the Pueblo world (E. C. Adams 1991; Crown 1994). Aspects of this new ritual system focused on fertility and community well-being, and may have helped to integrate newly aggregated populations (Crown 1994). Spielmann (1998:154) has argued that a new ideology and ritual practices were adopted in much of the Rio Grande area during this time and that large glaze-painted bowls were a necessary part of the communal feasting associated with this new ritual system. Graves and Eckert (1998) see the coinciding temporal and spatial distributions of glaze-painted pottery and a new rock art style, as well as a shared iconography between these material traits, as indications that residents of the central and lower Rio Grande regions were conveying messages concerning their participation in a new belief system.

The presence of glaze wares at some central Rio Grande sites may reflect the participation of villagers in regional and interregional exchange networks (Habicht-Mauche 1995; Nelson and Habicht-Mauche, chap. 11, this vol.; Snow 1981). Intervillage interaction established through exchange may have provided greater sociopolitical security during the massive demographic upheaval (Braun and Plog 1982) of the 1200s and 1300s. Participation in certain exchange networks may have marked participation in regional alliances. Spielmann (1994) has suggested that regional alliances, or clustered confederacies, developed in the protohistoric Rio Grande region between politically equivalent villages for limited purposes, such as mutual defense (Spielmann 1994: 50–51). However, regional ties need not have been formal alliances between pueblos (Habicht-Mauche 1995); rather, they may have been loose social relationships between individuals from separate villages who were bound by kinship ties, reciprocal social relations, recurring economic interactions, and/or ritual obligations.

Immigration, new ritual practice, and exchange are not mutually exclusive possibilities; as vessels may serve various utilitarian functions, so may they also be used in various social contexts. For example, glaze technology may have been associated with the adoption of a new ritual system, but immigrants from the Western Pueblo region may have introduced that ritual system. Similarly, glaze-painted vessels may reflect participation in exchange networks between villagers who were bound by similar belief systems. It is this possibility of glaze-painted pottery being associated with multiple social processes that I explore in the next section.

Black-on-White to Glaze-on-Red: The Case Studies

The Data Set

I examined data from three central Rio Grande sites (see fig. 1.2): Pueblo del Encierro (LA 70), Tijeras Pueblo (LA 581), and Hummingbird Pueblo (LA 578). For comparison, I also examined the northern Rio Grande site of Arroyo Hondo (LA 12). I relied on site reports from Pueblo del Encierro (Snow 1976; Warren 1976), Tijeras (Cordell 1975; Warren 1980), and Arroyo Hondo (Habicht-Mauche 1993a; Lang 1993; Olinger 1993). I was also able to personally examine the glaze ware assemblage from each of these three sites. Data from Hummingbird Pueblo come entirely from my own research at that village (Eckert 1999, 2001). These sites were chosen because they are contemporaneous, well reported, have well-defined ceramic seriations, and provided the data necessary for my analysis.

Although these sites all have complex occupation histories, it is the late-thirteenth- and fourteenth-century occupation at each site that I am concerned with here. At this time, Pueblo del Encierro consisted of at least seven pit rooms and an unknown number of associated surface rooms (Snow 1976). Tijeras Pueblo was initially occupied in the late 1200s and grew by accretion, so that by the 1360s this site consisted of approximately two hundred rooms (Cordell 1975). Arroyo Hondo had two fourteenth-century occupations, with a hiatus between them (Creamer 1993): Component 1 (AD 1300–1345) consisted of twenty-four roomblocks organized around ten plazas; Component 2 (AD 1370–1415) consisted of nine roomblocks organized around three plazas. This latter component is estimated to have had approximately two hundred rooms. Although Hummingbird Pueblo was occupied in the late thirteenth century, the size and layout of this early structure is uncertain. In the fourteenth century, Hummingbird Pueblo consisted of approximately two hundred rooms organized around at least three plazas (Eckert 1999; Eckert and Cordell 2004).

This study relies heavily on identifying decorative ceramic styles and

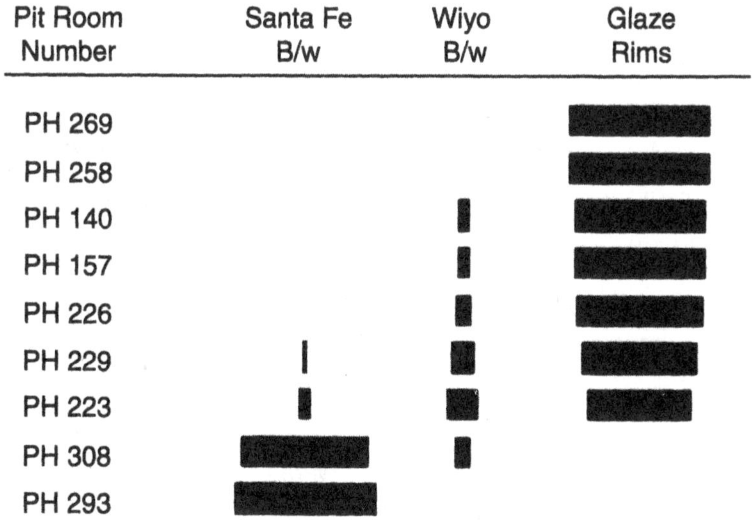

Pit Room Number	Santa Fe B/w	Wiyo B/w	Glaze Rims
PH 269			███
PH 258			███
PH 140		▮	███
PH 157		▮	███
PH 226		▮	███
PH 229	▮	▬	███
PH 223	▮	▬	███
PH 308	███	▮	
PH 293	███		

Fig. 9.1. Seriation of glaze rims (including early transitional, aberrant, Western Pueblo, and Glaze A) and most common black-on-white wares at Pueblo del Encierro, broken down by pithouse (from Warren 1976).

production proveniences. However, different archaeologists with different research questions analyzed the artifacts from each site (Eckert 2001; Habicht-Mauche 1993a; Warren 1976, 1980). As a result, the data are not entirely compatible. For example, Helene Warren (1976) combined transitional glaze ware, Western glaze ware, and Rio Grande Glaze A in her ceramic counts from Pueblo del Encierro, while Judith Habicht-Mauche (1993a) and Richard Lang (1993) separated these types from Arroyo Hondo. I have tried to control for these differences when possible and address such issues as they arise in the following analysis.

The White Ware to Glaze Ware Transition

There is considerable variation in how rapidly the glaze ware tradition replaced the white ware tradition at any particular village, or if it ever replaced it. Examination of ceramic seriations created for all four sites suggest it may be more appropriate to discuss how much the two traditions overlapped. Once introduced, glaze ware appears to have quickly replaced the local white ware at both Pueblo del Encierro (see fig. 9.1) and Hummingbird Pueblo (see fig. 9.2). At Arroyo Hondo and Tijeras, glaze ware never completely replaced white ware. Glaze ware eventually con-

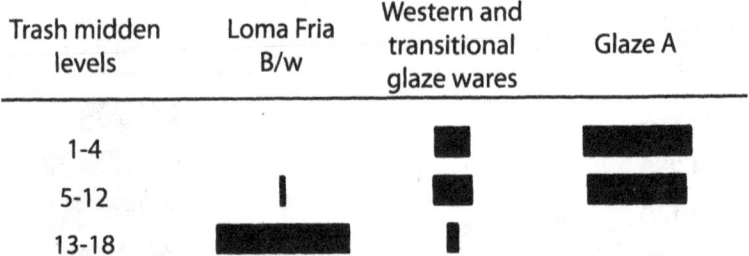

Fig. 9.2. Seriation of glaze wares and most common white wares at Hummingbird Pueblo (LA 578) (from Eckert 1999).

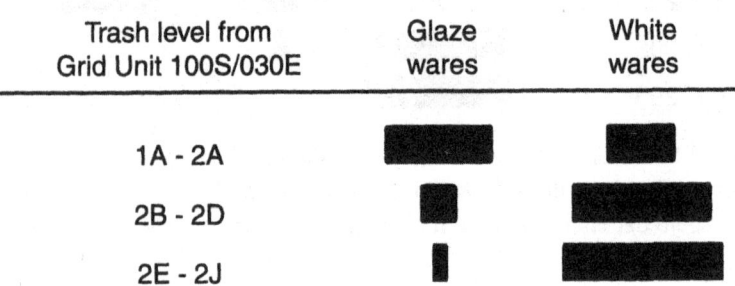

Fig. 9.3. Seriation of glaze wares (including Western glaze ware, transitional glaze ware, and Glaze A) and white wares at Tijeras Pueblo (LA 581) (adapted from Burtchard 1975).

stituted approximately 61 percent of the decorated pottery at Tijeras (see fig. 9.3). At Arroyo Hondo, glaze ware at its peak made up only about 20 percent of the decorated ceramic assemblage (see fig. 9.4).

Clearly, then, glaze technology was not wholeheartedly adopted once introduced into the Rio Grande Valley. As discussed above, the spread of glaze technology has been explained as the result of Western Pueblo immigrants moving into the region (Reed 1949:169–70; Shepard 1942:197–99; Warren 1976) or the adoption of a new ritual system by Rio Grande residents (Graves and Eckert 1998:279; Spielmann 1998). However, these explanations do not address why, at some sites, the local white ware tradition was dropped quickly and completely, while at other sites the white ware tradition continued. Understanding the variation in this shift in ceramic traditions requires closer scrutiny of the production and distribution of the wares at each site.

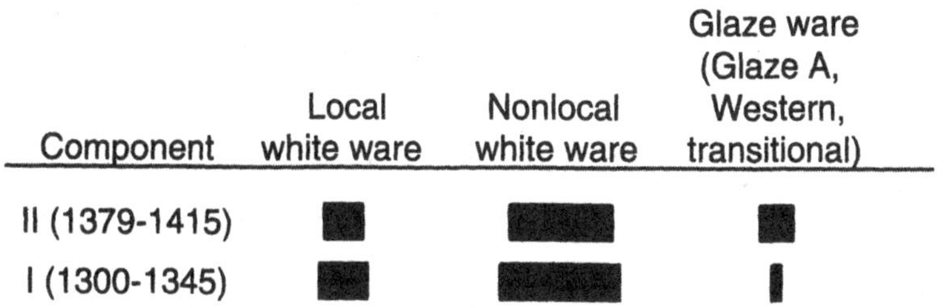

Component	Local white ware	Nonlocal white ware	Glaze ware (Glaze A, Western, transitional)
II (1379–1415)	■	■■	■
I (1300–1345)	■	■■	∣

Fig. 9.4. Seriation of Rio Grande glaze wares and white wares at Arroyo Hondo (LA 12), broken down by temporal components (adapted from Lang 1993; Habicht-Mauche 1993a, 1995).

Production Sources for the Black-on-White Types

The two most common white wares at Pueblo del Encierro were Santa Fe Black-on-white and Wiyo Black-on-white (Warren 1976). Warren (1976:B134) argued that "the variety of temper types suggests that most or all of Santa Fe Black-on-white vessels were intrusive to the pueblo" (table 9.1). Although Wiyo Black-on-white was primarily produced in the region north of the village, Warren argued that some of it *might* have been produced locally at Pueblo del Encierro (Warren 1976). This argument is based on the presence in some sherds of a dark-colored pumice temper similar to pumice found in the surrounding area.

Santa Fe Black-on-white, Wiyo Black-on-white, and Galisteo Black-on-white were all found at Tijeras Pueblo (Warren 1980). All of the Wiyo Black-on-white, and the occasional Galisteo Black-on-white and Santa Fe Black-on-white (Warren did not provide exact numbers in her report), are thought to have been exchanged. The majority of the white wares—Santa Fe Black-on-white and Galisteo Black-on-white—were produced locally (Warren 1980). The predominant temper in these types is quartz mica schist, mineralogically similar to the schist that occurs about one mile west of the site.

Only one common carbon-painted white ware, Loma Fria Black-on-white, was found at Hummingbird Pueblo. This type is almost exclusively tempered with sherd-tempered sherd and a combination of igneous and metamorphic rocks native to the clay (table 9.1) (Eckert 2001). The type shows a range of surface treatments, including well-polished slip, washy slip, and self-slip. Loma Fria Black-on-white is believed to have been made either at the thirteenth-century component of Hummingbird Pueblo, or at other nearby thirteenth-century sites.

Table 9.1
Percent Temper by Ceramic Type for Pueblo del Encierro,
Hummingbird Pueblo, and Arroyo Hondo

Temper	Ceramic Types		
	Pueblo del Encierro		
	Santa Fe B/w	Wiyo B/w	Glaze
Siltstone	21	0	0
Sherd and siltstone	14	2	0
Light pumice	34	0	1
Dark pumice (local?)	1	97	0
Sherd	27	1	11
Basalt (local)	0	0	87
Other	3	0	1

Temper	Hummingbird Pueblo		
	Loma Fria B/w	Western and transitional glaze wares	Glaze A
Olivine diabase	0	0	9
Mixed igneous rock	0	0	27
Pumice	0	4	9
Lithic sand	0	0	5
Sherd-tempered sherd	12	19	5
Sherd with mixed rocks (local)	88	78	45

Temper	Arroyo Hondo				
	Galisteo B/w	Santa Fe B/w	Rowe B/w	Wiyo B/w	Glaze A
Ashy clay	0	23	14	14	0
Lithic sand (local)	0	8	57	0	0
Pumiceous ash (local)	0	31	0	0	0
Ash	0	0	0	86	0
Basalt	0	0	0	0	0
Latite	0	0	0	0	6
Augite monzonite	43	0	0	0	24
Weathered igneous rock	43	0	0	0	19
Sherd-tempered sherd	14	15	29	0	16
Latite-tempered sherd	0	0	0	0	16
Basalt-tempered sherd	0	0	0	0	13
Other	0	23	0	0	6

Source: Compiled from Warren 1976, Eckert 2001, and Habicht-Mauche 1993a.

Habicht-Mauche (1993a) conducted an extensive study of the white wares at Arroyo Hondo that can only be briefly touched on here. Based on petrography (Habicht-Mauche 1993a) and x-ray fluorescence (Olinger 1993), she has argued that two white ware types were being locally produced at Arroyo Hondo: Rowe Black-on-white, *var. Poge*, which is tempered with lithic sand, and Santa Fe Black-on-white, *var. Pindi*, which is tempered with pumiceous ash (table 9.1). She argues that the presence of these two very different white ware traditions reflects the multiethnic composition of the population living within the village (Habicht-Mauche 1999). Other variants of Santa Fe Black-on-white, as well as Galisteo Black-on-white and Wiyo Black-on-white, found at Arroyo Hondo were produced elsewhere in the northern and central Rio Grande regions.

Production Sources for the Early Glaze Paint Vessels

Warren (1976) identified Rio Grande Glaze A (produced in the Rio Grande region), Western Pueblo Glaze Ware (produced in the Western Pueblo region), transitional glaze ware (produced in the Rio Grande region, but apparently copied from Western Pueblo Glaze Ware), and aberrant glaze ware (any glaze-painted sherd that does not fit into the recognized glaze ware typologies) at Pueblo del Encierro. She argued that the appearance of glaze paint at the site was the product of immigrants moving into the area, and that the high number of aberrant glaze ware sherds probably represented experimentation by Western Pueblo potters with local materials. In my reevaluation of glaze wares from the fourteenth-century pithouses at Pueblo del Encierro, I found only five sherds that could be classified as Western Pueblo Glaze Ware. Further, the classification of aberrant glaze ware included sherds with unusual rim forms, rims with no glaze decoration, misfired glaze paint, and the occasional truly aberrant or unusual glaze paint. Only these latter two categories suggest experimentation with new materials and, again, the number of these sherds is very low ($n = 13$). The vast majority of glaze wares found in the fourteenth-century component of Pueblo del Encierro are Rio Grande Glaze A sherds that were locally produced with crushed basalt temper (table 9.1).

Warren (1980) found that Western Pueblo Glaze Ware and transitional glaze ware make up approximately 20 percent of the glaze-decorated pottery at Tijeras, with the remainder of the glaze wares being Rio Grande Glaze A; my reevaluation of this assemblage confirms her findings. Half of the Rio Grande Glaze A, as well as the transitional glaze ware, are tempered with the same mica schist as the local white ware and assumed to have been produced locally (Warren 1980). (However, recent petrographic analysis by Habicht-Mauche and Ginn [2004] suggest that much of the transitional glaze ware at Tijeras may have been coming from the lower Rio Puerco.) Most (Warren did not provide exact numbers in her report) of the remainder of the Rio Grande Glaze A are tempered with crushed basalt that Warren (1980) believed was exchanged from pueblos located in the Albuquerque area. However, basalt tempers come from a variety of locations, including the lower Rio Puerco around Hidden Mountain, the Rio Abajo south of the modern town of Belen, around the modern town of Bernalillo, and from the Cochiti area on the west side of the Rio Grande.

Western Pueblo Glaze Ware, transitional glaze ware, and Rio Grande Glaze A have all been identified at Hummingbird Pueblo (Eckert 2003). The earliest glaze assemblage at Hummingbird Pueblo consists only of Western Pueblo Glaze Ware. The majority of transitional glaze ware and almost half of the Rio Grande Glaze A are tempered with the same material as the carbon-painted white ware that they replace—a mix of sherd-tempered sherd and rock native to the clay (table 9.1). Further, these locally produced glaze wares exhibit the same combination of surface treatments as the previously produced white ware—that is, a combination of well-polished slips, washy slips, and self-slips (Eckert 2001). This suggests that the indigenous potters adopted glaze ware technology, as Western Pueblo potters almost always produced their glaze ware with thick, well-polished slips (Carlson 1970). Finally, the majority of nonlocal Rio Grande Glaze A pottery is tempered with mixed igneous rock sourced to Hidden Mountain and believed to have been exchanged from Pottery Mound, a village about twenty miles south of Hummingbird Pueblo (Eckert 2001).

The majority of glaze ware vessels from Arroyo Hondo are Rio Grande Glaze A, although trace amounts of Western Pueblo Glaze Ware, transitional glaze ware, and Rio Grande Glaze B were also recovered from the site (Habicht-Mauche 1993a:21). None of these recovered glaze wares were produced at the site, but instead were produced in at least three archaeological districts south of Arroyo Hondo (Habicht-Mauche 1995). Although changes in exchange networks are suggested by changes in both nonlocal temper materials (table 9.1) and the percentage of glaze ware coming into the site through time (Habicht-Mauche 1995), at no time did the residents of Arroyo Hondo produce their own glaze ware.

Design Style and Iconography

Design style and iconography have been central in arguments for immigration, as well as in interpretations in favor of the adoption of a new ritual system in the Rio Grande region. Ceramic vessels identified as "Western Pueblo copies" produced with local materials, or transitional glaze ware as discussed above, have been presented as evidence of immigrant potters living within Rio Grande villages. These "copies" often have a different internal logic in terms of design layout, motif repetitions, and exterior design elements when compared to the locally produced white ware that they replace (Eckert 2003). This argument extends from the assumption that only immigrants familiar with western decorative techniques could have successfully produced nearly identical copies of Western Pueblo pottery (see chaps. 4 and 10, this volume, for expansions of this argument). The introduction of an entirely new suite of decorative motifs, along with glaze technology, has been used as evidence to support the notion that glaze-painted pottery was associated with a new ritual system (Eckert 2003; Graves and Eckert 1998). The logic behind this argument lies in the assumption that such icons were used either to signal participation in a new ritual system, as daily reminders to newly converted participants, or both.

A systematic design analysis has been performed only on pottery from Hummingbird Pueblo (Eckert 2003) and Arroyo Hondo (Habicht-Mauche 1993a). At Hummingbird Pueblo, locally produced white ware was predominantly decorated with banded design layouts divided into simple paneled sections. Geometric designs with solid filler were the most common elements used to fill these sections. Although many of the glaze-painted vessels were decorated with a layout similar to the black-on-white vessels, a new suite of icons was detected on the glaze-painted pottery. These icons included eyes, serpents, clouds, lightning, birds, feathers, and masked figures—all icons associated with new ideological developments believed to be spreading across the Pueblo world at this time (E. C. Adams 1991; Crown 1994).

At Arroyo Hondo, white wares were predominantly decorated with either banded designs or pendent figure layouts (Habicht-Mauche 1993a: 47–53). Geometric designs with both solid and hatched filler were the most common design elements, although birds and eyes were present on some black-on-white vessels. Glaze-painted sherds with identifiable de-

Table 9.2
Summary of Data Discussed in Chapter

	Pueblo del Encierro	Tijeras Pueblo	Hummingbird Pueblo	Arroyo Hondo
Highest obtained glaze percentage	100%	61%	100%	20%
White ware source	nonlocal	mostly local	mostly local	mostly nonlocal
Western and transitional glaze wares present?	trace amounts	yes	yes	trace amounts
Glaze A source	local	50% local 50% nonlocal	50% local 50% nonlocal	nonlocal
New suite of icons	unknown	unknown	yes	no

signs were rare at Arroyo Hondo, but appear to have been most commonly painted in a pendent design layout. Design elements seem to have been similar to those on the white wares.

Summary

The patterning associated with the introduction of glaze technology at each examined village varies (table 9.2). Three of the four sites examined produced their own glaze-decorated pottery, while the residents of Arroyo Hondo received all of their glaze-painted vessels through exchange. There is also no correlation between the transition to glaze technology at a site and the continued production of white wares: the residents of Tijeras Pueblo and Arroyo Hondo continued to produce white wares, while the residents of Hummingbird Pueblo and Pueblo del Encierro stopped production. All four sites had at least a few transitional glaze ware sherds (or "copies" of Western Pueblo glaze ware); however, Tijeras Pueblo and Hummingbird Pueblo had substantially more than the other two sites examined. The glaze ware vessels at Hummingbird Pueblo appear to be decorated with a suite of icons not present on the previous local white ware tradition, while few icons were recorded on the glaze wares from Arroyo Hondo; unfortunately, similar data concerning ceramic decoration is currently unavailable from Tijeras Pueblo and Pueblo del Encierro.

The Adoption of Glaze-Painted Pottery in the Central Rio Grande Area

The relationship between design style, technology, production source, and social behavior is exceedingly complex. Clearly, however, glaze technology was adopted differently at different villages within the central Rio Grande region and cannot be explained simply through the presence of immigrants, the adoption of a new ritual system, or the creation and maintenance of exchange networks. Instead, the presence of glaze technology at any one village was the result of the complex web of social interactions that reflected villagers' attempts to negotiate the complex, and often contradictory, dynamics of a newly formed social landscape. The data presented here allows for evaluation of the association of glaze technology with these three interrelated social processes.

Immigrants and Diverse Social Groups

Each newly settled village must have comprised a different combination of social, ethnic, and linguistic groups. Evidence for diverse populations is found at each of the pueblos examined above. For example, Habicht-Mauche (1993a, 1999) argues that Arroyo Hondo was composed of various indigenous groups struggling to find a compromise between village integration and maintenance of multiethnic identities. I have argued elsewhere (Eckert 2003) that the residents of Hummingbird Pueblo were immigrants from the Western Pueblo region as well as indigenous groups. Based on the finding that there are few decorative or technical similarities between the indigenous carbon-painted and newly adopted glaze-painted traditions at Pueblo del Encierro, Warren (1976) argued that the presence of glaze wares at this village was the result of immigrants. There are technical similarities between the glaze-painted pottery at Pueblo del Encierro and glaze-painted pottery produced in the region south of the site (Warren 1976). Thus, it is plausible that a new social group of potters from outside the immediate area moved into the pueblo during the 1300s, bringing a Rio Grande glaze ceramic tradition with them. Although the question of immigration into Tijeras Pueblo has not been systematically explored, the substantial presence (20 percent of glaze wares) of Western Pueblo and locally produced transitional glaze wares (or Western Pueblo copies) at this site suggests the potential presence of Western Pueblo immigrants living within the village alongside an indigenous, white ware-producing group.

Ritual Practice

It appears that as immigrants and indigenous groups were moving over the landscape, new ritual practices were moving with them (Eckert and Cordell 2004; Graves and Spielmann 2000; Spielmann 1998). The glaze ware vessels at Hummingbird Pueblo are decorated with a suite of icons not present on the previous local white ware. This suite of icons has been related to a southwestern regional earth/fertility cult that coalesced from earlier traditions during the large-scale migrations of the late 1200s and early 1300s (Crown 1994). Whether this ritual system was adopted wholesale at Hummingbird Pueblo from another region (possibly along with immigrants moving into the village), or was the result of residents selecting aspects from a broader suite of pan-Pueblo concepts, is difficult to know without comparative data from other sites. The evidence suggests, however, that both immigrants and indigenous residents of Hummingbird Pueblo readily adopted aspects of a new ritual system and that glaze-decorated pottery played a role in this new system.

There is no evidence for the introduction of a new suite of icons on glaze ware bowls at Arroyo Hondo. Further, as discussed above, Spielmann (1998:154) argues that an important aspect of the new ritual system adopted in much of the central and lower Rio Grande regions included communal feasting. She examined bowl rim sizes from six Rio Grande sites, arguing that glaze-painted bowls should exhibit a bimodal distribution in size within villages where community feasting was practiced, with larger bowls being the ones used in feasts. Arroyo Hondo is the only site in her sample where glaze ware bowls do not exhibit a bimodal size distribution. This village seems to have had only small glaze ware bowls, suggesting that they did not participate in the feasting activities in which large glaze bowls were used (Spielmann 1998:257). Unfortunately, similar data concerning ceramic decoration and bowl size is unavailable from Pueblo del Encierro and Tijeras Pueblo; however, the data presented in this chapter indicate that residents of these two villages adopted glaze wares differently than residents of Hummingbird Pueblo or Arroyo Hondo, suggesting that different social, and possibly ritual, processes were at work in each village.

Exchange Networks

The exchange of glaze-painted vessels between villages suggests that these vessels also played a role in intervillage social dynamics. Aggregation into villages, along with immigration within and between regions, would have had important consequences for intervillage social networks. Immigrants would not have had as large a kin-based network available to them in their new residence as they once did in their traditional homeland. Similarly, local groups aggregated into large villages would have found that access to some social networks required more time and effort than they once did.

Habicht-Mauche (1993a, 1995) has argued that the presence of glaze wares at Arroyo Hondo, along with nonlocal white ware, was the result of village residents participating in regional and interregional exchange networks. These networks were part of a broader system of interaction that linked various villages in the northern and central Rio Grande valleys and helped to stabilize intervillage relations. Although Arroyo Hondo was the only site examined where glaze wares were acquired exclusively through exchange, many of the glaze-painted vessels at the other three sites in this study were also acquired through participation in trade networks. The data presented here cannot provide details concerning the nature of these trade networks; however, the different percentages of exchanged vessels, along with the variation in exchange partners, suggests that residents at each village participated in regional and interregional interactions both at different scales and intensities. Further, as noted by Nelson and Habicht-Mauche (chap. 11, this vol.), the nature of such interactions changed over time.

Conclusions

Glaze-decorated pottery in the early Pueblo IV period in the central Rio Grande appears to have articulated with different, and multiple, social processes at each village examined. This period was marked by the movement of different sociolinguistic groups between various villages, working and reworking different aspects of ritual, social organization, and political structure. As a result, it was a period of social, political, and ideological uncertainty. It should not be surprising, then, that the articulation between glaze-painted pottery and these various social processes was dynamic and fluid. As a result, the ceramic data collected by archaeologists, at best, often seem to reflect multiple scales of social processes and, at worst, seem contradictory. This is because ceramic data reflect the struggle of each potter on a daily basis to negotiate various social strategies concerning her family, ethnic group, ritual society, and exchange networks within a socioreligious system that was not static but involved continued maintenance and re-creation.

Acknowledgments

An earlier version of this chapter, entitled "Black-on-White to Glaze-on-Red: Community Formation and Transformation in the Middle Rio Grande," was presented at the Sixty-seventh Annual Meeting for the Society for American Archaeology in Denver, Colorado. The chapter has benefited greatly from comments provided by various authors in this volume as well as several anonymous reviewers. I am most grateful to Deborah Huntley, Judith Habicht-Mauche, and Linda Cordell for insightful comments and discussion on issues pertaining directly to this chapter. Anthony Thibodeau of the Laboratory of Anthropology in Santa Fe graciously provided access to the Pueblo del Encierro collections despite my request coming at the last minute. I am also grateful to Michael Lewis of the Maxwell Museum for providing access to portions of the Tijeras and Hummingbird Pueblo collections, as well as the School of American Research for providing access to the Arroyo Hondo collection. Analysis of the Hummingbird Pueblo data was funded by grants from the Arizona State University Graduate College and the National Science Foundation, whose support is gratefully acknowledged.

10

Inferring Social Interactions from Pottery Recipes

Rio Grande Glaze Paint Composition and Cultural Transmission

Cynthia L. Herhahn

The development of Rio Grande glaze paint technology from the late thirteenth to seventeenth century has intrigued southwestern archaeologists since the 1910s. Part of the enduring interest stems from the craftsmanship and artistry evident in the vessels, but a large part stems from the possibility of addressing broader anthropological questions of technology transfer, social interaction, migration, and the contexts in which these occur. The spatial and temporal patterning in glaze paint "recipes" holds clues to the nature of social interactions, the possibility of population movements, and the social and economic contexts of production and consumption of glaze paint pottery. Fundamentally, the issues addressed in this chapter include the hoary dichotomy of migration versus diffusion, although more nuanced than the 1950s version.

Here I will examine similarities and differences in glaze paint preparation and firing techniques, which constitute recipes for producing a glaze vessel, to suggest which of the two related processes of migration and diffusion through social interaction dominated the observed transfer of technology. In this chapter, I use compositional analysis of glaze paints to trace the spread of glaze paint technology from west to east and then follow the trajectory of glaze paint recipe development in the Rio Grande Valley to its eventual establishment as a fixed recipe sometime after AD 1450. Based on the spatial and temporal structure of the changes in glaze paint composition, which is the result of interplay of paint ingredients and firing techniques, I argue that levels of intergroup transmission of knowledge were high during the fourteenth and fifteenth centuries, suggesting intense social interaction among glaze-paint-producing villages. I will argue further that this interaction had much to do with the demographic upheaval of the fourteenth century and that intergroup interaction was both a necessary precondition to, and a consequence of, migration on a household scale (cf. Cordell 1995; Duff 1998). After AD 1450 the overwhelming homogeneity in glaze paint recipes still indicates high intergroup transmission, but the context of that transmission changes from residential mobility and demographic fluidity to maintaining an economic system based on specialization and intraregional trade operating within a ritual context (Snow 1981; Spielmann 1998).

Cultural Transmission, Intergroup Interaction, and Migration

The late 1200s to the 1600s in the northern Southwest was a time of significant changes in demography, social networks, and decorated ceramic traditions. Technological aspects of ceramic traditions can be particularly fruitful in tracking and understanding the more significant social changes because the spread of glaze paint technology is a clear case of cultural transmission of technology, or in Lemonnier's terms, "technical borrowing" (Lemonnier 1993:21). Technological attributes tend to have low visibility (Carr 1995) and are often directly observable only during the production process, thus making it difficult to replicate the process without some knowledge of it. This makes the study of technology transfer particularly useful for examining patterns of migration and intergroup interaction occurring within a ritual or economic context. In the view presented here, migration and interaction (or diffusion) are complementary rather than contradictory processes. Clearly, as recent research on migration has pointed out, migrating groups do not choose to relocate to areas about which they have no knowledge (Anthony 1990; Brown and Sanders 1981; Burmeister 2000; Cameron 1995; Cordell 1995; Duff 1998). In general, groups migrate to areas with which they are familiar either because some members of the group have visited in the past or because they have contact with groups or individuals living in the area from whom they can obtain information. These two situations entail some degree of social interaction between resident groups and potential immigrant groups.

This connection between social interaction, which can engender diffusion of ideas and technology, and immigration further blurs the distinction made between these two processes, and provides additional explanation for the persistent problems in identifying migrations in prehistory (Cordell 1995) aside from those identified as "site-unit intrusions." However, as recent treatments of migration have argued, migrations are quite common in human societies (Anthony 1990; Cameron 1995; Lekson 1996), an observation corroborated by modern Pueblo views on migration (Naranjo 1995). Thus, it is likely that migration was an important factor in the spread of glaze paint technology, but perhaps not significantly more important than diffusion, as migration is unlikely to occur without social interaction and information exchange, which are linchpins in the process of diffusion. Because of the considerable overlap in the material record of migration and diffusion, and the improbability that one would occur without the other, my arguments for social interaction and diffusion do not dismiss migration as one process by which glaze paint technology spread. Evidence for diffusion of glaze paint technology supports the claim that the preconditions for migration were in place (i.e., knowledge of or familiarity with the area and current inhabitants), but the data are insufficient to argue that migration actually occurred.

Glaze Paint Pottery, Regional Cults, Migration, and Transmission

Rio Grande Glaze Paint Technology

The Rio Grande glaze paints from central New Mexico are not "true glazes" in that they do not constitute a coating of glass over the entire surface of the vessel (Rice 1987). These glaze paints are lead-based paints that are applied as a decoration rather than a coating like Near Eastern and Chinese glazes and frits (Biek and Bayley 1979; Hatcher et al. 1994; Hedges and Moorey 1975; A. Lane 1947; Redford and Blackman 1997; Shangraw 1977). This distinction is significant because the technology of an allover glaze is more complex than that of decorative glaze paint and requires a different kind of recipe. Glaze coatings have a specific range of recipes that involve the addition of silica, which forms the network of a glaze; alumina, which strengthens the network, preventing it from running; and colorants, which add or change the color of the fired glaze. These mixtures are then fired in complex kilns under well-controlled firing conditions. Based on observations on thin sections of Rio Grande glaze paint pottery and replication and laboratory experiments (Herhahn and Blinman 1999), I argue that these paints were produced through a different, less formal technology than glaze coatings, and that the technology was a modification and recombination of techniques with a history of use by Rio Grande potters. This is evident in the use of mineral pigments and in some aspects of firing technology, both of which are explored briefly following a description of decorative glaze paint production.

Based on experimental data, I believe Rio Grande glaze paint was produced using a mixture of manganese, copper, or lead applied to slipped vessels, then wood fired only once in a relatively informal pit or platform. Firing temperatures are estimated to have ranged from approximately 700° to 900° centigrade (Shepard 1956/1980). At these temperatures, the paint begins to melt. This occurs because, in general, oxides of metals such as manganese, copper, and lead, melt at relatively low temperatures, and the addition of these oxides to silica and alumina often lowers the melting points of these otherwise refractory materials. Once a melt forms, the liquid phase dissolves the underlying slip. This process is indicated by examination of petrographic thin sections in which the glaze/slip interface is visible, and is supported by experiments (Herhahn and Blinman 1999) conducted on test tiles painted with nothing more than powdered galena (PbS) and water. When analyzed for composition, the fired paints contained silica, alumina, iron, and other elements not found in galena but found in red-firing clays, suggesting that these constituents became incorporated into the glaze during firing. Therefore, I believe that much of the silica and alumina found in Rio Grande glaze paints is the result of the interaction of these metallic colorants and the clay slip to which they are applied. The implication is that the postfiring glaze paint composition is likely to differ significantly in silica and alumina content from the actual paint recipe applied to the prefired vessel, and that the "recipe" to which I refer in this chapter is actually the outcome of a combination of the paint mixture and choice of firing techniques, particularly those influencing atmosphere, maximum temperature, and soak time.

Several steps in the production process described above have precedents in earlier Rio Grande pottery production. In terms of materials, mineral pigments were in use for centuries on types such as Lino Black-on-gray and Kwahe'e Black-on-white prior to the adoption of carbon paint around AD 1150 with the advent of Santa Fe Black-on-white. Mineral-painted Chupadero Black-on-white continued to be produced in the Rio Abajo as late as AD 1545 (Hayes, Young, and Warren 1981:72). Firing technology for glaze-painted red wares differs from black-on-white technology only in firing atmosphere. Red wares were fired in a relatively oxygen rich atmosphere, while Rio Grande white wares were fired in a neutral to oxygen-poor atmosphere. However, the firing facilities appear to be similar between Santa Fe Black-on-white and later glaze wares.

Excavated Santa Fe Black-on-white pit kilns are "shallow, oval basins" measuring approximately 1.6–1.7 m long by 1.1 m wide, with depth ranging from 9 to 26 cm (Post and Lakatos 1995:145). Glaze ware firing areas have been identified on the surface at the Galisteo Basin site of San Lazaro, but these have not been excavated. Based on surface observations, they are similar in size and shape, and differ only in depth and the lack of a "smothering layer" in the glaze ware firing areas (Eric Blinman, personal communication 2003). It is beyond the scope of this chapter to compare in detail the *chaîne opératoire* (Lemonnier 1993) of black-on-white and glaze wares, but this brief discussion indicates that there are precedents in the Rio Grande for several key aspects of glaze ware production. This suggests that the change in technology was an adaptation of existing techniques rather than a dramatic change to an entirely different suite of techniques. The major changes involved the choice of particular mineral pigments, the clays that would fire to the strong reds seen in early Rio Grande glaze wares, and the combination of previously known techniques that would produce the desired effect of a vitreous black paint on a red background. The point to be made here is that the transfer of technology among southwestern potters involved both aesthetics and knowledge of materials and techniques. The particular suite of techniques to produce black glaze on a red vessel may have been developed in the Western Pueblo area and been introduced *as a suite* into the Rio Grande, but it was a suite that was compatible with existing production processes and therefore relatively likely to be adopted and adapted (cf. Lemonnier 1993).

Spread of Glaze Paint Technology

Broad regional patterning in the composition of southwestern glaze paints was identified almost sixty years ago (Hawley 1938; Shepard 1942; Snow 1982), as copper glaze was produced in eastern Arizona and western New Mexico and lead glaze in central New Mexico (also see chaps. 4 and 6 in this vol.). The temporal and spatial patterning has been interpreted as evidence for technological transfer, and perhaps migration, from west to east. In many interpretations, glaze paint technology was discovered accidentally and then developed into skilled artistry in eastern Arizona during the thirteenth century (Carlson 1970; De Atley 1986; Kidder 1917a; Mera 1935). Rio Grande potters "learned" the technology from Zuni area potters (Shepard 1936, 1942; Warren 1981; Wendorf and Reed 1955), who learned it from the upper Little Colorado potters. In this scenario, Rio Grande potters did not develop the technology on their own, but learned it from others farther to the west through some kind of interaction. As Huntley's (chap. 6, this vol.) lead isotope data and Eckert's (chap. 9, this vol.) decorative and technological style data show, this scenario is overly simplistic. It appears that glaze-paint-producing groups in the northern Southwest were alternately innovators and recipients of technology within a system of social interactions on both local and regional scales.

A possible context in which this interaction could have occurred is developed by Patricia Crown and involves the spread of a regional cult represented in ceramics by the spread of the Pinedale style (Crown 1994). Implicit in this model for the spread of red-slipped glaze-painted ceramics is a certain level of intergroup interaction on a pan-northern Southwest scale. In Crown's formulation, the regional cult facilitated intraregional migration by downplaying cultural differences between resident and immigrant groups. Crown's model is significant because it incorporates both migration, which may have brought western potters to the Rio Grande, and the social use of glaze paint pottery, the technology of which allows examination of the different degrees to which the technological knowledge was successfully transmitted among different pottery-producing communities in the Rio Grande Valley. Higher degrees of similarity are to be expected with migration, a situation in which interaction and cultural transmission of technological knowledge are more direct than in a context of occasional face-to-face interaction or word-of-mouth transmission. The data presented here are used to examine how successfully the technology transferred, resulting in highly similar paint recipes suggestive of migration versus less direct transmission, resulting in highly variable recipes suggestive of less direct interaction or diffusion.

Methodology. The ceramic data used in this analysis come primarily from earlier analyses on Rio Grande glaze paint pottery by Herhahn and Huntley (Herhahn 1995; Herhahn and Huntley 1996; Huntley and Herhahn

1996). Suzanne De Atley's (1986) published glaze paint compositional data of Fourmile Polychrome were also used in the current analysis. The reader is referred to De Atley's pioneering study (De Atley 1986) for the methodology by which those data were collected.

The Rio Grande Glaze Ware ceramics investigated by Herhahn and Huntley and used in this study are from excavations conducted by Katherine Spielmann of Arizona State University at Gran Quivira and Quarai, two pueblos in the Salinas area east of the Rio Grande Valley, New Mexico, that were occupied from the 1300s to the late 1600s. The Salinas area falls outside of the Rio Grande Valley proper, but prehistoric populations are affiliated culturally with the Rio Grande based on decorated ceramic types and architectural layout and style. Petrographic analyses (Capone 1995; Herhahn 1996; Warren 1981) suggest that Quarai was a significant producer of glaze wares during the 1500s, but had access to glaze-decorated ceramics produced in other Rio Grande pueblos throughout its occupation. Gran Quivira was never a major producer of glaze-decorated ceramics, but did import large quantities of pottery from other pueblos (Herhahn 1996; Warren 1981). Thus, the sample of Rio Grande Glaze Ware ceramics analyzed for this study represents ceramics produced throughout the Rio Grande, although their archaeological provenance is limited to the Salinas area.

Because of the importance of the spatial and temporal variations in glaze paint composition to understanding the spread of glaze paint technology, division of the sample by temporally diagnostic rim form and spatially diagnostic paste/temper characteristics was carried out prior to sampling for compositional analysis. Thus, Spielmann's collections from the Salinas area, which had been sorted by rim form into Rio Grande Glaze Ware groups A through F (as defined by Mera 1933; see Eckert, chap. 3, in this vol.), were sampled for compositional analysis. The provenance of each rim sherd was determined through visual examination of tempering materials, informed and guided by ceramic petrography (Herhahn 1995, 1996; D. L. Jones 1995). Examination of the ceramic paste allowed each sherd to be related to a production area within the Rio Grande Valley by referencing the materials observed to those observed by other researchers (Capone 1995; Habicht-Mauche 1993a; Shepard 1942; Warren 1979, 1980, 1981). The general locations of these production areas are indicated in figures 1.1 and 1.2. Grog temper is associated with the Albuquerque and Acoma areas; augite latite (equivalent to Herhahn's "augite diorite"

[1996]) with the Galisteo Basin, probably San Marcos; Tonque andesite with Tonque Pueblo; vitric basalt with the Lower Rio Puerco; hornblende diorite with Ábo and hornblende gneiss with Quarai, both or which are in the Salinas area (Capone 1995; Shepard 1942; Warren 1979, 1981).

Although tempering material in Rio Grande Glaze Ware is generally indicative of production area, there are also temporal changes in tempering material. For most Rio Grande glaze groups, the rim form itself is the most temporally diagnostic attribute. However, Glaze A, which falls at the beginning of the Rio Grande Glaze Ware sequence and dates between AD 1315 and 1425, also shows temporal variation in tempering material. Based on stylistic and stratigraphic information, grog temper appears in the earliest glaze wares produced in the Rio Grande Valley, Los Padillas Glaze Polychrome, which dates to as early as AD 1300 (Shepard 1942; Warren 1979). The use of grog temper continues with the production of Agua Fria Glaze-on-red, which is also produced with mineral temper. Other Glaze A types (Cieneguilla Glaze-on-yellow, Pottery Mound Glaze Polychrome, San Clemente Polychrome) are produced almost exclusively with mineral temper, a trend that continues throughout the remainder of the glaze sequence. As with most temporal transitions in any diagnostic attribute, the transition from grog to mineral temper is not abrupt, and it is not possible to distinguish unequivocally early and late Glaze A purely on the basis of temper. However, because the initial production of Rio Grande glaze wares is critical to the understanding of the development of this technology, it is important to consider them separately.

It should also be noted that only five Glaze B sherds were analyzed, owing to the rarity of this group in the collections we used. Glaze B data are presented here, but are of little utility in making temporal inferences about technological change. The potential problems associated with excluding Glaze B from a discussion of temporal trends in glaze paint composition are mitigated by the more restricted geographical distribution and short duration of Glaze B production (Mera 1933; Eckert, chap. 3, this vol.).

Following the characterization of Spielmann's collections of glaze rim sherds from Gran Quivira and Quarai ($n = 1,600$) by rim form and temper and paste characteristics, a sample of 143 Glaze A through F bowl rim sherds tempered with six distinct materials was selected for compositional analysis of the glaze paint. The sample was analyzed by the author and Deborah Huntley for a number of studies conducted between 1994 and 1996 (Herhahn 1995; Herhahn and Huntley 1996; D. L. Jones 1995).

Glaze composition was measured using an electron microprobe housed in the Arizona State University Chemistry Department. The percentages by weight of ten different glaze constituents, determined as mineral oxides, were measured for each sample by wavelength dispersive spectroscopy (WDS). WDS was chosen over energy dispersive spectroscopy (EDS) because WDS is able to distinguish between lead and sulfur, the two elements that combine to form galena, the likely material used in producing paints. The disadvantage of using WDS is that the number of WDS spectrometers on the ASU microprobe limited the number of elements that could be analyzed at one time. Because of this limitation, several elements that are sometimes present in small quantities were eliminated from the analysis. The most notable of these is zinc (Deborah Huntley, personal communication, 1995). The data collected by Herhahn and Huntley were renormalized to be consistent with De Atley's (1986) data from Fourmile Ruin, which did not include data for titanium dioxide (TiO_2). This was done by eliminating the data for TiO_2, then renormalizing to 100 percent. The weight percent data were then converted to molecular proportion to eliminate the effect of different molecular weights. This conversion involved dividing the normalized weight percent of each oxide by the molecular weight of that oxide, then normalizing to 1. The effect of this conversion gives each oxide equal weight in the analysis, rather than allowing heavier oxides to dominate.

Since multivariate analyses (Herhahn 1995) showed that most of the structure in the data was provided by lead oxide (PbO), copper oxide (CuO), manganese oxide (MnO), and silicon dioxide (SiO_2), only the oxides added as paint ingredients (PbO, CuO, MnO) are discussed here. To examine the spatial and temporal patterning in the various paint constituents, a series of log-log scale bivariate plots of molecular proportions or ratios of molecular proportions were created. Ratios of PbO to MnO and PbO to CuO were chosen to plot so that the relationship among the three variables could be represented in a bivariate plot, rather than a triangular plot. The log-log scale was chosen to spread the data points out more evenly along the axes to facilitate pattern identification. Additional categorical variables were introduced into each plot by varying the plot symbol of each data point to reflect provenance or temporal period.

Results. The first relationship explored is the association, if any, between glaze paint tradition (e.g., Fourmile Polychrome, Zuni glazes, early Rio Grande glazes, later Rio Grande glazes) and the choice of colorant. This

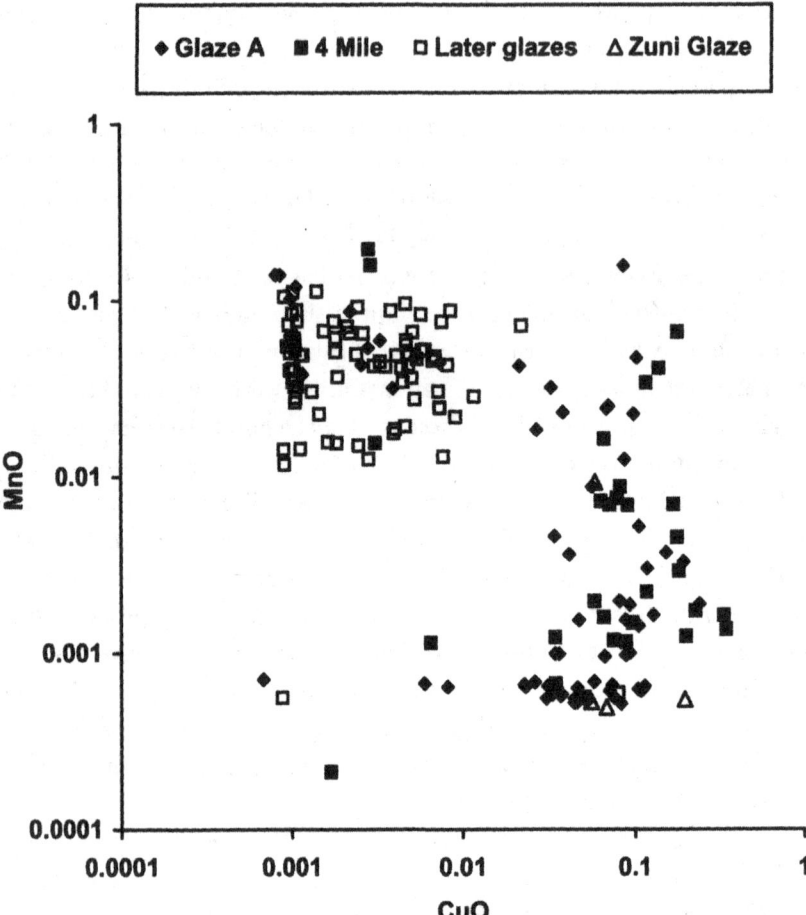

Fig. 10.1. Mol proportion of manganese oxide plotted against mol proportion of copper oxide, each on a log scale. Pottery types represented include Rio Grande Glaze A, Fourmile Polychrome, later Rio Grande Glaze Ware (B–F), and Zuni Glaze Ware.

was accomplished by means of a bivariate plot (see fig. 10.1) of the molecular proportion of MnO to CuO, with each data point plotted with a symbol indicating the group to which it belongs. De Atley's Fourmile Polychrome samples exhibit some variability, but mostly plot in the copper-rich part of the graph (the right third of the plot). This colorant strategy is also used by a large proportion of the Glaze A paints in the sample, and by the small number of Zuni glaze wares in the sample. A second colorant strategy is used by a smaller proportion of the Glaze A potters and all of the later Rio Grande glaze producers. This strategy involves the use of manganese as a colorant and the near exclusion of copper.

At first glance, it is tempting to interpret the use of copper as a colorant by Rio Grande potters as evidence for a high level of intergroup transmission between western glaze producers here represented by a few examples of Zuni glaze wares and Fourmile Polychrome. However, there is more to glaze production that just colorant. The fluxing agent is also extremely important. I have argued elsewhere (Herhahn and Blinman 1999) that the basic glaze recipe in Rio Grande glaze wares involves powdered galena as the flux, with an added colorant, either copper or manganese. When the flux component of the glaze paint recipe is factored in, it is apparent that the recipe used to produce most Zuni and Rio Grande glaze wares is distinct from Fourmile Polychromes. This is shown in a bivariate scatter plot (see fig. 10.2) of the ratio of manganese to lead versus the ratio of copper to lead on a log-log scale. The latter tend to be lower in lead than the Rio Grande glaze paints (see Fenn, Mills, and Hopkins, chap. 4, this vol.). This suggests that although the copper-rich colorant strategy appears to derive from a far western model, early Rio Grande glaze producers use a recipe more similar to that of Zuni glaze wares, although slightly more rich in lead (see Huntley, chap. 6, this vol.).

An additional deviation from the western colorant model and Zuni paint recipe is also seen in Glaze A paints on vessels with several different types of mineral temper, some from the Galisteo Basin and some from the central Rio Grande Valley. This deviation involves use of manganese-lead paint rather than copper-lead paint. This paint recipe came into use during the production of mineral-tempered Glaze A, which may place it slightly later than sherd-tempered Glaze A, perhaps the later 1300s. Following the invention of manganese-lead paints in the late 1300s, nearly all cases in our sample, which includes more than seven production areas, use this basic recipe containing manganese and lead (see figs. 10.2 and 10.3).

This pattern suggests the rapid and complete adoption of the general PbO/MnO recipe. Figure 10.3 shows the temporal trends by production area. In this log-log plot of the ratio of MnO to PbO plotted against the ratio of CuO to PbO, the production areas that engaged in glaze production of more than two glaze rim forms are shown. The initials in parentheses after each glaze rim form indicate the production area. "AD" indicates likely production in the area of San Marcos Pueblo in the

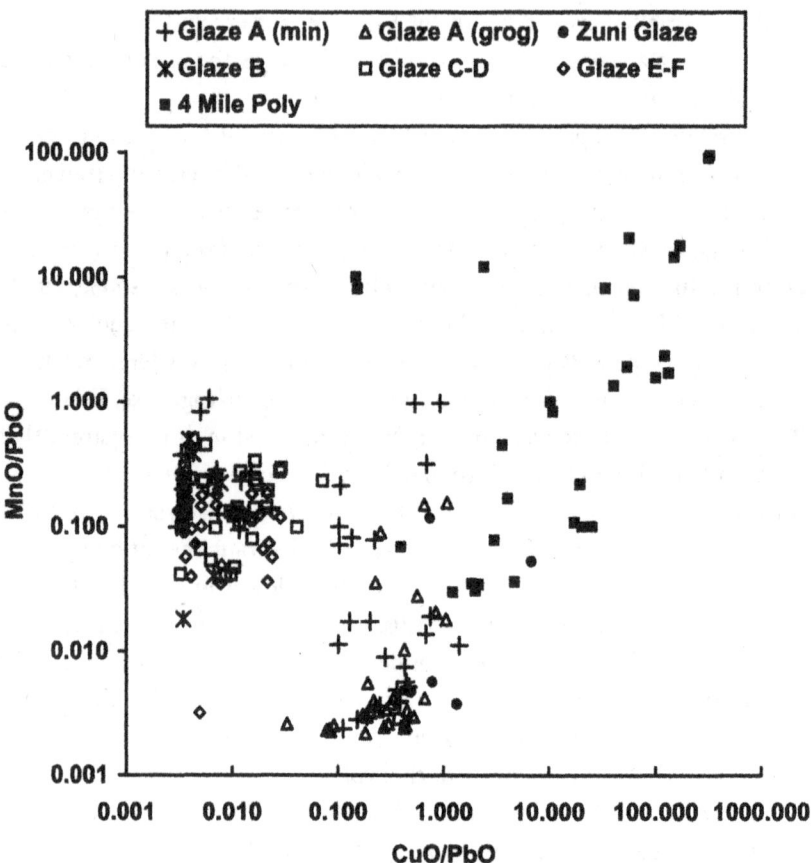

Fig. 10.2. The ratio of the mol proportion of manganese oxide to lead oxide plotted against the ratio of mol proportion of copper oxide to lead oxide, each on a log scale. Pottery types represented include Rio Grande Glaze A (mineral tempered), Rio Grande Glaze A (grog tempered), Rio Grande Glaze B, Rio Grande Glaze Ware C–D, Rio Grande Glaze Ware E–F, Fourmile Polychrome, and Zuni Glaze Ware.

Galisteo Basin, "vb" indicates the Lower Rio Puerco area, and "ta" indicates the area of Tonque Pueblo also in the Galisteo Basin. Minor temper types/production areas are not included in this graph, but their distribution is very similar. This plot shows that all paints produced after Glaze A, and some paints on mineral-tempered Glaze A, plot in the manganese-lead region of the graph. This suggests that starting sometime in the late 1300s, a rapid and complete shift toward manganese and away from copper as a colorant occurred.

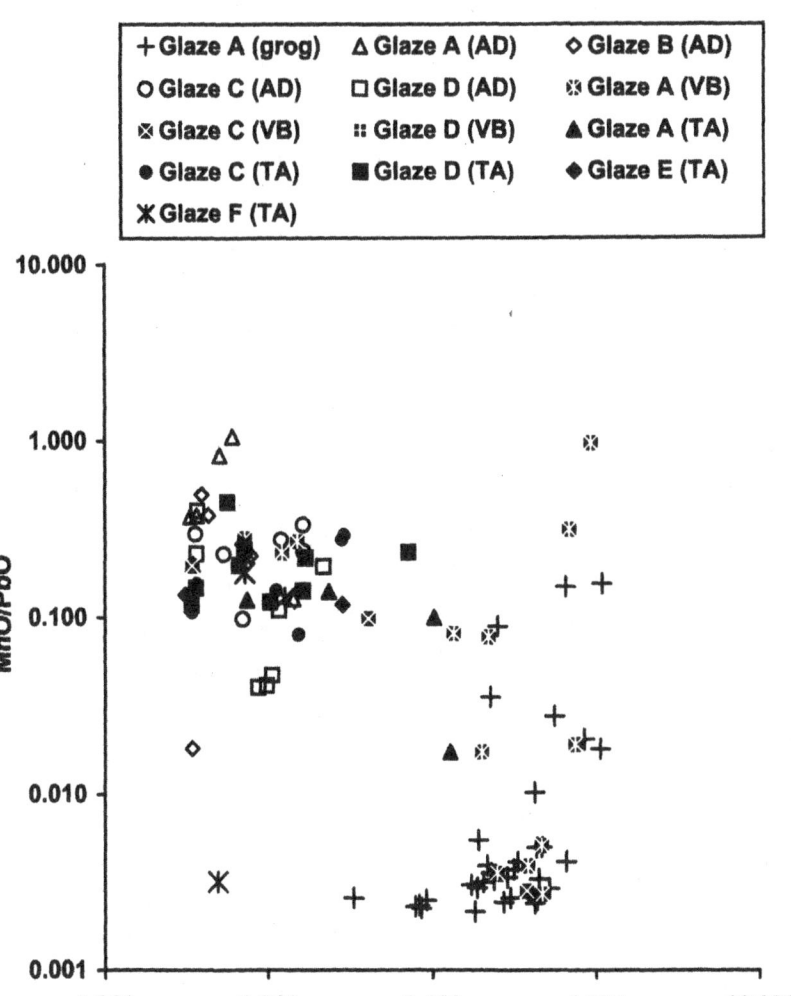

Fig. 10.3. The ratio of the mol proportion of manganese oxide to lead oxide for Rio Grande Glaze Ware plotted by temper type against the ratio of mol proportion of copper oxide to lead oxide, each on a log scale.

In summary, there are two basic trends visible in the glaze paint data presented here. First, there appear to be similarities in glaze paint recipes between early Rio Grande glazes and Zuni glazes. There is a basic, underlying similarity between Zuni and Fourmile Polychrome glazes, but at a coarser scale. Second, once glaze paint technology was established in the Rio Grande Valley; Rio Grande potters developed a distinct recipe that utilized manganese as a colorant over copper, as was used in the initial Rio Grande glaze paint production. The implications for the social dynamics of the fourteenth through seventeenth centuries will now be discussed.

Discussion

The data presented here cover a span of three hundred years, from the 1300s to the 1600s in the Rio Grande Valley. This relatively long time span provides the opportunity to explore the changing role of glaze paint pottery during this dynamic period. First I will address the origin and spread of this technology, then turn to the development of the technology following its establishment in the Rio Grande Valley.

The first appearance of purposeful glaze paint pottery in the northern Southwest corresponds to a time of demographic upheaval. It has long been suggested that migrants from the area that is now eastern Arizona brought first glaze paint pottery, then the technology to produce it, to Zuni. From there, the technology spread to the Rio Grande Valley. The compositional data discussed in this chapter support this general trajectory, but also open the possibility that the spread may not have been linear from eastern Arizona to Zuni to the Rio Grande, a possibility raised also by data presented by Huntley (chap. 6, this vol.). Zuni glazes and early Rio Grande glazes are similar in composition, and it is not clear which area was using this particular recipe first.

Based on Huntley's data (chap. 6, this vol.) showing that St. John's and Zuni glazes used Rio Grande Valley ore sources, it is perhaps not surprising that there is some similarity in the paint recipes. In fact, Zuni glazes and early Rio Grande Glaze A are quite similar, and there is a notable deviation in Glazes B through F, which is when Galisteo potters began to dominate glaze ware production in the east and when Zuni potters shifted their lead ore procurement to the south. The implication here may be that the technology was introduced to the Rio Grande by St. Johns/White Mountain Red Ware tradition glaze paint producers who used Cerrillos lead in their paints. The potters would have had the opportunity to interact with both Zuni area groups, based on proximity, and Rio Grande groups, based on direct procurement of ore or through trade, both of which would have engendered some contact. However, compositional data alone cannot resolve whether actual migration occurred.

Based on several lines of evidence, I argue that most of the technology transfer that occurred among glaze-paint-producing groups in the northern Southwest during the thirteenth and fourteenth centuries occurred through intergroup social interactions that may have also facilitated migration of peoples. In other words, more intergroup interaction and transmission occurred than actual migration, although migration almost certainly did occur (see in particular Eckert, chap. 9, this vol.). This is based on (1) the improbability of migration without knowledge of the target area gained through some kind of interaction, (2) the presence of a moderately large population in the Rio Grande (Duff 1998) at the time that this technology arrived, and (3) the access to Western Pueblo red wares through the Acoma and Laguna areas that were not depopulated until after this technological change was already well under way (Roney 1996). Furthermore, there is evidence of experimentation with glaze paint recipes by fourteenth-century Rio Grande potters (seen in fig. 10.2 by the wide range of variation in recipes used), suggesting that this was an unfamiliar combination of techniques. The "experiments" to which I refer are not evident on the graph shown here because when subjected to analysis with the electron microprobe they did not have an actual glaze layer. The paint appeared as a very thin (about 1 μ or less) layer. In three cases, the paint was indistinguishable from the slip in cross-section and is probably manganese alone; the other contained some lead but was primarily composed of iron. Sherds in this group tend to be grog or sherd-tempered Glaze A, which is thought to have been the earliest Glaze A produced (Warren 1976, 1979). Mineral-tempered Glaze A, thought to be somewhat later but still in the 1300s, is also present in the group.

Once glaze paint pottery is produced regularly in the Rio Grande Valley, the recipe by which it is produced follows a unique trajectory not seen in Zuni glaze wares, which fall out of production relatively early (Schachner, chap. 7, this vol.). Rio Grande glaze paints, initially produced using copper as the primary colorant, become fixed on a manganese-lead mixture. The rapidity and completeness of this change to manganese-lead paints has implications for social interaction and cultural transmission among groups in the region and for the social and economic organization of the region on a more general level.

Exchange of Knowledge or Trade of Materials?

Following the initial production of glaze paints in the 1300s by several villages in the Rio Grande Valley, that technological knowledge appears to have been transmitted successfully throughout the area, suggesting intense intergroup interaction. However, it is less clear what precisely was being transmitted. It is possible that just the knowledge of the recipe and the necessary raw materials were transmitted from Galisteo potters to all other areas of the Rio Grande. Another possible mechanism is that the Galisteo Basin Glaze A potters discovered a lead source with associated manganese oxides (a common co-occurrence with lead ores) that resulted in a superior glaze. If they were able to control access to this source and produce it as a trade "commodity," they could have traded to other Rio Grande potters. This would produce the pattern that Nelson and Habicht-Mauche (chap. 11, this vol.) clearly demonstrate, where the same lead source, Cerrillos, was used to produce glaze paint on vessels with varied production locales.

However, even if potters in different areas were using the identical lead ore or prepared paint, the major and minor element composition may vary because of differences in knowledge of firing techniques. By combining major and minor element compositional analysis of fired glaze paints with isotopic studies, it should be possible to examine the scale at which knowledge of other steps in the production process was shared, such as firing techniques. If the paints are isotopically identical, but compositionally different, this would suggest that the glaze paint (either as raw material or prepared paint) was distributed within a network that did not involve transmission of knowledge of other aspects of the production process.

Trade of glaze raw materials carries many of the same implications for social interactions within the Rio Grande Valley as transfer of knowledge, although perhaps on differing scales, as Nelson and Habicht-Mauche (chap. 11, this vol.) point out. Trade of materials does, however, carry different economic implications, which are not discussed in depth here. Whether the similarities in glaze paint composition in later glazes across production areas are the result of intergroup transmission of knowledge or intergroup exchange of materials, both suggest a high degree of social interaction among potters, if not larger communities.

The impetus and the context for this interaction and the production of the pottery itself may come from the ritual use of glaze bowls, as suggested by Spielmann (1998). As populations "settled in," and the large-scale population movements of the fourteenth century subsided, increasingly large and long-occupied villages became widespread. This may have fostered the development of intervillage dependencies (either economic or ritual) that had the effect of tying together villages with distinct community identities (perhaps Crown's "sects" [1994]). These issues are not likely to be resolved with reference to glaze paint composition and isotopic signatures alone. However, the existing data suggest that the high levels of intergroup interaction evidenced by patterning in glaze paint composition had shifted from minimizing between-group differences and facilitating demographic fluidity (cf. Crown 1994) to an increasingly economic focus predicated on village specialization and local exchange (Snow 1982; Spielmann 1998, cf. Ford 1972).

Conclusions

This study of glaze paint recipes inferred from composition has identified strong trends in recipe development in the Rio Grande Valley. Early in the glaze paint sequence (ca. AD 1300) potters generally followed a western glaze paint model exemplified by Fourmile Polychrome and Zuni Glaze Ware. However, Rio Grande potters did not follow the model very closely, as is evident in the spread of Glaze A compositions, shown in figures 10.2 and 10.3. I have argued here that this pattern is consistent with cultural transmission of technology through indirect means such as occasional interaction and word of mouth. Glaze A potters likely did not learn this technology from western potters in the context of production, precluding migration as a primary mechanism of glaze paint technology spread. The compositions are too different and too variable.

Shortly after the advent of glaze paint technology in the Rio Grande Valley, Galisteo Basin potters began making glaze paint containing manganese instead of copper as a colorant. This recipe spread rapidly to other glaze-producing villages, and the composition is remarkably similar regardless of production location or time period. This pattern is more suggestive of direct transmission of glaze paint technology or trade of glaze paint materials among Rio Grande potters. Both scenarios suggest regular interaction of potters from different communities. Based on the conclusions drawn by other researchers in the Rio Grande Valley regarding the development of village specialization during the latter part of the glaze sequence (Snow 1981; Spielmann 1998), I suggest that the context in which this regular interaction occurred was increasingly dominated by developing and maintaining economic interdependence among villages. However, paint composition alone cannot resolve whether the recipe or the paint as commodity was transmitted.

Regardless of the context within which interaction occurred among villages in the Rio Grande Valley in the centuries following AD 1275, tracking changes in glaze paint composition and lead isotope signatures will continue to provide information on the nature and spatial structure of social and economic interactions. Although the case presented here is particular to southwestern glaze paints, the level of detail that is possible by combining compositional analysis with isotopic studies facilitates the study of migrations in prehistory and allows questions of social interaction to be addressed more convincingly. By examining transmission of a technology that has a social and economic function, it is possible to begin to examine the role that artisans such as potters play in fostering social interaction, as well as the benefit they reap from it.

Acknowledgments

This analysis would not have been possible without the support of Katherine Spielmann, who provided access and the opportunity to analyze her collections from the Salinas area. I also thank Deborah Huntley for years of collaboration on Rio Grande glaze paints and access to her compositional data from Glazes E and F. Eric Blinman has also been a tremendous source of insights on glaze paint production, and my thinking on glaze paints has been enriched by our collaborations. Additional thanks go to Judith Habicht-Mauche, Suzanne Eckert, and Deborah Huntley for organizing such a productive and engaging SAA symposium. I am also grateful to Linda Cordell and Miriam Stark for their insightful comments and discussion on the original presentation. Rory Gauthier, Marianne Tyndall, and three anonymous reviewers provided helpful comments on earlier drafts of this chapter. Any omissions or errors remain my responsibility.

11

Lead, Paint, and Pots

Rio Grande Intercommunity Dynamics
from a Glaze Ware Perspective

Kit Nelson and Judith A. Habicht-Mauche

Intercommunity dynamics during the Pueblo IV period (AD 1300–1600) in the Rio Grande area of New Mexico have been portrayed in terms of discrete systems of sociopolitical and economic alliance (Snow 1981; Upham 1982; Upham and Reed 1989; Wilcox 1981, 1984) that are based, in part, on the geographic clustering of sites (Upham 1982; Upham and Reed 1989) in areas or districts that mirror historically defined ethnolinguistic provinces (Barrett 1997; Habicht-Mauche 1993a). These models of alliance have been variably interpreted as hierarchical polities (Wilcox 1991), complex tribes (Habicht-Mauche 1993a, 1993b), or clustered confederacies (Spielmann 1994). However, our research, based on the petrographic and lead isotope analyses of Rio Grande Glaze Ware pottery and paints, indicates that intercommunity interaction during the Pueblo IV period in the central Rio Grande was much more dynamic and complex than these alliance models would seem to suggest, especially when viewed from the perspective of individual sites through time.

Results of these analyses show that while some goods, such as finished glaze ware vessels, circulated largely within geographic clusters or districts, other materials, such as raw lead ores, were more widely distributed among the Rio Grande pueblos and beyond. The differential distribution of these goods denotes the presence of multiple, crosscutting exchange networks that functioned within different social and economic contexts and at different geographic and social scales. For example, while some exchange networks may have been focused on establishing and maintaining close social ties between households within neighboring communities, other exchanges may have linked individuals, households, and communities to larger networks of interregional interaction that extended throughout the Rio Grande Glaze Ware area. We argue that alliance models that focus on defining abstract organizational structures at a regional or interregional scale have obscured the real multiscalar and contextual dimensionality of intercommunity dynamics during the Pueblo IV period in the Rio Grande area and should be replaced by models that focus on examining how exchange is mobilized by individuals and groups in small- to medium-scale societies to construct, maintain, and contest specific social relationships and identities within various arenas of interaction.

Models of Pueblo IV Intercommunity Dynamics

Proposed models of Pueblo IV intercommunity dynamics in the Rio Grande area have been based primarily on three lines of evidence, including the geographic clustering of sites, historic information on ethnolinguistic identities and boundaries, and the distribution of specific ceramic styles or types. The fourteenth and fifteenth centuries witnessed a major restructuring of Rio Grande society as rapidly growing local and immigrant populations became increasingly concentrated in large, nucleated towns. In turn, these nucleated settlements tended to cluster geographically within specific river drainages or basins (see Mera 1940). These marked changes in settlement structure and distribution have led various researchers to characterize the Pueblo IV period in the Rio Grande as one of emerging intercommunity sociopolitical and economic alliances defined by the patterning of settlements in geographic space (F. Plog 1979; Snow 1981; Upham 1982; Upham and Reed 1989; Wilcox 1981, 1984). Upham (1982) and Upham and Reed (1989) argue that the uniform distribution between site clusters reflects the maintenance of regional systems as these relate to the "management of human interaction."

These geographic settlement clusters tended to mirror ethnolinguistic divisions or provinces identified by the earliest Spanish explorers and colonial administrators during the sixteenth century (Barrett 1997; Riley 1987). Such similarities have been used as evidence to support the development of ethnolinguistically based polities, tribes, and/or confederacies in the Rio Grande area during late precontact times (Habicht-Mauche

1993a; Spielmann 1994; Wilcox 1984). These researchers, however, differ markedly in their view of the organizational structure and complexity of these ethnolinguistic clusters, with some favoring more hierarchical models (e.g., Wilcox 1984, 1991) while others argue for more nonhierarchical, segmental (e.g., Habicht-Mauche 1993a, 1993b), or sequential models (e.g., Spielmann 1994).

The distribution of locally distinctive ceramic styles, types, and technologies has been used as supportive evidence for segmenting the Pueblo IV Rio Grande landscape into a series of ethnolinguistic districts or provinces (e.g., Habicht-Mauche 1993a). At the same time, the widespread exchange of various raw materials and finished products has been interpreted as evidence for the presence of larger and more integrated networks of regional and interregional interaction that crosscut local ethnic boundaries (Habicht-Mauche 1993a, 1998; Snow 1981; Wilcox 1981, 1984). Studies of the production and distribution of Rio Grande glaze-painted pottery have been central to many of these debates.

Earlier Studies of Rio Grande Glaze Ware Production and Exchange

Previous mineralogical characterization studies indicated that Rio Grande Glaze Ware vessels were exchanged widely throughout the Eastern Pueblo area and beyond (Shepard 1942, 1965; Warren 1969, 1970, 1979). In addition, these data seemed to suggest that certain districts or even specific sites dominated the Rio Grande Glaze Ware industry at different times in the past. According to Shepard (1942), the Galisteo district in the east-central Rio Grande region (see fig. 1.1) came to dominate glaze ware production during the Intermediate Glaze Ware period (AD 1450–1515), replacing earlier centers of production in the Albuquerque, Zia, and Santa Domingo areas. By the Late Glaze Ware period (AD 1515–1700), the Galisteo district's dominance had waned, with a number of more localized centers of production emerging throughout the Rio Grande area.

Later studies by Warren (1969, 1970, 1979) appeared to confirm this general pattern of interregional production and exchange. However, Warren's work also showed that the earliest red-slipped Rio Grande Glaze Ware vessels (Los Padillas Polychrome and Agua Fria Glaze-on-red) were produced at many more communities throughout the Rio Grande area than Shepard initially identified. Warren also argued that the pueblo of

San Marcos (LA 98), in the Galisteo district, was the primary producer of early yellow-slipped glaze-painted pottery (Cieneguilla and Largo Glaze-on-yellow), while Tonque Pueblo (LA 240), located just to the south and west of the Galisteo district, was the predominant interregional supplier of Intermediate Glaze Ware vessels (see Eckert, chap. 3, this volume, for a detailed discussion of the Rio Grande Glaze Ware sequence).

These interpretations have been used by other researchers to support the existence of a highly integrated interregional network of economic interaction and sociopolitical alliance, supported by a system of community-based craft specialization and the widespread exchange of raw materials and finished products (Habicht-Mauche 1993a, 1998; Snow 1981; Wilcox 1981, 1984). However, such systemic sociopolitical and economic models fail to consider the dynamic and contingent nature of exchange relationships as these are constituted within shifting fields of power, interest, and identity.

Shepard and Warren's methodological approach to the study of Rio Grande Glaze Ware production and exchange tended to reinforce these generalized systemic models by focusing on reconstructing broad regional patterns and temporal trends in the distribution of locally distinctive temper types. For example, although Shepard examined samples of glaze-painted pottery from over forty different sites located throughout the Rio Grande area (notes in Shepard Archives at University of Colorado, Boulder), her published report on this study (Shepard 1942) presents only temper type distributions and percentages at the level of whole districts or regions. Her unpublished notes also demonstrate that she was a very skilled petrographer who recognized and recorded multiple and nuanced petrographic differences among mineralogically similar materials. However, in her publications she tended to lump similar tempering materials from the same geological region into very generalized categories. The best example of this practice is her "andesite" temper group. This category encompasses a diverse mix of intermediate volcanic rock tempers of varying textures and compositions that can be attributed to multiple production sites throughout the Galisteo and eastern Santo Domingo basins.

Warren (1969, 1970, 1979) based her interpretations of regional patterns of glaze ware production and exchange on the isoclinal distribution of specific temper types across broad regions of the Rio Grande culture area through time. She paid less attention to the diversity of temper types present at any particular site. She also rarely examined permanent thin sections, making it difficult for her to make fine-grained distinctions between mineralogically similar tempering materials. In addition, both Shepard and Warren worked primarily with relatively small, grab-bag-selected surface collections, which limited their ability to examine smaller, intradistrict or intrasite scales of diversity.

This broad regional approach to the study of Rio Grande Glaze Ware production and exchange tended to mask a great deal of local diversity and complexity in resource selection, scales of production, and patterns of intercommunity interaction, both through time and across space. As a result, the organizational models developed to explain these data have emphasized macroscale systemic processes whose coherence and integration may be more an artifact of the focus and scale of our analyses than a true reflection of day-to-day social and economic practices. In place of these traditional macroscale approaches, we argue that Pueblo IV intercommunity dynamics in the Rio Grande area need to be examined from the microscale perspective of daily household and community practices. We begin that process by examining the diverse local, regional, and interregional strategies of exchange reflected in the variable distributions of finished Rio Grande Glaze Ware vessels as compared to the lead ores required for glaze paint production. Our results show that while glaze ware pots tended to circulate within networks of interaction that tended to reinforce local community and ethnolinguistic identities, specialized raw materials such as lead ore moved through systems of interaction that linked individuals and communities on a larger regional and interregional scale.

Methodology

Our research comparatively examines the changing patterns of Rio Grande Glaze Ware production and exchange using pottery from four Pueblo IV archaeological sites located in the central Rio Grande region of New Mexico: San Marcos (LA 98), Pueblo Blanco (LA 40), Cieneguilla/Tzeguma (LA 16), and Kuapa (LA 3444) (see fig. 1.2). This sample of Rio Grande Glaze Ware pottery is drawn from stratified midden deposits excavated in 1988 by the Rio Grande Research Project, directed by Winifred Creamer and Jonathan Haas.

The four sites used in this study are all located in or adjacent to the Galisteo Basin, an area that figures prominently in regional models of

Rio Grande Glaze Ware production and exchange. Both San Marcos and Pueblo Blanco are located within the Galisteo Basin proper (see figs. 1.1 and 1.2) and are part of a geographic cluster of large, multi-roomblock towns that define this archaeological district during the Pueblo IV period. Although these two sites are within the same archaeological district, ethnohistoric evidence suggests that San Marcos may have contained a linguistically and culturally mixed population (i.e., Keres and Tanos) (Barrett 1997). Therefore, one might expect this diversity to be reflected in the structure of the community's external exchange relationships.

Cieneguilla (aka Tzeguma) Pueblo lies outside the Galisteo Basin, to the north along the Santa Fe River. Although not located within the Galisteo Basin proper, it is often associated with the Galisteo cluster as part of the Tano (Southern Tewa) ethnolinguistic province (N. Nelson 1914, 1916; Wendorf and Reed 1955). Kuapa, on the other hand, is part of a separate cluster of large Pueblo IV sites situated along the Rio Grande near the modern pueblo of Cochiti in the Santo Domingo Basin district. This district lies within the historic homeland of the Keres-speaking Pueblos. As a result, it might be expected, based on ethnolinguistic alliance models, that Kuapa would be outside the immediate social and economic sphere of the predominantly Tano-speaking Galisteo Basin pueblos, despite its geographic proximity to those communities.

Two types of analyses, petrographic thin-section analysis of ceramic pastes and lead isotopic analysis of glaze paints, were carried out on this sample. The same sample of sherds was used for both types of analyses to produce comparable results. One hundred and sixty-five bowl rim sherds were chosen for analysis using a stratified random sampling procedure, which assured that sherds representing the entire glaze ware sequence at each site were examined. We attempted, wherever possible, to sample at least ten sherds from each glaze rim group (Glazes A–F) from each site. The Early (A and B) and Intermediate (C and D) Rio Grande Glaze Ware types were well represented at all four sites; however, the Late (E and F) Glaze Ware types were well represented only at San Marcos and Kuapa (table 11.1). As noted in chapter 3 of this volume, Glaze A rim forms were produced throughout the Rio Grande Glaze Ware sequence, potentially complicating the interpretation of the Early Glaze Ware group. However, we attempted to mitigate this problem by selecting samples from stratigraphically excavated contexts.

Petrographic thin-section analysis was carried out to mineralogically

Table 11.1
Ceramic Sample by Site and Glaze Ware Period

Site	Laboratory of Anthropology (LA) Number	Glaze Ware Periods Represented	Total Number of Samples
Kuapa	3444	Glaze A, B, C, D, E, F	22
San Marcos	98	Glaze A, B, C, D, E, F	61
Pueblo Blanco	40	Glaze A, B, C, D, E	40
Cieneguilla	16	Glaze A, B, C, D	42
Total			165

characterize ceramic tempers and pastes. This analysis was used to identify sources of vessel production and to trace patterns of finished vessel exchange. The locus of production for each temper type was determined by comparison with previous petrographic work in the Rio Grande area (Habicht-Mauche 1993a; Shepard 1942; Warren 1970, 1979, 1981) (table 11.2).

Arnold's (1985) ethnoarchaeological studies demonstrated that nonindustrial potters typically procure tempering materials from sources located less than 1 km from the production site. Shepard's (1942) maps showing the geological distribution of the various tempering materials used by Rio Grande Glaze Ware potters tend to support this assessment. Rio Grande potters appear to have been extremely conservative in their use of highly specific, local tempering materials through time (Capone, chap. 12, this vol.; Habicht-Mauche 1993a; Shepard 1942). As Capone argues in chapter 12 of this volume, such patterning suggests that temper choice defined local "technological styles" (following Lechtman 1977) of pottery production in the Rio Grande Valley and may have been used to mark the identity of specific, local "communities of practice" within the region (see Stark, chap. 2, this vol.). This conservatism in local tempering practices made it possible for us to petrographically source most of the bowl rims we examined to a particular district, cluster of sites, or, in some instances, a specific manufacturing center. This level of precision allowed us to define regional and interregional networks of interaction based on glaze ware production and exchange.

Isotopic analysis was conducted to establish the source of lead ores used to produce glaze paints. Rio Grande glaze-painted pottery was decorated

Table 11.2
Source Location of Temper Types

Temper Type	Source Location	Reference
intergranular basalt (IGB) *(Warren's San Felipe basalt)*	Santo Domingo Basin	Habicht-Mauche 1993a; Shepard 1942; Warren 1981
rhyolite tuff (RH) *(Shepard's devitrified tuff)*	Pajarito Plateau	Shepard 1942; Warren 1979, 1981
augite latite/monzonite (AUM) *(Warren's San Marcos latite; Shepard's andesite, in part)*	San Marcos Pueblo	Habicht-Mauche 1988, 1993a; Warren 1979, 1981
various augite and/or hornblende latite porphories (HB1) (AUL) (HB3) *(Shepard's andesite, in part)*	Galisteo Basin	Habicht-Mauche 1993a; Warren 1979, 1981
hornblende latite ash (HB2) *(Warren's Tonque latite; Shepard's andesite, in part)*	Tonque Pueblo	Habicht-Mauche 1993a; Warren 1969, 1979, 1981
sherd	Albuquerque area	Habicht-Mauche 1993a; Shepard 1942; Warren 1979, 1981
vitrophyric basalt (VB1), (VB2)	Bernalillo area and/or Cochiti area	Shepard 1942
syenite (SY)	Estancia Basin (Abó Pueblo)	Warren 1981
sandstone (SS)	Pecos Pueblo	Habicht-Mauche 1988; Shepard 1942; Warren 1981

with a lead-based paint that vitrified upon firing. Lead was critical to glaze paint production because it acted as a flux, lowering the melting point of silica and allowing glass to form at the low temperatures typical of the open or pit firings used by Rio Grande potters (see Herhahn, chap. 10, for more detailed discussion of Rio Grande glaze paint technology and firing). The lead needed to produce glaze paints was available from surface veins of galena (lead sulfide ore) located throughout the Rio Grande Rift Valley and adjacent highlands (see fig. 1.2). Each of these deposits formed within a unique and complex geological environment, characterized by temporally separated episodes of vulcanism and intrusion and marked by its own distinct signature of stable lead isotope ratios (Habicht-Mauche et al. 2000). Habicht-Mauche's laboratory has pioneered a technique for isotopically sourcing the lead in glaze paint using inductively coupled plasma mass spectroscopy (ICP-MS) (Habicht-Mauche et al. 2000, 2002). This technique allowed us to trace the acquisition and exchange of lead ores used in glaze paint production, separate from the production and exchange of finished glaze ware vessels.

Results of Analysis

Petrographic analysis revealed that all four sites have distinct glaze ware temper profiles (table 11.3), indicating the presence of very diverse and dynamic local strategies of intercommunity interaction and exchange. San Marcos was clearly an important glaze ware production center. Between one-third and one-half of the Rio Grande Glaze Ware sherds sampled from San Marcos were made locally at the site during all time periods. Similarly, Cieneguilla/Tzeguma's glaze ware assemblage is dominated by weathered augite monzonite temper throughout its sequence, suggesting that the site had very close bilateral ties to the pueblo of San Marcos. San Marcos glaze ware pottery also is very common at Pueblo Blanco, but this site had considerable amounts of glaze-painted pottery from other sites in the Galisteo Basin as well, suggesting that its relationship with communities throughout the district were more broad based and complex, certainly when compared to San Marcos or Cieneguilla. Like San Marcos, Pueblo Blanco had some glaze ware vessels from Tonque, but this source never eclipses the importance of the local Galisteo Basin sources at the site.

The site of Kuapa revealed the most dynamic and complex history of shifting exchange relationships. The early glazes from the site were domi-

Table 11.3
Relative Frequency of Glaze Ware Pottery from Different Source Areas by Site and by Glaze Period Based on Petrographic Identification of Temper

Site	Source Area	Early (Glaze A–B)	Intermediate (Glaze C–D)	Late (Glaze E–F)
Cieneguilla/ Tzeguma	San Marcos	41.2%	50.0%	not present
	Galisteo Basin	35.3%	25.0%	not present
	Santo Domingo Basin	5.9%	0.0%	not present
	Bernalillo/Cochiti	11.8%	0.0%	not present
	Estancia Basin (Abó)	5.9%	25.0%	not present
Kuapa	San Marcos	5.2%	5.3%	0.0%
	Galisteo Basin	11.8%	10.5%	20.0%
	Santo Domingo Basin	23.5%	0.0%	0.0%
	Bernalillo/Cochiti	47.1%	26.3%	0.0%
	Tonque	5.2%	52.6%	60.0%
	Albuquerque	0.0%	5.3%	0.0%
	Pajarito Plateau	5.2%	0.0%	20.0%
Pueblo Blanco	San Marcos	8.3%	45.0%	16.7%
	Galisteo Basin	58.3%	35.0%	66.7%
	Bernalillo/Cochiti	8.3%	5.0%	0.0%
	Tonque	25.0%	15.0%	16.7%
San Marcos	San Marcos	50.0%	36.0%	28.6%
	Galisteo Basin	45.5%	60.0%	42.9%
	Santo Domingo Basin	4.5%	0.0%	0.0%
	Tonque	0.0%	4.0%	14.3%
	Pajarito Plateau	0.0%	0.0%	7.1%
	Pecos	0.0%	0.0%	7.1%

nated by a variety of basalt tempers that most probably have their origin either locally in the western Santo Domingo Basin or, further south, in the Bernalillo area. However, the majority of the Intermediate and Late Period glazes from the site were probably manufactured in the vicinity of Tonque Pueblo, in the eastern periphery of the Santo Domingo district. San Marcos and the other Galisteo Basin communities, on the other hand, never seem to have been particularly important sources of glaze ware pottery at Kuapa.

Not surprisingly, San Marcos, Pueblo Blanco, and Cieneguilla all had

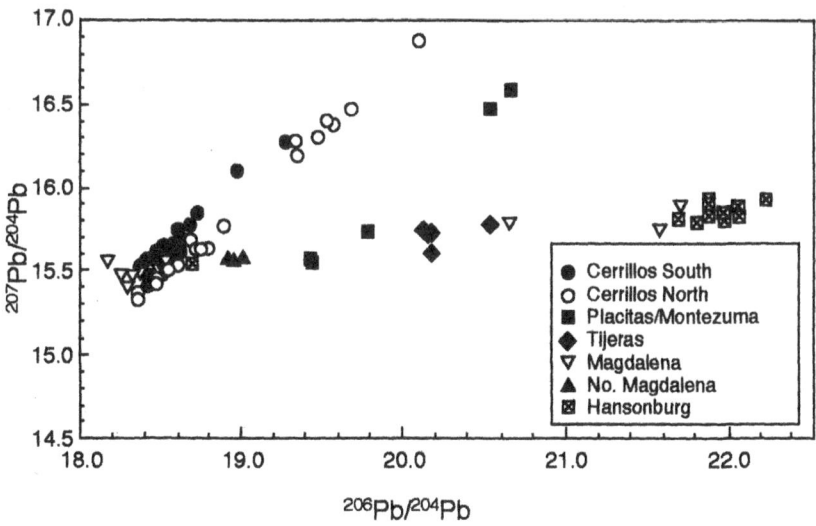

Fig. 11.1. Stable lead isotope ratios for New Mexico lead ores.

strong ties to other Galisteo Basin sites, but the exact structure of intercommunity relationships differed markedly among the sites. In contrast, Kuapa's closest exchange ties appear to have been with other sites in the Santo Domingo Basin throughout the sequence, although the orientation of those ties within the district shifted somewhat over time (from the western to the eastern side of the district). For all four sites, the closest and most sustained exchange relationships appear to have been with other communities in the same geographic cluster or archaeological district.

The patterns of exchange revealed by the isotopic fingerprinting of lead used in glaze paint production are completely different from those revealed by petrographically tracing the exchange of whole, finished vessels. Despite the presence of multiple geologically and isotopically distinct sources of lead ore in the central Rio Grande Valley (see fig. 11.1), ICP-MS analysis showed that glaze ware potters in this region of the valley were extremely selective in their use of lead for glaze paint production (see fig. 11.2). In particular, potters from production sites located throughout the central Rio Grande Valley preferentially utilized lead ore from a single source area located in the southern Cerrillos Hills, even when other sources of lead were readily available locally (Habicht-Mauche et al. 2000; see also Huntley, chap. 6). This dominance of the Cerrillos lead source is evident throughout the entire Rio Grande Glaze Ware sequence, from its

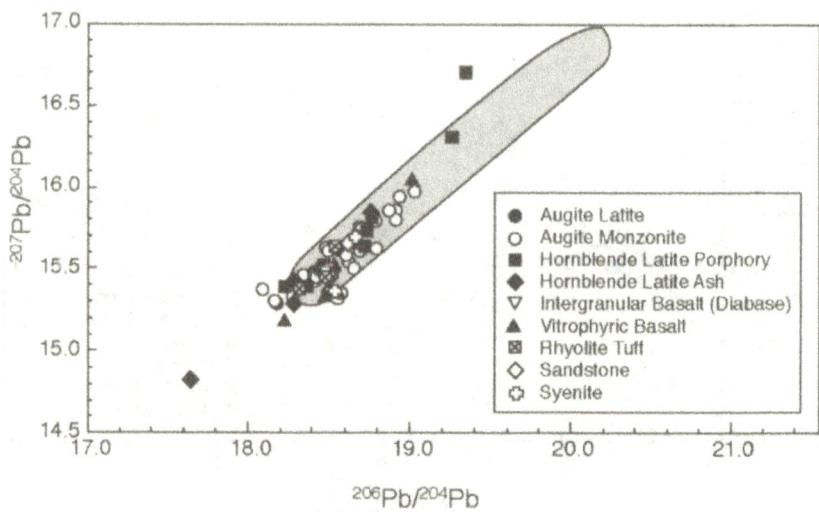

Fig. 11.2. Stable lead isotope ratios for Rio Grande glaze paints by temper type. Samples from all four sites and all periods are represented. Shaded area shows distribution of measured lead isotope ratios for Cerrillos district ores.

beginnings around the turn of the fourteenth century through its demise at the end of the seventeenth century. There are no apparent geological, technological, or economic reasons why this lead source should have been preferred so strongly over other sources in the region. Thus, we must look to other social and cultural factors to explain this patterning.

Rio Grande Intercommunity Dynamics from a Glaze Ware Perspective

Immigrants from the Zuni and/or Acoma area most likely introduced glaze paint technology to the southern Rio Grande Valley around the turn of the fourteenth century (Eckert 2003, and chaps. 3 and 9 in this volume; but see Herhahn, chap. 10, for an alternative perspective). However, locally produced glaze-painted pottery did not become widely distributed throughout the central Rio Grande until after AD 1350 (Habicht-Mauche 1993a). As Herhahn (chap. 10) aptly points out, the development of the Rio Grande glaze-painted pottery tradition involved a complex mix of innovation and borrowing, with specific aspects of technological knowledge and practice being alternately shared or guarded as these ideas moved through multiple and intersecting networks of social interaction that functioned at a variety of local, regional, and interregional scales.

The introduction of the ceramic designs, painting techniques, and slip colors that characterize Rio Grande Glaze Ware has been associated with the spread of new religious ideas and practices (E. C. Adams 1991; Crown 1994; Eckert 2003; Spielmann 1998). These new religious practices included, but were not limited to, certain aspects of what has come to be recognized ethnographically as Katsina ritualism. They involved public feasts, dances, and ritual performances that provided contexts where new social identities and roles were both constituted and contested. On the one hand, such practices may have been critical to the integration of the large nucleated towns and settlement clusters that came to dominate the Rio Grande landscape at this time. On the other hand, they created sites of potential conflict and competition that reinforced certain social differences within and among these emergent communities.

Nevertheless, evidence for the emergence of a new and widespread regional art style, as reflected in the distribution of shared design motifs and iconographic elements on Rio Grande glaze-painted pottery (Graves and Eckert 1998; Morgan 2002), rock art (P. Schaafsma 1992), and kiva murals (Brody 1991), suggests that certain religious ideas and practices transcended local household, community, and ethnolinguistic boundaries. Thus, these feasts and performances also may have served as important public and ceremonial arenas where broader intercommunity and interregional networks of interaction and alliance were negotiated and reaffirmed.

Spielmann (1998) has demonstrated that relatively large bowls dominated early Rio Grande Glaze Ware assemblages. This pattern suggests that glaze-painted vessels may have played an increasingly important role in public rituals and feasts during the Pueblo IV period in the Rio Grande area. Kiva mural illustrations of polychrome bowls filled with food and other offerings, either placed on altars or associated with katsinas (e.g., Hibben 1975), also indicate that glaze-painted pottery may have played a prominent role in ceremonial contexts. However, the ubiquitous and widespread distribution of glaze-painted vessels within southern and central Rio Grande sites suggests that they also functioned routinely within the more mundane domestic context of daily food preparation, storage, and service. As a result, glaze-painted vessels and the raw materials used in their production may have circulated among households and communities through a variety of diverse, yet intersecting, arenas of social, economic, and/or ceremonial exchange. Thus, by tracing patterns of glaze paint production and distribution, we can begin to model how various intercommunity networks of interaction were constituted and sustained through exchange at a local, regional, and interregional scale.

Examining Exchange at Multiple Scales

A comparison of the two data sets examined in the present study shows that raw lead ore and finished glaze-painted vessels were each circulating through distinct arenas of exchange that differed markedly in both organizational structure and geographic scale. Exchange is defined here as any of a broad range of contexts or practices through which material goods or services are transferred among individuals or social groups, including, but not limited to, economic trade, gift giving, and ritual exchange.

The Local Production and Exchange of Whole Pots. Finished glaze ware pots were produced and distributed within spheres of intercommunity interaction in which no one site dominated production or distribution. This study found no evidence to support Warren's (1970) argument for the dominance of first San Marcos and later Tonque Pueblo as the primary suppliers of glaze-painted ceramics in the central Rio Grande Valley. Both sites were clearly major centers of glaze ware production that exported large numbers of ceramics to other sites throughout the region and beyond (see Leonard, chap. 13, this vol.). But, rather than shifting from one source to another, from San Marcos to Tonque, the individual sites examined here appear to have maintained strong exchange connections with either San Marcos (e.g., Cieneguilla), Tonque (e.g., Kuapa), or, more rarely, with both communities (e.g., Pueblo Blanco), and these relationships appear to have remained fairly constant throughout the glaze ware sequence at each site.

Our petrographic studies also seemed to suggest that, during the Pueblo IV period in the Rio Grande, people were more likely to exchange finished glaze ware vessels with other people within their local settlement cluster or district than with people from adjacent clusters or districts—in other words, with those people or groups with whom they may have shared a common language and/or a common sense of origin and identity. The development of exchange relationships and contexts that constituted and reinforced a common sense of identity may have been particularly important for communities, such as San Marcos, whose populations appear, on the basis of ethnohistoric information (see Barrett 1997), to have been actually quite ethnically and linguistically diverse in their origins.

Nevertheless, the patterns of intercommunity glaze ware vessel exchange that were revealed by this petrographic study varied significantly from site to site and through time, both between sites in the same district and between sites in adjacent districts. These patterns suggest that social relationships associated with Rio Grande Glaze Ware vessel exchange were probably negotiated in a fairly ad hoc and dynamic manner at the level of household-to-household or social segment-to-social segment, both within and across communities, and may at times have extended beyond the boundaries of local settlement clusters. When examined from the perspective of individual sites and their specific histories of glaze ware production and exchange, there appears to be no credible evidence for the control of glaze ware production and exchange by any specific site or local ethnolinguistic group or for the management of these exchange networks by an overarching regional or interregional polity.

The Regional Acquisition and Circulation of Lead Ore. The widespread use of Cerrillos lead for glaze paint production throughout the central Rio Grande, as shown by lead isotope analysis, may be related to maintaining much larger networks of interregional relationships. Huntley (chap. 6, this vol.) has demonstrated that during the late thirteenth century Zuni potters also preferred the use of lead (and possibly copper) from the Cerrillos Hills for glaze paint production. However, their use of Cerrillos lead drops off considerably in later periods as they switched to lead from sources located farther south in the Magdalena Mountains, near Socorro. These new lead sources were not particularly closer to Zuni than the older Cerrillos source (see fig. 1.2). One possible reason for this shift could be that Zuni's access to Cerrillos lead may have been curtailed by the rise of local centers of glaze ware production in the central Rio Grande after around AD 1320 or by changing patterns of interregional interaction that crosscut the late prehistoric Southwest. In contrast, however, the isotopic data suggest that within the central Rio Grande region itself access to lead from the Cerrillos Hills deposits was not limited to potters from any particular district or cluster of production sites. Thus, the use of Cerrillos lead linked these production centers in a larger, regional "community of practice" that, unlike temper choice, transcended local communities and settlement clusters. Herhahn (chap. 10, this vol.) has demonstrated a similar pattern based on the distribution of glaze paint "recipes" in the Rio Grande Valley.

Lead for glaze paint production within the central Rio Grande could have been acquired in any of the following four ways: open access direct acquisition, controlled access direct acquisition, the exchange of raw ore, or the exchange of premixed paint. In a system of open access direct acquisition, individual potters or their assistants would have mined raw lead ore directly from surface deposits in the Cerrillos Hills, with no restriction on their access to these deposits. Controlled access direct acquisition would have been similar, but ownership or control of the Cerrillos lead deposits by a specific community or lineage segment within a community may have been acknowledged and respected by potters from other communities who would have offered gifts or other goods in exchange for access to the deposits. The alternative to direct acquisition, either open or controlled, would have been for lead to circulate through trade networks, either in the form of raw ore or premixed paint.

The lead isotope data tentatively support a model of direct acquisition rather than trade, since the isotopic signatures of glaze paints on pots manufactured at San Marcos are somewhat more homogeneous than the glaze paints on pots produced at other sites, suggesting that the latter paints were made using ores that came from a wide variety of deposits within the Cerrillos Hills, and possibly reflect some mixing of ores (Habicht-Mauche et al. 2000). In addition, the fact that our lab has sourced chunks of galena recovered from archaeological contexts at Tonque Pueblo to the Cerrillos Hills (Habicht-Mauche 2002) also strongly indicates that lead was being obtained as raw ore and processed into glaze paint pigments by individual potters from the various potting communities within the central Rio Grande.

The current data do not allow us to clearly distinguish between the alternative models of open or controlled direct acquisition. However, the process of controlled direct acquisition is well attested to ethnographically among the Rio Grande Pueblos for a variety of raw materials and resources (Ellis 1981). The site of San Marcos Pueblo (LA 98), known to have been a major producer of glaze-painted pottery, is located immediately adjacent to the most important lead deposits in the southern Cerrillos Hills. Its location would have put it in an ideal position to control access to the mineral deposits of the Cerrillos Hills, which included ritually important deposits of turquoise as well as lead. Nevertheless, if such ownership or control existed, San Marcos does not appear to have restricted access to the extent that central Rio Grande potters from other glaze-ware-producing sites were compelled to develop new or alternative sources of lead.

Why the Cerrillos lead source should have dominated central Rio Grande glaze ware production so completely is unclear and difficult to determine archaeologically. Perhaps it was partly a by-product of the technological conservatism that characterizes potters from nonindustrial, nonmarket-based societies. Since early glaze ware potters had proven the technological viability of Cerrillos lead as a flux, the policy of later potters in the central Rio Grande might have been to just "not mess with success." Alternatively, the widespread preference for Cerrillos lead may have been linked to its natural association with and proximity to ritually important deposits of turquoise, and in turn to the cosmological significance of the Cerrillos Hills themselves. A third alternative is that while finished glaze ware vessels may have circulated through public or ceremonial arenas that reinforced local and regional identities and relationships, certain rare or highly specialized raw materials, such as lead ore, may have moved through very different contexts of interaction. These latter networks may have functioned at a much broader regional or interregional scale, linking households and lineage segments from more widely dispersed and ethnically diverse communities through ties of complementarity and dependency that crosscut local settlement clusters and transcended emerging local identities. The value and significance of Cerrillos lead may have been defined reflexively within the context of the relationships and interactions that structured its acquisition and distribution on a regional and interregional scale.

When viewed from a broad, interregional perspective, the end result of such a process may resemble what Wilcox (1984) has called an "interethnic division of labor." However, when we examine the acquisition and distribution of Cerrillos lead from the perspective of individual glaze ware potters or potting groups within communities, we see the result, not of an abstract, overarching organizational system, but of choices and strategies made in response to local needs and individual interests, as constituted within culturally defined realms of value and meaning.

Discussion and Conclusions

In this chapter we have explored some of the dynamics of intercommunity interaction during the Pueblo IV period in the central Rio Grande from the varying perspectives of regional lead ore acquisition versus local glaze ware vessel production and exchange. We have examined these dynamics by tracing the production and exchange of finished glaze ware vessels using petrographic analysis and by identifying the source of lead ores used in glaze paint production through isotopic analysis. These two data sets revealed two very different patterns and contexts of exchange and interaction.

The petrographic data suggested that finished glaze ware vessels circulated through social and ceremonial arenas that tended to define emerging local and regional identities. We see these exchanges as part of both conscious and unconscious practices that tended to reinforce the appearance of coherent identities and stable relationships that were probably more imagined than real within the fractured, postmigration social landscape of the Pueblo IV central Rio Grande.

The isotopic analyses indicated that potters in the central Rio Grande region favored the use of the Cerrillos Hills lead source near San Marcos Pueblo, even though other surface deposits of lead were readily available in the area. This highly selective and specialized pattern of raw material acquisition linked households from diverse and widely scattered communities into broader regional and interregional networks of economic complementarity and dependency. However, the value of the Cerrillos lead source may have been based more on its social and symbolic significance than on the raw economics of supply and demand.

This evidence tends to challenge social organizational models that view the Pueblo IV Rio Grande landscape as segmented into highly coherent and well-bounded regional alliances or ethnolinguistic polities (e.g., Upham and Reed 1989; Wilcox 1981). Nor do these data justify thinking about intercommunity interaction in terms of a highly integrated economic system based on community specialization or an interethnic division of labor (e.g., Habicht-Mauche 1993a, 1993b; Wilcox 1984). Rather, what is highlighted by the Rio Grande Glaze Ware data is that different objects and materials circulated through different arenas and contexts of interaction defining complementary and crosscutting social relationships and identities on a local, regional, and interregional scale.

Acknowledgments

Special thanks go to the National Science Foundation (SBR-9602123), the Clements Center for Southwest Studies of Southern Methodist University, and the Social Sciences Division and Academic Senate at UCSC for support of this research. This project would not have been possible without the use of ceramic collections made available by Winifred Creamer (Northern Illinois University) and Jonathan Haas (Field Museum) and additional ore samples provided by the New Mexico Mineral Museum in Socorro and Dave Hill of Archaeological Research and Technology, Inc., in Austin. We thank them for their generosity. We would also like to thank the administrative and curatorial staff at the University of Colorado Museum in Boulder for their assistance in accessing and photographing material from the Anna O. Shepard thin section archives. This material was extremely useful for helping us clarify and standardize our petrographic identifications. Deirdre Morgan prepared the thin sections, under the guidance of Bruce Tanner in the Mineral Preparations Laboratory at UCSC. The methodology used to fingerprint lead ores and source glaze paints was originally developed by Habicht-Mauche, in collaboration with A. Russell Flegal (Environmental Toxicology, UCSC), Homer Milford (formerly of the New Mexico Department of Energy, Minerals, and Natural Resources Division), and Stephen Glenn (formerly of the Department of Anthropology, UCSC). Rob Franks of the Marine Sciences Institute at UCSC provided invaluable technical assistance and support for the ICP-MS analyses. Helen Cole of Graphic Services at UCSC redrafted the two figures for this chapter.

12

Rio Grande Glaze Ware Technology and Production

Historic Expediency

Patricia Capone

Rio Grande glaze ware technology and organization of production contribute to a sense of technological style when examined through time. Lechtman's notion of technological style submits that "technological behavior is characterized by the many elements that make up technological activities . . . which are unified non-randomly in a complex of formal relationships," and that "the format or package defined by these relationships . . . is stylistic in nature" (Lechtman 1977:10). This notion attributes elements of style to any stage of technique of manufacture or technology. Technological style, similar to decorative style, can be a window into culture and its associated behaviors, and can reflect trends in social dynamics through time.

Alongside the notion of technological style, this study employs historic, ethnohistoric, and ethnographic analogy for reflecting on the organization of production and social dynamics during preceding periods. Cautionary tales from various ethnoarchaeological situations indicate that analogy should be employed mindfully to avoid pitfalls such as oversimplification (as noted by Arnold 1991). With this in mind, some insights into the organization of production and social dynamics are suggested in light of historic, ethnohistoric, and ethnographic frameworks from Puebloan and other cultures. Furthermore, such understanding may contribute to cross-cultural generalizations in contexts, such as other mission or colonial contexts, that may have some analogous elements.

The implications of glaze ware technology and its stylistic attributes offer understanding of social dynamics and of technology and culture more broadly. The relationships are explored within the theoretical framework of the social potential of things, as advocated by Appadurai (1986). Within this framework, Puebloan ceramic technological style is envisioned as representing an initial step in imbuing glaze wares with social potential. Ceramic technology then forms a baseline in the social history of ceramic items. Cultural biographies of glaze wares in the specific settings considered here set the stage for understanding the social history of glaze wares. Two key themes of this study are the social potential of technological choice and producer-consumer relations as they are represented through aspects of glaze wares.

Puebloan Ceramic Technology: Durability and Flexibility of Style

Puebloan ceramic technological style is envisioned here as a set of approaches to ceramic technology and manipulations of that technology that are "manifest expressions of cultural patterning" (Lechtman 1977:4). This study explores elements of durability and flexibility within the style. For example, a particular set of techniques within this style is maintained over eight hundred years, from the thirteenth century through the present. These maintained techniques may be viewed as a core ensemble of techniques. The core ensemble of techniques reflects durability within the style as well as the aspects of culture that contribute to their maintenance, while other techniques and their concomitant behavioral patterns appear more flexible to change. The idea that "technological performance is supported by a set of underlying values" guides this approach (Lechtman 1977:10). While glaze wares were not produced after the historic period, certain aspects of their technology are emphasized even into present-day twenty-first-century Puebloan ceramics. Aspects subject to change during the Mission and Revolt periods are revealed in this study. What factors contribute to maintaining some aspects of Puebloan ceramic technology and to developing a sense of durability within the style of Puebloan ceramic technology? What are factors of change?

Table 12.1
Aspects of Technology and Their Associated Petrographic Characteristics Used in This Study

Aspect of Technology	Petrographic Characteristic
processing of raw material or choice of raw material source	average grain size of large fraction coarse:fine distribution (C:f) inclusion grain size frequency
choice of raw material firing or raw material source	inclusion (temper) composition optic state color (oxidation/reduction)
construction technique	birefringence void frequency

Measuring Patterns in Glaze Ware Technology: Methodology and Sampling Strategy

Petrographic analysis was chosen for its utility in exploring production location and technology. This petrographic study explores evidence for the following technological behaviors: processing of raw materials, construction technique, firing behavior, and choice of raw materials. The petrographic characteristics that contribute especially to understanding these for glaze wares are grain size, frequency, relative proportions of coarse to fine material, optical activity and birefringence (or brightness and light patterning of the micromass), and patterning of voids and color (table 12.1).

These petrographic analyses offer a detailed view of the final periods of glaze ware manufacture in two areas in the Rio Grande region: the Salinas area and the Cochiti area (see fig. 1.1). These analyses relate technological behavior over the pre-Mission period (ca. 1490–1650) through the Revolt and post-Revolt periods (ca. 1680–1700). The aspect of this study in the Salinas area of the south-central Rio Grande spans the earlier of the periods: pre-Mission period (approximately 1490–1650, Glaze D–E samples) through the Mission period (approximately 1650–80, Glaze F). The subsequent Revolt and post-Revolt periods (ca. 1680–1700) form the focus on Kotyiti Pueblo in the Cochiti area of the northern Rio Grande.

The data set from the Salinas area consists of 161 sherd samples from

Table 12.2
Number of Samples from the Salinas Area

Salinas Area Pueblo	LA Number	Number of Samples
Abó	97/3933	90
Gran Quivira	120	16
Quarai	95	29
Tenabo	240	26
Total		161

four pueblos: Abó, Gran Quivira, Quarai, and Tenabo (table 12.2) (see fig. 1.2). The samples derive from various projects, all of which are curated by the Laboratory of Anthropology. Most of the samples derive from excavations by Toulouse (1949) and Dutton (1981, 1985) at Abó; Baldwin (1988) at Tenabo; and Spielmann (1993) at Quarai. The remainder are from surface surveys by Dutton at Abó; Mera (1940) at Abó, Gran Quivira, and Quarai; and Warren at Abó and Gran Quivira. The sherds were selected by means of a judgmental sample for representation of both pre-Mission and Mission periods and spatial variety within each pueblo. The Kotyiti data set consists of 112 sherds from Nels Nelson's 1912 excavations curated at the American Museum of Natural History. These sherds were collected from numbered rooms by means of a judgmental sample.

Each sample was examined in thin section under a petrographic microscope. The system of petrographic description used here follows that developed by Whitbread (1989). The system includes characteristics of fabric texture and raw material composition, both of which are explored in this study for their utility in understanding production location and technology of glaze wares (table 12.1). *Fabric* refers to the arrangement, size, shape, frequency, and composition of its three main components—micromass, inclusions, and voids. Micromass is often regarded as the fired-clay matrix and comprises particles smaller than about 15 μ. Inclusions are frequently thought of as temper added by the potter, but may also be naturally occurring particles in the clay, which lack plasticity and are usually larger than 15 μ. They serve to inhibit cracking of the fabric. Voids are open vesicles in the fabric, which may exhibit distinguishing arrangements, size, or shape. Each of these three components provides insight into geographic location and technology of ceramic production.

Resulting Patterns in Glaze Ware Technology: Expediency and Standardization

Technological style of glaze wares tends toward increasing expediency when examined from pre-Mission through the Revolt and post-Revolt periods (ca. AD 1490–1700). Some aspects of glaze ware technology continue through time, while others change. In particular, petrographic evidence illustrates a tendency toward continuity in aspects of temper material choice and a trend toward a more expedient version of a core ensemble of ceramic techniques, whose basic elements are maintained throughout glaze ware history.

Pre-Mission and Mission Periods: Salinas Area Results

Petrographic characteristics of Salinas area glaze wares reveal marked trends toward ceramics that are more expediently produced and less standardized from the pre-Mission to the Mission period. The characteristics of grain size, frequency, relative proportions of coarse to fine material, optical activity and birefringence (or brightness and light patterning of the micromass), patterning of voids, and color are important for understanding trends in glaze ware technology (table 12.1).

Although raw materials appear to remain constant, they undergo less processing through time. This is especially evident through the larger overall grain size and higher frequency of large grains in Mission-period glaze wares (table 12.3). Construction technique becomes more expedient, with less compaction of the body coils. Less compaction results in characteristic patterns of large voids and characteristic arrangements of clay particles. Similarly, more expedient Mission-period firings produced more varied results. Results include the presence of higher optical activity overall and increased variation in color (less consistent oxidation). Together these suggest expediency, less standardization, and perhaps reorganization of firing behavior (Capone 1995:258). Figure 12.1 illustrates characteristics of a typical pre-Mission glaze ware, while figure 12.2 highlights changes in Mission-period glaze wares. It is notable, however, that these shifts occur with the same core ensemble of technology: the same basic techniques of construction (smoothed coils) and firing (open, non-kiln format), which endure throughout Pueblo ceramic history.

In sum, prominent patterns for the pre-Mission- and Mission-period Salinas area are (1) trend toward more expedient technology, (2) conti-

Table 12.3
Summary of Technologically Informative Petrographic Characteristics of Pre-Mission Period and Mission Period Sherds from the Salinas Area and Revolt-Reconquest Period Sherds from Kotyiti

Petrographic Characteristic	Salinas Pre-Mission Period Sherds	Salinas Mission-Period Sherds	Kotyiti Revolt-Reconquest-Period Sherds	Technological Significance
average grain size of large fraction	400 μ	600–800 μ	700–900 μ	diachronic change in processing of raw material or choice of material
coarse:fine distribution (c:f)	single-spaced	close-spaced or single-spaced	close-spaced or single-spaced	same as above
inclusion grain size frequency (c:f 10 μ)	50:50	60:40	60:40	same as above
inclusion (temper) composition	Abó and Tenabo: hornblende diorite Gran Quivira: biotite felsite Quarai: hornblende gneiss	same as pre-mission	not applicable	diachronic continuity of choice of raw material
optic state	slightly active	moderately active	moderately active to active	diachronic change in firing or choice of raw material
color oxidation/ reduction)	more consistent	not consistent	not consistent	diachronic change in firing or raw material
birefringence	undifferentiated	undifferentiated	undifferentiated	diachronic continuity of construction technique

Table 12.3
Continued

Petrographic Characteristic	Salinas Pre-Mission Period Sherds	Salinas Mission-Period Sherds	Kotyiti Revolt-Reconquest-Period Sherds	Technological Significance
void frequency (average)	4%	7–10%	7–10%	diachronic change in construction technique

nuity in temper choice, and (3) continuity of core ensemble of ceramic technology.

Revolt and Post-Revolt Periods: Kotyiti Area Results

Later, in the subsequent Revolt and post-Revolt periods (approximately 1680–1700) at Kotyiti Pueblo in the Cochiti area of the northern Rio Grande, petrographic signs of expedient technology in glaze wares appear to continue. Even within expediency, a uniform temper material is adopted at Kotyiti as the standard selection, while other suitable materials are readily available. Study by Robert Preucel (Capone and Preucel 2002) and myself suggests that this uniformity of temper type at Kotyiti is similar to a pre-Revolt pattern of village-based uniformity in glaze ware temper type. This uniformity is especially interesting at Kotyiti because Kotyiti was formed by representatives of three previously separate villages coming together during the Pueblo Revolt. Their united adoption of one new material as standard may suggest some degree of social unity. Social unity also is suggested by residential integration at Kotyiti (Capone and Preucel 2002).

Implications for Organization of Production

These elements of technology reflect on organization of production when they are examined within Costin's framework (1991:9). Costin's framework for understanding organization of production is particularly suited to understanding Pueblo culture because it allows exploration of nuances between dispersed and nucleated settlement production systems and various levels of specialists. Archaeological and historical evidence suggests

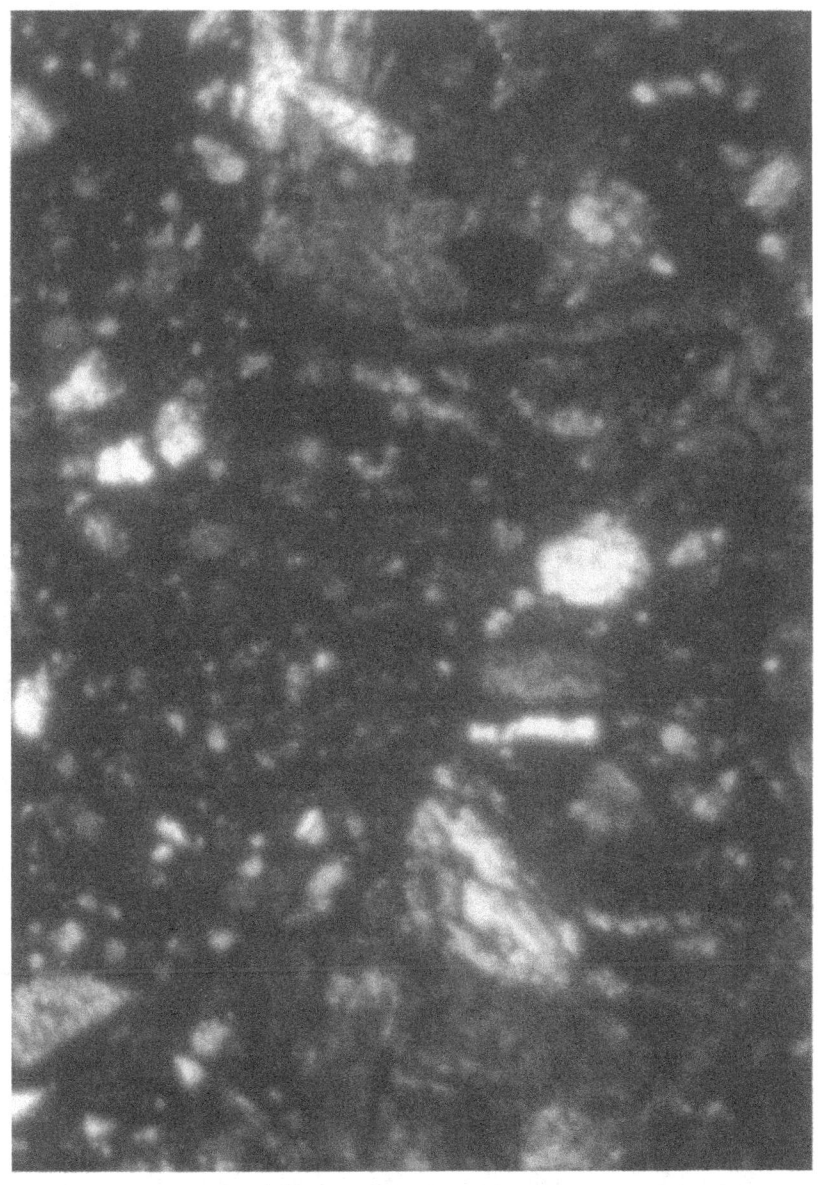

Fig. 12.1. Petrographic thin section of pre-Mission-period glaze ware.

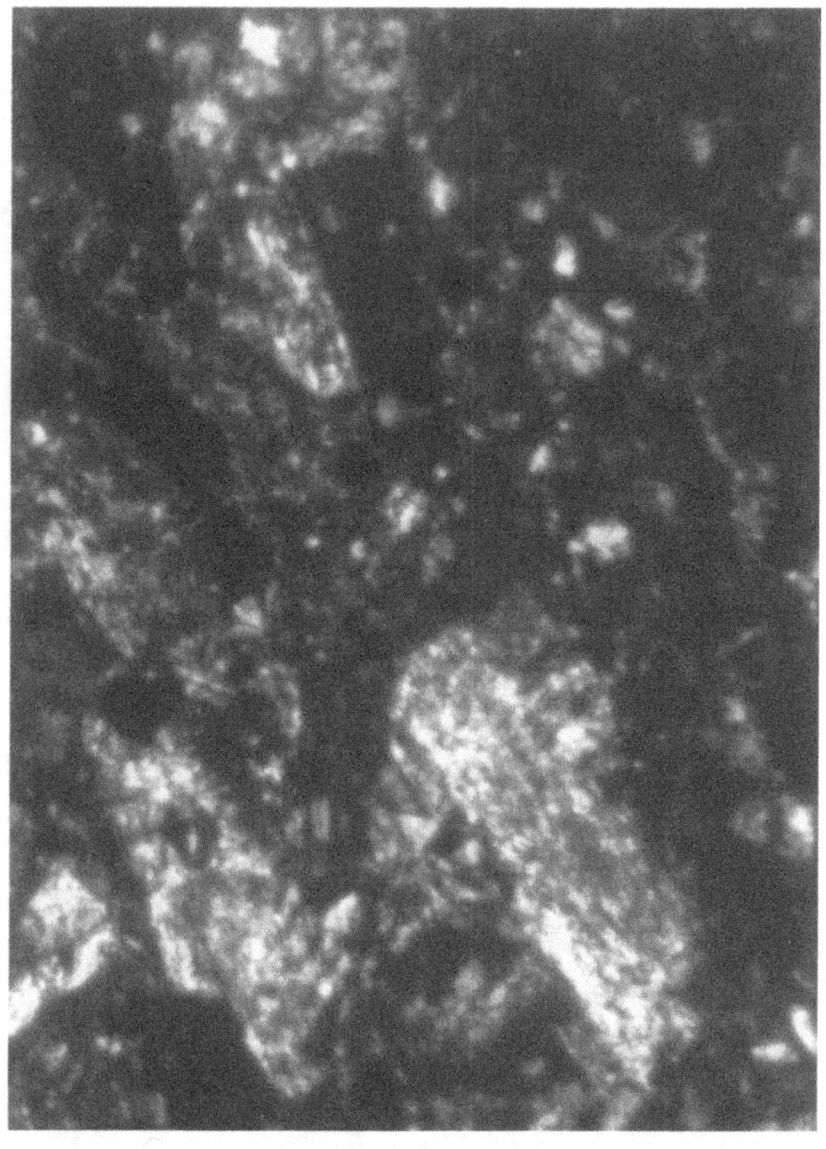

Fig. 12.2. Petrographic thin section of Mission-period glaze ware.

these for Pueblo culture (summarized in Capone 1995). Costin's framework offers four parameters:

1. *Context* refers to the "affiliation of producers," which is likely to have been independent in pre-Mission Pueblo culture given current understanding.
2. *Concentration* refers to "geographic organization of production," which has been shown to be dispersed or present in most pre-Mission communities in the Rio Grande. Nucleation has been suggested for certain locations, most notably the Galisteo Basin for Glazes C–D (Shepard 1942; Warren 1969) and Abó Pueblo for Mission-period glaze wares (Capone 1995).
3. *Scale* refers to "composition of production unit," which is difficult to assess for glaze ware production owing to the paucity of evidence for work areas. Based on ethnohistoric and ethnographic information, collaboration among potters may have played an important role, such as in kin-based group firing, raw material collection, or in forming and painting a piece (Capone 1999; Guthe 1925; Wyckoff 1985).
4. *Intensity* refers to the "amount of time spent on craft," which is inferred to have been seasonal and part-time for pre-Mission glaze wares based on ethnographic and ethnoarchaeological analogy (Arnold 1991; Dittert and Plog 1980).

Factors Relating to Organization of Production

Trends in Mission-period technology, reflecting greater expediency and less standardization, taken together with Mission-period factors potentially relevant to the organization of production, suggest that shifts in the organization of production begin to emerge. Review of literature on protohistoric Pueblo culture (archaeological, ethnohistorical, and historical) identifies a number of common factors that could have affected the organization of ceramic production:

1. introduction of new political officers and associated transformations of sociopolitical organization;
2. transformation of aspects of prestige associated with feasting and gifting;
3. transformation of prestige associated with the control of marriage;
4. demands on Pueblo labor by mission and civil personnel;

5. mission supply networks as an exchange-structuring factor among mission pueblos;
6. demand for certain ceramics owing to changes in their use;
7. the mission program goal of producing mission pueblo economic autonomy;
8. creation of new social alliances (e.g., traditionalist and progressive factionalism).

These factors suggest potential shifts in the context of production toward a more attached brand of production, shifts in concentration toward less nucleation and increased autonomy, and reduction in scale toward degradation of collaborative groups. Given that demand probably increased, intensity may have increased to meet it. The historically known factors most relevant for these changes may include demands on Pueblo labor by missions and potential transformations in the structure of prestige associated with feasting, gift giving, and control of marriage into which mission personnel attempted insertion. These factors likely influenced context of production toward a slightly more attached brand of specialization where mission personnel were owed ceramics by Puebloan villagers in a patronage or tribute-style relationship. That relationship may have been based partially in preexisting Puebloan notions of prestige and gifting (Gutiérrez 1991). Lastly, mission goals of village economic autonomy likely contributed to more dispersed concentration of production (Capone 1995).

The Interpretation of Expediency Results

The expediency of glaze ware technological style, which is seen to continue into the Revolt period at Kotyiti, likely relates to factors known about this tumultuous period. Historically known factors such as population relocation, limitations on travel, and potential effects of these on previous interaction relationships (Preucel 2002) could have impacted concentration, scale, and intensity of production. Concentration could have changed because of the shift in settlement pattern toward mesa-top stronghold locations. Limitations on travel could have affected scale by encouraging village self-sufficiency. Both factors could have affected intensity through the disruption of travel patterns and interaction relationships. In the absence of a pre-Revolt sample at Kotyiti, one can only suggest that Revolt-period technological style is more expedient than pre-

Mission glaze ware technology based on the understanding of Mission-period technology suggested by Salinas area data. A more secure comparison for future study would explore the technological styles of pre-Revolt glaze wares at the three villages whose populations are believed to have contributed to the formation of Kotyiti: Cochiti, San Felipe, and San Marcos. Notably, the core ensemble of techniques continues throughout occupation of Kotyiti from the Revolt period until residents left in approximately 1700.

Temper Choice: A Measure of the Social Potential of Glaze Wares?

The Mission-period continuity of temper types at Abó Pueblo in the Salinas area is especially striking in light of the trend toward increased expedience. The material is not the most readily available. The chosen hornblende diorite occurs 1–5 km from the village, while suitable material abounds within the village and is used in the nondecorated wares. This pattern suggests that there is a shared conception of the type of temper that is appropriate for use in glaze wares. This idea is supported by the distinctive rock types that are used consistently as glaze ware tempers at numerous villages (Shepard 1942). The regionwide pattern of technology suggests that there may be a regionwide conception of temper. This is an important aspect in the cultural biography of the glaze wares studied here. To some degree, social identity, such as village identity, may be signaled through temper. Possible village identity in temper suggests an aspect of the social potential of glaze wares and merits further study—for example, exploring the producer-consumer relations and the implications of distributions of glaze wares across space and time with village identity and temper in mind.

At Kotyiti, temper material of Tshirege tuff is adopted uniformly with the founding of the village. This specific material, which is among a number of potential temper materials readily available on the mesa top, is used in the vast majority of glaze wares that were produced at the village (Capone and Preucel 2002). Notably, the same material is present in all samples of my pilot study of utility wares from the village. The Kotyiti plaza pueblo also conveys a theme of uniformity, as it was planned and constructed as a unit. I suggest that these expressions of unity at a village, which was composed of refugees from three previous villages, are notable.

These patterns of uniformity may reflect a social identity of broader unity than suggested here for villages prior to the Revolt period. In other words, they may reflect less emphasis on expression of intervillage difference and more emphasis on pan-Puebloan commonalities during the Revolt and post-Revolt periods.

Continuity in temper material and its possible role in maintenance of village identity suggests that village identity was important during the late prehistoric and Mission periods, but perhaps less emphasized during the Revolt and post-Revolt periods. Today, village and family are emphasized as important social units by many Puebloan potters. This is evidenced by adherence to identifiable family styles and village styles, which play prominent roles in the contemporary ceramic market (Dillingham 1994).

Cross-Cultural Interest: Cultures in Contact

Understanding these factors contributes to exploring meanings of ceramic technology across cultures. The roles of traditionalism, producer-consumer relations, individual artist choice, and pragmatism have potential for interest across cultures. Situations of culture contact such as missions or other colonial structures that involve domination, resistance, and challenges to preexisting behaviors, may be especially conducive to exploring these themes.

Technological choices of contemporary and past Puebloan potters shed light on how behavior influences technology. The adoption of expedient technology during the Mission period can be viewed as a pragmatic choice based in the Mission-period factors described above. The stresses on context of production, scale, and intensity were likely to have been important in the pragmatic choice of expediency. Contemporary Puebloan potters identify particular aspects of technology as subject to pragmatic technological choices. Some aspects of technology are open to compromise, while others are not. Further exploration of this may offer insight into past cultures and across cultures and in particular whether generalized patterns develop across other situations of culture contact where stresses of control of production, scale, and intensity may have been active factors. Among factors of culture contact that may be affecting today's potters is the demand of a market economy, which emphasizes a degree of dependability. Pragmatic choices for today's Pueblo potters include use of modern technology, such as an electric kiln if the vagaries of an outdoor fire present too great a risk (Capone 1999:52).

Traditionalism may be defined as adherence to prescribed behavior rooted in the past. Emphasis on aspects of traditionalism in contemporary Puebloan ceramic technology is suggestive of a cultural/technological insurance policy for a successful product. Some aspects of technology are treated with reverence as unchangeable tradition. Initial discussions with contemporary potters highlight aspects of technique that are considered traditional and an essential element of their work along with individual expression (Capone 1998, 1999). Choice of raw material, including temper, is suggested by contemporary potters to be a particularly important quality to maintain (Capone 1998). Some potters say their understanding of the meanings of temper material is important to their selection. For example, Acoma potters' use of sherd temper symbolizes the support of the ancestors for the pot through the addition of the ancestral spirit, which is in turn symbolized by the pot as it embarks on its social life (Lewis, Lewis Mitchell, and Lewis Garcia 1990). This area of inquiry would be interesting to pursue given the diachronic emphasis on inclusion material choice discussed here and the demonstration that this choice is imbued with meaning for contemporary potters. San Ildefonso potters ground temper on their metates earlier this century (Guthe 1925:21). One wonders if the grinding of temper mirrored the grinding of corn to Pueblo people and if some symbolism of corn grinding was attributed to temper. This analogy is further supported by the fact that the unusual type of rock used for temper at Abó is present at the village in only one other form, as manos. This line of inquiry could be explored further through discussion with contemporary potters and additional research in ethnohistoric accounts.

Issues of social identity in the choice of raw material are interesting for cross-cultural study. Arnold has also suggested cultural significance in temper choice among contemporary Maya potters (Arnold 1967). He recounts how Shepard questioned the connection and suggested he was attributing mineralogical knowledge to the potters (Arnold 1991:330). Study of Neolithic stone axes in Britain, which explores the "social and material conditions under which those objects were originally produced" suggests that raw material and its association with the place the material originated is pivotal in understanding the "changing character and social context of axe circulation and deposition across the country as a whole"

(Bradley and Edmonds 1993). These studies indicate that the degree to which choice of raw material and technology play a role in initially imbuing an object with social potential is a rich avenue for study.

The trend toward a more expedient style of technology combines with ethnohistoric and ethnographic information to suggest new types of alliances between social groups within the village of Abó, or shifts in producer-consumer relations. One new alliance may result from the incorporation of mission personnel into the system of supply and consumer demand for ceramics. Another may form along the lines of traditionalist/progressive sodalities that have been described for historic and modern pueblos (Titiev 1944; Wyckoff 1985). The change in technological style within the continuation of the major theme (or core ensemble of techniques) suggests active transformation of technology, which is rooted in pre-Mission identity. Emphasis on elements of pre-Mission identity suggests that changes in consumer demand may have been the most potent factor in developing expediency. Changes in demand, and their social consequences, also may be informative for cross-cultural studies.

Conclusions

Arnold's approach of ceramic ethnoarchaeology suggests that the best broad theories will be those based on the unique physical and chemical characteristics of ceramics themselves. Along those lines, I suggest that exploring conservatism in technology, such as that seen here in the core ensemble of techniques, and the aspects of that technology that continue into today's market economy may be interesting and may shed light on technological choices and socioeconomic strategies across cultures. Market economy and demand for traditional goods can confound the ethnoarchaeology in prehistoric analogy. However, understanding what is emphasized as traditional may be enlightening. Two lessons are clear for interpreting the past: awareness of the ever-changing nature of tradition over the past century, and identification of essentialist qualities that are so linked to Pueblo culture that their compromise would be untenable today. Exploration of meanings of temper, a seemingly immutable category of material in Puebloan ceramics, and exploration of what constitutes core technologies may be informative inquiries and lead to additional theory. Stark suggests that these areas, technological styles, "provide more stable and resilient patterning of social boundaries than does iconological style"

(Stark 1999: 42). The emerging patterns in glaze ware technology and their implications for other ceramic types may support the idea that technology is a fruitful area for future study of social dynamics and ways in which the creation of things imbues them with social potential.

Acknowledgments

I thank Robert Preucel for direction of the Kotyiti Project and support of my petrographic study of Kotyiti wares within the project through the University of Pennsylvania Museum and the University Research Foundation; Katherine Spielmann for her direction of related projects in the Salinas area; the American Museum of Natural History for loan of ceramics from Kotyiti; the Laboratory of Anthropology, Museum of New Mexico, Santa Fe, for loan of ceramics from Kotyiti and the Salinas area; and the University Museum at the University of Colorado for access to the Shepard petrographic reference collection.

13
Directionality and Exclusivity of Plains-Pueblo Exchange during the Protohistoric Period, AD 1450–1700

Kathryn Leonard

Much archaeological research has been directed toward understanding the economic and ecological character of Plains-Pueblo interaction (Baugh 1984, 1991; Habicht-Mauche 1988; Speth 1991; Spielmann 1982, 1991a, 1991b, 1994; Wilcox 1991). Building on this previous research, this study utilizes Rio Grande Glaze Ware ceramic temper data to elucidate the geographical directionality of Plains-Pueblo trade ties and evaluate the level of exclusivity with which these ties were maintained during the Protohistoric period (AD 1450–1700). Drawing on available ethnographic data on hunter-gatherer and horticulturist exchange and Spanish historical descriptions of Plains-Pueblo interaction, I further explore the likelihood of individuals' participation in interethnic political alliances and inherited trade partnerships.

I examine Plains-Pueblo exchange using a macroscopic technique of temper identification on glaze ware sherds recovered from sixty-three archaeological sites located on the Llano Estacado escarpment of the Texas Panhandle. Although designated generally as protohistoric Plains, these sites constitute two separate geographic areas commonly associated with two distinct archaeological complexes: Tierra Blanca and Garza (Hughes 1989). The results of this analysis suggest that while Plains residential groups maintained highly exclusive trade ties with specific pueblos, the geographical directionality of these ties varied between complexes. Thus, the vision of Plains-Pueblo exchange that emerges from my study is one of a network of independent, long-term, and socially embedded interethnic trade ties.

While ecological and economic considerations must have factored into the various Plains and Pueblo groups' decisions to engage in the complementary exchange of corn and bison products, I argue that it was not merely the demand for material objects, but also the social relationships, that maintained the system as a whole. While the precise social mechanisms that linked Plains individuals with their Pueblo peers eludes archaeological discussion, this study represents an attempt to better characterize the structure, or "rules and resources" (following Giddens 1984), within which the social agents of Plains and Pueblo exchange operated. In grounding this research in an explicit structure and agency-based perspective, it becomes possible to recast Plains-Pueblo exchange as a dynamic force, shaping not only the economic but also the social realm of interethnic relations.

Protohistoric Occupation of the Rio Grande and the Llano Estacado

The Rio Grande region (see fig. 1.1), in comparison with other areas of the Greater Southwest, experienced a relatively late florescence of cultural activity. However, by the time of Coronado's 1540 *entrada* into the Southwest, the population of the Rio Grande was organized into a series of large, often multistoried pueblo villages bound together by a complex series of ritual and economic relationships. Glaze ware ceramics have been frequently cited as evidence for this complex system of intraregional exchange emerging in the protohistoric Rio Grande. It is also about this time that many of the large border pueblos, such as Pecos and Gran Quivira, intensified exchange relations with the Plains.

The Llano Estacado (see fig. 1.1) represents a vast track of arid "hauntingly flat" grassland that extends east of the Rio Grande into what is familiarly known as the Texas Panhandle (Kessell 1987:22). Although much archaeological attention has been directed toward an understanding of Plains hunter-gatherers, the Llano Estacado may be geographically conceived as the "crossroads" of the southwestern and Plains cultural adaptations. While the historic inhabitants of the Llano Estacado are typically portrayed as nomadic bison hunters (i.e., Apache, Comanche), a substantial semisedentary population of Caddoan horticulturists has been both ethnohistorically and archaeologically documented (Baugh 1991).

In much of the literature on West Texas archaeology, sites of the Protohistoric period are ascribed to one of two culture complexes (see fig. 1.2). Sites ascribed to the Tierra Blanca Complex (AD 1450–1650) are situated in the canyons of the Red River drainage system, primarily in the vicinity of Palo Duro and Tierra Blanca Creek. Sites ascribed to the Garza Complex (AD 1450–1650) fall within a broader geographical area, located in the Caprock Canyons north of the Brazos River and arguably extending into western Oklahoma. In addition to the obvious geographical differences, these sites also possess more subtle differences in terms of lithic technology and subsistence.

While the ethnic distinctions drawn by Coronado's chroniclers (Castañeda 1990) suggest the existence of two contemporaneous, yet ethnically distinct, groups of Plains peoples, attempts to link the Tierra Blanca and Garza complexes definitively to the ethnohistoric Querecho and Teya are tenuous, at best. My reluctance to ascribe ethnicity to these sites involves the potential hazard of reifying archaeological constructs that, although generally useful, have been alternately qualified as "ill-defined," "misunderstood," and "vague" in the literature of West Texas archaeology (Boyd 1997:368, 380). Nevertheless, while the archaeological basis of the Garza/Tierra Blanca distinction bears consideration, the almost two hundred kilometer distance between the two sets of sites remains a clear point of separation. Thus, for the purposes of this analysis, sites from these two areas are considered as two separate archaeological entities that I will refer to as "complexes."

Plains-Pueblo Exchange: Archaeological and Historical Studies

The ecological aspect of Plains-Pueblo exchange has been most thoroughly addressed by Spielmann (1982, 1991a, 1991b) and Speth (1991). In addition, Baugh (1984, 1991) employed a world systems approach to an understanding of Plains-Pueblo relations. Although these studies have taken an ecological perspective on horticulturist/hunter-gatherer interaction, they also lay the groundwork for analyses focused on the social dynamics of Plains-Pueblo exchange. The consequent vision of trade emerging from these studies involves the nutritionally complementary exchange of bison meat for corn. However, as later work by Spielmann, Schoeninger, and Moore (1990) suggests, Plains-Pueblo mutualism may have also had a nondietary dimension. Spielmann (1989) has subsequently suggested that a portion of Pueblo exchange with Plains hunter-gatherers may have stemmed from the demand for bison hides, which may have been used as garments. This suggestion of interethnic trade for items of essentially nonsubsistence value lays the groundwork for further studies into the social dimensions of Plains-Pueblo exchange.

Several other archaeologists have integrated the social component of Plains-Pueblo interaction into their research. Drawing on ethnographic analogy, Speth (1991) hypothesizes that Pueblo-Plains mutualistic exchange may have been intensified through the process of hypergyny, the exogamous marriage of hunter-gatherer women into Pueblo households. Such marital patterns, Speth argues, intensified the degree of competition among Plains men for mates. This competition, in turn, "fostered increasing economic specialization and encouraged or reinforced mutualistic exchange relationships between the two systems" (Speth 1991:22). Speth's suggestion of hypergynous marriage on the part of Plains women is countered by the work of Judith Habicht-Mauche (1988). She interprets the adoption of a new technology for manufacturing culinary ware in Plains archaeological assemblages as indicative of the marriage of Pueblo potters (i.e., women) into Plains groups, a pattern not typically observed among ethnographic populations of farmers and hunters. Regardless of whether such marriage patterns can be archaeologically elucidated, Habicht-Mauche argues that the Plains adoption of this new technological style would necessitate prolonged interethnic contact between women. The intensity of interethnic contact portrayed in her study would have to be maintained through the exchange of technological information via learning frameworks (i.e., long-term observation).

Numerous historical documents also preserve a record of Plains-Pueblo interaction. During Coronado's initial foray into the Rio Grande area in 1540, the Spanish chronicler Castañeda noted the presence of nomadic peoples wintering outside "under the eaves" of Pecos Pueblo (Winship 1896). Fray Alonso de Benavides describes Indians, "including their women and children," traveling to Pecos Pueblo for trade during the late summer months until mid-October (Benavides 1954). Similar descriptions of Plains encampments for the purpose of exchange are recorded by DeSosa for Taos and Picuris pueblos (Hammond and Rey

1966). The Chamuscado-Rodriguez expedition (1581) also received reports of frequent exchange with Plains hunter-gatherers from informants at San Marcos Pueblo in the Galisteo Basin (Hammond and Rey 1966). The observations preserved in these historical accounts thus suggest that Plains-Pueblo exchange did not occur on an ad hoc "encounter" basis. Rather, trade involved the movement of entire Plains social units to the pueblo locality. Despite the equivocal evidence of seasonality of exchange, the documentary records consistently suggest that trade occurred over sustained periods.

While historical accounts provide some hints of the seasonal timing and general organization of the Plains-Pueblo exchange event, the social dynamics of such exchange are not as clearly manifest. In other words, it is unclear whether specific residential groups of Plains people repeatedly traveled to the same pueblos for trade or instead maintained trade relations with multiple pueblos. Nevertheless, historical records do document what appear to be strong interethnic relationships between various Rio Grande pueblos and distinct Plains hunter-gatherers. The Teyas-Jumanos and Seven Rivers Apaches are often linked to the Tompiro-speaking pueblos of the Salinas district (Benavides 1954; Scholes 1937), while the Faraones Apaches are commonly associated in trade with Pecos Pueblo (A. B. Thomas 1935). Bandelier (1892), Hickerson (1994), and Riley (1997) link Piro-speaking pueblos with the nomadic Manso and Suma populations of the El Paso area. Conversely, relations of enmity are recorded between the Tiwa-speaking pueblo of Quarai and the Seven Rivers Apaches, as well as between the Tewa and the Faraones Apaches (Hackett 1937; A. B. Thomas 1935).

Archaeological Expectations

The periodic encampment of hunter-gatherers in proximity to sedentary pueblos, coupled with the long-term, seasonal nature of the exchange event, undoubtedly involved the negotiation of social relationships between the Plains people and Pueblo Indians on both an individual and group basis. While the resolution of the archaeological record prohibits an appreciation of the precise nature of exchange ties between the actual individuals participating in the exchange event, the aggregate actions of such individuals may be gleaned by examining exchange ties at the group level. For purposes of this analysis, I define the hunter-gatherer group as a residential unit comprising multiple, and likely related, families. Where necessary, I have attempted to distinguish my use of the residential "group" as the analytical unit responsible for site-specific archaeological phenomena from other uses of *group* to refer to broader archaeological complexes or hunter-gatherer ethnic distinctions (e.g., Querechos vs. Teyas) *writ large*.

The social dynamics of Plains-Pueblo exchange may be elucidated through archaeological investigations of the intensity of hunter-gatherer ties to the various Rio Grande pueblos. Specifically, it may be possible to determine archaeologically whether a Plains group that repeatedly occupied the same Plains village consistently traded with a single pueblo or pueblo cluster. If, as the historical accounts suggest, Plains groups repeatedly traveled to the same pueblos for exchange, one would expect sherds recovered from Plains sites on the Llano Estacado to be dominated by a single source. Apparently exclusive exchange ties would also corroborate Spielmann's characterization of "trade partners" as the institutionalized set of social relationships through which interethnic exchange occurs (Spielmann 1991a).

While a finding of *exclusivity* supports the characterization of trade partnerships as the social mechanism structuring Plains-Pueblo exchange, such findings would not conform to known hunter-gatherer strategies of risk minimization. Assuming that Plains groups had knowledge of the variable productivity of different areas of the Rio Grande, the desire to avoid agricultural shortfalls would be reflected in the maintenance of multiple trade partnerships. This strategy—in ecological terms referred to as "buffering"—has been thoroughly documented by Spielmann (1991a) for a variety of ethnographic groups. The microclimatic shifts and corresponding variability in agricultural production documented by Rautman (1993) for prehistoric central New Mexico suggests that a buffering strategy involving the maintenance of extensive trade ties presents itself as a viable model for Plains-Pueblo interaction. Such a buffering strategy in which a Plains group's decision is based solely on economic exigency and the presence of a reliable agricultural surplus would find archaeological expression in a Plains ceramic assemblage with multiple Puebloan temper types.

In defining the research problem, I examine social relationships in terms of two analytical variables: exclusivity and directionality. In choosing these variables, I hope to quantitatively ascertain the intensity of relations engendered between specific groups of Plains hunter-gatherers and

Pueblo communities. *Exclusivity* is defined here as the degree to which one group's trade of a complex of goods is with a single other group. Investigations of the degree of exclusivity of Plains-Pueblo exchange can provide insight into the social preferences of trade in the context of other risk-minimizing strategies, such as buffering, that may favor trade with multiple groups.

While I use the concept of exclusivity to gauge the intensity of exchange ties at the level of the residential group, such a concept does not fully address the question of whether such trade preferences occur at the level of the mobile residential group, or whether the decision with whom to conduct trade is rooted in a broader *cultural preference* in interethnic social relations. As such, I use the concept of directionality to gauge whether residential groups that share some level of social identification also share trade relations with the same external groups. Thus, the term *directionality* is defined here as the degree to which groups that share a common cultural tradition also share a common focus of long-distance exchange. As the archaeological distinctions between the Garza and Tierra Blanca complexes have often been cited as evidence for the existence of contemporary, yet ethnically distinct, groups of Plains hunter-gatherers, I use these categories as a comparative framework for evaluating the degree of directionality within these two regions.

It is important to note that while I discuss the concepts of directionality and exclusivity as they apply to the interethnic social relationships generated by long-distance exchange, my data address only a single side of the exchange equation. That is, even if Plains trade relations with the Rio Grande pueblos may be characterized as highly directional and highly exclusive, the same may not be true for the Pueblos themselves. It seems plausible that a Plains residential group might trade exclusively with a single pueblo, while a Pueblo household might maintain trade ties with a variety of groups. Furthermore, regionally (and perhaps ethnically) distinct Plains complexes may have had a highly directional trade focus on a single pueblo or pueblo cluster, while the pueblo itself had a more diffuse trade focus on multiple complexes. While the nature of the data prohibits further elucidation of this problem, the question of symmetry in the social dynamics of Plains-Pueblo exchange remains a provocative topic for future research.

In this study, both directionality and exclusivity will be assessed through an examination of the various temper types (indicating the pueblo cluster of production) represented in the glaze ware ceramic assemblages from Plains sites. Exclusivity can be gauged through an examination of the relative homogeneity of temper types represented at a single site. Directionality, on the other hand, can only be ascertained through an examination of the glaze ware temper data at the level of the archaeological complex. As such, a high degree of directionality will result in a high degree of temper homogeneity between sites identified as Tierra Blanca Complex and those identified as Garza Complex.

Data and Methods

While the majority of Tierra Blanca Complex and Garza Complex sites sampled in this study are known only by surface observation, excavation data are available for several sites. Blackburn (41RD20) and Tierra Blanca (41DF3) represent well-documented Tierra Blanca Complex sites, and Montgomery (41FL17), Floydada Country Club (41FL1), Bridwell (41CB27), Headstream (41KT51), and Longhorn (41KT53) represent well-documented Garza Complex sites. All of these sites may be considered residential base camps, with ephemeral structures defined by rock rings. However, there are qualitative differences both in location and in scale. First, while Tierra Blanca encampments are located on the actual Llano Plain, broadly distributed along tributaries of the Tierra Blanca and Canadian River drainages, sites of the Garza Complex are generally found in more protective confines and riparian environments, such as Blanco Canyon (Boyd 1997). Second, while Tierra Blanca Complex sites such as Blackburn and Tierra Blanca may have at least two components of occupation, the extremely large size and multicomponent nature of Garza Complex sites appear to reflect not only an areally extensive occupation, but also an occupation that may have extended over several hundred years (Boyd 1997:395).

A total of 2,050 glaze ware sherds from sixty-three sites ascribed to either the Tierra Blanca or Garza complexes were analyzed in this study (Leonard 2000). The bulk of these materials represent multiple episodes of surface collection by amateur archaeologists on highly deflated sites. Thus, with the exception of sites A264 and A152 (excavated by Spielmann 1982), intrasite provenience data are nonexistent. Several sites examined in this study (41FL1, 41CB27, and 41FL17) were excavated by amateur archaeological groups (Parker 1982; Word 1963, 1965). However, provenience data from these excavations were not preserved.

For purposes of this analysis, sites were divided into three tiers according to sample size. The first tier includes sites with glaze ware sample sizes of eighty sherds or more. The second tier includes sites with glaze ware sample sizes of fifty to eighty sherds. The third tier comprises sites with glaze ware assemblages of fewer than ten sherds. The grouping of sites in tiers was designed to prevent sites with smaller sample sizes from having a disproportionate influence on patterning.

Exclusivity of Trade Ties

The homogeneity of temper types present in each Plains site's glaze ware ceramic assemblage can be used to evaluate the exclusivity of that site's trade ties with Rio Grande pueblo clusters. Glaze ware assemblages from sites of both the Tierra Blanca and Garza complexes are characterized by the presence of relatively few temper types. More importantly, these temper types can often be linked to a single area of production. Multiple temper types are associated with glaze ware production in the Galisteo Basin (augite latite and hornblende andesite) and the Salinas area (hornblende diorite, hornblende gneiss, biotite diorite, and sherd). For purposes of analysis, these temper types have been collapsed into a single source area.

Source distributions indicative of high levels of exclusivity are found in a preponderance of sites ascribed to the Tierra Blanca Complex. The three sites with the largest ceramic assemblages have temper sources represented in very similar proportions (see fig. 13.1). The Galisteo Basin tempers augite latite (San Marcos) and hornblende andesite (Tonque) predominate, constituting between 78.7 percent and 88.0 percent of the total ceramic assemblage. Hornblende diorite (Abó), sherd, and sandstone (Quarai) temper indicative of trade with the Salinas pueblos are also present in almost identical proportions. This same pattern is also present among the "second tier" sites examined, with Galisteo Basin tempers constituting between 62.2 percent and 100 percent of the ceramic assemblages (see fig. 13.1). Although the glaze ware assemblages of these second-tier sites do not precisely mirror those of the first-tier sites, the smaller sample sizes of these sites are expected to somewhat skew the various proportions of tempers represented.

Despite the obvious differences among the specific tempers represented at individual sites, glaze ware ceramic assemblages of Garza Complex sites are also dominated by a single source (see fig. 13.2). This is most dramatically apparent at the Bridwell site (41CB27), where 90.0 percent

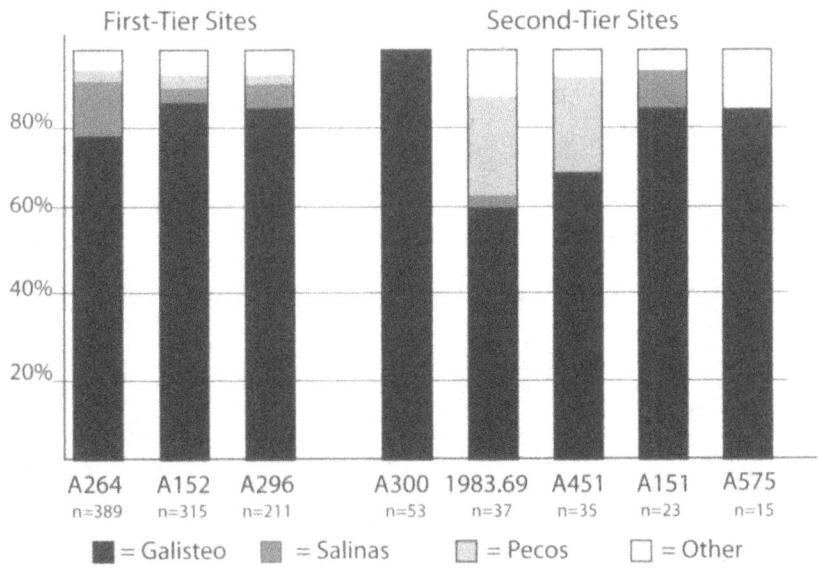

Fig. 13.1. Glaze ware source areas for first- and second-tier Tierra Blanca sites.

of the glaze ware sherds sampled are sourced to the Galisteo Basin. At the Montgomery site (41FL17), 68.2 percent of the sherds sampled derive from the Salinas district. At the Floydada Country Club site (41FL1) and site 41MY1, 81.3 percent and 66.8 percent of the sherds sampled are sandstone tempered, interpreted as trade with Pecos Pueblo. This same pattern of site-level exclusivity is also evident among the second-tier sites sampled (see fig. 13.2).

As the bar charts do not immediately convey a high degree of trade exclusivity among Garza Complex sites, I have further analyzed the distribution of glaze ware source areas for the Garza Complex using Simpson's C statistic. Simpson's C is typically employed as a measure of concentration, or dominance, of a particular type within a population (Pielou 1975). The measure has values ranging from 0 (minimal dominance) to 1 (perfect dominance) that represent the probability that any two items selected from a distribution (with replacement) will be of the same type or class (Kintigh 2002; Pielou 1975). As the concept of exclusivity, in operational terms, refers to the dominance of a single source area for sherds within an individual glaze ware assemblage, this measure is particularly well suited to address this question.

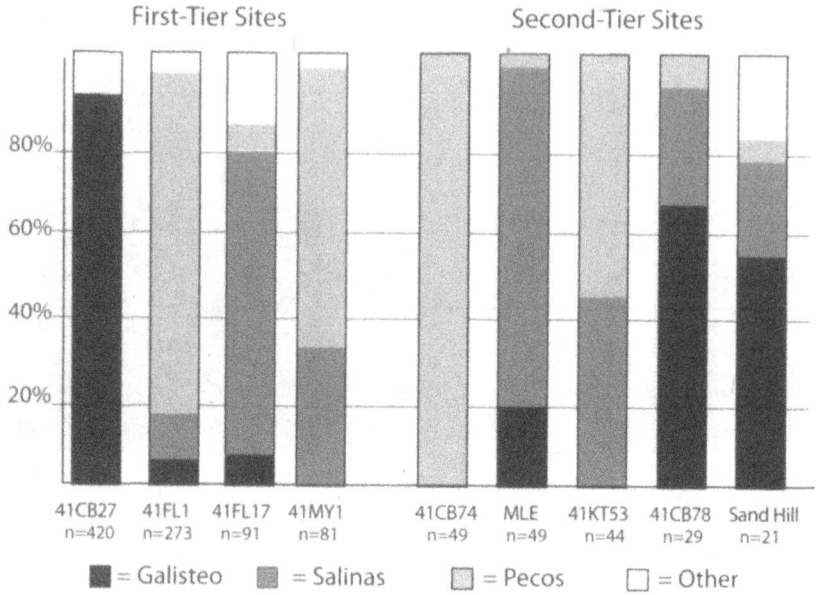

Fig. 13.2. Glaze ware source areas for first- and second-tier Garza Complex sites.

Using Kintigh's (2002) EVALC program, a Simpson's C is first calculated for an actual assemblage with its specified type proportions. Using the sample sizes of the actual assemblages, a large number of Monte Carlo samples are then randomly generated using proportions in an observed population. The distribution of Simpson's C values for the random samples is used to estimate the probability of obtaining a C value greater than or equal to the C value of the original sample. A low probability associated with obtaining an observed C value as high or higher than the original C value suggests that the observed concentration in the sample is unlikely to occur by chance.

To generate the reference population, I averaged the proportions of glaze ware source areas for all Tierra Blanca and Garza Complex sites to create a model population against which the observed populations' (Garza Complex sites) C values can be compared. This model population was intended to simulate a scenario of minimal exclusivity, in which a Plains group's trade occurred with all three pueblo clusters in roughly similar proportions. A Monte Carlo simulation of 10,000 runs was employed for the evaluation of each assemblage. As presented in table 13.1, with the ex-

Table 13.1
Simpson's C Values Generated for Garza Complex Sites

	Source Areas				Sample Size	Simpson's C	p Value
	Salinas	Galisteo	Pecos	Other			
Population	19%	53%	22%	6%	—	0.37	—
Garza Complex Site							
41CB27	1%	91%	1%	8%	419	0.83	< 0.001
41FL1	11%	5%	81%	3%	273	0.68	< 0.001
41FL17	73%	8%	3%	16%	91	0.56	< 0.001
41MY1	33%	0%	67%	0%	81	0.56	< 0.001
41CB74	0%	0%	100%	0%	49	1.00	< 0.001
MLE No ID*	80%	18%	2%	0%	49	0.67	< 0.001
41KT53	43%	0%	57%	0%	44	0.51	< 0.019
41CB78	28%	66%	7%	0%	29	0.51	< 0.064
Sand Hill	24%	52%	5%	19%	21	0.37	< 0.604

*"MLE" refers to an unprovenienced collection at the Museum of the Llano Estacado in Plainview, Texas. "No ID" refers to collections that are not provenienced to a specific site but for which the general location of recovery is known.

ception of Sand Hill, all of the Garza Complex sites' C values were greater than the original "model" population's C value of 0.37. These values suggest that, with the possible exceptions of 41CB78 and Sand Hill, the results are highly significant. Furthermore, the extremely low p values suggest that the probability of obtaining concentrations this high is unlikely to be the result of sampling error.

Directionality of Trade Ties

While the shared degree of exclusivity suggests that the overall system of Plains-Pueblo exchange was characterized by the long-term persistence of interethnic trade ties, an evaluation of the directionality of these ties suggests that geographically distinct groups (i.e., Garza and Tierra Blanca peoples) may have possessed very different ways of organizing long-distance exchange. Sites of the more northerly Tierra Blanca Complex have a strong directional focus of exchange with the pueblos of the Galisteo Basin. Evidence of this relationship is borne out of the consistently high percentage of glaze ware ceramics at Tierra Blanca Complex sites with tempers indicative of production at the Galisteo Basin pueblos of San Marcos and Tonque.

In contrast to the Tierra Blanca pattern, sites of the more southerly Garza Complex have a small degree of geographical directionality. Not only do sites of the Garza Complex have ceramic assemblages with tempers indicative of production areas other than the Galisteo Basin, these sites also appear to have exchange ties that are differentially distributed among the other Rio Grande pueblos. The presence of what appears to be a diverse set of trade ties within the Garza Complex is particularly interesting in terms of the extreme geographic proximity of these sites. For example, the Bridwell site, Floydada Country Club site, and Montgomery site are all located within approximately two kilometers of one another, within the protected confines of Blanco Canyon.

Not only do the Garza sites possess a low overall directional focus of exchange, they also seem to reflect a different pattern of exchange altogether. That is, while the Tierra Blanca sites form a cohesive unit, Garza sites appear to be distinguished from one another in terms of their exchange ties. The differences in the geographic directionality of exchange ties among sites of the Tierra Blanca and Garza complexes are particularly evident when the percent contributions of each of the three known production areas are plotted against one another. As the resultant triangular plot demonstrates (see fig. 13.3), sites of the Tierra Blanca Complex cluster tightly together at a single vertex, reflecting ceramic assemblages indicative of exchange with the Galisteo Basin, while sites of the Garza Complex are located near all three of the vertices of the plot, reflecting ceramic assemblages indicative of exchange with all three of the major production areas.

Considerations for Interpreting Results

While the contrasts between the glaze ware assemblages of sites of the Tierra Blanca and Garza complexes are readily apparent, the interpretation of this contrast is less straightforward. On the one hand, the observed differences in the degree of directionality may be the product of differences in the structure of trade relations by two contemporary Plains populations. On the other hand, these differences could also reflect a shift in the foci of Pueblo trade over time. The issue here is one of contemporaneity.

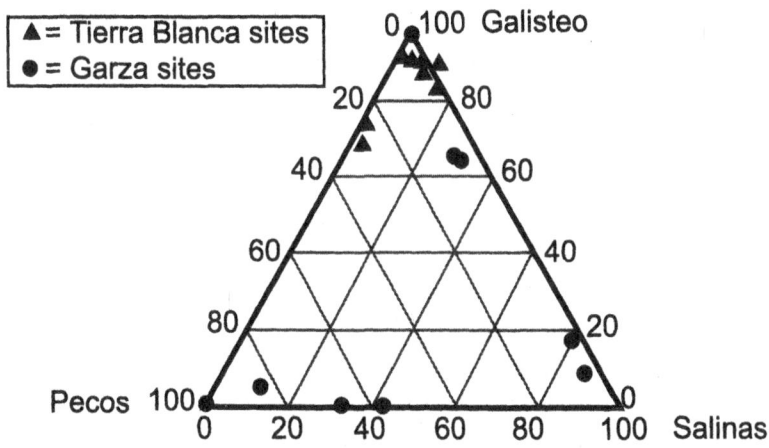

Fig. 13.3. Triangular coordinate plot of glaze ware source areas.

Thus, it is necessary to address what role, if any, time contributes to the observed patterning.

Texas Panhandle archaeologists have long lamented the problem of dating protohistoric sites of the Southern Plains (Boyd 1997). Where possible, dating of Tierra Blanca and Garza sites has been helped by the small amounts of glaze ware bowl rims recovered through excavation (e.g., Spielmann 1991b; Boyd et al. 1993). Eleven bowl rims were recorded for sites of the Tierra Blanca Complex, while thirty-two bowl rims were recorded for sites of the Garza Complex (table 13.2). Both the Garza sites and the Tierra Blanca sites have Glaze C and D bowl rims; however, the Garza sites are distinguished by the presence of Glaze E and F bowl rims (see fig. 13.4). The co-occurrence of Glaze C and D indicates a chronological interpretation of the Tierra Blanca sites as dating between AD 1425 and 1525. The additional presence of Glaze E and F at the Garza Complex sites extends their occupation further into the historic period, dating through the end of the 1600s. However, the presence of sizable amounts of Glaze C and D bowl rims on both Tierra Blanca and Garza sites suggests a substantial amount of temporal overlap between these two complexes.

This pattern is also borne out by the available radiocarbon data (compiled by Boyd 1997:372, 383–88). Although there are clearly more radiocarbon dates recovered from Garza site contexts ($n = 53$) than from Tierra Blanca site contexts ($n = 8$), some clear patterns may be discerned (see fig. 13.5). Like the glaze bowl rim data, the radiocarbon data suggest at

Table 13.2

Total Bowl Rims Recorded for Tierra Blanca and Garza Complex Sites

	Bowl Rim Form							
Site	A	B	C	C/D	D	E	F	Total
Tierra Blanca Sites								
A152	0	0	1	0	0	0	0	1
A264	0	0	2	0	5	0	0	7
A106	0	0	0	0	1	0	0	1
A474	0	0	1	0	0	0	0	1
A419	0	0	1	0	0	0	0	1
Total	0	0	5	0	6	0	0	11
Garza Complex Sites								
41MY1	0	0	5	0	0	2	2	9
41CB27	2	0	2	0	3	1	0	8
41FL1	0	0	0	0	0	0	3	3
41CB64	0	0	0	0	0	0	2	2
Word No ID[a]	0	0	0	0	0	1	2	3
41KT53	0	0	0	1	0	0	1	2
Lynn No ID[b]	0	0	1	0	0	0	0	1
MLE No ID[c]	0	0	1	0	2	0	1	4
Total	2	0	9	1	5	4	11	32

Note: "No ID" refers to collections that are not provenienced to a specific site but for which the general location of recovery is known.

[a] "Word" refers to the collection of Jim Word.

[b] "Lynn" to the collection of Alvin Lynn.

[c] "MLE" refers to an unprovenienced collection at the Museum of the Llano Estacado in Plainview, Texas.

least partial contemporaneity between sites of these two complexes, with the bulk of dates falling in the AD 1400 to 1550 range. However, Garza Complex sites have also yielded radiocarbon dates from the mid-1600s as well as a smaller cluster of dates from the early 1800s (see fig. 13.5).

The hypothesized long-term occupation of Garza Complex sites, when compared to Tierra Blanca sites, is particularly interesting in light of the exclusivity of glaze ware sources observed among the Garza Complex sites. It suggests that certain hunter-gatherer groups may have maintained trade ties with specific pueblos or pueblo clusters for extended periods. Two of the three sites that have rims indicative of Middle Glaze- (C and D) and Late Glaze- (E and F) period occupations also exhibit continuity

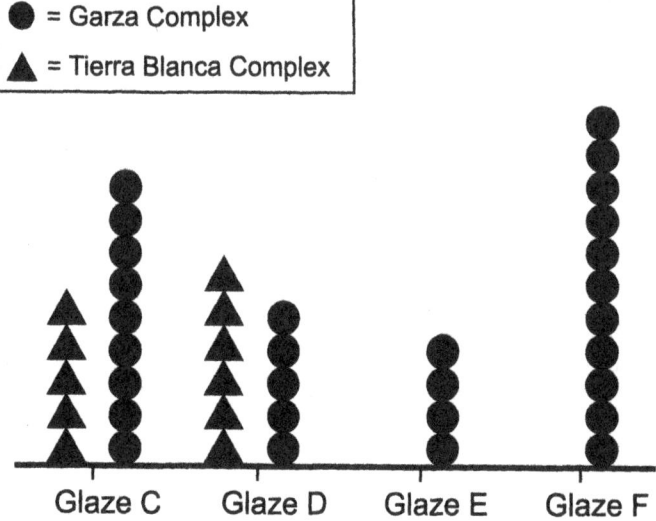

Fig. 13.4. Distribution of glaze ware rims by rim form: Garza Complex and Tierra Blanca Complex sites.

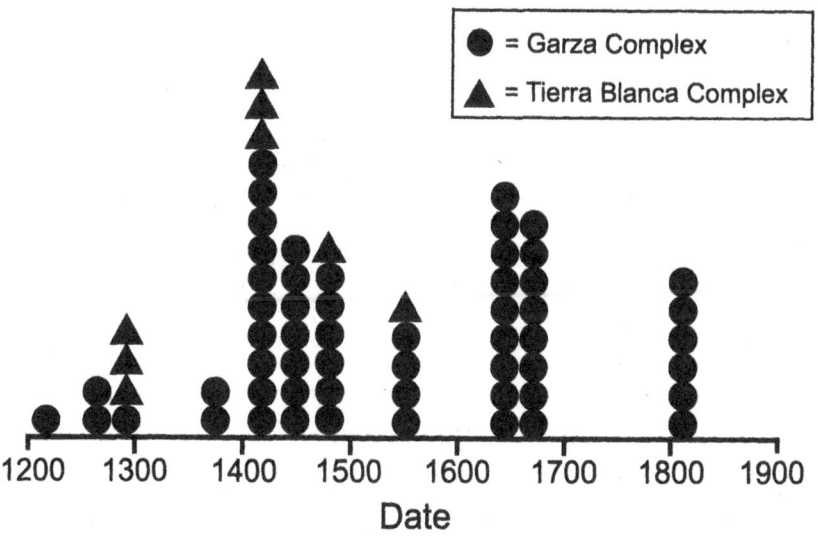

Fig. 13.5. Radiocarbon intercept dates: Garza and Tierra Blanca Complex sites.

Table 13.3
Garza Complex Rims by Time Period and Source

		Galisteo		Salinas		Pecos		
Occupation	Site	Middle Glaze (C/D)	Late Glaze (E/F)	Middle Glaze (C/D)	Late Glaze (E/F)	Middle Glaze (C/D)	Late Glaze (E/F)	Total
Early	41CB27	5						5
Early and Late	MLE No ID[a]			2	1	1		4
	41MY1			5	2		2	9
	41KT53				1	1		2
Late	41FL1				3			3
	41CB64				2			2
	Word No ID[b]				3			3
Total		5		7	12	2	2	28

Note: "No ID" refers to collections that are not provenienced to a specific site, but for which the general location of recovery is known.
[a] "MLE" refers to an unprovenienced collection at the Museum of the Llano Estacado in Plainview, Texas.
[b] "Word" refers to the collection of Jim Word.

in the source of glaze ware ceramics (table 13.3). For example, at 41MY1, there are five Middle Glaze and two Late Glaze rims indicative of exchange with the Salinas pueblos. The addition of two Late Glaze rims sourced to Pecos Pueblo suggests that although the inhabitants of this site may have expanded trade to include another pueblo, they still maintained their established trade ties with the Salinas district.

Discussion

On a broad level, I have attempted to evaluate the general structure of Plains-Pueblo exchange by assessing the degree of directionality and exclusivity manifested in ties of exchange. However, on a more theoretical level, I believe this study may also approach the "precise nature" of the social relationships engendered through interethnic exchange (Boyd 1997:419). In the following discussion, I evaluate the results of the temper distribution data in terms of the ethnohistoric record of Plains-Pueblo relations and current ethnographic literature on hunter-gatherer and agriculturist interaction. In so doing, I hope to explore the means by which exchange operated in the construction of meaningful social relations between Plains and Pueblo communities, as well as individuals.

Directionality and the Development of Interethnic Social Alliances

The distribution of glaze ware temper types on Plains sites suggests that the Tierra Blanca and Garza complexes possessed a different degree of directional focus in terms of their exchange ties with Rio Grande pueblos. The pattern observed among the Garza sites of Blanco Canyon is particularly interesting, because despite their close proximity, the Montgomery, Bridwell, and Floydada Country Club sites all have radically different glaze ware sources. This pattern suggests that extended families or smaller bands that identified with one another in terms of subsistence lifestyle, and perhaps even ethnicity, may have independently constructed external relations of exchange.

Alternatively, the high degree of site level exclusivity and lack of regional directionality evident in the Pueblo trade ties of sites in the Blanco Canyon area may stem from the particular environmental setting. With its perennial water source, lush vegetation, abundant fauna, and protected environs, Blanco Canyon provided a temporary haven for groups seeking to avoid the harsh winters of the Llano. Historically, the area around Blanco Canyon was known as Quitaque, a rendezvous point for highly mobile bands of Apache, Wichita, and Comanche (Loomis and Nasatir 1967). If each of these groups possessed trade ties with different pueblos but repeatedly wintered at the same Blanco Canyon encampment, the archaeological signature would be one of geographically proximate sites with very different glaze ware sources. Thus, the low degree of regional directionality evident in this area may be owing to the particular context of repeated seasonal reoccupation by multiple, far-ranging groups, each with *stable* trade ties, rather than the presence of multiple trade ties within a single "territory" of hunter-gatherers.

While there are no data to suggest that the groups residing within the confines of Blanco Canyon were politically aligned against one another, the independence of their trade ties with the Pueblos does suggest that they did not operate as a cohesive unit in terms of long-distance exchange. The high degree of directionality and uniform trade ties apparent among sites of the Tierra Blanca Complex, on the other hand, suggests that groups in this area shared a common conception of not only *how* long-distance trade should be conducted but also with *whom* it should be conducted. If the Tierra Blanca Complex indeed represents the prehistoric equivalent of the historic Querecho, then the highly directional nature of these sites' trade ties with the Galisteo Basin may reflect durable bonds between ethnically distinct Plains and Pueblo households or residential units.

Spanish colonial records lend some support to this interpretation of the existence of strong social, and perhaps political, alliances between the Rio Grande pueblos and ethnically distinct bands of Plains hunter-gatherers (A. B. Thomas 1935). Spanish attempts at managing the Plains trade fairs at Pecos Pueblo repeatedly stress the long-term, intensive nature of ties between the Pecos and the Faraones Apaches, "who are accustomed to come to their pueblo most years" (Governor Panuela, in Kessell 1987).[1] Similar observations of Plains-Pueblo co-residence have been preserved in early Spanish accounts of trade occurring at Gran Quivira, a large Tompiro pueblo in the Salinas district. In fact, it seems likely that the early Spanish name for Gran Quivira, "Las Humanas," was used to distinguish the "ethnically Plains" character of the Pueblo (Hammond and Rey 1945:66). While Fray Alonso de Benavides' description of Gran Quivira stresses its role as a center of Plains-Pueblo trade, other accounts further suggest the pueblo was home to a considerable population of ethnically Plains people.

Exclusivity of Exchange and Inherited Trade Partnerships

While the results of this study suggest the presence of highly exclusive and highly persistent trade ties between specific groups of Pueblo villagers and specific groups of Plains hunter-gatherers, the question still remains: how, precisely, were such strong interethnic ties maintained? In their cross-cultural study of hunter-gatherer/horticulturist interaction, Spielmann and Eder (1994:308) cite inherited trade partnerships as a common means by which such groups "maintain predictable economic ties." Ethnographic examples of exclusive and inherited trade-partnerships between agriculturists and hunter-gatherers have been documented between adult males in numerous ethnographic groups (Gubser 1965; Harding 1967; J. T. Peterson 1978), including the Tewa and the Jicarilla Apache of the North American Southwest (Ford 1972).

The social and economic linkage of households is a common result of such trade partnerships. Household bonds are strengthened not only by wife sharing, but also by child fostering and inherited dyadic relationships between males (Harding 1967). Among the Tewa and the Jicarilla Apache, Ford observed inherited trade partnerships linking families for over three generations. These families would spend major holidays, such as Christmas and feast days, together each year (Ford 1972:33). The almost "familial" quality of these interethnic relations of exchange may be ascribed, in part, to the inherited nature of the trade partnership. However, in a very real sense, such trade partnerships between unrelated individuals may ultimately be responsible for the activation of kin-based relations (Gubser 1965; Healey 1990).

While my discussion of hunter-gatherer agriculturist trade partnerships has focused on relationships between adult males, such partnerships may have also been formed by Plains and Pueblo women. Wiessner (1997) has previously noted the construction of fictive kin relationships between !Kung San women who participate in the *hxaro* trade partnership (Wiessner 1997:120). The presence of such relationships between protohistoric Plains and Pueblo women may have provided the long-term, intensive social context Habicht-Mauche (1988) identifies as critical for the transfer of ceramic technological knowledge.

Conclusion

The capacity for exchange to construct meaningful social relationships between individuals may elude archaeological discussion. However, the reflexive monitoring of action by *individuals* is the essential generative component of social systems (Giddens 1984). In order to explore the means by which "social systems are produced as transactions between agents," we must first examine the system that structures such interaction (Giddens 1984:95); this is a task to which archaeological investigations are particularly well suited. While ethnohistoric documents and ethnographic modeling may provide us with gleanings into the more *emic* and, furthermore, microscale, social constructions of Plains-Pueblo exchange, archaeological analyses directed at evaluating the geographical directionality and exclusivity of trade ties more precisely approach the rules and resources that make such constructions possible.

The rules and resources of Plains-Pueblo exchange were characterized by both rigidity and diversity in social relations. The high degree of exclusivity apparent in the glaze ware assemblages of almost all Plains sites sampled implies the existence of relatively formal ties of exchange between individual Plains and Pueblo communities. The long-term persistence of these ties may, in turn, have been maintained through such social institutions as marriage (Speth 1991) or the inherited trade partnership.

The apparent differences in the degree of directionality evident in Garza Complex and Tierra Blanca Complex long-distance trade ties further suggest that, on a systemic level, the social framework of Plains-Pueblo exchange was also characterized by a high degree of social flexibility. As the Garza Complex sites of Blanco Canyon most dramatically indicate, Plains hunter-gatherers possessed trade ties with various Rio Grande pueblos independent of the trade ties maintained by their neighbors. However, as the more northerly Tierra Blanca sites suggest, other sets of Plains groups focused their energies on long-distance exchange with a single pueblo or pueblo cluster.

As Ford (1972:43) exhorts, "regional trade is a form of foreign policy" in which "each society interacts on different terms." While our understanding of Plains-Pueblo trade is far from complete, this study has contributed a fuller appreciation of the archaeological variability and concomitant complexity of social interaction involved in intersocietal exchange. Furthermore, this study has raised questions regarding the manner by which individuals, through the construction and maintenance of meaningful social relationships, shape the structure of the exchange system.

Acknowledgments

This chapter is based on research conducted for my master's thesis at Arizona State University. Thanks to my M.A. committee, co-chairs Michelle Hegmon and Kate Spielmann, Keith Kintigh, and Arleyn Simon, for their guidance and insightful comments. Thanks to the staff of the Panhandle Plains Historical Museum, the Crosby County Pioneer Memorial Museum, the Floyd County Historical Museum, the Museum at Texas Tech, and the Museum of the Llano Estacado for facilitating access to their collections. Alvin Lynn and the late Jim Word also generously provided me with access to their private collections. This chapter has also benefited from conversations with Douglas Boyd, Jack Hughes, Christopher Lintz, Leslie Nogue, Regge Wiseman, and the editors of this volume. This research was conducted during my tenure as a National Science Foundation graduate fellow. Funding was also provided by the Graduate College and Department of Anthropology at Arizona State University.

14

Rio Grande Glaze Paint Ware in Southwestern Archaeology

Linda S. Cordell

> The methods of studying pottery get better all the time, but the pottery stays about the same.
> —R. F. Burgh (1959:40)

This volume is particularly timely because after a very long hiatus in technological analyses of Rio Grande glaze paint ware, there is a great deal of sophisticated new research being carried out by ceramic technologists, archaeologists, and anthropologists. Additionally, although much of the seminal work in southwestern archaeology took place at large Pueblo IV sites of the late pre-Hispanic period (Kidder 1917b; Kroeber 1916; N. Nelson 1914) where glaze paint ware was used, there have been decades of neglect of that era that is only now being remedied (E. C. Adams and Duff 2004; Spielmann, ed., 1998). This new research encourages a fuller understanding of the production, use, and movement of glaze paint ware within diverse social contexts.

This chapter is composed of four sections. I first briefly and broadly characterize the Pueblo IV period, as defined by the contributors to this volume, and the kinds of questions archaeologists have brought to their research on this time in Pueblo history. I then discuss the early history of technological analysis of Rio Grande glaze paint ware, especially the pioneering work of Anna O. Shepard (Kidder and Shepard 1936; Shepard 1942). While she was not the first to examine thin sections of ancient pottery, Shepard was the first archaeologist to use thin sections and other analytical techniques systematically, and she developed rigorous methods to study ceramic technology in the U.S. Southwest and Mesoamerica (Bishop and Lange 1991; Cordell 1991). I describe the context of Shepard's work on the glaze paint wares in order to explicate why the many leads she offered were ignored by southwestern archaeologists until quite recently. The discussion of Shepard's work provides a framework within which I then focus, in the third section, on some of the contributions in this volume. I conclude with lingering questions and suggest directions for future research.

Pueblo IV: Prelude to the Pueblos Today

The Pueblo IV period is generally dated AD 1300 to 1500. As a developmental stage in the original Pecos Classification (Kidder 1927), Pueblo IV refers to the time when much of the Pueblo area, especially the San Juan region, was depopulated and ends with the Spanish *entradas* into the Southwest in 1539 and 1540. Reflecting recent refinements in dating as well as information about the archaeological chronology of the Mogollon Mountains, Pueblo IV is variously dated by the authors in this volume to 1250/1300 to 1540/1600/1700. The earlier beginning date is the result of new information about the timing of depopulation of much of the northern portion of the Ancestral Pueblo homeland (Duff and Wilshusen 2000). The later ending date of 1600 or 1700 for Pueblo IV, used by some of the authors, incorporates a Protohistoric period during which Pueblos and other indigenous peoples were only loosely tied to European polities and economies (Adams and Duff 2004; Wilcox 1981). In any case, Pueblo IV was a dynamic period in the cultural history of Ancestral Pueblo peoples. It was the time during which Pueblo peoples moved away from the Colorado Plateau and San Juan River drainage, and when settlement also contracted dramatically in much of traditional Mogollon territory. It was also a time when very large settlements were established in the Rio Grande drainage, in the ancestral Zuni and Hopi regions, in the Salinas area of east-central New Mexico, and in northern Chihuahua, Mexico. Some of these new and large settlements were deserted in the fifteenth and sixteenth centuries, while others continue to be occupied by Pueblo peoples today. In addition to the pre-Hispanic depopulation of enormous areas of Ancestral Pueblo homeland, the expanded chronology of Pueblo IV used by authors in this volume includes the trauma of the Spanish entradas, diverse responses to European conquest, subsequent Spanish colonization, the Pueblo Revolt of 1680, and the reconquest of 1692–96 (Cordell 1989; Preucel 2002). I was particularly pleased to have been asked to discuss the chapters in this book, because having spent my field career investigating Pueblo IV sites in the Rio Grande region and having thought about the broader issues raised by that work (Cordell, Doyel, and Kintigh 1994), I wanted to learn how archaeological understanding of the cultural dynamics of that period has been improved by the renewed study of glaze paint pottery.

Archaeologists who have tried to understand the events and processes of the Pueblo IV period have tended to approach them either looking forward from the regional depopulations and migrations of the late 1200s or backward from today as the basis of modern Pueblo sociolinguistic distributions that were severely disturbed by the Spanish Conquest (Eckert and Cordell 2004; Habicht-Mauche, chap. 1, this vol.; Whiteley 2004). Looking forward from the massive migrations of the late thirteenth century, many archaeologists (e.g., Habicht-Mauche, chap. 1, this vol.; Eckert, chap. 3, this vol.; Huntley, chap. 6, this vol.) focus on the dramatic color schemes of glaze paint ware and the novelty of the colors, since previous painted wares among Ancestral Pueblos were largely black-on-white, as a method of signaling affiliation in pan-regional ritual systems that could have united people from different regions and cultural backgrounds. At the end of this chapter, I note some difficulties I have with this interpretation.

Looking backward from ethnographic portrayals of Pueblo villages, and the modern political designations of most individual Pueblo villages as federally recognized tribes, has encouraged some scholars to project political, economic, and social autonomy of single villages into the Pueblo IV period. Linguistic and ethnohistorical discussions, however, focus on interactions among villages within clusters that share a common language, such as Tewa or Keres. From an archaeological perspective, either one that looks forward from the 1200s or back from today, no model of autonomous, independent Pueblo IV villages makes sense. Rather, regional depopulations and subsequent population aggregation would have integrated people with diverse histories into single settlements. Each settlement would therefore include groups who had historic ties to different settlements (Duff 2002; Eckert, chap. 3, this vol.; Nelson and Habicht-

Mauche, chap. 11, this vol.). Settlement instability at various times during Pueblo IV would have lowered single village population levels below those needed to sustain ceremonial life or ensure demographic continuity (Zubrow 1974). The clustered linguistic groupings of villages today and ethnohistoric accounts also encourage us to doubt that Pueblo IV villages were autonomous in social, ritual, and political terms. For these reasons, crucial issues for Pueblo IV are understanding how and in what ways Ancestral Pueblo communities were organized beyond the village level, and how they were linked through exchange, leadership, and/or shared belief systems (e.g., E. C. Adams 2002; E. C. Adams and Duff 2004; Cordell 1989, 1997; Cordell, Doyel, and Kintigh 1994; Crown 1994; Duff 2002; Habicht-Mauche, chap. 1, this vol.; Mills 2000; Spielmann 1998).

The contributors to this volume use pottery, specifically glaze paint ware, as a means toward understanding the nature and dynamics of the organization and interactions among Pueblo IV settlements at the district and regional levels. These discussions are not examples of "pots are people." Rather, the chapters focus on exploring the ways in which pottery technology, decoration, and exchange inform us about dynamic social interactions. The reasons why glaze paint ware technology and Pueblo IV socioreligious and political organization are linked topics are embedded in the history of southwestern archaeology. Although that history is not discussed in the chapters in this volume, I believe it is important to understand why some research topics have long been neglected while others have not. I discuss some of that history to elucidate the major strengths, weaknesses, and implications of the present volume for increased understanding of some of the dynamics of Pueblo IV organization.

Miss Shepard's Bombshell

The Rio Grande Glaze Ware sequence was first established by Alfred Vincent Kidder, the acknowledged dean of modern southwestern archaeology, through his excavations at Pecos Pueblo, New Mexico. Pecos Pueblo, occupied between about 1300 and 1838, was the largest of the late pre-Hispanic to Historic period pueblos (Kidder 1924; Kidder and Shepard 1936). Kidder selected Pecos for excavation, he tells us in his characteristically explicit fashion, because it had the longest documented history of continuous occupation of the Rio Grande Pueblo ruins, had been described in Spanish documentary history, had a known abandonment date, and had very deep trash deposits that promised (although in fact did not yield) materials of considerable antiquity (Kidder 1924).

Kidder worked in the days before tree-ring and radiocarbon dating. Excavation at Pecos Pueblo provided an excellent opportunity to demonstrate the utility of the then new techniques of stratigraphic excavation and ceramic seriation to chronicle change over time. In addition to proving the usefulness of stratigraphy, another of Kidder's objectives in excavating Pecos Pueblo was to write a history of the development of a local, household, decorative art based on the supposition that the pottery at Pecos had been locally produced (Kidder 1936:xxiii). Shepard conducted her study of petrographic thin sections of the pottery of Pecos long after Kidder's excavation had ended and Kidder's manuscript on the glaze paint pottery was nearing completion. As is well known, Shepard demonstrated that huge quantities of pottery found at Pecos had not been made there. Kidder (1936:xxiii) wrote of the "bombshell Miss Shepard's findings have thrown into the research":

> It has always been assumed that potting was one of the regular household tasks of every Pueblo woman; that each town was in this regard self-sufficient. But if whole classes of pottery, such as Glaze I and Biscuit, were imported, we must postulate an extraordinary volume of trade and allow for a compensating outward flow of other commodities. Furthermore, we must believe that the production of vessels at the source of supply was much greater than was needed for home consumption, in other words, that rudimentary commercial manufacturing was practiced. (Kidder 1936:xxiii)

Yet, Shepard's findings, especially the implications of her findings at Pecos and much of her later work, were ignored by southwestern archaeologists for more than forty years. Southwestern archaeologists could not give up the idea of autonomous villages that were in all important respects analogous to ethnographically known pueblos. As I have elaborated elsewhere (Cordell 1991), accepting the implication of Shepard's work that in at least some respects, such as craft production and exchange, modern pueblos are not analogs for ancient Pueblo villages, even those like Pecos that had a known documentary history, would have undermined the direct historical approach and much of the theoretical structure of U.S. culture-historical archaeology. To allow for disjunction between the late pre-Hispanic era and the period of ethnographic observation would open the door to the "conjectural history" of Adolph F. Bandelier and Lewis Henry Morgan. Continuity from present to past was considered necessary for the development of a science of human culture. Shepard's notion that with the development of Rio Grande glaze paint ware there seemed to have been rudimentary commercial production for market exchange was antithetical to scholars who believed that all Pueblo communities, past and present, were economically and socially independent and autonomous.

Many archaeologists writing about the Rio Grande region acknowledged that Pecos Pueblo had been a major center for trade between the Pueblos and Plains groups (Riley 1987:278-79; Schroeder 1979:435-36), but there was no discussion of how production and exchange among Pueblo communities might have been organized at the village or regional level, nor how glaze paint production technology might have been differentially distributed among Rio Grande pueblos. Shepard's work suggested economic ties among villages. Kidder's work continued to assume village-level economic autonomy, because his science required continuity in organization and structure from the present to the past. Kidder's (1924, 1927, 1958) broad understanding of the chronology of southwestern culture history placed the origin of Pecos Pueblo in the 1300s. It was a town among many that would have been influenced by the major social upheavals and migrations that transpired in the Southwest between about 1250 and 1540. Yet, Kidder did not develop a social history of this era, let alone one that included discussion of craft specialization and regional exchange. Although Pecos, like other large Pueblo IV towns, would have been influenced by major social upheavals and migrations, Kidder continued to view Pecos as economically and socially autonomous.

In 1942 Shepard published *Rio Grande Glaze Paint Ware: A Study Illustrating the Place of Ceramic Technological Analysis in Archaeological Research*, a work that is cited by many of the authors in this volume. I provide the full title here, because it describes her intent so well. Shepard did not use her work on the Pecos pottery to rewrite Rio Grande archaeology, but to provide a case study in ceramic technology in which she argues that the ceramic technologist and archaeologist need to work together. Sadly, however, the monograph is another example of the many ways in which technologist and archaeologist seem only to talk past each other. As Raymond H. Thompson (1991) points out, Shepard's explicitly stated goal for the Ceramic Technology Project that she directed for the Carnegie Institution was to conduct basic research—that is, to do the crucial systematic investigation that would apply to a variety of problems, "rather than to provide facilities analysis to be used for miscellaneous and unrelated identifications" (Shepard 1938:24).

Shepard's approach, though perhaps essential from the perspective of the development of the science of ceramic technology, discouraged close collaborations with field archaeologists who would have brought their interpretive problems, probably often as miscellaneous identifications, to Shepard's attention. I think that it is often within the context generated by largely mundane and routine field identifications that collaborative research develops and is sustained. It is of particular interest to me, in the context of the development of archaeology, that the authors in the present volume are not solely or specifically ceramic technologists. Rather they are archaeologists who have developed expertise in ceramic technological analysis in order to assist them in resolving questions about social interactions and social change. Nevertheless, the incomplete integration of ceramic technology and anthropological archaeology is a matter that continues to haunt us and to which I return later in this chapter.

Kidder's (1942) foreword to Shepard's (1942) glaze paint ware study acknowledges the implications of Shepard's study, but then moves away from them, unlike several chapters in this volume. First, Kidder comments on Shepard's findings:

> But that thousands of vessels were transported many miles and evidently exchanged for some product not possessed by their makers seriously modifies our previous conception of Pueblo economics; and the making of a few vessels of foreign types in villages which already had well-standardized wares is perhaps *evidence of a willingness to experiment or perhaps of the marrying into these communities of potters from other towns*—in either event, important new problems are raised. (Kidder 1942:i, emphasis mine)

The contexts and means of what today would be termed technology transfer are at the core of contributions to this volume by Fenn, Mills, and Hopkins, by Leonard, by Schachner, and by Herhahn. Kidder believed that traditional potters were willing to experiment, rather than mechanically follow custom. This raises questions about the contexts in which experimentation is encouraged, and it resonates with the chapters in this volume by Huntley and by Van Keuren. Although Kidder himself was not ready to address these matters in the 1940s, he chided archaeologists for not more closely associating with ceramic technologists, who like Shepard, exemplified the methods of science.

According to Kidder (1942:ii), "archaeologists ... are scandalously loose and reckless thinkers" because they attempt to reconstruct the workings of man's mind from woefully fragmentary data. "And by inference from such inferences we [archaeologists] strive to trace the complex series of events — the migrations, the wars, the developments and clashes of societies and cults — which took place throughout the millennia of prehistoric time" (Kidder 1942:ii).

Kidder (1942) then, both sagaciously and despairingly, explains what was needed in his day:

> The trouble, I think, lies in over-eagerness to justify our [archaeological] existence by producing historical results when our purely archaeological data are as yet entirely insufficient for that purpose — at a time when research in ethnology, on the psychology of preliterate peoples, and upon the multitudinous environmental and physiological factors which have shaped the course of human events has not gone far enough to allow us safely to draw any but the most tentative conclusions. (Kidder 1942:ii)

Kidder lamented not only the imperfection of archaeological data but also a lack of anthropological or psychological theory that would allow developing robust, or even perhaps just plausible, inferences about human history. At the same time, he notes that "until more is known as to how far research in ceramic technology should be carried in any given case, the work itself must to a considerable extent be experimental and exploratory" (Kidder 1942:iv). Conducting ceramic technological analyses was also relatively expensive and required many well-trained individuals like Shepard, and then as now did not offer or assure regular employment. Finally, Kidder noted that encouraging teamwork in ceramic technology and archaeology would be difficult, because "the type of individual interested in mastering the physical and chemical sciences upon which research in ceramic technology is based, is unlikely to be attracted to the archaeological field" (Kidder 1942:iv).

Times have changed and archaeologists are no longer — if they ever were — solely those with strong backs. I would note, of course, that Kidder wrote at a time when, according to him, archaeologists were of two sorts: "the hairy-chested and hairy-chinned" (Kidder 1949:xi). Today, I suspect that the greater number of women in archaeology, neither hairy-chested nor hairy-chinned, may lead to more archaeological research using the methods of the physical and chemical sciences. However, I also believe that the high-tech equipment of current ceramic technology (microprobes, mass spectrometers, and lasers) appeals to archaeologists regardless of their gender.

In sum, Shepard's discovery that there was a significant amount of trade within the Rio Grande glaze paint area was underappreciated in her day. The notion of village economic and social autonomy prevailed. Shepard was always concerned about the adequacy of her samples, potential problems with geological maps, and the lack of precision in some of her measurements given the instrumentation available to her (Shepard 1942). Properly cautious, Shepard (1942:139) noted that it was possible that raw materials, rather than vessels, were being exchanged and that systematic geologic mapping might not have been accomplished at the appropriate scale to reveal local sources for materials thought to have been imported.

It would require major changes in American archaeology for Shepard's work to be rediscovered, reevaluated, and accepted. Beginning with Walter W. Taylor (1948), of course, and the formulators and proponents of processual archaeology (e.g., Binford 1962; Longacre 1970) archaeologists refused to accept the limited nature of archaeological data as an excuse for a failure to do anthropology or at least address some anthropological issues, such as postmarital residence patterns and potentially including matters such as Kidder's clashes of societies and cults. I believe it is also significant that when southwestern archaeologists did rediscover Shepard's work after nearly half a century, it was not her work on the pottery of Pecos that drew their attention. Rather, they focused on her 1939 study in which she identified the temper in cooking vessels excavated from Pueblo Bonito in Chaco Canyon as sanidine basalt that originated at sources some eighty kilometers from Chaco Canyon. This work suggested that there was widespread trade or exchange of vessels and that such movement included huge quantities of common, unpainted cooking wares. Archaeologists would evaluate and reconfirm Shepard's discovery in the context of new excavation and analysis of what has come to be understood as a regionally organized system centered in Chaco Canyon (Toll 2001). It has been easier to accept "rudimentary commercial manufacturing" (Kidder 1936:xxiii) in the situation of a temporally remote, regionally organized polity centered in Chaco Canyon than it has been to question the status of the inhabitants of Pecos, who were described in Spanish and English chronicles as being decidedly Pueblo Indians living in a politically and economically autonomous village and whose descendants live in Pueblo villages today.

Glaze Paint Ware Reappraised

In the reappraisal of her 1942 study, Shepard (1965) presented three unresolved questions and a hypothetical reconstruction for the introduction of glaze paint ware. The first two questions involved the paint. Had the first Rio Grande potters to use glaze paint secured raw ores from Western Pueblos, or had they developed a local source? How many sources of lead ore did the Rio Grande potters have when production of glaze paint ware flourished? The final question was whether in the later glaze period potters were intentionally modifying the recipe of the glaze paint in order to produce a glaze that became runny and overflowed lines, or if that effect reflected a lack of technological control. Without the technical instrumentation to use lead isotopes to determine the source of the lead ore used in the paint, as Huntley (chap. 6, this vol.) and Nelson and Habicht-Mauche (chap. 11, this vol.) do, Shepard relied on copper content as reported for Western Pueblo glaze paint ware and Rio Grande glaze paint ware to suggest source areas. While copper and lead may occur together geologically (Huntley, chap. 6, this vol.), the copper content Shepard examined can result from the glaze recipe and not necessarily reflect the source of the lead ore.

There are two fascinating results of Shepard's approach, one prescient and the other possibly misleading. Shepard's chemical analyses suggested that the glaze paint used on early glaze-painted ware made in the Rio Grande area had high copper content that matched the glaze paint recipes determined spectrographically on Western Pueblo glaze-painted pottery sherds from the Zuni region. This led Shepard to the insight that it had been the paint or ores rather than the pots that were exchanged (Shepard 1965:79). This conclusion matches Huntley's (chap. 6, this vol.) discovery that the isotope signature of glaze paint on early (AD 1275 to 1325) Zuni glaze-paint-decorated wares, from the Zuni region, matches the Cerrillos lead source near Santa Fe some two hundred miles distant. What is possibly misleading is that the analysis that Shepard relied on as a standard for Western Pueblo glaze paint ware was derived from archaeological materials from the Zuni region that may have been decorated with pigment made from ores from Cerrillos or another Rio Grande region source or, as likely, with pigment in which the glaze paint recipe was modified by the addition of copper. Shepard's analysis of glaze paint recipe or composition revealed that the western sherds either could have been painted with pigment made from ores from the Rio Grande region or that the glaze recipe for these sherds included abundant copper. The kind of analysis Shepard used to infer a Zuni or western origin for Rio Grande glaze paint cannot discriminate ore sources. Geological sources must be determined through analysis of isotopes (Habicht-Mauche et al. 2000; Huntley, chap. 6, this vol.).

In either case, Shepard's hypothetical reconstruction has "a friendly trader" agreeing to bring the potters of the Rio Grande "a little of the mysterious paint" (Shepard 1965:80). Hence, as Shepard noted prophetically, it is the paint, and not the pot, that is the commodity. Shepard continues:

> [The Rio Grande] hunters had noticed patches of various colored earths in the Ortiz Mountains, which had been used as body paint during ceremonials and for Kiva frescoes. Potters now tried these colored earths. After a number of trials, they were again successful. These people of the Albuquerque district now had pottery to trade. They sought trade especially with the people of the Galisteo Basin who controlled the turquoise mines, but their ware also passed into all parts of the valley. (Shepard 1942:80)

Shepard, in her narrative reconstruction, ties the acquisition of glaze paint to knowledge of pigments related to kiva rituals and body paint. The idea that glaze paint ware functioned in ritual contexts or was associated with kiva murals and body decoration is also suggested by Spielmann (1998), by Eckert (chap. 3, this vol.), and by Van Keuren (chap. 5, this vol.). However, as Fenn, Mills, and Hopkins (chap. 4, this vol.) remind us, it may be a logical leap to suggest that Ancestral Pueblo potters were motivated to produce a shiny black pigment. Fenn, Mills, and Hopkins and other authors in this volume, especially Eckert and Herhahn, emphasize that prior to the development of the glaze paint series of wares, most painted pottery in the northern Southwest was black-on-white. The black-on-white color scheme is achieved by firing pottery in a neutral to reducing atmosphere. The glaze-painted wares fire to a red background color achieved by allowing air to circulate during firing, an oxidizing atmosphere. Potters needed a paint composition that would remain black when the pot was fired in an oxidizing atmosphere. Otherwise they might have produced red-on-red, which would not have been visually successful. Rather than attempting to produce shiny or glassy painted designs, it is at least as likely that they were simply trying to produce red pottery with black paint decoration. Herhahn's (chap. 10, this vol.) warning that we recognize glaze paint as *paint*, and not as incipient overall glazing technology, is crucial.

The tie Huntley (chap. 6, this vol.) makes between the Cerrillos mines as an ore source and the early Zuni glaze paint wares is both intriguing and potentially misleading. The selection of Cerrillos is fascinating because as Fenn, Mills, and Hopkins (chap. 4, this vol.) and Herhahn (chap. 10, this vol.) point out, a variety of more readily available materials could have been used for pigment. Cerrillos is intriguing because, as Shepard (1965) notes, it is a source of turquoise, and likely the source for turquoise found at the Great Houses of Chaco Canyon (Mathien 1986). It is fascinating to speculate and wonder if the ores from Cerrillos were valued and widely exchanged because they came from a sacred place where one also found the blue green stone that had been known to people throughout the Southwest from the time of the ascendancy of Chaco Canyon. Use of the Cerrillos source by the potters at Zuni may have been a continuation of their use of the Cerrillos mines for turquoise when their ancestors were part of a network centered at Chaco Canyon. On the other hand, this scenario is potentially misleading if the earliest glaze paint ware was being made in the Rio Grande or in several areas including the Rio Grande, and was valued because the ore pigment was available and fired black on a red background and not because the pigment was associated with a ritually important source. The assumed temporal priority of western glaze paint ware is something I address briefly again below.

Finally, Shepard (1942:218) investigated the runny character of the late glaze paint. She concluded that the fluid late glazes were a product of different glaze recipes that included more lead, and did not signal a lack of manual control over the paint (Shepard 1942:218). Shepard did not suggest what may have motivated potters to produce runny paints. Recently, Spielmann, Mobley-Tanaka, and Potter (1999) have proposed that use of runny paints deliberately hid design elements from Spanish missionaries and colonists.

Kidder's (1942) reluctance to write culture history on the basis of pottery technology was based on two considerations. First, the techniques of ceramic technology were still considered experimental. Second, there were no data from ethnography and paleoenvironmental reconstructions or theory from ethnology or psychology that would encourage him to reconstruct past behavior. Later in his career, Kidder (1958:217–28) berated himself for having written a potsherd-centered history of Pecos Pueblo and attempted to remedy this by exploring the geographic and linguistic origins of Tanoan speakers in general and specifically of the Pecos Indians. This he believed could be explored through locating the source of migrants to Pecos who could have introduced glaze paint technology (Kidder 1958:256). Because Shepard (1942, 1965) argued that glaze-painted ware had reached Pecos most immediately and directly from the relatively proximate Galisteo Basin but earlier on from much farther west in the Zuni region, Kidder argued that Tanoan speakers migrated into the Rio Grande and Upper Pecos valleys from the region of the Western Pueblos of Zuni and Acoma. Hence, Kidder accepted Shepard's conclusion that production of glaze paint ware was a Western Pueblo invention. Nelson and Habicht-Mauche (chap. 11, this vol.) indicate that Shepard (1942) presented her data for glaze production areas in a generalized way that homogenized sources of raw materials. This has led to interpretations that suggest more specialization at the village or district level, and her conclusion is open to question. Because Kidder did not accept the implications of Shepard's suggestion that enormous quantities of glaze paint ware had been exchanged over long distances, he focused on the possible directions of migration. Kidder also did not incorporate Shepard's findings that, in some cases, pigment ores were being distributed independently of the pots. That too might have suggested production in contexts that transcended household or village organization.

In sum, the chapters in this volume derive from and reflect on a complicated set of debates about Ancestral Pueblo culture history. These debates involve judgments about whether or not Ancestral Pueblo communities in the fourteenth and fifteenth centuries were economically, socially, and politically independent of one another and whether or not Ancestral Pueblos had "rudimentary commercial manufacturing" (Kidder 1936:xxiii) of glaze paint wares. The arguments were not resolved in Kidder and Shepard's time and are only now being resumed. In Kidder's day, there was concern about the reliability of Shepard's analytical methods as well as whether there was good "theory" for inferring social organization and change from material culture (Kidder 1942:ii). The production and distribution of glaze-paint-decorated ware were not debated within the context of events, people, or processes of Ancestral Pueblo culture history.

Fast Forward

Kidder's (1942:ii) concerns about the reliability of technological analyses and the process of inference in archaeology have substantially been allayed in modern archaeology. As amply demonstrated by all the contributions to this volume, technological analysis of ceramics, if not routine, has certainly moved far beyond the experimental stage. Analytical techniques and instrumentation provide quantitative, as well as qualitative, data. The number of ceramic analytic studies gives us much better coverage than we had in the past. Also heartening are the instances, such as Fenn, Mills, and Hopkins (chap. 4, this vol.), Herhahn (chap. 10, this vol.), and Leonard (chap. 13, this vol.) in which authors incorporate the results of previous analyses, demonstrating that we can and do build on past research. The paleoenvironmental reconstructions that Kidder (1942:ii) wished to include, while never as detailed as one would wish, are perhaps better documented than they are for any other part of the world, largely because of the remarkable work of the Laboratory of Tree-Ring Research at the University of Arizona (J. S. Dean 1996; Dean and Van West 2002; Rose, Dean, and Robinson 1981). Finally, modern survey and excavation have once again focused on the Pueblo IV period, yielding very high quality contextual information (e.g., as reported in E. C. Adams and Duff 2004; Duff 2002; Habicht-Mauche 1993a; Mills, ed., 2000; Mills and Herr 1999; Nelson and Schachner 2002; Spielmann, ed., 1998; and the chapters in this book). And yet, we have not written the culture history that would "trace the complex series of events—the migrations, the wars, the developments and clashes of societies and cults" (Kidder 1942:ii)—nor have we precisely described the social lives of glaze paint ware for which Habicht-Mauche (chap. 1, this vol.) encourages us to strive.

In our comments at the symposium from which this volume derives, Miriam Stark and I called for the specification of theory to guide interpretation. In this volume, Habicht-Mauche and Stark draw on the perspectives offered by practice theory (Bourdieu 1977). Stark (chap. 2, this vol.) also calls on the anthropology of technology (Lemonnier 1986) and the use of *chaîne opératoire* as an analytic research tool (Dobres 2000; Leroi-

Gourhan 1993, Stark 1998 and chap. 2, this vol.). I agree that all of these sources offer useful perspectives, as demonstrated by many of the contributors to this volume. Nevertheless, I also find that there seems to be something missing within these theoretical constructs that is necessary in order to link them to archaeological data and to develop confidence in our inferences about dynamic culture history. One problem derives from the focus on production afforded by ceramic technological analysis, rather than what we see archaeologically, which is the distribution of pottery from contexts of production to their locations of use, final discard, and eventual recovery. If we are to explore the social lives of pots, we will need to address their complete life histories. Another problem relates to the scale and precision of focus on individual agents, be they mindful or unaware actors, and the aggregate nature of archaeological data. I explore each of these briefly within the context of questions about the ultimate source of glaze paint ware technology and the mechanisms of transfer of that technology. Finally, I comment briefly on one general challenge of integrating anthropology and archaeology.

Ceramic technology focuses our attention on the geological provenance of materials and on, in the case before us in this volume, preHispanic methods of production. Archaeologists find ceramics most often in the context of their final use and discard. Especially for the glaze-paint-decorated wares, we anticipate that the loci of production and archaeological recovery were not the same. We seem to lack theory that focuses on distribution and the consumer end of the pottery life cycle. The studies that have used a chaîne opératoire approach have so far focused on production rather than distribution and consumption. I realize this is not a fault of the chaîne opératoire perspective itself. Rather, the approach requires expansion. In this volume, the chapters by Capone, Van Keuren, and Leonard call for such a change in vantage point toward understanding distribution and consumption. For Capone, expedient production, as she defines it, was a response to the demands for quantity by the Spanish consumers of the pottery in the Mission period. Theory relating to the influence of consumer demands on production could be expanded using comparative ethnographic and ethnoarchaeological data, such as that provided by Arnold's (1999) study of modern Maya tourist pottery and Stark's (1999) study of Kalinga pottery. A different perspective on relationships between producers and consumers of Rio Grande Glaze Ware is given by Spielmann, Mobley-Tananka, and Potter (1999), who argue that the runny quality of seventeenth-century glaze ware can be interpreted as an act of resistance in which Pueblo potters obscured indigenous designs from the Spanish. For Van Keuren, it becomes important to understand what is "acceptable" to the eventual users or viewers of Fourmile Polychrome vessels. Whether or not, or in what ways, the design errors Van Keuren notes in the copies of White Mountain Red Ware were acceptable to the eventual populations in which they were adopted requires an understanding both of consumer demands and what I think of as literacy in the semantics of design. The latter is also an issue that requires a larger theoretical and comparative perspective. For example, similar problems arise, although in a very different context, in the study of literacy among some classes of Maya scribes (Houston 1993). Leonard's concern is also with the distribution, not the production, of glaze paint ware on the southern Great Plains. While the technological aspects of the ceramics she is dealing with allow her to specify production source locations, the mechanisms that operated to distribute the wares on the Plains remain difficult to discern. In addition, while Leonard is appropriately concerned about the nature of her sample, the broad geographic and temporal frameworks within which her data are situated suggest any number of distribution scenarios. This might be a situation in which computer simulation is a useful tool for further analysis.

The very complicated issues surrounding the origins of glaze paint technology in the Zuni and Rio Grande regions (Huntley, chap. 6, this vol.; Herhahn, chap. 10, this vol.) involve problems of definition, of distribution, and of scale. Huntley finds one variety of St. Johns Polychrome at Zuni that is painted with a glaze paint the ore source for which is most likely Cerrillos. St. Johns Polychrome is one of the most widely distributed of all southwestern pottery types with no concentration of tree-ring dates (Breternitz 1966; Hawley 1936); although Breternitz (1966:93) gives best dates of between 1200 and about 1300. St. Johns is considered indigenous to sites in the upper Little Colorado and is present at Pecos, at Albuquerque area sites, in Chaco Canyon, at Kinishba, on the Pajarito Plateau, in the Jeddito area, and elsewhere (Breternitz 1966:93). At how many of these locations and occurrences is the variety of St. Johns decorated with glaze paint? Among those that are decorated with glaze paint, what are the sources of the pigment ores? Huntley also found Cerrillos lead/copper ore in Heshotauthla Polychrome, a type that is also very widely distributed and about which the same questions need to be asked. Kwakina, the third Zuni glaze type that Huntley (chap. 6, this vol.) examined is not as widely distributed as the other two types.

Huntley (chap. 6, this vol.) notes that the St. Johns Polychrome she studied from the Zuni region shows intraregional variation in clay sources. Schachner (chap. 7, this vol.) cites work from the Silver Creek area indicating a restricted suite of clays for the type. At this point, we do not know how many sources of production of the clay body there were for St. Johns Polychrome and how variable they might have been from one district or site cluster to another. St. Johns Polychrome is predominantly sherd tempered, although sand may also be included. For this reason, petrographic identification of temper will not be sufficient to determine the locations in which the type was manufactured; chemical characterization of clays will be required.

Although Shepard's (1965) work, discussed above, and Huntley's work in this volume provide strong evidence that the glaze paint used in St. Johns Polychrome was exchanged independently of the clay body, we do not at this point know how many different sources of the paint there were. Our only information on the geological provenance of the St. Johns Polychrome glaze pigment lead ore comes from pottery from sites at Zuni and Huntley's sample, indicating the Cerrillos ores as source. We do not know what was being exchanged in all cases, whether ore, paint, finished vessels, or clay bodies. I believe that future research needs be directed toward a reexamination and reevaluation of variability within St. Johns Polychrome and other early Western Pueblo glaze types, such as Heshotauthla; however, that research alone will not be sufficient to understand the potential social contexts of the use—and discard—of these types. Research must also focus on the archaeological contexts within which these glaze-painted types and variants occur. Where and when does the glaze variety, for example, constitute more than a small percentage of the decorated wares at specific sites? Until we understand how St. Johns Polychrome and its physical constituents (clays, temper, pigment ores) were distributed, the ultimate source of the type is just one of many queries. While we may be able to describe the context of St. Johns Polychrome in Huntley's sample from Zuni, we need a large geographic area and a statistically reliable sample of contexts to begin to define the social fabric within which this pottery moved.

A number of the chapters in this volume, specifically contributions by Nelson and Habicht-Mauche, Laumbach, and Schachner, and Eckert's discussion of black-on-white to glaze-on-red, describe social networks at a regional scale from the perspective of predominantly site-specific or site cluster contexts. Although the contributors to this volume accept the notion that pre-Hispanic Pueblo villages were not economically and socially autonomous, they nevertheless vary in their scrutiny of issues of simultaneous occupations among sites. It makes a big difference in all discussions of social networks that the communities involved be demonstrably contemporary. How sure are we that neighboring sites were participating in different social networks rather than being chronologically separated? Are we, in some cases, describing a social network when the behavior might have been a relocation of the same people from one settlement to another? Laumbach's very careful analysis of the context of Pinnacle Ruin is a model for the inquiry that is required. As Laumbach shows, different scenarios for the establishment of Pinnacle Ruin and the ceramic assemblage at that site depend on the size of the immigrant group and the occupational status of neighboring communities. This is not easy, because we know from excavations that Pueblo IV sites frequently were occupied either for relatively short periods or often have lacunae in their occupation histories.

All of our discussions of social networks call for further development of theory. It seems unlikely that networks of economic exchange are the equivalents of ethnic or linguistic groups, although it is often difficult for us to separate these conceptually. As we know, group affiliations and their tangible markers are mutable, contextual, and may not be visible in aggregated archaeological data (Cordell and Yannie 1991; Preucel in press). We need more studies like that of James Skibo, Michael Schiffer, and Nancy Kowalski (1989) that go back to archaeological data to reevaluate previous inferences about postmarital residence that were based on distributions of pottery design elements in Ancestral Pueblo sites. We need to worry about whether or not the scale of our observations fits the scale of our interpretations. I suspect that one reason that so many authors rely on Patricia Crown's (1994) conclusion that the Salado Polychromes represent a regional cult is that the scale of Crown's analysis is appropriate to the kinds of networks they have in mind. Yet, Crown was, correctly, looking at iconography. She was not describing a regional cult on the basis of details of the technology of production, many of which, such as variation in clay bodies or ore sources, may not be visible in the finished products. The invisible details may indeed reflect habitus and may have much more to do with networks of learning and enculturation than with shared rituals or ideologies. We need to know more about the contexts of distribution and especially of use to begin to develop bridging arguments that assign social meaning to technologically distinct wares. We need more studies like Crown's (1994) study of iconography, and the study by Spielmann, Mobley-Tanaka, and Potter (1999) of style and social resistance. We also need more studies like Spielmann's (1998) comparison of Rio Grande White Ware bowl sizes and Rio Grande Glaze Ware bowl sizes. She argues that the large bowls that are prominent in early Rio Grande glaze assemblages signal large numbers of consumers and a different, more public, ritual context of use. These studies focus on markedly visible attributes of pottery that arguably display information about affiliation.

None of us underestimates the difficulty of moving from archaeological data to anthropological interpretations, from pots and potsherds to interactions among people over time. I have suggested that we need more analyses at scales appropriate to the aggregate nature of much archaeological data that are the products of cultural and natural formation processes (Schiffer 1987). I believe that ethnoarchaeological and ethnohistoric research, ceramic life-history studies, and computer simulations will be useful in this endeavor. Shepard's work (Kidder and Shepard 1936; Shepard 1942) showed us the ways that technological analysis of archaeological ceramics could illuminate social interaction and social change. The contributors to this volume follow her direction and move us forward with studies that enhance our understanding of the culture history of the Southwest, add to anthropological studies of material culture, and, not incidentally, provide a better understanding of the diverse social lives of pots.

Acknowledgments

I thank the editors of this volume for inviting my participation and for their fine editorial suggestions. This chapter has benefited from comments from the archaeology lunch group at the University of Colorado, Boulder: Douglas Bamforth, Catherine Cameron, Arthur Joyce, Steve Lekson, Payson Sheets, and especially Richard Wilshusen. I gratefully acknowledge, although I did not always follow, excellent editorial advice from Norman Yoffee. None of these gracious individuals is responsible for the final product.

Notes

Chapter 5. Decorating Glaze-Painted Pottery in East-Central Arizona

1. Fourteenth-century White Mountain Red Ware types rarely exhibit a full glaze, as other authors in this volume point out (see Fenn, Mills, and Hopkins, chap. 4, this vol.).

Chapter 6. From Recipe to Identity: Exploring Zuni Glaze Ware Communities of Practice

1. Based on a recent ceramic seriation (Huntley 2004; Huntley and Kintigh 2004), excavated assemblages from Heshotauthla, Cienega, Mirabal, Atsinna, and Pueblo de los Muertos and surface collections from Box S Pueblo can be classified as relatively early and late components within the Pueblo IV period. The Lower Pescado Village collection was not included in the seriation but appears to fall within the late portion of the Pueblo IV period.

2. Herhahn (chap. 10, this vol.) identifies lead-manganese glaze paints as characteristic of certain Rio Grande Glaze A glazes. While the glazes discussed in this chapter are on grog-tempered sherds and thus likely made in the Zuni region, the high-manganese paints may indicate close ties with early Rio Grande potters.

3. T-tests were used to evaluate the statistical significance of differences between the groups (see Huntley 2004:table 7.4).

4. Fisher's Exact test is commonly used instead of the chi-square statistic to compute exact probabilities for 2 × 2 contingency tables involving relatively small sample sizes (D. H. Thomas 1986:291). For a given 2 × 2 table, Fisher's Exact probability in-

dicates the likelihood of obtaining a result where the observed cell frequencies deviate as much or more than the expected cell frequencies if the variables being examined are truly independent. I used the FISHER program available in Kintigh's (2002) *Tools for Quantitative Archaeology* to compute probabilities.

5. See Huntley (2004) for sample proveniences, as well as a complete discussion of sample preparation and analysis procedures.

6. A regression line is defined as the best-fit straight line between data points on a bivariate scatter plot (Shennan 1997:136–37).

7. Herhahn (chap. 10, this vol.) reports that Rio Grande Glaze A paints are compositionally similar to Zuni glazes, but that post-AD 1400 glazes differ in overall lead content and use of colorants. Moreover, glaze replication experiments (Herhahn 1995, chap. 10, this vol.; Herhahn and Blinman 1999) suggest that Rio Grande glazes can be made using a simple mixture of powdered ore and water. Thus, Rio Grande glaze technology did not necessarily involve the use of glaze recipes requiring multiple raw materials in specific proportions.

Chapter 7. The Decline of Zuni Glaze Ware Production in the Tumultuous Fifteenth Century

1. For the purposes of this chapter, when using the term Zuni Glaze Ware, I am referring to Kwakina Polychrome, Heshotauthla Black-on-red and Polychrome, Pinnawa Glaze-on-white, and Kechipawan Polychrome. In some cases, Kwakina and Heshotauthla are grouped with White Mountain Red Ware (see Carlson 1970).

2. Another glaze-painted ceramic type is found at Zuni, but its relationship to the Zuni Glaze Ware sequence discussed here is questionable. Hawikuh Polychrome was produced after the construction of missions at Halona:wa (Zuni Pueblo) and Hawikku in 1629 and ceased production during the Pueblo Revolt of 1680. A break of approximately 100–175 years occurred between the production of this type and the primary Zuni Glaze Ware sequence. Hawikuh Polychrome is quite different in form and style from earlier Zuni types (Mills 1995, 2002a; Woodbury and Woodbury 1966:331–34), suggesting little continuity in ceramic traditions. Various authors have suggested its manufacture was spurred on by missionization and probably the movement of Rio Grande or Acoma potters to the Zuni area (Mills 1995, 2002a; Seventh Southwestern Ceramic Seminar 1965; Woodbury and Woodbury 1966:334). Thus while this chapter refers to the demise of Zuni Glaze Ware production, readers might also be interested in exploring references discussing its "revival" and subsequent decline over a short span almost two centuries later (Mills 1995, 2002a).

3. Sherds from some glaze-painted Hawikuh types are present in level 6 and above at Zuni Middle Village. This could be interpreted as evidence for continuity in the glaze ware sequence, but I would suggest that their presence is most likely the result of minor mixing of deposits. Only forty-two sherds of Hawikuh types were identified in the excavation unit (levels 6 through 10). For comparison, forty-nine definitively post-Pueblo Revolt matte-painted polychrome sherds (see Mills 2002a) were found in the same levels (Mills 2002b). A similar explanation probably accounts for some

of the earliest occurrences of Hawikuh types in the Hawikku trench as well (levels 5 through 8). Mixing in the Hawikku trench is attested to by the presence of small amounts of Black-on-red ceramics throughout, a category Hodge apparently reserved for Pueblo III types (Smith, Woodbury, and Woodbury 1966:171).

4. Note that these results derive from post-AD 1400 examples, thus yielding a different result from studies by Duff (2002) or Huntley (chap. 6, this vol.) that focused on pottery produced during the fourteenth century and identified a diversity of sources for Zuni Glaze Ware. This change may relate to dramatic shifts in settlement location discussed later in this chapter.

Chapter 13. Directionality and Exclusivity of Plains-Pueblo Exchange during the Protohistoric Period

1. The relationship between the Faraones Apaches and the prehistoric archaeological complexes of the Texas Panhandle is not clear. In the ethnohistoric literature, the Faraones are repeatedly distinguished from the Jumano and Teya. However, they are often conflated with the Querecho.

Bibliography

Adams, E. C.
1991 *The Origin and Development of the Pueblo Katsina Cult*. Tucson: University of Arizona Press.
1994 The Katsina Cult: A Western Pueblo Perspective. In *Kachinas in the Pueblo World*, edited by P. Schaafsma, 35–46. Albuquerque: University of New Mexico Press.
2002 *Homol'ovi, An Ancient Hopi Settlement Cluster*. Tucson: University of Arizona Press.

Adams, E. C., and A. I. Duff, eds.
2004 *The Protohistoric Pueblo World, AD 1275–1600*. Tucson: University of Arizona Press.

Adams, J. A.
1976 Issues for a Closed-Loop Theory of Motor Learning. In *Motor Control: Issues and Trends*, edited by G. E. Stelmach, 87–107. New York: Academic Press.

Anthony, D. W.
1990 Migration in Archaeology: The Baby and the Bathwater. *American Anthropologist* 92:895–914.

Anyon, R.
1987 Prehistoric Cultures. In *An Archaeological Reconnaissance of West-Central New Mexico: The Anasazi Monuments Project*, edited by A. P. Fowler, J. R. Stein, and R. Anyon, 20–28. Report submitted to the New Mexico Office of Cultural Affairs, Historic Preservation Division, Santa Fe.

Appadurai, A.
1986 Introduction: Commodities and the Politics of Value. In *The Social Life of Things: Commodities in Cultural Perspective*, edited by A. Appadurai, 3–63. Cambridge: Cambridge University Press.

Arensberg, C. M.
1961   The Community as Object and as Sample. *American Anthropologist* 63 (2): 241–64.

Arnold, D. E.
1967   *Sak Lu'um in Maya Culture: And Its Possible Relation to Maya Blue.* Department of Anthropology Research Reports, no. 2. Urbana: University of Illinois.
1970   The Emics of Pottery Design from Quinea, Peru. PhD diss., Department of Anthropology, University of Illinois, Urbana.
1985   *Ceramic Theory and Cultural Process.* Cambridge: Cambridge University Press.
1991   Ethnoarchaeology and Investigations of Ceramic Production and Exchange: Can We Go Beyond Cautionary Tales? In *Ceramic Legacy of Anna O. Shepard*, edited by R. Bishop and F. Lange, 321–45. Niwot: University Press of Colorado.
1999   Advantages and Disadvantages of Vertical-Half Molding Technology: Implications for Production Organization. In *Pottery and People, a Dynamic Interaction*, edited by J. M. Skibo and G. M. Feinman, 59–80. Salt Lake City: University of Utah Press.

Arnold, D. E., H. A. Neff, and R. L. Bishop
1991   Compositional Analysis and "Sources" of Pottery: An Ethnoarchaeological Approach. *American Anthropologist* 93:71–90.

Arnold, D. E., H. A. Neff, R. L. Bishop, and M. D. Glascock
1999   Testing Interpretative Assumptions of Neutron Activation Analysis: Contemporary Pottery in Yucatán, 1964–1994. In *Material Meanings: Critical Approaches to the Interpretations of Material Culture*, edited by E. S. Chilton, 61–84. Salt Lake City: University of Utah Press.

Aronson, M. A., and P. Fournier
1993   Models for Technological Innovation: An Ethnoarchaeological Project in Pino Suarez, Mexico. In *The Social and Cultural Contexts of New Ceramic Technologies*, edited by W. D. Kingery, 33–74. Westerville, OH: American Ceramic Society.

Aronson, M. A., J. M. Skibo, and M. T. Stark
1994   Production and Use Technologies in Kalinga Pottery. In *Kalinga Ethnoarchaeology: Expanding Archaeological Method and Theory*, edited by W. A. Longacre and J. M. Skibo, 83–111. Washington, DC: Smithsonian Institution Press.

Audouze, F.
2002   Leroi-Gourhan, a Philosopher of Technique and Evolution. *Journal of Archaeological Research* 10 (4): 277–306.

Baldwin, S. J.
1983   A Tentative Occupation Sequence for Abó Pass, Central New Mexico. *COAS* 1 (2): 12–28.
1988   Tompiro Culture, Subsistence, and Trade. PhD diss., University of Calgary, Alberta, Canada.

Bandelier, A. F.
1892   *Final Report of Investigations among the Indians of the Southwestern United States.* Cambridge: J. Wilson and Sons.

Barrett, E. M.
1997   *The Geography of Rio Grande Pueblos Revealed by Spanish Explorers, 1540–1598.*

Research Paper Series, no. 30. Albuquerque: Latin American Institute, University of New Mexico.

Barth, F.
1969   Introduction. In *Ethnic Groups and Boundaries: The Social Organization of Culture Difference*, edited by F. Barth, 9–38. Boston: Little, Brown & Company.

Baugh, T. G.
1984   Southern Plains Societies and Eastern Frontier Pueblo Exchange during the Protohistoric Period. *Papers of the Archaeological Society of New Mexico* 9:154–67.
1991   Ecology and Exchange: The Dynamics of Plains-Pueblo Interaction. In *Farmers, Hunters and Colonists*, edited by K. A. Spielmann, 107–27. Tucson: University of Arizona Press.

Benavides, F. A. de
1954   *Benavides' Memorial of 1630*. Edited by C. J. Lynch. Translated by P. P. Forrestal. Washington, DC: Academy of American Franciscan History.

Bernardini, W.
2002   The Gathering of the Clans: Understanding Ancestral Hopi Migration and Identity, AD 1275–1400. PhD diss., Arizona State University.

Biek, L., and J. Bayley
1979   Glass and Other Vitreous Materials. *World Archaeology* 11 (1): 1–25.

Binford, L. R.
1962   Archaeology as Anthropology. *American Antiquity* 28:217–25.

Bishop, R. L., and F. W. Lange, eds.
1991   *The Ceramic Legacy of Anna O. Shepard*. Niwot: University Press of Colorado.

Bleed, P.
2001   Trees or Chains, Links or Branches: Conceptual Alternatives for Consideration of Stone Tool Production and Other Sequential Activities. *Journal of Archaeological Method and Theory* 8 (1): 101–27.

Blinman, E.
1988   The Interpretation of Ceramic Variability: A Case Study from the Dolores Anasazi. PhD diss., Washington State University.

Blinman, E., and C. D. Wilson
1993   Ceramic Perspectives on Northern Anasazi Exchange. In *The American Southwest and Mesoamerica: Systems of Prehistoric Exchange*, edited by J. E. Ericson and T. G. Baugh, 65–94. New York: Plenum.

Bourdieu, P.
1977   *Outline of a Theory of Practice*. Translated by Richard Nice. Cambridge: Cambridge University Press.

Boyd, D. K.
1997   *Caprock Canyonlands Archaeology: A Synthesis of the Late Prehistory and History of Lake Alan Henry and the Texas Panhandle-Plains*, vol. II. Reports of Investigations, no. 110. Austin, TX: Prewitt and Associates.

Boyd, D. K., J. Peck, S. Tanka, and K. W. Kibbler, eds.
1993   *Data Recovery at Justiceburg Reservoir (Lake Alan Henry), Garza and Kent Counties, Texas, Phase III, Season 2*. Reports of Investigations, no. 88. Austin, TX: Prewitt and Associates.

Bradley, R., and M. Edmonds
1993   *Interpreting the Axe Trade: Production and Exchange in Neolithic Britain.* Cambridge: Cambridge University Press.

Braun, D. P., and S. Plog
1982   Evolution of "Tribal" Social Networks: Theory and Prehistoric North American Evidence. *American Antiquity* 47 (3): 504–24.

Breternitz, D. A.
1966   *An Appraisal of Tree-Ring Dated Pottery in the Southwest.* Anthropological Papers of the University of Arizona, no. 10. Tucson: University of Arizona Press.

Breternitz, D. A., A. H. Rohn Jr., and E. A. Morris
1974   *Prehistoric Ceramics of the Mesa Verde Region.* Flagstaff, AZ: Northern Arizona Society of Science and Art.

Brody, J. J.
1964   Design Analysis of the Rio Grande Glaze Pottery of Pottery Mound, New Mexico. Master's thesis, University of New Mexico.
1991   *Anasazi and Pueblo Painting.* Albuquerque: University of New Mexico Press.

Brown, L. A., and R. L. Sanders
1981   Toward a Development Paradigm of Migration with Particular Reference to Third World Settings. In *Migration Decision Making: Multidisciplinary Approaches to Microlevel Studies in Developed and Developing Countries*, edited by G. F. DeLong and R. W. Gardner, 149–85. New York: Pergamon Press.

Browning, C., M. Sale, D. T. Kirkpatrick, and K. W. Laumbach
1992   *MOTR Site: Excavation at Site LA 72859, an El Paso Phase Structure on Ft. Bliss, Otero County, New Mexico.* Report no. 8927. Tularosa, NM: Human Systems Research.

Burgh, R. F.
1959   Ceramic Profiles in the Western Mound at Awatovi, Northeastern Arizona, *American Antiquity* 25 (2): 184–202.

Burmeister, S.
2000   Approaches to an Archaeological Proof of Migration. *Current Anthropology* 41 (4): 539–67.

Burtchard, G. C.
1975   Teaching Assistant Report 1975 Season. In *The 1975 Excavation of Tijeras Pueblo, Cibola National Forest, New Mexico*, edited by L. S. Cordell, 80–99. Archaeological Report, no. 5. Albuquerque: USDA Forest Service, Southwestern Region.

Bushnell, G.H.S.
1955   Some Pueblo IV Pottery Types from Kechipaun, New Mexico, USA. *Anais do XXXI Congresso Internacional de Americanistas, São Paula 1954,* 2:657–65. São Paula: Editora Anhembi.

Bushnell, G.H.S., and A. Digby
1955   *Ancient American Pottery.* New York: Pitman.

Cain, D. P.
2002   An Analysis of Three American Indian Archaeofaunal Assemblages from the Cañada Alamosa, New Mexico. Master's thesis, University of Colorado.

Calhoun, C., E. LiPuma, and M. Postone, eds.
1993　*Bourdieu: Critical Perspectives.* Chicago: University of Chicago Press.

Cameron, C.
1995　Migration and the Movement of Southwestern Peoples. *Journal of Anthropological Archaeology* 14:104–24.

Capone, P.
1995　Mission Pueblo Ceramic Analyses: Implications for Protohistoric Networks and Cultural Dynamics. PhD diss., Harvard University.
1998　The Wright Collection of Southwestern Pottery: Perspectives in Pottery Making and Collecting. In *Makers and Markets: The Wright Collection of Twentieth-Century Native American Art,* edited by P. Drooker, 35–84. Cambridge, MA: Peabody Museum Press.
1999　One and All Traditions: Views on the Radcliffe Symposium on Pottery Traditions of the Pueblo Southwest. *The Studio Potter* 28 (1): 52–56.

Capone, P., and R. W. Preucel
2002　Ceramic Semiotics: Women, Pottery, and Social Meanings at Kotyiti Pueblo. In *Archaeologies of the Pueblo Revolt: Identity, Meaning, and Renewal in the Pueblo World,* edited by R. W. Preucel, 99–113. Albuquerque: University of New Mexico Press.

Carlson, R. L.
1970　*White Mountain Redware: A Pottery Tradition of East-Central Arizona and West-Central New Mexico.* Anthropological Papers of the University of Arizona, no. 19. Tucson: University of Arizona.
1982　The Polychrome Complexes. In *Southwestern Ceramics: A Comparative Review,* edited by A. H. Schroeder, 210–234. *The Arizona Archaeologist* 15. Phoenix: Arizona Archaeological Society.

Carmichael, D. L.
1986　*Archaeological Survey in the Southern Tularosa Basin of New Mexico.* Publications in Anthropology, no. 10, El Paso Centennial Museum, University of Texas at El Paso.

Carr, C.
1995　A Unified, Middle-Range Theory of Artifact Design. In *Style, Society, and Person: Archaeological and Ethnological Perspectives,* edited by C. Carr and J. Neitzel, 171–258. New York: Plenum Press.

Castañeda, P. de
1990　*The Journey of Coronado.* Edited by G. C. Winship. Reprint. New York: Dover Publications.

Chaiklin, S., and J. Lave, eds.
1996　*Understanding Practice: Perspectives on Activity and Context.* New York: Cambridge University Press.

Childs, S. T.
1991　Style, Technology, and Iron Smelting in Bantu-Speaking Africa. *Journal of Anthropological Archaeology* 10:332–59.

Childs, S. T., and D. Killick
1993   Indigenous African Metallurgy: Nature and Culture. *Annual Review of Anthropology* 22:317–37.

Clark, J. J.
2001   *Tracking Prehistoric Migrations, Pueblo Settlers among the Tonto Basin Hohokam.* Anthropological Papers of the University of Arizona, no. 6. Tucson: University of Arizona Press.

Colton, H. S.
1955   *Pottery Types of the Southwest No. 3A and 3B.* Flagstaff, AZ: Museum of Northern Arizona Ceramic Series.

Colton, H. S., and L. L. Hargrave
1937   *Handbook of Northern Arizona Pottery Wares.* Museum of Northern Arizona, Bulletin 11. Flagstaff.

Cordell, L. S.
1975   *The 1974 Excavation of Tijeras Pueblo.* Archaeology Report, no. 5. Albuquerque, NM: USDA Forest Service, Southwestern Region.
1989   Durango to Durango: An Overview of the Southwest Heartland. In *Columbian Consequence: Archaeological and Historical Perspectives on the Spanish Borderlands West*, edited by D. H. Thomas, 17–40. Washington, DC: Smithsonian Institution Press.
1991   Anna O. Shepard and Southwestern Archaeology, Ignoring a Cautious Heretic. In *The Ceramic Legacy of Anna O. Shepard*, edited by R. L. Bishop and F. W. Lange, 132–53. Niwot: University Press of Colorado.
1995   Tracing Migration Pathways from the Receiving End. *Journal of Anthropological Archaeology* 14 (2): 203–11.
1997   *Archaeology of the Southwest.* 2nd ed. New York: Academic Press.
2002   Discussion of "The Social Life of Pots: Glaze Wares and Cultural Transformation in the Late Prehistoric Southwest." Symposium presented at the 67th Annual Meeting of the Society for American Archaeology, Denver.

Cordell, L. S., D. E. Doyel, and K. W. Kintigh
1994   Process of Aggregation in the Prehistoric Southwest. In *Themes in Southwest Prehistory*, edited by G. J. Gumerman, 109–35. Santa Fe, NM: Advanced Seminar Series, School of American Research.

Cordell, L. S., and V. J. Yannie
1991   Ethnicity, Ethnogenesis, and the Individual: A Processual Approach toward Dialogue. In *Processual and Postprocessual Archaeologies: Multiple Ways of Knowing the Past*, edited by R. W. Preucel, 96–107. Occasional Papers, no. 10. Carbondale: Center for Archaeological Investigations, Southern Illinois University.

Costin, C. L.
1991   Craft Specialization: Issues in Defining, Documenting, and Explaining the Organization of Production. In *Archaeological Method and Theory*, vol. 3, edited by M. B. Schiffer, 1–56. Tucson: University of Arizona Press.

Creamer, W.
1993   *The Architecture of Arroyo Hondo Pueblo, New Mexico.* Santa Fe, NM: School of American Research Press.

2002 Regional Interactions and Regional Systems in the Protohistoric Rio Grande. In *The Archaeology of Regional Interaction*, edited by M. Hegmon, 99–118. Boulder: University Press of Colorado.

Creamer, W., J. Haas, K. Nelson, D. Burdick, L. Renken, and A. Wenzel
2002 Ceramic Analysis of Intra- and Intersite Occupation at Protohistoric Pueblos in the Northern Rio Grande. In *Traditions, Transitions, and Technologies: Themes in Southwestern Archaeology*, edited by S. Schlanger, 59–70. Boulder: University Press of Colorado.

Crown, P. L.
1994 *Ceramics and Ideology: Salado Polychrome Pottery*. Albuquerque: University of New Mexico Press.
1996 Change in Ceramic Design Style and Technology in the 13th to 14th Century Southwest. In *Interpreting Southwestern Diversity: Underlying Principles and Overarching Patterns*, edited by P. R. Fish and J. J. Reid, 241–47. Anthropological Research Papers 48. Tempe: Arizona State University.
1998 Changing Perspectives on the Pueblo IV World. In *Migration and Reorganization: The Pueblo IV Period in the American Southwest*, edited by K. A. Spielmann, 293–99. Arizona State University Anthropological Research Papers 51. Tempe: Arizona State University.
1999 Socialization in American Southwest Pottery Decoration. In *Pottery and People: A Dynamic Interpretation*, edited by J. M. Skibo and G. M. Feinman, 25–43. Salt Lake City: University of Utah Press.
2001 Learning to Make Pottery in the Prehispanic Southwest. *Journal of Anthropological Research* 57 (4): 451–69.

Crown, P. L., and W. H. Wills
2004 Commensal Politics in the Prehispanic Southwest: An Introductory Review. In *Identity, Feasting, and the Archaeology of the Greater Southwest*, edited by B. J. Mills, 153–72. Boulder: University Press of Colorado.

Crozier, W. R., and A. J. Chapman
1984 The Perception of Art: The Cognitive Approach and its Context. In *Cognitive Processes in the Perception of Art*, edited by W. R. Crozier and A. J. Chapman, 3–25. Amsterdam: Elsevier.

Cushing, F. H.
1896 Outlines of Zuni Creation Myths. In *Thirteenth Annual Report of the Bureau of American Ethnology, 1882–1883*, 467–521. Washington, DC: Smithsonian Institution.

Dana, E. S.
1932 *A Textbook of Mineralogy, with an Extended Treatise on Crystallography and Physical Mineralogy*. Revised and edited by W. E. Ford. 4th ed. New York: John Wiley & Sons.

Davis, E. L.
n.d. Field Notes from 1961 Season. Manuscript on file at National Park Service Office, Mesa Verde National Park, Colorado.
1964 Anasazi Mobility and Mesa Verde Migrations. PhD diss., University of California.

Dean, J. S.
1996   Demography, Environment, and Subsistence Stress. In *Evolving Complexity and Environmental Risk in the Prehistoric Southwest*, edited by J. A. Tainter and B. B. Tainter, 25–56. Reading, MA: Addison Wesley.

Dean, J. S., W. H. Doelle, and J. D. Orcutt
1994   Adaptive Stress, Environment, and Demography. In *Themes in Southwest Prehistory*, edited by G. J. Gumerman, 53–86. Santa Fe, NM: School of American Research Press.

Dean, J. S., and C. Van West
2002   Environment-Behavior Relationships in Southwestern Colorado. In *Seeking the Center Place: Archaeology and Ancient Communities in the Mesa Verde Region*, edited by M. D. Varien and R. H. Wilshusen, 81–100. Salt Lake City: University of Utah Press.

Dean, R. M.
2001   Social Change and Hunting During the Pueblo III to Pueblo IV Transition, East-Central Arizona. *Journal of Field Archaeology* 28:271–85.

De Atley, S. P.
1986   Mix and Match: Traditions of Glaze Paint Preparation at Four Mile Ruin, Arizona. *Ceramics and Civilization*. Vol. 2, *Technology and Style*, edited by W. D. Kingery, 297–329. Columbus, OH: American Ceramic Society.

Dietler, M., and I. Herbich
1994   Ceramics and Ethnic Identity: Ethnoarchaeological Observations on the Distribution of Pottery Styles and the Relationship between the Social Contexts of Production and Consumption. In *Terre cuite et société: La céramique, document technique, économique, culturel*, edited by D. Binder and F. Audouze, 459–72. XIVe Rencontre internationale d'archéologie et d'histoire d'Antibes. Juan-les-Pins: Éditions APDCA.
1998   Habitus, Techniques, Style: An Integrated Approach to the Social Understanding of Material Culture and Boundaries. In *The Archaeology of Social Boundaries*, edited by M. T. Stark, 264–80. Washington, DC: Smithsonian Institution Press.

Dillingham, R.
1994   *Fourteen Families in Pueblo Pottery*. Albuquerque: University of New Mexico Press.

Di Peso, C. C., J. B. Rinaldo, and G. J. Fenner
1974   *Casas Grandes: A Fallen Trading Center of the Gran Chichimeca*. Vol. 6, *Ceramic and Shell*. Dragoon, AZ: Amerind Foundation, and Flagstaff, AZ: Northland Press.

Dittert, A. E., Jr.
1959   Culture Change in the Cebolleta Mesa Region, Central Western New Mexico. PhD diss., University of Arizona.
1998   The Acoma Culture Province during the Period AD 1275–1500: Cultural Disruption and Reorganization. In *Migration and Reorganization: The Pueblo IV Period in the American Southwest*, edited by K. A. Spielmann, 81–89. Anthropological Research Papers, no. 51. Tempe: Arizona State University.

Dittert, A. E., and F. Plog
1980   *Generations in Clay*. Flagstaff, AZ: Northland Press.

Dobres, M. A.
1999 Of Paradigms and Ways of Seeing: Artifact Variability as if People Mattered. In *Material Meanings: Critical Approaches to the Interpretation of Material Culture*, edited by E. S. Chilton, 7–23. Salt Lake City: University of Utah Press.
2000 *Technology and Social Agency: Outlining a Practice Framework for Archaeology*. Malden, MA: Blackwell.
Dobres, M. A., and C. Hoffman
1994 Social Agency and the Dynamics of Prehistoric Technology. *Journal of Archaeological Method and Theory* 1 (3): 211–58.
Dobres, M. A., and J. E. Robb
2000 Agency in Archaeology: Paradigm or Platitude? In *Agency in Archaeology*, edited by M. A. Dobres and J. E. Robb, 3–18. London: Routledge.
Dongoske, K. E., M. Yeatts, R. Anyon, and T. J. Ferguson
1997 Archaeological Cultures and Cultural Affiliations: Hopi and Zuni Perspectives in the American Southwest. *American Antiquity* 62:600–608.
Dornan, J.
2002 Agency and Archaeology: Past, Present, and Future Directions. *Journal of Archaeological Method and Theory* 9 (4): 303–29.
Duff, A.I.L.
1998 The Process of Migration in the Late Prehistoric Southwest. In *Migration and Reorganization: The Pueblo IV Period in the American Southwest* edited by K. A. Spielmann, 31–52. Arizona State University Anthropological Research Papers, no. 51. Tempe: Arizona State University.
2000 Scale, Interaction, and Regional Analysis in Late Pueblo Prehistory. In *The Archaeology of Regional Interaction: Religion, Warfare, and Exchange across the American Southwest and Beyond*, edited by M. Hegmon, 71–98. Boulder: University of Colorado Press.
2002 *Western Pueblo Identities: Regional Interaction, Migration, and Transformation*. Tucson: University of Arizona Press.
Duff, A.I.L., and R. H. Wilshusen
2000 Prehistoric Population Dynamics in the Northern San Juan Region, AD 950–1300. *Kiva* 66 (1): 167–90.
Dutton, B. P.
1981 Excavation Tests at the Pueblo Ruins of Abo. In *Collected Papers in Honor of Erik Kellerman Reed*, edited by A. Schroeder, 177–95. Albuquerque, NM: Albuquerque Archaeological Society Press.
1985 Excavation Tests at the Pueblo Ruins of Abo. In *Prehistory and History in the Southwest: Collected Papers in Honor of Alden C. Hayes*, edited by N. Fox, 91–104. Albuquerque: Archaeological Society of New Mexico.
Eckert, S. L.
1999 Report on the 1998 Excavations at Hummingbird Pueblo, New Mexico. Paper presented at the Sixty-fourth Annual Meeting of the Society for American Archaeology, Chicago.
2001 Pueblo IV Identity and Community Formation along the Lower Rio Puerco

drainage. Paper presented at the Sixty-sixth Annual Meeting of the Society for American Archaeology, New Orleans.
2003   Social Boundaries, Immigration, and Ritual Systems: A Case Study from the American Southwest. PhD diss., Arizona State University.

Eckert, S. L., and L. S. Cordell
2004   Pueblo IV Community Formation in the Central Rio Grande Valley (Albuquerque, Cochiti, and Lower Rio Puerco Districts). In *The Protohistoric Pueblo World, AD 1275–1600*, edited by E. C. Adams and A. I. Duff, 35–42. Tucson: University of Arizona Press.

Eden, M.
1961   On the Formalization of Handwriting. In *Structure of Language and Its Mathematical Aspects*, 83–88. Proceedings of the Twelfth Symposium in Applied Mathematics. Providence: American Mathematical Society.

Eggan, F.
1950   *Social Organization of the Western Pueblos*. Chicago: University of Chicago Press.

Eighth Southwestern Ceramic Seminar
1966   Rio Grande Glazes. Museum of New Mexico, Santa Fe, NM. September 23–24, 1966.

Ellis, F. H.
1974   Anthropology of Laguna Pueblo Land Claims, Docket #227, Claimants Ex. #92. In *Pueblo Indians III*. New York: Garland.
1981   Comments on Four Papers Pertaining to the Protohistoric Southwest. In *The Protohistoric Period in the North American Southwest, AD 1450–1700*, edited by D. R. Wilcox and W. B. Masse, 410–33. Anthropological Research Papers, no. 24. Tempe: Arizona State University.

Elson, M. D., M. T. Stark, and D. A. Gregory
2000   Tonto Basin Local Systems: Implications for Cultural Affiliation and Migration. In *Salado*, edited by J. S. Dean, 167–91. Albuquerque: University of New Mexico Press.

Emerson, T. E., and D. L. McElrath
2001   Interpreting Discontinuity and Historical Process in Midcontinental Late Archaic and Early Woodland Societies. In *The Archaeology of Traditions: Agency and History before and after Columbus*, edited by T. R. Pauketat, 195–217. Gainesville: University Press of Florida.

Ezzo, J. A., C. M. Johnson, and T. D. Price
1997   Analytical Perspectives on Prehistoric Migration: A Case Study from East-Central Arizona. *Journal of Archaeological Science* 24:447–66.

Ferguson, L.
1992   *Uncommon Ground: Archaeology and Early African America, 1650–1800*. Washington DC: Smithsonian Institution Press.

Ferguson, T. J.
2002   Dowa Yalanne: The Architecture of Zuni Resistance and Social Change during the Pueblo Revolt. In *Archaeologies of the Pueblo Revolt: Identity, Meaning, and Renewal in the Pueblo World*, edited by R. W. Preucel, 33–44. Albuquerque: University of New Mexico Press.

Ferguson, T. J., and Richard Hart
1985   *A Zuni Atlas*. Norman: University of Oklahoma Press.
Fewkes, J. W.
1904   Two Summers' Work in Pueblo Ruins. In *Twenty-second Annual Report of the Bureau of American Ethnology*, pt. 1, 1–196. Washington, DC: Government Printing Office.
Fish, P. R., S. K. Fish, G. J. Gumerman, and J. J. Reid
1994   Toward an Explanation for Southwestern "Abandonments." In *Themes in Southwest Prehistory*, edited by G. J. Gumerman, 135–64. Santa Fe, NM: School of American Research Press.
Ford, R.
1972   Barter, Gift or Violence: An Analysis of Tewa Intertribal Exchange. In *Social Exchange and Interaction*, edited by E. N. Wilmsen, 21–45. Museum of Anthropology, University of Michigan Anthropological Papers, no. 46. Ann Arbor: University of Michigan.
Frankel, D.
2000   Migration and Ethnicity in Prehistory Cyprus: Technology as Habitus. *European Journal of Archaeology* 3 (2): 167–87.
Friedrich, M. H.
1970   Design Structure and Social Interaction: Archaeological Implications of an Ethnographic Analysis. *American Antiquity* 35:332–43.
Giddens, A.
1979   *Central Problems in Social Theory: Action, Structure, and Contradiction in Social Analysis*. London: Macmillan Press.
1984   *The Constitution of Society*. Berkeley and Los Angeles: University of California Press.
Glascock, M. D.
1992   Characterization of Archaeological Ceramics at MURR by Neutron Activational Analysis and Multivariate Statistics. In *Chemical Characterization of Ceramic Pastes in Archaeology*, edited by H. Neff, 11–26. Monographs in World Archaeology, no. 7. Madison, WI: Prehistory Press.
Goldfrank, E.
1970   *Isleta Paintings*. Introduction by Elsie Clews Parsons. Washington, DC: Smithsonian Institution Press.
Gomolak, A. R., and T. L. Knight
1990   Ceramic Analysis. In *Excavations in the South Room Block of Gallinas Springs Pueblo (LA 1178), A Large Town of the Gallinas Mountain Phase (Late Pueblo III–Early Pueblo IV) on the Mogosazi Frontier*, edited by J. B. Bertram, A. R. Gomolak, S. R. Hoagland, T. L. Knight, E. Garber, and K. J. Lord, 8:1–55. Albuquerque, NM: Chambers Group. On file at USDA Forest Service, Albuquerque.
Gosselain, O. P.
1992   Technology and Style: Potters and Pottery among the Bafia of Cameroon. *Man*, n.s., 27:559–86.
1998   Social and Technical Identity in a Clay Crystal Ball. In *The Archaeology of So-*

cial Boundaries, edited by M. T. Stark, 78–106. Washington, DC: Smithsonian Institution Press.

1999   In Pots We Trust: The Processing of Clay and Symbols in Sub-Saharan Africa. *Journal of Material Culture* 4:205–30.

2000   Materializing Identities: An African Perspective. *Journal of Archaeological Method and Theory* 7:187–217.

Graves, M. W.

1994a   Community Boundaries in the Late Prehistoric Puebloan Society: Kalinga Ethnoarchaeology as a Model for the Southwestern Production and Exchange of Pottery. In *The Ancient Southwest Community: Models and Methods for the Study of Prehistoric Social Organization*, edited by W. H. Wills and R. D. Leonard, 149–69. Albuquerque: University of New Mexico Press.

1994b   Kalinga Social and Material Culture Boundaries: A Case of Spatial Convergence. In *Kalinga Ethnoarchaeology: Expanding Archaeological Method and Theory*, edited by W. A. Longacre and J. M. Skibo, 13–49. Washington, DC: Smithsonian Institution Press.

1998   The History of Method and Theory in the Study of Prehistoric Puebloan Pottery Style in the American Southwest. *Journal of Archaeological Method and Theory* 5:309–33.

Graves, W. M., and S. L. Eckert

1998   Decorated Ceramic Distributions and Ideological Developments in the Rio Grande Valley, New Mexico. In *Migration and Reorganization: The Pueblo IV Period in the American Southwest*, edited by K. Spielmann, 263–84. Anthropological Research Papers 51. Tempe: Arizona State University.

Graves, W. M., and K. A. Spielmann

2000   Leadership, Long-Distance Exchange, and Feasting in the Protohistoric Rio Grande. In *Alternative Leadership Strategies in the Prehispanic Southwest*, edited by B. J. Mills, 45–59. Tucson: University of Arizona Press.

Gubser, N. J.

1965   *The Nunamiut Eskimos: Hunters of Caribou*. New Haven, CT: Yale University Press.

Guthe, C. E.

1925   *Pueblo Pottery Making: A Study at the Village of San Ildefonso*. New Haven, CT: Yale University Press.

Gutiérrez, R. A.

1991   *When Jesus Came, the Corn Mothers Went Away*. Stanford, CA: Stanford University Press.

Habicht-Mauche, J. A.

1988   An Analysis of Southwestern-Style Utility Ware Ceramics from the Southern Plains in the Context of Protohistoric Plains-Pueblo Interaction. PhD diss., Harvard University.

1993a   *The Pottery from Arroyo Hondo Pueblo, New Mexico: Tribalization and Trade in the Northern Rio Grande*. Arroyo Hondo Archaeological Series, vol. 8. Santa Fe: School of American Research.

1993b   Town and Province: Sociopolitical Change among the Northern Rio Grande

Pueblos. Unpublished manuscript on file at Department of Anthropology, University of California, Santa Cruz.
1995 Changing Patterns of Pottery Manufacture and Trade in the Northern Río Grande Region. In *Ceramic Production in the American Southwest*, edited by B. J. Mills and P. L. Crown, 167–93. Tucson: University of Arizona Press.
1998 The Production and Exchange of Rio Grande Glaze-Painted Pottery: New Approaches to Old Questions. Paper presented at the Sixty-third Annual Meeting of the Society for American Archaeology, Seattle.
1999 Struggling to Make Community along the Northern Rio Grande. Paper presented at the Sixty-fourth Annual Meeting of the Society for American Archaeology, Chicago.
2002 Report on Galena Ore Sample from Tonque Pueblo (LA 240). Report submitted to Richard Bice and Albuquerque Archaeology Society, Albuquerque.

Habicht-Mauche, J. A., and S. Ginn
2004 The Origins of Glaze Painted Pottery in the Central Rio Grande. Paper presented at the Sixty-ninth Annual Meeting of the Society for American Archaeology, Montreal.

Habicht-Mauche, J. A., S. T. Glenn, H. Milford, and A. R. Flegal
2000 Isotopic Tracing of Prehistoric Rio Grande Glaze-Paint Production and Trade. *Journal of Archaeological Science* 27:709–13.

Habicht-Mauche, J. A., S. T. Glenn, M. P. Schmidt, R. Franks, H. Milford, and A. R. Flegal
2002 Stable Lead Isotope Analysis of Rio Grande Glaze Paints and Ores Using ICP-MS: A Comparison of Acid Dissolution and Laser Ablation Techniques. *Journal of Archaeological Science* 29:1043–54.

Hackett, C. W., ed.
1937 *Historical Documents Relating to New Mexico, Nueva Vizcaya, and Approaches Thereto, to 1773, Collected by Adolph F. A. Bandelier and Fanny R. Bandelier.* Vol. 3. Washington, DC: Carnegie Institution.

Hagstrum, M. B.
1995 Creativity and Craft: Household Pottery Traditions in the Southwest. In *Ceramic Production in the American Southwest*, edited by B. J. Mills and P. L. Crown, 281–99. Tucson: University of Arizona Press.

Hammond, G., and A. Rey, eds.
1945 *Fray Alonso de Benavides Revised Memorial of 1634.* Albuquerque: University of New Mexico Press.
1966 *The Rediscovery of New Mexico, 1580–1594.* Albuquerque: University of New Mexico Press.

Hardin, M. A.
1983 The Structure of Tarascan Pottery Painting. In *Structure and Cognition in Art*, edited by D. K. Washburn, 8–24. Cambridge: Cambridge University Press.
1984 Models of Decoration. In *The Many Dimensions of Pottery: Ceramics in Archaeology and Anthropology*, edited by S. E. van der Leeuw and A. C. Pritchard, 573–601. Amsterdam: Albert Egges Van Giffen Instituut voor Prae-en Protohistorie, Cingvla VII, Universiteit van Amsterdam.

Hardin, M. A., and B. J. Mills
2000   The Social and Historical Context of Short-Term Stylistic Replacement: A Zuni Case Study. *Journal of Archaeological Method and Theory* 7:139–63.

Harding, T. C.
1967   *Voyagers of the Vitiaz Straits*. American Ethnological Society Monograph, no. 44. Seattle: University of Washington Press.

Harker, R., C. Wilkes, and C. Mahar
1990   *An Introduction to the Work of Pierre Bourdieu: The Practice of Theory*. London: Macmillan.

Hatcher, H., A. Kaczmarczyk, A. Scherer, and R. P. Symonds
1994   Chemical Classification and Provenance of Some Roman Glazed Ceramics. *American Journal of Archaeology* 98 (3): 431–56.

Haury, E. W.
1934   *The Canyon Creek Ruin and the Cliff Dwellings of the Sierra Ancha*. Medallion Papers, no. 14. Gila Pueblo, Globe, AZ.
1958   Evidence at Point of Pines for a Prehistoric Migration from Northern Arizona. In *Migrations in New World Culture History*, edited by R. H. Thompson, 1–8. University of Arizona Bulletin 29:2, Social Science Bulletin 27. Tucson: University of Arizona Press.
1985   *Mogollon Culture in the Forestdale Valley, East-Central Arizona*. Tucson: University of Arizona Press.

Haury, E. W., and L. L. Hargrave
1931   *Recently Dated Pueblo Ruins in Arizona*. Smithsonian Miscellaneous Collections 82 (11). Washington, DC: Smithsonian Institution.

Hawley, F. G.
1936   *Field Manual of Prehistoric Southwestern Pottery Types*. University of New Mexico Bulletin 291. Reprint, Millwood, NY: Kraus Co., 1977.
1938   Chemical Analysis of Prehistoric Southwestern Glaze-Paint, with Components. In *Classification of Black Pottery Pigments and Paint Areas*, by F. M. Hawley and F. G. Hawley, 15–27. University of New Mexico Bulletin 321. Anthropological Series 2 (4). Albuquerque: University of New Mexico Press.

Hawley, F. M., and F. G. Hawley
1938   *Classification of Black Pottery Pigments and Paint Areas*. University of New Mexico Bulletin 321, Anthropological Series 2 (4): 3–14. Albuquerque: University of New Mexico Press.

Hayden, B.
1995   The Emergence of Prestige Technologies and Pottery. In *The Emergence of Pottery: Technology and Innovation in Ancient Societies*, edited by W. K. Barnett and J. W. Hoopes, 257–65. Washington, DC: Smithsonian Institution Press.

Hayes, A. C., J. N. Young, and A. H. Warren
1981   *Excavation of Mound 7: Gran Quivira National Monument, New Mexico*. Publications in Archaeology 16. Washington, DC: National Park Service.

Hays, K. A.
1989   Katsina Depictions on Homol'ovi Ceramics: Toward a 14th-Century Pueblo Iconography. *Kiva* 54 (3): 297–313.

Hays-Gilpin, K., and E. van Hartesveldt
1998   *Prehistoric Ceramics of the Puerco Valley: The 1995 Chambers-Sanders Trust Lands Ceramic Conference*. Ceramic Series, no. 7. Flagstaff, AZ: Museum of Northern Arizona.

Healey, C. J.
1990   *Maring Hunters and Traders: Production and Exchange in the Papua New Guinea Highlands*. Berkeley and Los Angeles: University of California Press.

Hedges, R.E.M., and P.R.S. Moorey
1975   Pre-Islamic Ceramic Glazes at Kish and Nineveh in Iraq. *Archaeometry* 17 (1): 25–43.

Hegmon, M.
1998   Technology, Style, and Social Practice: Archaeological Approaches. In *The Archaeology of Social Boundaries*, edited by M. T. Stark, 264–79. Washington, DC: Smithsonian Institution Press.

Hegmon, M., M. C. Nelson, R. Anyon, D. Creel, S. A. LeBlanc, and H. J. Shafer
1999   Scale and Time Space Systematics in the Post-AD 1100 Mimbres Region of the North American Southwest. *Kiva* 65 (2): 143–66.

Hegmon, M., M. C. Nelson, and M. J. Ennes
2000   Corrugated Pottery, Technological Style, and Population Movement in the Mimbres Region of the American Southwest. *Journal of Anthropological Research* 56:217–40.

Hegmon, M., M. C. Nelson, and S. Ruth
1998   Abandonment, Reorganization, and Social Change: Analyses of Pottery and Architecture from the Mimbres Region of the American Southwest. *American Anthropologist* 100:148–62.

Hensler, K. N., and E. Blinman
2002   Experimental Ceramic Technology or, the Road to Ruin(s) Is Paved with (Cracked) Pots. In *Traditions, Transitions, and Technologies: Themes in Southwestern Archaeology*, edited by Sarah H. Schlanger, 366–85. Boulder: University Press of Colorado.

Herbich, I.
1987   Learning Patterns, Pottery Interaction, and Ceramic Style among the Luo of Kenya. *African Archaeological Review* 5:193–204.

Herhahn, C. L.
1995   An Exploration into Technology Transfer in the 14th Century Middle Rio Grande Valley, New Mexico: A Compositional Analysis of Glaze Paints. Master's thesis, Arizona State University.
1996   Glaze Ware Petrographic Analysis Descriptive Report for Gran Quivira (LA 120), Quarai (LA 95), Pueblo Colorado (LA 476), and Pueblo Blanco (LA 51). Manuscript on file, Department of Anthropology, Arizona State University, Tempe.

Herhahn, C. L., and E. Blinman
1999   Materials Science Meets the Artisan: A Look at Innovation through Experiments with Lead-glazed Paints from the American Southwest. Paper presented at the Sixty-fourth Annual Meeting of the Society for American Archaeology, March 24–28, Chicago.

Herhahn, C. L., and D. L. Huntley
1996   Technology Change and Craft Specialization in the Protohistoric Rio Grande Valley, New Mexico. Paper presented at the Sixty-first Annual Meeting of the Society for American Archaeology, April 10-14, New Orleans.

Hibben, F. C.
1975   *Kiva Art of the Anasazi at Pottery Mound.* Las Vegas, NV: KC Publications.

Hickerson, N.
1994   *The Jumanos: Hunters and Traders of the South Plains.* Austin: University of Texas Press.

Hill, J. N.
1970   *Broken K Pueblo: Prehistoric Social Organization in the American Southwest.* Anthropological Papers of the University of Arizona, no. 18. Tucson: University of Arizona Press.

Hill, J. N., and R. K. Evans
1972   A Model for Classification and Typology. In *Models in Archaeology*, edited by D. L. Clarke, 231–73. London: Methuen.

Hinde, R. A.
1976   Interactions, Relationships, and Social Structure. *Man* 11 (1): 1–17.

Hitchcock, R. K., and L. E. Bartram Jr.
1998   Social Boundaries, Technical Systems, and the Use of Space and Technology in the Kalahari. In *The Archaeology of Social Boundaries*, edited by M. T. Stark, 12–59. Washington, DC: Smithsonian Institution Press.

Hodge, F. W.
1924   Pottery of Hawikuh. *Indian Notes* 1 (1): 8–15.
1937   *History of Hawikuh, New Mexico: One of the So-Called Cities of Cibola.* Los Angeles: Southwest Museum.

Honea, K.
1968   Material Culture: Ceramics. In *The Cochiti Dam Archaeological Salvage Project, Part 1: Report on the 1963 Season.* Assembled by C. H. Lange. Museum of New Mexico Research Records, no. 6. Santa Fe: Museum of New Mexico Press.

Hosler, D.
1986   The Origins, Technology, and Social Construction of Ancient West Mexican Metallurgy. PhD diss., University of California.
1994   *The Sounds and Colors of Power: The Sacred Metallurgical Technology of Ancient West Mexico.* Cambridge, MA: MIT Press.
1996   Technical Choices, Social Categories, and Meaning among the Andean Potters of Las Animas. *Journal of Material Culture* 1:63–90.

Houston, S. D.
1993   *Hieroglyphs and History at Dos Pilas, Dynastic Politics of the Classic Maya.* Austin: University of Texas Press.

Howell, T. L., and K. W. Kintigh
1996   Archaeological Identification of Kin Groups Using Mortuary and Biological Data: An Example from the American Southwest. *American Antiquity* 61:537–54.

Hughes, J. T.
1989　Prehistoric Cultural Developments on the Texas High Plains. *Bulletin of the Texas Archaeological Society* 60:1-55.

Human Systems Research
1974　Technical Manual, 1973 Survey of the Tularosa Basin, The Research Design. Tularosa, NM: Human Systems Research.

Huntley, D. L.
2004　Technological Style, Exchange, and the Organizational Scale of Pueblo IV Zuni Society. PhD diss., Arizona State University.

Huntley, D. L., and C. L. Herhahn
1996　The Role of Technological Change and Resources in the Development of Rio Grande Valley Craft Specialization. Paper presented in the symposium "Technological Innovation in Social Context: The Development and Change of Pottery-Making Traditions," at the 1996 Chacmool Conference, Calgary, Alberta, Canada.

Huntley, D. L., and K. W. Kintigh
2004　Archaeological Patterning and Organizational Scale of Late Prehistoric Settlement Clusters in the Zuni Region of New Mexico. In *The Protohistoric Pueblo World, AD 1275-1600*, edited by A. I. Duff and C. Adams, 62-74. Tucson: University of Arizona Press.

Huntley, D. L., K. A. Spielmann, J. A. Habicht-Mauche, C. L. Herhahn, and A. R. Flegal
In press　Local Recipes or Distant Commodities? Lead Isotope and Chemical Compositional Analysis of Glaze Paints from the Salinas Pueblos, New Mexico. *Journal of Archaeological Science*.

Hurlbut, C. S., Jr., and C. Klein
1977　*Manual of Mineralogy*. 19th ed. New York: John Wiley & Sons.

Jenkins, R.
1992　*Pierre Bourdieu*. London: Routledge.

Jones, D. L.
1995　Identifying Production Groups within a Single Community: Rio Grande Glaze-Decorated Ceramics at Quarai Pueblo. Master's thesis, Arizona State University.

Jones, S.
1997　*The Archaeology of Ethnicity*. London: Routledge.

Jones, T. L., G. M. Brown, L. M. Raab, J. L. McVickar, W. G. Spaulding, D. J. Kennett, A. York, and P. L. Walker
1999　Environmental Imperatives Reconsidered: Demographic Crises in Western North America during the Medieval Climatic Anomaly. *Current Anthropology* 40 (2): 137-40.

Kaldahl, E. J., S. Van Keuren, and B. J. Mills
2004　Migration, Factionalism, and the Trajectories of Pueblo IV Period Clusters in the Mogollon Rim Region. In *The Protohistoric Pueblo World, AD 1275-1600*, edited by A. Duff and E. C. Adams, 85-94. Tucson: University of Arizona Press.

Kalentzidou, O.
2000　Discontinuing Traditions: Using Historically Informed Ethnoarchaeology in the Study of Evros Ceramics. *Journal of Archaeological Method and Theory* 7:165-86.

Keith, S. B., D. E. Gest, E. DeWitt, N. W. Toll, and B. A. Everson
1983   *Metallic Mineral Districts and Production in Arizona.* Tucson: Arizona Bureau of Geology and Mineral Technology, Geological Survey Branch.

Kessell, J.
1987   *Kiva, Cross, and Crown: The Pecos Indians and New Mexico 1540–1840.* Tucson, AZ: Southwest Parks and Monuments Association.

Kidder, A. V.
1917a   Notes on the Pottery of Pecos. *American Anthropologist* 19:325–60.
1917b   *Old North Pueblo of Pecos: The Condition of the Main Pecos Ruin.* Papers of the School of American Archaeology, no. 38. Santa Fe: School of American Research.
1924   *An Introduction to the Study of Southwestern Archaeology, with a Preliminary Account of the Excavations at Pecos.* Papers of the Southwestern Expedition, no. 1. New Haven, CT: Publication for the Department of Archaeology, Phillips Academy, Andover, MA, by the Yale University Press, 1924. Reprint, New Haven, CT: Yale University Press, 1962.
1927   Southwestern Archaeological Conference. *Science* 66:489–91.
1936   Introduction to *The Pottery of Pecos*, vol. 2, edited by A. V. Kidder and A. O. Shepard, xvii–xxxi. Papers of the Phillips Academy Southwestern Expedition, no. 7. New Haven, CT: Yale University Press.
1942   Foreword to *Rio Grande Glaze Paint Ware: A Study Illustrating the Place of Ceramic Technological Analysis in Archaeological Research*, by A. O. Shepard, i–iv. Contributions to American Anthropology and History, vol. 7, no. 39. Washington, DC: Carnegie Institution of Washington.
1949   Introduction to *Prehistoric Southwesterners from Basket-maker to Pueblo*, by C. A. Amsden, xi–xiv. Los Angeles: Southwest Museum.
1958   *Pecos, New Mexico: Archaeological Notes.* Papers of the Robert S. Peabody Foundation for Archaeology, vol. 5. Andover, MA: Phillips Academy, the Foundation.

Kidder, A. V., and A. O. Shepard
1936   The Glaze-Paint, Culinary, and Other Wares. In *The Pottery of Pecos*, vol. 2. Phillips Academy Papers of the Southwest Expedition, no. 7. New Haven, CT: Yale University Press.

Kingery, W. D.
1960   *Introduction to Ceramics.* New York: John Wiley & Sons.

Kintigh, K. W.
1985a   Social Structure, the Structure of Style, and Stylistic Patterns in Cibola Pottery. In *Decoding Prehistoric Ceramics*, edited by B. A. Nelson, 35–74. Carbondale: Southern Illinois University Press.
1985b   *Settlement, Subsistence, and Society in Late Zuni Prehistory.* Anthropological Papers of the University of Arizona, no. 44. Tucson: University of Arizona Press.
1996   The Cibola Region in the Post-Chacoan Era. In *The Prehistoric Pueblo World: AD 1150–1350*, edited by M. A. Adler, 131–44. Tucson: University of Arizona Press.
2000   Leadership Strategies in Protohistoric Zuni Towns. In *Alternative Leadership Strategies in the Prehispanic Southwest*, edited by B. J. Mills, 95–116. Tucson: University of Arizona Press.
2002   *Tools for Quantitative Archaeology: Programs for Quantitative Analysis in Archae-*

ology. Available from author at School of Human Evolution and Social Change, Arizona State University, Tempe, AZ.

Kloberdanz, T. J.
1975   Volga Germans in Old Russia and in Western North America: Their Changing World View. *Anthropological Quarterly* 48 (4): 209–22.

Knecht, H.
1993   Splits and Wedges: The Techniques and Technology of Early Aurignacian Antler Working. In *Before Lascaux: The Complex Record of the Early Upper Paleolithic*, edited by H. Knecht, A. Pike-Tay, and R. White, 137–62. Boca Raton, FL: CRC Press.

Knight, T. L.
1981   Ceramics of LA 1178, Gallinas Springs, New Mexico. Jicarilla Archaeological Services, Dulce. Manuscript on file at the USDA Forest Service, Cibola National Forest, Albuquerque, NM.

Kolb, M. J., and J. E. Snead
1997   It's a Small World After All: Comparative Analyses of Community Organization in Archaeology. *American Antiquity* 62 (4): 609–28.

Kramer, C.
1985   Ceramic Ethnoarchaeology. *Annual Review of Anthropology* 14:77–102.

Kramer, C., and Douglas, J. E.
1992   Ceramics, Caste, and Kin: Spatial Relations in Rajasthan, India. *Journal of Anthropological Archaeology* 11:187–201.

Kroeber, A. L.
1916   *Zuni Potsherds*. Anthropological Papers of the American Museum of Natural History, vol. 18, pt. 1. New York: The Trustees.
1917   *Zuni Kin and Clan*. Anthropological Papers of the American Museum of Natural History, vol. 18, pt. 2. New York: The Trustees.

Kuwanwisiwma, L.
2002   *Hopit Navotiat*, Hopi Knowledge of History: Hopi Presence on Black Mesa. In *Prehistoric Culture Change on the Colorado Plateau: Ten Thousand Years of History on Black Mesa*, edited by S. Powell and F. E. Smiley, 161–63. Tucson: University of Arizona Press.

Lane, A.
1947   *Early Islamic Pottery*. London: Faber and Faber.

Lane, J. F.
2000   *Pierre Bourdieu: A Critical Introduction*. London: Pluto Press.

Lang, R. W.
1993   Additional Report: Analysis and Seriation of Stratigraphic Ceramic Samples from Arroyo Hondo Pueblo. In *The Pottery from Arroyo Hondo Pueblo, New Mexico: Tribalization and Trade in the Northern Rio Grande*, by J. Habicht-Mauche, 166–81. Santa Fe, NM: School of American Research Press.

Laumbach, K. W.
1992   *Reconnaissance Survey of the National Park Service Ojo Caliente Study Area, Socorro County, New Mexico*. Human Systems Research Report 9132, Tularosa, NM: Human Systems Research.

2000   *Canada Alamosa Project: A Preliminary Report on the 1999 Field Season*. Human Systems Research Report 9917. Las Cruces, NM.

2001   *Cañada Alamosa Project: A Preliminary Report on the 2000 Research Season, Featuring Excavations at the Pinnacle Ruin, Cañada Alamosa, New Mexico*. Human Systems Research Report 2011. Las Cruces, NM: Human Systems Research.

Laumbach, K. W., and D. T. Kirkpatrick

1983   *The Black Range Survey: A 2% Archaeological Sample of State Lands in Western Sierra County, New Mexico*. Cultural Resources Management Division, report no. 566. Las Cruces: New Mexico State University.

Laumbach, K. W., and T. S. Laumbach

2001   Reflections on Pinnacle Ruin and Its Impact on the Canada Alamosa Project. In *Cañada Alamosa Project: A Preliminary Report on the 2000 Research Season, Featuring Excavations at the Pinnacle Ruin, Cañada Alamosa, New Mexico*, compiled by Karl Laumbach, 89–97. Human Systems Research Report 2011. Las Cruces, NM: Human Systems Research.

Laumbach, K. W., and J. L. Wakeman

1999   Rebuilding an Ancient Pueblo: The Victorio Site in Regional Perspective. In *Sixty Years of Mogollon Archaeology*, edited by S. M. Whittlesey, 183–89. Tucson: SRI Press.

2001   Site Plan and Architecture. In *Cañada Alamosa Project: A Preliminary Report on the 2000 Research Season, Featuring Excavations at the Pinnacle Ruin, Cañada Alamosa, New Mexico*, compiled by K. Laumbach, 49–50. Human Systems Research Report 2011. Las Cruces, NM: Human Systems Research.

Lave, J.

1996   The Practice of Learning. In *Understanding Practice: Perspectives on Activity and Context*, edited by S. Chaiklin and J. Lave, 3–32. New York: Cambridge University Press.

Lave, J., and E. Wenger

1991   *Situated Learning: Legitimate Peripheral Participation*. New York: Cambridge University Press.

1996   Practice, Person, Social World. In *An Introduction to Vygotsky*, edited by H. Daniels, 143–50. London: Routledge.

LeBlanc, S. A.

1999   *Prehistoric Warfare in the American Southwest*. Salt Lake City: University of Utah Press.

2001   Warfare and Aggregation in the El Morro Valley, New Mexico. In *Deadly Landscapes: Case Studies in Prehistoric Southwestern Warfare*, edited by G. E. Rice and S. A. LeBlanc, 19–49. Salt Lake City: University of Utah Press.

Lechtman, H.

1977   Style in Technology—Some Early Thoughts. In *Material Culture: Styles, Organization, and Dynamics of Technology*, edited by H. Lechtman and R. S. Merrill, 3–20. St. Paul, MN: West.

1984   Andean Value Systems and the Development of Prehistoric Metallurgy. *Technology and Culture* 25 (1): 1–36.

Lechtman, H., and A. Steinberg
1979   The History of Technology: An Anthropological Point of View. In *The History and Philosophy of Technology*, edited by G. Bugliarello and D. B. Doner, 135–60. Champaign: University of Illinois Press.

Lehmer, D. J.
1948   *The Jornada Branch of the Mogollon*. University of Arizona Social Science Bulletin, no. 17. Tucson: University of Arizona.

Lekson, S. H.
1989   An Archaeological Reconnaissance of the Rio Grande Valley in Sierra County, New Mexico. *The Artifact* 27 (2): 1–102.
1996   Scale and Process in the Southwest. In *Interpreting Southwestern Diversity: Underlying Principles And Overarching Patterns*, edited by P. R. Fish and J. J. Reid, 81–86. Arizona State University Anthropological Papers, no. 48. Tempe: Department of Anthropology, Arizona State University.
2001a   Mesa Verde Migrations and the Test Excavations at the Pinnacle Ruin. In *Cañada Alamosa Project: A Preliminary Report on the 2000 Research Season, Featuring Excavations at the Pinnacle Ruin, Cañada Alamosa, New Mexico*, compiled by K. Laumbach, 10–32. Human Systems Research Report 2011. Las Cruces, NM: Human Systems Research.
2001b   Dating the Pinnacle Ruin. In *Cañada Alamosa Project: A Preliminary Report on the 2000 Research Season, Featuring Excavations at the Pinnacle Ruin, Cañada Alamosa, New Mexico*, compiled by K. Laumbach, 85–89. Human Systems Research, Report 2011. Las Cruces, NM: Human Systems Research.

Lekson, S. H., C. P. Nepstad-Thornberry, B. E. Yunker, T. S. Laumbach, D. P. Cain, and K. W. Laumbach
2002   Migrations in the Southwest: Pinnacle Ruin, Southwestern New Mexico. *Kiva* 68 (2): 73–101.

Lekson, S. H., and A. S. Rorex
1987   *Archaeological Survey of the Cottonwood Spring and Indian Tank Sites, Doña Ana County, New Mexico*. Human Systems Research, Report 8634. Tularosa, NM: Human Systems Research.

Lemonnier, P.
1986   The Study of Material Culture Today: Towards an Anthropology of Technical Systems. *Journal of Anthropological Archaeology* 5:147–86.
1992   *Elements of an Anthropology of Technology*. Ann Arbor: Museum of Anthropology, University of Michigan.
1993   Introduction to *Technological Choices: Transformation in Material Cultures Since the Neolithic*, edited by P. Lemonnier, 1–35. New York: Routledge.

Leonard, K.
2000   Directionality and Exclusivity of Plains-Pueblo Exchange in the Protohistoric Period (AD 1450–1700). Master's thesis, Arizona State University.

Leroi-Gourhan, A.
1993   *Gesture and Speech (La geste et la parole)*. Translated from the French by A. B. Berger. Cambridge, MA: MIT Press.

Lewis, L., E. Lewis Mitchell and D. Lewis Garcia
1990   *Daughters of the Anasazi.* VHS. Produced and directed by John Anthony. 28 min. Indianapolis: Second Sight Productions.

Lightfoot, K. G., A. Martinez, and A. M. Schiff
1998   Daily Practice and Material Culture in Pluralistic Social Settings: An Archaeological Study of Culture Change and Persistence from Fort Ross, California. *American Antiquity* 63 (2): 199–222.

Lindsay, A. J., Jr.
1987   Anasazi Population Movements to Southeastern Arizona. *American Archaeology* 6 (3): 190–98.

Livingstone Smith, A.
2000   Processing Clay for Pottery in Northern Cameroon: Social and Technical Requirements. *Archaeometry* 42: 21–42.

Loney, H. L.
2000   Society and Technological Control: A Critical Review of Models of Technological Change in Ceramic Studies. *American Antiquity* 65:646–68.

Longacre, W. A.
1970   *Archaeology as Anthropology: A Case Study.* Anthropological Papers of the University of Arizona, no. 17. Tucson: University of Arizona Press.

Longacre, W. A., and M. T. Stark
1992   Ceramics, Kinship, and Space: A Kalinga Example. *Journal of Anthropological Archaeology* 11:125–36.

Loomis, N. M., and A. P. Nasatir
1967   *Pedro Vial and the Roads to Santa Fe.* Norman: University of Oklahoma Press.

Lyons, P. D.
2003   *Ancestral Hopi Migrations.* Anthropological Papers of the University of Arizona, no. 68. Tucson: University of Arizona Press.

Mahias, M.
1993   Pottery Techniques in India: Technical Variants and Social Choice. In *Technological Choices: Transformation in Material Cultures since the Neolithic*, edited by P. Lemonnier, 157–80. London: Routledge.

Marshall, M. P.
1982   *Excavations at Nuestra Señora de Dolores Pueblo (LA 6777), A Prehistoric Settlement in the Tiquex Province.* Albuquerque: Office of Contract Archaeology, University of New Mexico.
1987   *Archeological Investigations in a 16th–Early 17th Century Piro Pueblo in the Village of San Antonio, New Mexico.* Albuquerque: Office of Contract Archaeology, University of New Mexico.

Marshall, M. P., and H. J. Walt
1984   *Rio Abajo: Prehistory and History of a Rio Grand Province.* Santa Fe, NM: State Historic Preservation Division.

Mathien, F. J.
1986   External Contact and the Chaco Anasazi. In *Ripples in the Chichimec Sea: New Considerations of Southwestern-Mesoamerican Interactions*, edited by F. J. Mathien and R. H. McGuire, 220–42. Carbondale: Southern Illinois University Press.

Mera, H. P.
1933   *A Proposed Revision of the Rio Grande Glaze-Paint Sequence.* Technical Series Bulletin, no. 5. Santa Fe: Laboratory of Anthropology.
1935   *Ceramic Clues to the Prehistory of North Central New Mexico.* Technical Series Bulletin, no. 8. Archaeological Survey/Laboratory of Anthropology. Ann Arbor, MI: Edwards Brothers.
1939   *Style Trends of Pueblo Pottery in the Rio Grande and Little Colorado Cultural Areas from the Sixteenth to the Nineteenth Century.* Santa Fe, NM: [Baltimore: Waverly Press, Inc.].
1940   *Population Changes in the Rio Grande Glaze-Paint Area.* Laboratory of Anthropology. Technical Series Bulletin, no. 9. Santa Fe: University of New Mexico.

Miksa, E. J., and J. M. Heidke
2001   It All Comes Out in the Wash: Actualistic Petrofacies Modeling of Temper Provenance, Tonto Basin, Arizona, USA. *Geoarchaeology* 16 (2): 177–222.

Mills, B. J.
1995   The Organization of Protohistoric Zuni Ceramic Production. In *Ceramic Production in the American Southwest*, edited by B. J. Mills and P. L. Crown, 200–230. Tucson: University of Arizona Press.
1998   Migration and Pueblo IV Community Reorganization in the Silver Creek Area, East-Central Arizona. In *Migration and Reorganization: The Pueblo IV Period in the American Southwest*, edited by K. A. Spielmann, 65–81. Anthropological Research Papers, no. 51. Tempe: Arizona State University.
1999   Ceramics and the Social Contexts of Food Consumption in the Northern Southwest. In *Pottery and People, A Dynamic Interaction*, edited by J. Skibo and G. Feinman, 99–114. Salt Lake City: University of Utah Press.
2002a Acts of Resistance: Zuni Ceramics, Social Identity, and the Pueblo Revolt. In *Archaeologies of the Pueblo Revolt: Identity, Meaning, and Renewal in the Pueblo World*, ed. R. W. Preucel, 85–98. Albuquerque: University of New Mexico Press.
2002b Zuni Middle Village Ceramics Report to the Pueblo of Zuni. Manuscript on file, Zuni Cultural Resource Enterprise, Pueblo of Zuni, NM.
In press Ceramics, Identity, and the Question of Zuni-Mogollon Relationships. In *Zuni Origins: Anthropological Perspectives on Multiple Scales*, edited by D. A. Gregory and D. R. Wilcox. Tucson: University of Arizona Press and the Center for Desert Archaeology.

Mills, B. J., ed.
2000   *Alternative Leadership Strategies in the Prehispanic Southwest.* Tucson: University of Arizona Press.

Mills, B. J., and S. A. Herr
1999   Chronology of the Mogollon Rim Region. In *Living on the Edge of the Rim: Excavations and Analyses by the Silver Creek Archaeological Research Project, 1993–1998*, edited by B. J. Mills, S. A. Herr, and S. Van Keuren. Arizona State Museum Archaeological Series, no. 192. Tucson: Arizona State Museum.

Mills, B. J., S. H. Herr, S. L. Stinson, and D. Triadan
1999   Ceramic Production and Distribution in the Silver Creek Area. In *Living on the Edge of the Rim: Excavations and Analysis of the Silver Creek Archaeological Re-*

search Project 1993–1998, edited by B. J. Mills, S. H. Herr, and S. Van Keuren, 295–324. Arizona State Museum Archaeological Series, no. 192. Tucson: Arizona State Museum.

Minar, C. J.
2001   Motor Skills and the Learning Process: The Conservation of Cordage Final Twist Direction in Communities of Practice. *Journal of Anthropological Research* 57 (4): 381–405.

Minar, C. J., and P. L. Crown
2001   Learning and Craft Production: An Introduction. *Journal of Anthropological Research* 57:369–80.

Moerman, M.
1965   Ethnic Classification in a Complex Civilization: Who Are the Lue? *American Anthropologist* 67:1215–30.

Morgan, D.
2002   Symbolic Negotiations of Regional Identity in Rio Grande Glaze Ware Designs. Master's thesis, University of Northern Arizona.

Motsinger, T. N.
1992   The Rise and Fall of a Village Industry: Specialized Ceramic Production in Protohistoric New Mexico. Master's thesis, University of Northern Arizona.

Murdock, G. P.
1949   *Social Structure*. New York: Macmillan.

Naranjo, T.
1995   Thoughts on Migration by Santa Clara Pueblo. *Journal of Anthropological Archaeology* 14:247–50.

Neff, H.
2002   Quantitative Techniques for Analyzing Ceramic Compositional Data. In *Ceramic Production and Circulation in the Greater Southwest: Source Determination by INAA and Complementary Mineralogical Investigations*, edited by D. M. Glowacki and H. Neff, 15–36. Monograph 44. Los Angeles: Cotsen Institute of Archaeology at UCLA.

Neff, H., and D. M. Glowacki
2002   Ceramic Source Determination by Instrumental Neutron Activation Analysis in the American Southwest. In *Ceramic Production and Circulation in the Greater Southwest: Source Determination by INAA and Complementary Mineralogical Investigations*, edited by D. M. Glowacki and H. Neff, 1–14. Monograph 44. Los Angeles: Cotsen Institute of Archaeology at UCLA.

Neitzel, J. E.
2000   What Is A Regional System? Issues of Scale and Interaction in the Prehistoric Southwest. In *The Archaeology of Regional Interaction*, edited by M. Hegmon, 25–40. Boulder: University Press of Colorado.

Nelson, B. A., and S. A. LeBlanc
1986   *Short-Term Sedentism in the American Southwest: The Mimbres Valley Salado*. Albuquerque: University of New Mexico Press.

Nelson, M. C.
2000   Abandonment: Conceptualization, Representation, and Social Change. In *Social*

Theory in Archaeology, edited by M. B. Schiffer, 52–62. Salt Lake City: University of Utah Press.

Nelson, M. C., and M. Hegmon
1993 Archaeological Research on the Ladder Ranch. Eastern Mimbres Archaeological Project. Manuscript on file at Department of Anthropology, Arizona State University, Tempe.

Nelson, M. C., and G. Schachner
2002 Understanding Abandonments in the North American Southwest. *Journal of Archaeological Research* 10:167–206.

Nelson, N.
1914 *Pueblo Ruins of the Galisteo Basin, New Mexico*. Anthropological Papers of the American Museum of Natural History, no. 15, pt. 1. New York: The Trustees.
1916 Chronology of the Tano Ruins, New Mexico. *American Anthropologist* 18 (2): 159–80.

Nepstad-Thornberry, C.
2001 Macrofloral and Charcoal Analysis of Samples from Site LA 2292, The Pinnacle Ruin, Cañada Alamosa, New Mexico. In *Cañada Alamosa Project: A Preliminary Report on the 2000 Research Season, Featuring Excavations at the Pinnacle Ruin, Cañada Alamosa, New Mexico*, compiled by Karl Laumbach, 81–83. Human Systems Research Report 2011. Las Cruces, NM.

Nepstad-Thornberry, C., and S. H. Lekson
2001 Feature 1 — Midden Excavations. In *Cañada Alamosa Project: A Preliminary Report on the 2000 Research Season, Featuring Excavations at the Pinnacle Ruin, Cañada Alamosa, New Mexico*, compiled by K. Laumbach, 34–40. Human Systems Research Report 2011. Las Cruces, NM.

Nicklin, K.
1971 Stability and Innovation in Pottery Manufacture. *World Archaeology* 3:13–48.

Olinger, B.
1993 Appendix C: Summary of X-Ray Fluorescence Analysis. In *The Pottery from Arroyo Hondo Pueblo, New Mexico: Tribalization and Trade in the Northern Rio Grande*, by J. Habicht-Mauche, 157–65. Santa Fe, NM: School of American Research Press.

Ortner, S. B.
1984 Theory in Anthropology since the Sixties. *Comparative Studies in Society and History* 26 (1): 126–66.

Ortiz, A.
1969 *The Tewa World: Space, Time, Being, and Becoming in a Pueblo Society*. Chicago: University of Chicago Press.

Parker, W.
1982 *Archaeology of the Bridwell Site*. Crosbyton, TX: Crosby County Pioneer Memorial.

Pauketat, T. R.
2001a Practice and History in Archaeology: An Emerging Paradigm. *Anthropological Theory* 1 (1): 73–98.
2001b A New Tradition in Archaeology. In *The Archaeology of Traditions: Agency and*

History before and after Columbus, edited by T. R. Pauketat, 1–16. Gainesville: University Press of Florida.

2003 Resettled Farmers and the Making of a Mississippian Polity. *American Antiquity* 68:39–66.

Pelegrin, J.

1990 Prehistoric Lithic Technology: Some Aspects of Research. *Archaeological Review from Cambridge* 9 (1): 116–25.

Pelegrin, J., C. Karlin, and P. Bodu

1989 Chaînes opératoires: Un outil pour le préhistorien. In *Technologie Préhistorique*, edited by J. Tixier, 55–62. Notes et Monographies Techniques, no. 25. Paris: CNRS.

Peterson, J. T.

1978 *The Ecology of Social Boundaries: Agta Foragers of the Philippines*. Illinois Studies in Anthropology, no. 11. Urbana: University of Illinois Press.

Peterson, K. L.

1988 Climate and the Dolores River Anasazi. University of Utah Anthropological Papers, no. 113. Salt Lake City: University of Utah Press.

Pétrequin, P., and A. M. Pétrequin,

1999 La poterie en Nouvelle-Guinée: Savoir-faire et transmission des techniques. *Journal de la Société des Océanistes* 108:71–101.

Pfaffenberger, B.

1988 Fetishised Objects and Humanised Nature: Towards an Anthropology of Technology. *Man* 23:236–52.

1992 Social Anthropology of Technology. *Annual Review of Anthropology* 21: 491–516.

Pielou, E. C.

1975 *Ecological Diversity*. New York: Wiley.

Plog, F.

1979 Alternate Models of Prehistoric Change. In *Transformations, Mathematical Approaches to Cultural Change*, edited by C. Renfrew and K. L. Cooke, 221–36. New York: Academic Press.

Plog, S.

1980 *Stylistic Variation in Prehistoric Ceramics: Design Analysis in the American Southwest*. Cambridge: Cambridge University Press.

1983 Analysis of Style in Artifacts. *Annual Review of Anthropology* 12:125–42.

Plog, S., and J. Solometo

1997 The Never-Changing and the Ever-Changing: The Evolution of Western Pueblo Ritual. *Cambridge Archaeological Journal* 7 (2): 161–82.

Post, S. S., and S. A. Lakatos

1995 Santa Fe Black-on-White Pottery Firing Features of the Northern Rio Grande Valley, New Mexico. In *Of Pots and Rocks: Papers in Honor of A. Helene Warren*, edited by M. S. Duran and D. T. Kirkpatrick, 141–153. Albuquerque: Archaeological Society of New Mexico.

Potter, J.

2000 Pots, Parties, and Politics: Communal Feasting in the American Southwest. *American Antiquity* 65 (3): 471–92.

Pratt, F.
1985   A Perspective on Traditional Artistic Practices. In *Visual Order: The Nature and Development of Pictorial Representation*, edited by N. H. Freeman and M. V. Cox, 32–58. Cambridge: Cambridge University Press.

Preucel, R. W.
2002   Writing the Pueblo Revolt. In *Archaeologies of the Pueblo Revolt: Identity, Meaning, and Renewal in the Pueblo World*, edited by R. W. Preucel, 3–32. Albuquerque: University of New Mexico Press.
In press   Ethnicity, Ethnogenesis, and Southwestern Archaeology. In *One Hundred Years of Southwestern Archaeology: The Transformation of a Discipline*, edited by D. D. Fowler and L. S. Cordell. Tucson: University of Arizona Press.
2006   Ethnicity and Southwestern Archaeology. In *Southwest Archaeology in the Twentieth Century*, edited by L. S. Cordell and D. W. Fowler, 173–92. Salt Lake City: University of Utah Press.

Rautman, A.
1993   Resource Variability, Risk, and the Structure of Social Networks: An Example from the Prehistoric Southwest. *American Antiquity* 58 (3): 403–24.

Redford, S., and M. J. Blackman
1997   Luster and Fritware Production and Distribution in Medieval Syria. *Journal of Field Archaeology* 24 (2): 233–47.

Reed, E. K.
1949   Sources of Upper Rio Grande Pueblo Culture and Population. *El Palacio* 56:163–84.
1955   Painted Pottery and Zuñi History. *Southwestern Journal of Anthropology* 11:178–93.

Reed, S.J.B.
1993   *Electron Microprobe Analysis*. Cambridge: Cambridge University Press.

Reid, J. J.
1998   Return to Migration, Population Movement, and Ethnic Identity in the American Southwest. In *Vanishing River: Landscapes and Lives of the Lower Verde River*, edited by S. M. Whittlesey, R. Ciolek-Torrello, and J. H. Altschul, 629–38. Tucson: SRI Press.

Reid, J. J., and S. M. Whittlesey
1999   *Grasshopper Pueblo: A Story of Archaeology and Ancient Life*. Tucson: University of Arizona Press.

Renfrew, C.
1986   Varna and the Emergence of Wealth in Prehistoric Europe. In *The Social Life of Things: Commodities in Cultural Perspective*, edited by A. Appadurai, 141–68. Cambridge: Cambridge University Press.

Rice, P. M.
1984   Change and Conservatism in Pottery Producing Systems. In *The Many Dimensions of Pottery: Ceramics in Archaeology and Anthropology*, edited by S. E. van der Leeuw and A. C. Pritchard, 231–88. Amsterdam: University of Amsterdam.
1987   *Pottery Analysis: A Sourcebook*. Chicago: University of Chicago Press.

1996a   Recent Ceramic Analysis: 2, Composition, Production, and Theory. *Journal of Archaeological Research* 4: 165–202.
1996b   Recent Ceramic Analysis: 1, Function, Style, and Origins. *Journal of Archaeological Research* 4: 133–163.

Riggs, C. R.
2002   *The Architecture of Grasshopper Pueblo.* Salt Lake City: University of Utah Press.

Riley, C. L.
1987   *The Frontier People: The Greater Southwest in the Protohistoric Period.* Rev. ed. Albuquerque: University of New Mexico Press.
1997   The Teya Indians of the Southwestern Plains. In *The Coronado Expedition to Tierra Nueva: The 1540–1542 Route across the Southwest*, edited by R. Flint and S. C. Flint, 320–43. Niwot: University Press of Colorado.

Rinaldo, J. B.
1964   Notes on the Origins of Historic Zuni Culture. *The Kiva* 29:86–98.

Rinaldo, J. B., and E. Bluhm
1956   Late Mogollon Pottery Types of the Reserve Area. *Fieldiana Anthropology* 36 (7): 159–61. Chicago: Chicago Natural History Museum.

Robinson, W. J.
1981   Tree-Ring Dates from Atsinna. Letter on file, Laboratory of Tree-Ring Research, University of Arizona, Tucson.

Robinson, W. J., and R. Sprague
1965   Disposal of the Dead at Point of Pines, Arizona. *American Antiquity* 30:442–53.

Roe, P. G.
1980   Art and Residence among the Shipibo Indians of Peru: A Study in Microacculturation. *American Anthropologist* 82:42–71.

Roney, J. R.
1996   The Pueblo III Period in the Eastern San Juan Basin and Acoma-Laguna Areas. In *The Prehistoric Pueblo World AD 1150–1350*, edited by M. A. Adler, 145–69. Tucson: University of Arizona Press.

Roscoe, P. B.
1993   Practice and Political Centralisation: A New Approach to Political Evolution. *Current Anthropology* 34 (2): 111–40.

Rose, M. R., J. S. Dean, and W. J. Robinson
1981   *The Past Climate of Arroyo Hondo, New Mexico, Reconstructed from Tree Rings.* Arroyo Hondo Archaeological Series, no. 4. Santa Fe, NM: School of American Research Press.

Rouse, I.
1939   *Prehistory in Haiti: A Study in Method.* Yale University Publications in Anthropology, no. 21. New Haven, CT: Published for the Department of Anthropology, Yale University, by the Yale University Press.

Sackett, J. R.
1977   The Meaning of Style in Archaeology: A General Model. *American Antiquity* 43 (3): 369–80.
1982   Approaches to Style in Lithic Archaeology. *Journal of Anthropological Archaeology* (1): 59–112.

1985 Style and Ethnicity in the Kalahari: A Reply to Wiessner. *American Antiquity* 50 (1): 154–59.
1986 Isochrestism and Style: A Clarification. *Journal of Anthropological Archaeology* 5:266–77.
1990 Style and Ethnicity in Archaeology: The Case for Isochrestism. In *The Uses of Style in Archaeology*, edited by M. Conkey and C. Hastorf, 32–43. Cambridge: Cambridge University Press.

Sahlins, M. D.
1981 *Historical Metaphors and Mythical Realities: Structure in the Early History of the Sandwich Islands Kingdom.* Ann Arbor: University of Michigan Press.

Salzer, M. W.
2000 Temperature Variability and the Northern Anasazi: Possible Implications for Regional Abandonment. *The Kiva* 65:295–318.

Sassaman, K. E., and W. Rudolphi
2001 Communities of Practice in the Early Pottery Traditions of the American Southwest. *Journal of Anthropological Research* 57:407–25.

Schaafsma, C.
1969 The Pottery of Las Madres. Manuscript on file, Laboratory of Anthropology, Museum of New Mexico, Santa Fe.

Schaafsma, P.
1992 *Rock Art of New Mexico.* Santa Fe: Museum of New Mexico Press.

Schachner, G.
2001 Tracing Zuni Connections to the Hohokam: Integrating Archaeology, Oral Tradition, and Ethnography. Paper presented at the Sixty-sixth Annual Meeting of the Society for American Archaeology, New Orleans.

Schiffer, M. B.
1987 *Formation Processes of the Archaeological Record.* Albuquerque: University of New Mexico Press.
1988 The Structure of Archaeological Theory. *American Antiquity* 53:461–85.

Schiffer, M. B., and J. M. Skibo
1987 Theory and Experiment in the Study of Technological Change. *Current Anthropology* 28:595–622.
1997 The Explanation of Artifact Variability. *American Antiquity* 62 (1): 25–50.

Schiffer, M. B., J. M. Skibo, J. L. Griffiths, K. L. Hollenback, and W. A. Longacre
2001 Behavioral Archaeology and the Study of Technology. *American Antiquity* 66 (4): 729–38.

Schlanger, N.
1998 The Study of Techniques as an Ideological Challenge: Technology, Nation, and Humanity in the Work of Marcel Mauss. In *Marcel Mauss: A Centenary Tribute*, edited by W. James and N. J. Allen, 192–212. Methodology and History in Anthropology, vol. 1. New York: Berghhahn Books.

Scholes, F. V.
1937 Troublous Times in New Mexico, 1659–1670. *New Mexico Historical Review* XII:134–74, 380–452; XIII:63–84; XV:249–68, 369–417; XVI:15–40, 184–205, 313–27.

Schroeder, A. H.
1979 Pecos Pueblo. In *Handbook of North American Indians*, vol. 9, edited by A. A. Ortiz, 430–37. Washington, DC: Smithsonian Institution Press.

Sellet, F.
1993 Chaîne Opératoire: The Concept and its Applications. *Lithic Technology* 18 (1–2): 106–12.

Seventh Southwestern Ceramic Seminar
1965 Acoma-Zuni Pottery Types. Research Center, Museum of Northern Arizona, Flagstaff, AZ. September 24–25.

Shangraw, C. F.
1977 Early Chinese Ceramics and Kilns. *Archaeology* 30 (6): 382–93.

Shennan, S.
1993 After Social Evolution: A New Archaeological Agenda? In *Archaeological Theory: Who Sets the Agenda?* edited by N. Yoffee and A. Sherratt, 53–59. Cambridge: Cambridge Archaeological Press.
1997 *Quantifying Archaeology*. 2nd ed. Iowa City: University of Iowa Press.

Shepard, A. O.
1936 *The Pottery of Pecos*, vol. 2. Papers of the Phillips Academy Southwestern Expedition, no. 7. New Haven, CT: Yale University Press.
1938 Ceramic Technology. *Year Book* 37:159–61. Washington, DC: Carnegie Institution of Washington.
1939 Technology of La Plata Pottery. In *Archaeological Studies in the La Plata District, Southwestern Colorado and Northwestern New Mexico*, by E. H. Morris, 249–87. Washington, DC: Carnegie Institution of Washington.
1942 *Rio Grande Glaze Paint Ware: A Study Illustrating the Place of Ceramic Technological Analysis in Archaeological Research*. Contributions to American Anthropology and History, vol. 7, no. 39, pp. 129–262. Washington, DC: Carnegie Institution of Washington.
1956/1980 *Ceramics for the Archaeologist*. Washington, DC: Carnegie Institution of Washington.
1965 Rio Grande Glaze-Paint Pottery: A Test of Petrographic Analysis. In *Ceramics and Man*, edited by F. R. Matson, 62–87. Chicago: Aldine.

Sillar, B.
1997 Reputable Pots and Disreputable Potters: Individual and Community Choices in Present-Day Pottery Productions and Exchanges in the Andes. In *Not So Much a Pot, More a Way of Life*, edited by C. C. Cumberpatch and P. W. Blinkhorn, 1–20. Oxford: Oxbow Books.
2000 Dung by Preference: The Choice of Fuel as an Example of How Andean Pottery Production Is Embedded within Wider Technical, Social, and Economic Practices. *Archaeometry* 42:43–60.

Sillar, B., and M. S. Tite
2000 The Challenge of "Technological Choices" for Materials Science Approaches in Archaeology. *Archaeometry* 42:2–20.

Sinclair, A.
2000 Constellations of Knowledge: Human Agency and Material Affordance in Lithic

Technology. In *Agency in Archaeology*, edited by M. A. Dobres and J. Robb, 196–212. London: Routledge.

Skibo, J., M. B. Schiffer, and N. Kowlaski
1989   Ceramic Style Analysis in Archaeology and Ethnoarchaeology: Bridging the Analytic Gap. *Journal of Anthropological Archaeology* 8:388–409.

Smith, W.
1952   *Kiva Mural Decorations at Awatovi and Kawaika-a*. Papers of the Peabody Museum of Archaeology and Ethnology, no. 37. Cambridge: Harvard University Press.

Smith, W., R. B. Woodbury, and N.F.S. Woodbury
1966   *The Excavation of Hawikuh by Frederick Webb Hodge: Report of the Hendricks-Hodge Expedition, 1917–1923*. Contributions from the Museum of the American Indian, Heye Foundation, vol. 20. New York: Museum of the American Indian.

Snow, D. H.
1976   Description of the Architecture and Excavation Units at LA 70. In *Archaeological Excavations at Pueblo del Encierro, LA 70; Cochiti Dam Salvage Project, Cochiti, New Mexico: Final Report 1964–1965 Field Seasons*, edited by D. H. Snow, A8–A227. Laboratory of Anthropology Notes, no. 78. Santa Fe: Museum of New Mexico.
1981   Protohistoric Rio Grande Pueblo Economics: A Review of Trends. In *The Protohistoric Period in the North American Southwest, AD 1450–1700*, edited by D. R. Wilcox and W. B. Masse, 354–77. Anthropological Research Papers, no. 24. Tempe: Arizona State University.
1982   The Rio Grande Glaze, Matte-Paint, and Plainware Tradition. In *Southwestern Ceramics: A Comparative Review*, edited by A. H. Schroeder, 235–78. Phoenix: Arizona Archaeological Society.
1986   A Preliminary Ceramic Analysis, LA 120, Gran Quivira (1985): The Glazes and Black-on-White Wares. Manuscript on file, K. A. Spielmann, Arizona State University, Tempe.
1989   A Very Brief Overview of Rio Grande Glaze and Matte-Paint Ceramics. Manuscript prepared for New Mexico Archaeological Council, Rio Grande Ceramic Workshop, Santa Fe.
1997   "Por alli no ay losa ni se hace": Gilded Men and Glaze Pottery on the Southern Plains. In *The Coronado Expedition to Tierra Nueva: The 1540–1542 Route across the Southwest*, edited by R. Flint and S. C. Flint, 244–364. Niwot: University Press of Colorado.

Snow, D. H., and M. L. Stoller
1987   Outside Santa Fe in the Seventeenth Century. Paper presented at the Ethnic Relations in the Southwest Symposium, American Society for Ethno-History, Berkeley.

Speth, J.
1991   Some Unexplored Aspects of Plains-Pueblo Food Exchange. In *Farmers, Hunters, and Colonists*, edited by K. A. Spielmann, 18–35. Tucson: University of Arizona Press.

Spielmann, K. A.
1982   *Inter-Societal Food Acquisition among Egalitarian Societies: An Ecological Study*

of Plains-Pueblo Interaction in the American Southwest. PhD diss., University of Michigan.

1989 Colonists, Hunters, and Farmers: Plains-Pueblo Interaction in the Seventeenth Century. In *Columbian Consequences*, vol. 1, edited by D. H. Thomas, 101–13. Washington, DC: Smithsonian Institution Press.

1991a *Interdependence in the Prehistoric Southwest: An Ecological Analysis of Plains-Pueblo Interaction.* New York: Garland.

1991b Interaction amongst Non-Hierarchical Societies. In *Farmers, Hunters and Colonists*, edited by K. A. Spielmann, 1–17. Tucson: University of Arizona Press.

1993 The Evolution of Craft Specialization in Tribal Societies: Preliminary Report for the 1992 Excavation Season at Quarai Pueblo, New Mexico. Report submitted to the National Park Service, Southwestern Regional Office, Santa Fe, NM.

1994 Clustered Confederacies: Sociopolitical Organization in the Protohistoric Río Grande. In *The Ancient Southwestern Community: Models and Methods for the Study of Prehistoric Social Organization*, edited by W. H. Wills and R. D. Leonard, 45–54. Albuquerque: University of New Mexico Press.

1998 Ritual Influences on the Development of Rio Grande Glaze A Ceramics. In *Migration and Reorganization: The Pueblo IV Period in the American Southwest*, edited by K. A. Spielmann, 253–61. Anthropological Research Papers, no. 51. Tempe: Arizona State University.

Spielmann, K. A., ed.

1998 *Migration and Reorganization: The Pueblo IV Period in the American Southwest.* Anthropological Research Papers, no. 51. Tempe: Arizona State University.

Spielmann, K., and J. Eder

1994 Hunters and Farmers: Then and Now. *Annual Review of Anthropology* 23:303–23.

Spielmann, K. A., J. Mobley-Tanaka, and J. Potter

1999 Style and Resistance in the Seventeenth Century Salinas Province. Paper presented in the symposium "An Archeology of the Pueblo Revolt," Sixty-fourth Annual Meeting of the Society for American Archaeology, Chicago.

Spielmann, K. A., M. Schoeninger, and M. K. Moore

1990 Plains-Pueblo Interdependence and Human Diet at Pecos Pueblo, New Mexico. *American Antiquity* 55 (4): 745–65.

Spier, L.

1917 *An Outline for a Chronology of Zuni Ruins.* Anthropological Papers of the American Museum of Natural History, vol. 18, pt. 3. New York: The Trustees.

Stark, M. T.

1991 Ceramic Change in Ethnoarchaeological Perspective: A Kalinga Case Study. *Asian Perspectives* 30:193–216.

1993 Re-fitting the Cracked and Broken Facade: A Plea for Empiricism in the Collection and Use of Ethnoarchaeological Data. In *Archaeological Theory: Who Sets the Agenda?* edited by N. Yoffee and A. Sherratt, 81–92. Cambridge: Cambridge University Press.

1998 Technical Choices and Social Boundaries in Material Culture Patterning: An Introduction. In *The Archaeology of Social Boundaries*, edited by M. T. Stark, 1–11. Washington, DC: Smithsonian Institution Press.

1999 Social Dimensions of Technical Choice in Kalinga Ceramic Traditions. In *Material Meanings: Critical Approaches to the Interpretation of Material Culture*, edited by E. S. Chilton, 24–43. Salt Lake City: University of Utah Press.

2003 Current Issues in Ceramic Ethnoarchaeology. *Journal of Archaeological Research* 11 (3): 193–242.

Stark, M. T., ed.

1998 *The Archaeology of Social Boundaries*. Washington, DC: Smithsonian Institution Press.

Stark, M. T., R. L. Bishop, and E. Miksa

2000 Ceramic Technology and Social Boundaries: Cultural Practices in Kalinga Clay Selection and Use. *Journal of Archaeological Method and Theory* 7:295–331.

Stark, M. T., J. J. Clark, and M. D. Elson

1995 Causes and Consequences of Migration in the 13th Century Tonto Basin. *Journal of Anthropological Archaeology* 14:212–46.

Stark, M. T., and J. M. Heidke

1998 Ceramic Manufacture, Productive Specialization, and the Early Classic Period in Arizona's Tonto Basin. *Journal of Anthropological Research* 54 (4): 499–520.

Stark, M. T., and W. A. Longacre

1993 Kalinga Ceramics and New Technologies: An Ethnoarchaeological Perspective. In *The Social and Cultural Contexts of New Ceramic Technologies*, edited by W. D. Kingery, 1–32. Ceramics and Civilization, vol. 6. Waterville, OH: American Ceramics Society.

Stubbs, S. A., and W. S. Stallings Jr.

1953 *The Excavation of Pindi Pueblo, New Mexico*. Monographs of the School of American Research, no. 18. Santa Fe: Museum of New Mexico Press.

Sudar-Murphy, T., and K. W. Laumbach (with D. Ford)

1977 Analyses of Ceramic, Lithic, Bone, and Flotation Materials. In *Archeological Investigations in Cochiti Reservoir, New Mexico*. Vol. 2: *Excavation and Analysis 1975 Season*, edited by R. C. Chapman and J. V. Biella (with S. D. Bussey). Albuquerque: Office of Contract Archeology, University of New Mexico.

Summers, J.

1989 Motor Programs. In *Human Skills*, edited by D. Holding, 49–69. Chichester: John Wiley & Sons.

Tainter, J. A., ed.

n.d. Social and Economic Organization of Gallinas Springs Pueblo, A Report on the 1977 Excavations. On file at U.S. Department of Agriculture, Forest Service, Cibola National Forest, Albuquerque, NM.

Taylor, W. W.

1948 *A Study of Archeology*. Memoir 69, American Anthropological Association, Menasha.

Thomas, A. B.

1935 *After Coronado: Spanish Exploration Northeast of New Mexico, 1696–1727*. Norman: University of Oklahoma Press.

Thomas, D. H.
1986   *Refiguring Anthropology: First Principles of Probability and Statistics*. Prospect Heights, IL: Waveland Press.
1999   *Archaeology: Down to Earth*. 2nd ed. Fort Worth, TX: Harcourt Brace.
Thompson, R. H.
1991   Shepard, Kidder, and Carnegie. In *The Ceramic Legacy of Anna O. Shepard*, edited by R. L. Bishop and F. W. Lange, 11–41. Niwot: University Press of Colorado.
Titiev, M.
1944   *Old Oraibi: A Study of the Hopi Indians of Third Mesa*. Papers of the Peabody Museum of American Archaeology and Ethnology, vol. 22, no. 1. Cambridge, MA: The Museum.
Toll, H. W.
2001   Making and Breaking Pots in the Chaco World. *American Antiquity* 66:56–78.
Toulouse, J. H.
1949   *The Mission of San Gregorio de Abo*. Monograph of the School of American Research, no. 13. Albuquerque: University of New Mexico Press.
Triadan, D.
1997   *Ceramic Commodities and Common Containers: Production and Distribution of White Mountain Red Ware in the Grasshopper Region, Arizona*. Anthropological Papers of the University of Arizona, no. 61. Tucson: University of Arizona Press.
Triadan, D., B. J. Mills, and A. I. Duff
2002   From Compositional to Anthropological: 14th-Century Red-Ware Circulation and Its Implications for Pueblo Reorganization. In *Ceramic Production and Circulation in the Greater Southwest: Source Determination by INAA and Complementary Mineralogical Investigations*, edited by D. Glowacki and H. Neff, 85–97. Monograph 44. Los Angeles: Cotsen Institute of Archaeology of UCLA.
United States Geological Survey
1969   *Mineral and Water Resources of Arizona*. Prepared by the U.S. Geological Survey, the Arizona Bureau of Mines, and the U.S. Bureau of Reclamation. Arizona Bureau of Mines Bulletin, no. 180. Tucson: University of Arizona.
Upham, S.
1982   *Polities and Power: An Economic and Political History of the Western Pueblo*. New York: Academic Press.
Upham, S., P. L. Crown, and S. Plog
1994   Alliance Formation and Cultural Identity in the American Southwest. In *Themes in Southwest Prehistory*, edited by G. J. Gumerman, 183–210. Santa Fe, NM: School of American Research Press.
Upham, S., and L. S. Reed
1989   Regional Systems in the Central and Northern Southwest: Demography, Economy, and Sociopolitics Preceding Contact. In *Columbian Consequences*. Vol. 1: *Archaeological and Historical Perspectives on the Spanish Borderlands West*, edited by D. H. Thomas, 57–76. Washington, DC: Smithsonian Institution Press.
Van der Leeuw, S.
1993   Giving the Potter a Choice: Conceptual Aspects of Pottery Techniques. In *Tech-*

nological Choices: Transformation in Material Cultures since the Neolithic, edited by P. Lemonnier, 238–88. London: Routledge.

Vandiver, P. B.
1990   Ancient Glazes. *Scientific American* 262 (4): 106–13.

Van Keuren, S.
1999   *Ceramic Design Structure and the Organization of Cibola White Ware Production in the Grasshopper Region, Arizona*. Arizona State Museum Archaeological Series, no. 191. Tucson: Arizona State Museum, the University of Arizona.
2000   Ceramic Decoration as Power: Late Prehistoric Design Change in East-central Arizona. In *Alternative Leadership Strategies in the Prehispanic Southwest*, edited by B. J. Mills, 79–94. Tucson: University of Arizona Press.
2001   Ceramic Style and Reorganization of 14th Century Pueblo Communities in East-Central Arizona. PhD diss., University of Arizona.

Voll, C. B.
1961   The Glaze Paint Ceramics of Pottery Mound, New Mexico. Master's thesis, University of New Mexico.

Wallaert-Pêtre, H.
2001   Learning How to Make the Right Pots: Apprenticeship Strategies and Material Culture, A Case Study in Handmade Pottery from Cameroon. *Journal of Anthropological Research* 57 (4): 471–93.

Warren, A. H.
1969   Tonque: One Pueblo's Glaze Pottery Industry Dominated Middle Rio Grande Commerce. *El Palacio* 76 (2): 36–42.
1970   Notes on Manufacture and Trade of Rio Grande Glazes. *The Artifact* 8 (4): 1–7.
1974   Southern Variety of McElmo Black on White. *Pottery Southwest* 1 (2): 4.
1976   The Ceramic and Mineral Resources of LA 70 and the Cochiti Area. In *Archaeological Excavations at Pueblo del Encierro, LA 70, Cochiti Dam Salvage Project, Cochiti, New Mexico: Final Report 1964–1965 Field Seasons*, edited by D. H. Snow, B1–B184. Laboratory of Anthropology Notes, no. 78. Sante Fe: Museum of New Mexico.
1979   The Glaze Paint Wares of the Upper Middle Rio Grande. In *Archaeological Investigations in Cochiti Reservoir, New Mexico*. Vol. 4: *Adaptive Changes in the Northern Rio Grande Valley*, edited by J. V. Biella and R. C. Chapman, 187–216. Albuquerque: Office of Contract Archaeology, Department of Anthropology, University of New Mexico.
1980   Prehistoric Pottery of Tijeras Canyon. In *Tijeras Canyon, Analyses of the Past*, edited by L. S. Cordell, 149–68. Albuquerque: Maxwell Museum of Anthropology and University of New Mexico Press.
1981   A Petrographic Study of the Pottery. In *Contributions to Gran Quivira Archaeology*, edited by A. C. Hayes, 67–73. Publications in Archaeology, no. 17. Washington, DC: National Park Service, U.S. Department of the Interior.

Warren, A. H., and D. H. Snow
1976   Formal Descriptions of Rio Grande Glazes from LA 70. In *Archaeological Excavations at Pueblo del Encierro, LA 70; Cochiti Dam Salvage Project, Cochiti, New*

Mexico: *Final Report 1964–1965 Field Seasons*, assembled by D. H. Snow, C1–C34. Laboratory of Anthropology Notes, no. 78. Santa Fe: Museum of New Mexico.

Washburn, D. K.
1983   Toward a Theory of Structural Style in Art. In *Structure and Cognition in Art*, edited by D. Washburn, 138–64. Cambridge: Cambridge University Press.

Watson, J. B.
1990   Other People Do Other Things: Lamarckian Identities in the Kainantu Subdistrict, Papua New Guinea. In *Cultural Identity and Ethnicity in the Pacific*, edited by J. Linnekin and L. Poyer, 17–42. Honolulu: University of Hawai'i Press.

Watson, P. J., S. A. LeBlanc, and C. L. Redman
1980   Aspects of Zuni Prehistory: Preliminary Report on Excavations and Survey in the El Morro Valley of New Mexico. *Journal of Field Archaeology* 7: 201–18.

Weigand, P. C.
1975   Aboriginal West Mexican Glazes and Their Possible Relationship to the Southwest. *Pottery Southwest* 2 (2): 5–6.

Welsch, R., and J. Terrell
1998   Material Culture, Social Fields, and Social Boundaries on the Sepik Coast of New Guinea. In *The Archaeology of Social Boundaries*, edited by M. T. Stark, 50–77. Washington, DC: Smithsonian Institution Press.

Wendorf, F.
1950   *A Report on the Excavation of a Small Ruin Near Point of Pines, East Central Arizona*. Social Science Bulletin, no. 19. Tucson: University of Arizona.

Wendorf, F., and E. K. Reed
1955   An Alternative Reconstruction of Northern Rio Grande Prehistory. *El Palacio* 62:131–73.

Wenger, E. C.
1998   *Communities of Practice: Learning, Meaning, and Identity*. Cambridge: Cambridge University Press.

Whalen, M. E.
1978   *Settlement Patterns of the Western Hueco Bolson*. Publications in Anthropology, no. 6. El Paso: El Paso Centennial Museum, University of Texas.

Whitbread, I. K.
1989   A Proposal for the Systematic Description of Thin Sections towards the Study of Ancient Ceramic Technology. In *Archaeometry, Proceedings of the 25th International Symposium*, edited by Y. Maniatis, 127–38. Amsterdam: Elsevier.

White, L. T.
1962/1970   *Medieval Technology and Social Change*. New York: Oxford University Press.

Whiteley, P.
1988   *Deliberate Acts: Changing Hopi Culture through the Oraibi Split*. Tucson: University of Arizona Press.
2004   Social Formations in the Pueblo IV Southwest: An Ethnological View. In *The Protohistoric Pueblo World, AD 1275–1600*, edited by E. C. Adams and A. I. Duff, 144–55. Tucson: University of Arizona Press.

Whittlesey, S. M.
1974 Identification of Imported Ceramics through Functional Analysis of Attributes. *The Kiva* 40 (1–2): 101–12.

Wiessner, P. W.
1983 Style and Social Information in Kalahari San Projectile Points. *American Antiquity* 48:253–76.
1985 Style or Isochrestic Variation? A Reply to Sackett. *American Antiquity* 50:160–66.
1997 Hxaro: A Regional System of Reciprocity for Reducing Risk among the !Kung San. Vol. 1. PhD diss., University of Michigan.

Wilcox, D. R.
1981 Changing Perspectives on the Protohistoric Pueblos, AD 1450–1700. In *The Protohistoric Period in the North American Southwest, AD 1450–1700*, edited by D. R. Wilcox and W. B. Masse, 378–409. Arizona State University Anthropological Research Papers, no. 24. Tempe: Arizona State University Press.
1984 Multi-Ethnic Division of Labor in the Protohistoric Southwest. *Papers of the Anthropological Society of New Mexico* 9:141–56.
1991 Changing Contexts of Pueblo Adaptation, AD 1250–1600. In *Farmers, Hunters, and Colonists: Prehistoric and Historic Plains-Pueblo Exchange*, edited by K. A. Spielmann, 128–54. Tucson: University of Arizona Press.

Wilcox, D. R., and J. Haas
1994 The Scream of the Butterfly: Competition and Conflict in the Prehistoric Southwest. In *Themes in Southwest Prehistory*, edited by G. J. Gumerman, 211–38. Santa Fe: School of American Research Press.

Wilson, C. D.
1996 Ceramic Pigment Distributions and Regional Interaction: A Re-examination of Interpretations in Shepard's "Technology of La Plata Pottery." *The Kiva* 62 (1): 83–102.

Wilson, J. P., and A. H. Warren
1973 New Pottery Type Described, Seco Corrugated. *Awanyu* 1 (1): 12–13.

Winship, G. P.
1896 The Coronado Expedition. In *Bureau of Ethnology 14th Annual Report*, 329–613. Washington, DC: Smithsonian Institution, Government Printing Office.

Wobst, H. M.
1977 Stylistic Behavior and Information Exchange. In *Papers for the Director: Research Essays in Honor of James B. Griffin*, edited by C. E. Cleland, 317–42. Anthropological Papers, no. 67. Ann Arbor: Museum of Anthropology, University of Michigan.
1999 Style in Archaeology or Archaeologists in Style. In *Material Meanings: Critical Approaches to the Interpretation of Material Culture*, edited by E. Chilton, 118–32. Salt Lake City: University of Utah Press.

Woodbury, R., and N.F.S. Woodbury
1966 Decorated Pottery of the Zuni Area. In *The Excavation of Hawikuh by Frederick Webb Hodge: Report of the Hendricks-Hodge Expedition*, by W. Smith, R. Woodbury, and N. Woodbury, appendix II. Contributions from the Museum of the

American Indian, Heye Foundation, vol. 20. New York: Museum of the American Indian, Heye Foundation.

Word, J. H.
1963   Floydada Country Club Site (41FL1). *Bulletin of the Southern Plains Archaeological Society* 1:37–63.
1965   The Montgomery Site in Floyd County, Texas. *Bulletin of the South Plains Archaeological Society* 2:55–102.

Wyckoff, L.
1985   *Designs and Factions: Politics, Religion, and Ceramics on the Hopi Third Mesa*. Albuquerque: University of New Mexico Press.

Yoffee, N., and A. Sherratt, eds.
1993   *Archaeological Theory: Who Sets the Agenda?* Cambridge: Cambridge University Press.

Zedeño, M. N.
1994   *Sourcing Prehistoric Ceramics at Chodistaas Pueblo, Arizona: The Circulation of People and Pots in the Grasshopper Region*. Anthropological Papers of the University of Arizona, no. 58. Tucson: University of Arizona Press.
1995   The Role of Population Movement and Technology Transfer in the Manufacture of Prehistoric Southwestern Ceramics. In *Ceramic Production in the American Southwest*, edited by B. J. Mills and P. L. Crown, 115–41. Tucson: University of Arizona Press.
2002   Artifact Design, Composition, and Context: Updating the Analysis of Ceramic Circulation at Point of Pines, Arizona. In *Ceramic Production and Circulation in the Greater Southwest*, edited by D. M. Glowacki and H. Neff, 74–84. Monograph 44. Los Angeles: Cotsen Institute of Archaeology at UCLA.

Zier, C. J.
1976   *Excavations near Zuni, New Mexico: 1973*. Museum of Northern Arizona Research Paper, no. 2. Flagstaff: Museum of Northern Arizona.

Zubrow, E.B.W.
1974   *Population, Contact, and Climate in New Mexican Pueblos*. Anthropological Papers, no. 24. Tucson: University of Arizona.

Contributors

Patricia Capone. Peabody Museum of Archaeology and Ethnology, Harvard University, 11 Divinity Avenue, Cambridge, MA 02138. pcapone@fas.harvard.edu

Linda S. Cordell. University of Colorado Museum, 218 UCB, University of Colorado, Boulder, CO 80309. Linda.Cordell@colorado.edu

Suzanne L. Eckert. Department of Anthropology, Texas A&M University, 4352 TAMU, College Station, TX 77843-4352. sleckert@tamu.edu

Thomas R. Fenn. Department of Anthropology, University of Arizona, P.O. Box 210030, Tucson, AZ 87521-0030. tfenn@email.arizona.edu

Judith A. Habicht-Mauche. Department of Anthropology, University of California, 1156 High Street, Santa Cruz, CA 95064. judith@ucsc.edu

Cynthia L. Herhahn. Bandelier National Monument, 15 Entrance Road, Los Alamos, NM 87544. cynthia_herhahn@nps.gov

Maren Hopkins. Department of Anthropology, University of Arizona, P.O. Box 210030, Tucson, AZ 87521-0030. mhopkins@northlandresearch.com

Deborah L. Huntley. Southwest Archaeological Consultants, Inc., P.O. Box 8617, Santa Fe, NM 87504-8617. debhuntley@aol.com

Toni S. Laumbach. New Mexico Farm and Ranch Heritage Museum, 4100 Dripping Springs Road, Las Cruces, NM, 88011. toni.laumbach@state.nm.us

Kathryn Leonard. Arizona State Historic Preservation Office, Arizona State Parks, 1300 W. Washington St., Phoenix, AZ. KLeonard@pr.state.az.us

Barbara J. Mills. Department of Anthropology, University of Arizona, P.O. Box 210030, Tucson, AZ 87521-0030. bmills@email.arizona.edu

Kit Nelson. Department of Anthropology, Tulane University, 1021 Audubon Street, New Orleans, LA 70118. knelson1@tulane.edu

Gregson Schachner. School of Human Evolution and Social Change, Arizona State University, Tempe, AZ 85287-2402. schachner@asu.edu

Miriam T. Stark. Department of Anthropology, University of Hawai'i, 2424 Maile Way, Saunders 346, Honolulu, HI 96822. miriams@hawaii.edu

Scott Van Keuren. Natural History Museum of Los Angeles County, 900 Exposition Boulevard, Los Angeles, CA 90007. svankeur@nhm.org

About the Editors

Judith A. Habicht-Mauche is chair of the Department of Anthropology at the University of California, Santa Cruz. Professor Habicht-Mauche's research interests include the study of the organization of production and exchange of ancient pottery from the American Southwest and Southern Plains. She received her doctorate in anthropology from Harvard University in 1988. Her dissertation on interaction between Pueblo farmers of the Southwest and bison-hunting nomads of the Southern Plains won the 1988 Society for American Archaeology Dissertation Prize. In 1993, she published *The Pottery from Arroyo Hondo Pueblo, New Mexico: Tribalization and Trade in the Northern Rio Grande* with the School of American Research Press in Santa Fe. In 1997, Professor Habicht-Mauche was awarded an NSF grant, with geochemist A. Russell Flegal, to explore the application of lead isotope analysis, using ICP-MS, to the sourcing of glaze-painted ceramics from the Rio Grande Valley of New Mexico. A poster based on early results of this collaborative research won the Outstanding Poster Award (Professional Category) at the 1997 Annual Meeting of the Society for American Archaeology in Nashville, Tennessee. She has published articles in various regional, national, and international journals, including *Plains Anthropologist* and the *Journal of Archaeological Science*.

Suzanne L. Eckert has studied how pre-Hispanic Pueblo social dynamics articulate with material culture (especially pottery) for the past fifteen years. She has worked primarily in the Zuni, upper Little Colorado River, and central Rio Grande regions. She has examined the relationship between ritual organization and village size, how disease affected protohistoric demographic patterns, and the development and spread of ritual systems. Her dissertation work focused on how fourteenth-century Pueblo potters decorated their vessels to signal multiple, and often contradictory, aspects of their social identity. Recently graduated from Arizona State University with a PhD in anthropology, she taught at the University of California at Santa Cruz and the University of Utah before joining Texas A&M as assistant professor of anthropology. Her current research focuses on the spread of glaze technology into the Rio Grande region and the development and decline of ceramic technology in pre-colonial Samoa.

Deborah L. Huntley has spent more than a decade studying pre-Columbian social organization, ceramic exchange, craft specialization, and intraregional interaction in the American Southwest. She has conducted archaeological research in the central Rio Grande Valley and the Zuni region of New Mexico, as well as the southern coastal and desert areas of California. Her current research interests include understanding how ancestral Pueblo populations used technological and decorative styles of material culture to express multiple social identities and create social boundaries. She received her PhD from Arizona State University and is a project director for Southwest Archaeological Consultants in Santa Fe.

Index

Abó Pueblo, 204, 225, 227
Acoma Glaze Ware, series of types of, 43–47
Acoma region: experimentation in, 5; glaze ware technologies in, 27; technological practices in, 18
aesthetics: pottery and, ix, 183
agency theory, 21–22
American Southwest: state of archaeology in, 32
analytical techniques designated, 6
Appadurai, Arjun, 7, 10
archaeological sites, 8–9
archaeologists: and anthropology of technology approach, 18–20; archaeological ceramicists, 32; and *chaîne opératoire* approach, 10, 19; as consumers of external theory, 32; and the French approach, 19–20; and practice theory, 19–23
Arizona. *See* east-central Arizona
Arroyo Hondo, 53–54, 153, 166–78

Bailey Ruin site, 62, 64, 66–84, 103
black-on-white *vs.* glaze-painted ceramics: in central Rio Grande Valley, 13–14; in lower Rio Puerco region, 13–14
Bourdieu, Pierre, 11, 20–21
brushstroke sequences, 24, 94–97, 99, 101, 103–4
Bryant Ranch Pueblo site, 62–85; feasting at, 83

carbon paint wares, 15, 29; in Rio Alamosa region, 142–46, 149, 151, 154, 159–60; in Rio Grande Valley region, 164, 169, 172, 175, 182
Casas Grandes, 158; glaze-painted vessels in, 34, 38, 151
Cedar Creek Polychrome pottery, 35, 38–39, 64–65
central Rio Grande Valley region, 13, 15; black-on-white *vs.* glaze-painted ceramics in, 13–14; compositional analyses of ceramics in, 25; contact with Zuni region, 15; glaze wares in, 163–78; interaction, integration in, 14; migrations and, 175–76; pottery types in, 166–74; white ware production in, 29–30
ceramics: ethnoarchaeological research

on, 32; material characterization, tools for, ix. *See also* technological practices

chaîne opératoire approach, 10, 19

Chodistaas Pueblo, 66

Cibola White Ware, 37, 95; compositional analysis of, 66–83; replaced by red ware, 29; in Silver Creek area, 63–66

Cieneguilla (aka Tzeguma) Pueblo, 202, 205–6

communities of practice, 25–27; in east-central Arizona, 91–94, 99–103; future research in, 31–32; geographic clusters and, 26–27; glaze wares and, 12; practice theory and, 23; in Zuni Glaze Ware, 105–23

compositional analysis: of central Rio Grande ceramics, 25; of Cibola White Ware, 66–82; of Rio Grande Valley glaze wares, 184–92, 201–8, 218–23, 227–28; of White Mountain Red Ware, 66–82; of Zuni Glaze Ware, 109–20

copper-based pigments: experimentation with, 5; migrations and, 18; and shift to low-copper paints, 29

Cordell, Linda S., x

cultural biography of things, 10

cultural transmission, 30–31

diffusion and cultural transmission, 30–31

Early Contact Period, ix, x; glaze wares and, 10

east-central Arizona, 26; glaze wares in, 86–104

electron microprobe, ix

ethnoarchaeologists, 31–32

exchange networks: cultural preference and, 238; directionality of, 238–39; in east-central Arizona, 86–104; exclusivity and, 237–39; expansion of, 34; in Rio Grande Valley region, 54–55, 163–66, 172, 175–77, 197–98, 210–13

feasting: at Bryant Ranch Pueblo site, 83–84; in east-central Arizona, 101; pots used in, 5, 13; in Rio Grande Valley region, 165, 176, 209, 225–26; in Silver Creek region, 62–63, 82–85; in Zuni region, 107

formulas. *See* glaze paint recipes

Four Corners region: early use of glaze in, 17; experimentation in, 12; glaze wares in, 34, 60

Fourmile Polychrome pottery, 35, 38–40, 59, 64–65, 84–85; in east-central Arizona, 87–88, 90–91, 95–99, 101–4; as element in Zuni Glaze Ware, 128; miscoding of, 13; painting style of, 95–99; in Rio Grande Valley region, 185, 187–91, 195, 268

Fourmile Pueblo, 63

Fourmile Ruin site, 62, 66–67, 71, 78–80, 89, 97, 99

Fourmile-style pots, 13

Galisteo Pueblo, 53

Gallinas Springs Pueblo, 142, 146, 153–54, 156–58

Garza Complex sites, 232, 234, 238–39; glaze wares at, 239–49, 252

geochemical analysis, ix, 6

geographic clusters, 26–27

glaze paint recipes: colorants for, 5; and copper-based pigments, 5; in east-central Arizona, 87, 102; fluxes for, 5–6; high-lead, low-copper paints, 29; and lead-based pigments, 5; low-lead, high-copper paints, 29; in Mogollon Rim area, 29; in Mogollon Rim region, 28; in Rio Grande Valley region, 29, 164, 179–82, 184, 189, 191–95, 262–64; in Silver Creek region, 13, 60–61, 63, 66, 71, 74–75, 78–79, 81, 84–85; in Zuni region, 14, 28, 105, 108, 110, 112–13, 121–22

glaze wares: in Acoma region, 27; and anthropology of technology approach, 19–20; and brushstroke sequences, 24; and *chaîne opératoire* approach, 10, 19–20; changes in timing, nature, and

contexts of, 27–30; Cibola White Ware, 29; and communities of practice, 12; cultural transmission of, 30–31; design styles, 39, 58–59; distribution, 34–35; in east-central Arizona, 86–104; exchange patterns for, 6; in Four Corners region, 17, 34; at Garza Complex sites, 239–49, 252; ICP-MS analysis of, 6; INAA analysis of, 6; indigenous development of, 5; innovations in, 27–30; in Little Colorado region, 27, 40, 58, 65, 128, 135, 139, 184, 268; and local systems, local settlement clusters, 26; map of production areas, 36; meaning of, as things, 7, 10; migration effect on, 3, 5; in Mogollon Rim region, 27–28; optical petrography of, 6; origins of, 30; paint combinations, 57–58; petrographic analysis of, 15; and Plains-Pueblo exchanges, 232–52; and practice theory in archaeology, 19–23; and producer-consumer relationships, 24; production, 34–35; and Pueblo social life, 6; red ware, 29; and regional systems, 26; resource acquisition for, 6, 15; in Rio Alamosa region, 142–62; in Rio Grande Valley region, 27, 163–231, 253–71; series of types of, 35–56; in Silver Creek area, 60–85; slip color variations, 56–57; social contexts of changes in, 28–30; social history of, 10–11, 12–16; and social lives of pots, 23–25; stylistic analyses of, 6; technology adoption, 27; at Tierra Blanca Complex sites, 239–50, 252; typological analysis of, 6, 35–55; in western Mexico, 34; White Mountain Red Ware, 24; Zuni Glaze Ware, 105–41; in Zuni region, 27
Gran Quivira Pueblo, 136, 185, 186, 219, 233, 250
Grasshopper Pueblo, 89, 95, 97, 101

habitus, 11, 21–22; and communities of practice, 25

Heshotauthla Pueblo, 113
High Plains. *See* southern High Plains region
Hummingbird Pueblo, 31, 48, 166–70, 172–76, 178

ICP-MS analysis, ix, 6
ideologies: pottery and, ix
INAA analysis, ix, 6
inductively coupled plasma mass spectroscopy, ix, 6
instrumental neutron activation analysis, ix, 6
Isleta Pueblo, 107

Kotyiti Pueblo, 218

Late Precontact Period, ix, x, 3, 5; glaze wares and, 10. *See also* Pueblo IV period
lead-based pigments: experimentation with, 5; migrations and, 18; and shift to high-lead paints, 29; Zuni potters and, 24
Little Colorado region. *See* upper Little Colorado region
Llano Estacado escarpment, 232–34
local systems, local settlement clusters, 26
Lower Rio Puerco of the East Glaze Ware, 48
lower Rio Puerco region, 6, 14, 47, 136, 163, 172, 190; black-on-white *vs.* glaze-painted ceramics in, 13–14

macrogroups, 26
Matsaki Buff Ware, 25, 124, 129–33, 138–41
Mesa Verde, 142–46, 148–50, 153–55; culture area of, 142–43; immigrant community in, 15
Mexico. *See* western Mexico
microprobe, ix
migrations: and central Rio Grande Valley region, 175–76; cultural transmission and, 30–31; effect of, 3, 5; effect on

Index / 321

Rio Alamosa region, 142–62; and pottery production, 34; series of, 17–18; tracking by ceramics, 18
mineral paints, 29
Mogollon Rim region, 13; Cibola White Ware replaced by red ware in, 29; experimentation in, 28–29; glaze paint production in, 60; glaze ware technologies in, 27–28; migrants from, 28, 31; pottery production groups in, 25; Silver Creek area of, 60–85

New Archaeology, 22, 25
nucleated pueblos, 106, 109, 122
Nuestra Señora de Dolores Pueblo, 54–55

optical petrography of glaze wares, 6
ore sources, 8–9; for Rio Grande Glaze Ware, 192, 263–64, 268, 270; in Silver Creek region, 85; for Zuni Glaze Ware, 112–14, 116, 118–20

Pecos and Rio Grande Glaze Ware, series of types of, 49–56
Pecos Pueblo, 49, 55, 204, 235–36, 241, 248, 250, 256–58, 265
petrographic analysis, 15, 172, 182, 185, 197, 200, 202–3, 205–7, 210–11, 214, 218–24, 231, 257, 269
Picuris Pueblo, 235
Pindi Pueblo, 53
Pinedale Black-on-red and Polychrome pottery, 35, 37–39, 58–59; in Acoma Glaze ware, 44; in east-central Arizona, 87–88, 90, 95–96, 99, 101–3; at Pinnacle Ruin site, 152–53, 156–57, 161; in Rio Alamosa region, 147–49; in Rio Grande Valley region, 184; in Silver Creek region, 64–65, 71, 78–79, 81; in Zuni Glaze Ware, 40–42; in Zuni region, 128
Pinedale Pueblo, 38
Pinnacle Ruin site, 15; pottery types at, 144–53

Plains-Pueblo relations, 25, 27; and glaze ware exchange, 232–52
Point of Pines Pueblo, 89–90, 97
pottery design styles, 39; in east-central Arizona, 86–104; painting Fourmile style, 95–98
The Pottery from Arroyo Hondo Pueblo, New Mexico (Habicht-Mauche), 317
Pottery Hill site, 62–63, 82–83
pottery types: in central Rio Grande Valley region, 166–74; at Pinnacle Ruin site, 144–53; in Silver Creek area, 63–66, 72; typological analysis of, 6, 35–55; in Zuni villages, 105–41
practice theory in archaeology, 23; combined with *chaîne opératoire* approach, 20; framework, 19; and *habitus*, 21
producer-consumer relationships, 24, 217, 227, 230
Pueblo Blanco, 53, 201–3, 205–6, 210
Pueblo del Encierro, 55, 166–67, 169–71, 174–76, 178
Pueblo IV Period, 3, 254–56. See also Late Precontact Period

Quarai Pueblo, 107

Rattlesnake Point Pueblo, 40, 42
red ware: Cibola White Ware replaced by along Mogollon Rim region, 29. See also White Mountain Red Ware
regional systems, 26
resource acquisition, 6; by Zuni potters, 15
Rio Alamosa region, glaze wares in, 142–62
Rio Grande Glaze Paint Ware (Shepard), ix, 258
Rio Grande Glaze Ware: Kidder's work on, 256–58, 264–65; series of types of, 49–56; Shepard's work on, 255–66
Rio Grande Valley region: central, 13–15, 163–78; compositional analysis of glaze wares in, 184–92, 201–8, 218–23, 227–

28; cultural transmission in, 30–31; emulation of glaze wares by Zunis, 27; geographic clusters in, 26–27; glaze wares in, 49–56, 163–231, 253–71; and migrations between Western Pueblos, 17–18; multiple strategies of production in, 29; and Plains-Pueblo relations, 25, 27, 232–52; southern, 13, 15; technology adoption in, 27; trade in, 29

ritual practices, 13, 63, 82–85, 101–2, 126, 140, 233; diversification of, 31; migrants and, 139, 163, 176–77; migration effect on, 3, 5; new systems of, 6, 16, 34, 59–60, 87, 107–8, 164–66, 168, 173, 175; pots used in, 13; pottery and, ix; ritual exchange and, 210; and ritual functions of glaze ware vessels, 121, 194, 209, 255, 263–64, 271; and turquoise deposits, 212–13

St. Johns Polychrome pottery, 35–36, 38; at Pinnacle Ruin site, 152, 155–57; in Rio Alamosa region, 145–49; in Rio Grande Valley region, 192, 268–69; in Silver Creek region, 64–65, 71, 76, 78; and Zuni Glaze Wares, 40, 107, 127, 134; in Zuni region, 109–10, 112, 116–18

San Marcos Pueblo, 189, 204–6, 212, 214, 236

Silver Creek Archaeological Research Project (SCARP), 62

Silver Creek region, 13, 60; glaze wares in, 60–85

slip colors: in Acoma Glaze Ware series, 43–47; in White Mountain Red Ware series, 35–40; in Zuni Glaze Ware series, 40–43

"The Social Life of Pots" (symposium), x

social networks: migration effect on, 3, 5. *See also* exchange networks

southern High Plains region, 15; and Plains-Pueblo relations, 25, 27, 232–52

southern Rio Grande Valley, 13; contact with Zuni region, 15

southwestern America: state of archaeology in, 32

Stark, Miriam T., x

stylistic analyses of glaze wares, 6

technological changes: adoption of, 27; scope of, 28; social contexts of, 28–30

technological practices: adoption of, 18; and anthropology of technology approach, 18–20; and communities of practice, 25; as culturally embedded, 11; geochemical analysis tools and, ix; local practices, 29–30; pottery and, ix; and technological styles, 20; and technology of practice approach, 11

temper, 29. *See also* compositional analysis

Tierra Blanca Complex sites, 232, 234, 238–39; glaze wares at, 239–50, 252

Tijeras Pueblo, 53, 166, 168–69, 174, 176

Tonque Pueblo, 54–55, 186, 190, 200, 204, 206, 210, 212

Tonto Basin, 26

towns: growth of, 17

Tularosa style decorations, 35, 39

typological analysis: of Acoma Glaze Ware series, 43–47; differing traditions of, 35; at Garza Complex sites, 239–49, 252; of Lower Rio Puerco of the East Glaze ware series, 48; of Pecos and Rio Grande Glaze Ware series, 49–55; techniques for, 6; at Tierra Blanca Complex sites, 239–50, 252; of White Mountain Red Ware series, 35–40; of Zuni Glaze Ware series, 40–43

upper Little Colorado region: adoption of glaze ware technologies in, 18, 27; adoption of technology in, 18; experimentation in, 12; glaze wares in, 27, 40, 58, 65, 128, 135, 139, 184, 268; and Rio Grande Valley region, 184, 268; and Zuni Glaze wares, 128, 135, 139 western Mexico: glaze-painted polychrome ware in, 34; glaze ware traditions in, 17

Western Pueblo region: glaze ware technology adoption in, 27; migrations and, 17–18; and Plains-Pueblo relations, 25, 27, 232–52

Western Pueblos, 15

White Mountain Red Ware, 25; and brushstroke sequences, 24; compositional analysis of, 66–82; series of types of, 35–40; in Silver Creek area, 63–66

white ware production: continuance or replacement of, 29–30. *See also* Cibola White Ware

Zuni Glaze Ware: communities of practice, 105–23; compositional analysis of, 109–20; decline in production of, 124–41; decline of, 14; series of types of, 40–42; technology adoption in, 27; tradition abandonment, 28; and transition to Matsaki Buff Ware, 25, 124, 129–33, 138–41

Zuni potters: and lead-based glazes, 24; Rio Grande glaze wares emulated by, 27

Zuni Pueblo, 47, 128–29, 136

Zuni region: adoption of technologies in, 18; glaze ware technology adoption in, 27; migrations to, 28, 31; social dynamics in, 14–15